Michel Foucault's Force of Flight

Contemporary Studies in Philosophy and the Human Sciences

Series Editors:
Hugh J. Silverman and Graeme Nicholson

Published

* Also available in paperback

Michel Foucault's Force of Flight:

Toward an Ethics for Thought

———◆———

James W. Bernauer

Humanities Press
New Jersey ▼ London

B2430
F724
B47
1990

First published in 1990 by Humanities Press International, Inc.,
Atlantic Highlands, NJ 07716 and 3 Henrietta Street,
London WC2E 8LU

© James W. Bernauer, 1990

Reprinted in paperback 1992

Library of Congress Cataloging-in-Publication Data

Bernauer, James William.
    Michel Foucault's force of flight: toward an ethics for thought/
James W. Bernauer.
        p. cm. — (Contemporary studies in philosophy and the human
sciences)
    Bibliography: p.
    Includes index.
    ISBN 0-391-03635-1   ISBN 0-391-03740-4 (Pbk.)
    1. Foucault, Michel.   2. Foucault, Michel—Ethics.   3. Ethics,
Modern—20th century.   I. Title.   II. Series.
B2430.F724B47 1990
194—dc20   89-31526
                                                                    CIP

Printed in the United States of America

Contents

◆—

Abbreviations

———◆———

AS	*L'archéologie du savoir*
HF	*Histoire de la folie à l'âge classique*
IRE	Introduction to *Le rêve et l'existence*
LMC	*Les mots et les choses*
MPR	*Moi, Pierre Rivière, ayant égorgé ma mère, ma soeur et mon frère*
NC	*Naissance de la clinique*
OD	*L'ordre du discours*
PER	*Maladie mentale et personnalité*
PSY	*Maladie mentale et psychologie*
RR	*Raymond Roussel*
SP	*Surveiller et punir*
SS	*Le souci de soi*
UP	*L'usage des plaisirs*
VS	*La volonté de savoir*

Preface

◆

When I began this comprehensive examination of Michel Foucault's thought, nearly a decade ago, I regarded it as at once overdue and premature. At the time, there had been no attempt in the English language to consider Foucault's writings as a whole, although the body of his work was already twenty-five years old. Fortunately, this situation has changed dramatically, and a competent series of studies is now available to assist the reader of Foucault. Although my own work differs from these studies in its claim that the various elements in Foucault's work form a coherent ethics of thought, I have profited immensely from the various interpretations of Foucault's achievement that have been published in recent years both here and abroad. I regarded my study as premature because since Foucault was then only in his early fifties, his journey of thought could be considered far from complete. Despite all that he had achieved, there was much more to be anticipated. His untimely death in 1984 at the age of fifty-seven dashed that expectation. Death has forced upon his project a definitiveness that enables me to give his work a clear face, not a death mask but a precise shape inviting further recognition and encounter by his future readers.

This study began when I attended Foucault's 1979 lectures at the Collège de France; it ended at the 1988 Paris conference on "Foucault as Philosopher" that was sponsored by the research institute dedicated to continuing his paths of exploration, the Centre Michel Foucault. The international list of speakers was impressive, including, among others, Georges Canguilhem, Gilles Deleuze, François Ewald, François Wahl, Richard Rorty, Manfred Frank, Miguel Morey, Roberto Machado, Paul Veyne, and André Glucksmann. Despite the quality of the papers and discussions at this conference, I was struck by how difficult it still was to locate Foucault on the traditional philosophical landscape. As the newspaper reports on the conference concluded, Foucault seemed to preserve his enigmatic status in contemporary intellectual life. My own examination aims to lessen the enigma and accentuate the promise of Foucault's originality.

My work was made possible by the support of many people and institutions. It is a pleasure to acknowledge all of these debts, even if it is possible to name only a few here. I am especially obligated to the New York Province of the Society of Jesus for having provided me with the opportunity to participate in two years of courses and seminars with Michel Foucault in Paris. My students and colleagues at Boston College have provided an ideal environment for critical appropriation of Foucault's work, and the Graduate School has aided me with a semester's faculty fellowship. I want to express particular thanks to these members of the philosophy department: Peggy Bakalo, Louise Dietenhofer, Joseph Flanagan, and Tracey Stark. I am grateful to John Sallis, the Arthur J. Schmitt Professor in Philosophy at Loyola University in Chicago, for his patient encouragement of my efforts to write this book. I appreciate the dedicated professionalism of the staff and of my editor at Humanities Press, Judith Camlin. Professor Hugh Silverman originally interested me in the work of Foucault while I was a graduate student at the State University of New York at Stony Brook. I appreciate the support he extended to me as a student, and in the years since then, as a friend. Among the many who assisted me throughout the long period of research and writing, I wish to acknowledge in a special way my father, John, and my brothers Jack and Kenneth, as well as Maurice Belval, John and Patty Bowen-Moore, Daniel Defert, Edward Dougherty, Joseph Gauthier, James Pollock, David Rasmussen, William Richardson, Patrick Samway, and Pedro de Velasco. Finally, I am extremely grateful for the warm welcome and gracious assistance I received from Michel Foucault himself. The critical and modest attitude he exhibited in regard to his own work encouraged the greatest intellectual independence in my own approach to it. When he died, I mourned him personally as well as the premature end of my Foucault years. Now, however, the shock of sudden death has given way to a profound gratitude for the privilege of having had those years. My work is but a gesture of appreciation to him, for his thought and his humanity.

Department of Philosophy
Boston College
Chestnut Hill, Massachusetts

1

◆

Force of Flight, An Introduction

The title of this study of Michel Foucault's thought is borrowed from his meditation on a series of paintings, *Prisoners*, by the contemporary French artist Paul Rebeyrolle.[1] The paintings portray a dog that has been confined to a barred space, and follow the moods of the dog's imprisonment, his struggle with it, and the eventual escape of the animal out of the "black fortress of the past" into "storms of future color." Foucault admires the artist's style because the canvases are linked dynamically. They elaborate a spreading intuition, which requires an ordered multiplicity of different expressions but avoids concretion in a single meaning. The paintings form an "irreversible series, an irruption that cannot be mastered. Do not say: a history appears thanks to the juxtaposition of canvases; say rather: the movement which trembles at first and then shakes itself free from the canvas actually passes outside of its limits in order to inscribe itself and to continue on to the following canvas and to arouse them all in a single great movement which escapes them and leaves them hanging there in front of us. This series of paintings, instead of narrating that which has passed, makes a force pass whose history can be recounted as the wake of its flight and of its liberty." Rebeyrolle's work is "concerned less with a form than an energy; less with a presence than an intensity; less with a movement and an attitude than with an agitation, of a trembling that is contained only with difficulty." In addition to admiring the style, Foucault applauded Rebeyrolle's choice of imprisonment as a timely theme for contemporary viewers. "You have entered. Here you are surrounded by ten paintings which encircle a room, all of whose windows have been carefully closed. Is it now your turn to be in prison, just like the dogs you see standing up and knocking against the grills?" Imprisonment is a political theme, for it reveals the existence of a power that is constantly exercised, "commands that are barked from on high and from below."

1

Permanent incarceration is not the final message of these paintings, however, for the dog does manage to escape. But not, as might be expected, through the windows that appear in the first six paintings. As long as imprisonment triumphs, the windows are blank. "There is neither sky nor light: nothing from the interior hints at it; no longer does anything venture to penetrate. Rather than an exterior, there is a pure outside, neutral, inaccessible, without form." The emergence of a space of liberty does not occur until the "decisive moment" in the series is reached, when grays and whites yield to a canvas illuminated with an immense blue. "The canvas where this mutation is effected bears the title *Within (Dedans)*: an exchange starts and the within, despite itself, begins to open on to the birth of a space. The wall cracks from top to bottom; one might say that it is split by a great blue sword. The vertical, which showed power in the prominence of the stick, now opens up a liberty. The vertical sticks which secure the grating do not prevent the wall, which is beyond them, from cracking. A nose and paws press on and dig at the opening in a state of intense joy, of an electric quivering. In the struggle of men, nothing great is achieved by way of windows but everything is always achieved in the triumphant collapse of walls." While Foucault's writing often flashed with intense feeling, Rebeyrolle's *Prisoners* evoked a reflection that stands out in its passion. In the end, Foucault's passion is the eruption of his own uniqueness, for the meditation dramatically exposes the three faces of his intelligence: his singular style of thinking, his project's relentless disclosure of imprisonments, and finally, his work's exhilarating exhibition of escape. While "Force of Flight" is the title of only one of Foucault's writings, it is nevertheless that unanticipated portrait that captures both his spirit and his experience of thought.

1. FOUCAULT'S STYLE

A paradox has often appeared in the interpretations of Foucault by those critics who have successfully avoided simplistic readings of his work. While great ability is manifested in their analyses of him, this competence is frequently joined with a confession of ignorance about what Foucault is really doing. Thus, in a review of one of Foucault's last volumes, the historian John Boswell could praise it as a "rare pleasure, like watching fireworks of the mind," and at the same time plead that he was "unsure about what the book is discussing." His profession echoes a tradition of frustration. Earlier, Foucault's thought and style had been compared with an Escher drawing with "stairs rising to platforms lower than themselves, doors leading outside that bring you back inside." Another critic recommended that readers approach Foucault with the attitude Faulkner counseled for students of Joyce: the blind faith of the illiterate working through the Bible.[2] Although these images are amusing, they needlessly discourage the effort that reading Foucault requires, deserves, and rewards. His work is neither a maze nor does it demand a leap into the dark; the variety of subjects he has explored notwithstanding, there is a remarkable coherence to a body of work that spanned thirty years. The individual writings are stages on a path that is full of markers, the product of a remarkable intelligence.

While no one will deny that understanding Foucault requires effort, the reason for the difficulty of his thought is not to be sought in yet another conspiracy theory, namely, that Foucault is rebelling against the tradition of French clarity by deliberately aiming at obscurity.[3] The obvious reason for the difficulty in reading him and for the fact that his work has attracted the attention of diverse linguistic and academic communities is that in him there is a "powerful and genuine originality of thought," and that "he has a remarkable angle of vision, a highly disciplined and coherent one, that informs his work to such a degree as to make the work *sui generis* original."[4] In addition to his originality, much interpretation of Foucault's work has floundered on the difficulties of his style. Certainly he is willfully antisystematic. His perspective shifts from work to work, and he nurtures a dream of the intellectual as one "who is incessantly on the move, doesn't know exactly where he is heading nor what he will think tomorrow for he is too attentive to the present."[5] "Do not ask who I am and do not ask me to remain the same: leave it to our bureaucrats and our police to see that our papers are in order. At least spare us their morality when we write."[6] The key to understanding this desire is the recognition that Foucault was above all a teacher, and his works exhibit the style of what he took teaching to be: an incessant interrogation in the interest of examining how an issue is cast in the form of a problem.

The story of Foucault's life could largely be told through the geography of his teaching positions. Lille, Uppsala, Warsaw, Hamburg, Clermont-Ferrand, Tunisia, Vincennes, Paris. It was during his fourteen years at the Collège de France that Foucault achieved his greatest renown as a thinker and teacher. The cacophony of foreign tongues heard before each of his classes among the hundreds of students who filled the large lecture hall at the Collège testified to the audience that his work had found in other countries. Although the major languages into which he had been translated was a sign of an interest in his writings that extended far beyond the classroom, the best single indication of his thought's appeal was the tangible sense of excitement that possessed his auditors as they listened to him thinking aloud. The regular, almost monotone voice in which the words poured forth seemed irreconcilable with the bursts of dramatic images that exploded in his speech: word paintings in which Greek philosophers and Christian theologians, medical doctors and psychiatrists, those searching for truth and those inflicted with the passion for power found themselves depicted together with the figures of madmen, the dissected bodies of the dead, and the cowering expressions of the imprisoned and exploited. In hearing Foucault, many felt that the world we did in fact inhabit had found a craftsman to portray it. It was a very personal style of portrayal. Like Rebeyrolle, Foucault's teaching communicated an energy, an intensity, and an agitation. It was not so much the specific topics he treated that concentrated attention as it was the restlessness of his questioning, the deployment of a thinking that continually transgressed disciplinary bounds and its own most recent formulations. Foucault's thinking swept on to a series of problematics in which it struggled with itself and urged an activity upon his students. He left no teaching, but he did engrave a manner of questioning.

As a practitioner of the history of systems of thought, the title he gave to his Chair at the Collège and to his work in general, Foucault's investigations were directed not to philosophical truth but to the historically true: What kinds of knowledge functioned as true in different historical periods? How were they related to the exercise of power in constructing a type of normativity and a mode of relating to the self? His classroom inquiries pressed on his listeners the need to grasp the history of cultural development operating behind the ways we conceive of reason and its absence, behind the symptoms announcing our finitude, behind the disciplines we establish for directing human development, and finally, behind the technologies that shape our experience of our very selves, and our questioning of that experience. Two of the unique accents in Foucault's practice of teaching are thus the specific domains he chose as worthy of thought, and the approaches with which he experimented in order to make these domains thinkable. His cultural analysis worked on the relations formed within the intersection of three spheres: how a field of learning is constituted (knowledge); what forces are operating in relation to that learning (knowledge-power); how self-formation is tied to both (knowledge-power-liberty). His approach to these spheres was to problematize their historical appearance, that is, to exercise wonder regarding how these specific relations actually functioned and why they took on the configuration they did. While the study of the history of thought is the examination of the relations of knowledge-power-liberty or subjectivization, the practice of thought consists of grasping these relations as responses to particular cultural problematics. Foucault's style was employed not for the sake of resolving the problems that were discovered, but rather of overturning the unquestioned status that these historically contingent problematizations held in determining our contemporary practice of thought. It battled against that tyranny of intellect that assumes the unknown to be irrelevant, or that accepts the sufficiency of current lines of inquiry for eliminating our ignorance. If the ideal of good teaching is to leave students with questions, Foucault's left them principally with questions about their questions.

Recognizing this personal style does not mean that there is no legacy from Foucault's teaching and writing. Indeed, the aim of this study is a comprehensive reading of his work in the interest of making that legacy more precise and more suited for appropriation. The structure of this study organizes Foucault's work according to its stages of development, and respects the distinct forms of thinking he fashioned at each of these stages. Chapter 2, "From Man and Psychology to the Experience of Thought," is an account of Foucault's earliest writings (1954–1966) and of the psychological interrogation of man that characterized his first intellectual commitments. These writings exhibit as well the collapse of that original anthropological project and the emergence of a series of distinctive experiences in thinking. Four experiences define the basic stages in his intellectual journey as well as the operations for the conduct of inquiry that were fashioned from them. Chapter 3, "Cathartic Thinking," examines his work in the important years from 1966 to 1968. Cathartic thinking was Foucault's effort to comprehend and purge the epistemic conditions determining the major principles of current knowledge in the human sciences. The need for catharsis was personal, for an archaeology of the human sciences would reveal to Foucault why the question of man formed the ground of his initial philosophical-historical inquiries. Such a catharsis would also excavate the roots both of modern anthropological concern in general and of its major forms of investigation, hermeneutics and structuralism. Chapter 4, "Dissonant Thinking," considers the work of 1969 to 1971 and the first major formulation of his archaeological method. Archaeology defines itself as a way of thinking that, liberated from an anthropological project, seeks the emancipation of dissonance, the exposure of thought to reality as a multiplicity of events that need new, nondialectical orderings. Chapter 5, "Dissident Thinking," explores those writings from the period of 1972 to 1979, the time during which Foucault was engaged in an archaeology-genealogy of politics. His analysis entailed a dissent from contemporary society's forms of the distribution and practice of power, and from the types of understanding that conceal the grounds for these forms. The last chapter, "Ecstatic Thinking," explores the final and culminating stage in Foucault's development, his genealogy of desire and his statement of an ethical route for future intellectual inquiry.

In addition to these distinct experiences of thought that Foucault enunciated, any study of his work should recognize the three distinguishable levels on which he operated throughout his development. The first was his consideration of specific cultural and institutional practices. While it is necessary for an understanding of his thought to give some sense of these researches, the focus of this examination is to subordinate their detail to a second level: the methodological ambition of Foucault's work, its attempt to show how a history of our present could find its way. Archaeology and genealogy were the general terms he employed to indicate both this way and the possibility of a cooperative labor: the critical comprehension of our culture's limits on and options for the practice of freedom by those scattered individuals, intellectuals or activists, actual victims or future prey, for whom the promise of the modern age at its creation has been exploded by the destructiveness of its maturation. A third level on which Foucault's thought elaborates itself is more subtle, forcing this study to navigate between Scylla and Charybdis. While rendering a coherent account of Foucault's accomplishment as a whole, it has sought to avoid a common mistake, namely, the failure to appreciate that thought's fundamental experience of itself as a force of flight. Foucault's fidelity to this experience and to the style generated by it accounts for many features in his work that may prove annoying to a systematically oriented commentator. Nevertheless, the essential character of his thought is precisely this dynamic movement of relentless questioning that refuses to remain with one specific area of study and draw out fully the implications of a particular investigation. Foucault's style mirrors the fundamental urgency of his thought, which is less to convince than to agitate, to compel a desire for flight, to afflict the reader with a pressure or force. "The same force passes directly from the painter to the canvas, and from one canvas to that which follows it; from a trembling dejection and then a sorrow that is born, to a quivering of hope, to an endless flight"; the movement of this flight "has left you alone in the prison where you are now confined, dizzy from the passage of this force which is already now far from you and of which you see before you only its traces, the traces of what escapes."[7] This manner of experiencing thought is not new. Ever since Plato composed his parable of the cave, the notion of flight and escape has been a leading image for the activity of thought. A modern example would be Kant's definition of Enlightenment as an "Ausgang," as an exit or escape from the state of immaturity.[8] Nevertheless, Foucault's experience of thought was novel, for it was enunciated at a different time and for a different situation. If Foucault's fundamental experience of thought was flight and escape, it was because he found himself illuminating confinements that were striking in their extensiveness and subtlety.

2. CONFINEMENTS

No other contemporary philosophical thinker possessed Foucault's acute ability to discover and describe the confinements that imprison human life and thought: the confinement of the mad in the Age of Reason; the condemnation of the asylum's patients to the status of children; the internment of thought in the human sciences; the incarceration of prisoners in the penitentiary; the imprisonment of human identity within the cell of a sexual self; the fate of living in a carceral archipelago. His sensitivity to human confinement was a gift of early experience, of painful recollection. Michel Foucault was born on October 15, 1926, in Poitiers, between the unexpected slaughter of the First World War and the unanticipated sudden collapse of France in the face of the Nazis. His city lay on the frontier of the Occupied and Vichy zones, a place of uneasiness to which the city was no stranger. The great eighth-century battle of Poitiers, at which Christian and Muslim forces opposed one another in the decisive confrontation over the identity of future European civilization, was the most world-historical of the many conflicts and invasions that have traversed the city's history. Long a showpiece of Roman culture, a style to which its Christian centuries would remain attached, Poitier's physical memory continues to juxtapose the different epochs through which it has lived. Its local history opens with the boast, "Poitiers, city of all ages," a sense one often has when visiting its museum's rich archaeological collection or strolling its streets.[9]

And yet native to Foucault's young years was a particular sense of menace.

> What strikes me now when I try to recall those impressions is that nearly all the great emotional memories I have are related to the political situation. . . . The menace of war was our background, our framework of existence. Then the war arrived. Much more than the activities of family life, it was these events concerning the world which are the substance of our memory. I say "our" because I am nearly sure that most boys and girls in France at this moment had the same experience. Our private life was really threatened. Maybe that is the reason why I am fascinated by history and the relationship between personal experience and those events of which we are a part.[10]

In the years of his youth, this political awareness would be sharpened by other events, which educated him into a nuanced appreciation of the restrictions acting upon human life. As a student in Paris, where he initially engaged in Communist Party causes, Foucault ran into the limits that his Marxist professors could impose. His early interest in exploring the relations between politics and the human sciences was discouraged, and he speculated later on a possible reason for his teachers' lack of response:

> I wonder nevertheless whether among the intellectuals in or close to the PCF [French Communist Party] there wasn't a refusal to pose the problem of internment, of the political use of psychiatry and, in a more general sense, of the disciplinary grid of society. No doubt little was then known in 1955–60 of the real extent of the gulag, but I believe that many

sensed it, in any case many had a feeling that it was better not to talk about those things: it was a danger zone marked by warning signs.[11]

While these warning signs were very evident in the Poland of the 1950s, where Foucault spent a year at the University of Warsaw, his three years at the University of Uppsala made him especially aware of undeclared limitations. "At the moment when I left France, freedom for personal life was very sharply restricted there. At this time Sweden was supposed to be a much freer country. And there I had the experience that a certain kind of freedom may have, not exactly the same effects, but as many restrictive effects as a directly restrictive society. That was an important experience for me."[12]

The fruit of that experience became apparent in his later analyses of disciplinary practices and of such institutions as the asylum and the clinic. On a more general level, the bequest of these experiences was a superb training in recognizing the chains that could be forged by noble identities: modern, enlightened, humanistic. Foucault became suspicious of a modernity that proclaimed itself as a period of history, a victorious surpassing of a more or less archaic premodernity. He came to regard it not as a lucky location on a calendar but as an attitude with which one could approach reality. His attitude toward modernity was a commitment to the task of understanding the present, a task that for him was separable "from a desperate eagerness to imagine it, to imagine it otherwise than it is, and to transform it not by destroying it but by grasping it in what it is."[13] The conviction of enlightenment could become an even more dangerous delusion. Foucault refused what he called "the 'blackmail' of the Enlightenment," the demand that one be either for or against it.[14] The issue was more complicated than that. Foucault saw that the heritage of the Enlightenment period had become deeply problematic. Political decisions seemed to have become hostages of the technical rationality advanced. Its praise of a Reason with universal validity had been called into question by the angry challenges of those nonwestern cultures that were free to speak after the end of the colonial era. Finally, amid the destruction of the world wars, it became both a right and an obligation to ask what part that once-promising heritage had played in the "effects of a despotism where that hope was lost."[15] For Foucault, an enlightened ethos arises not from slavish faithfulness to the Enlightenment period's doctrinal elements but from a commitment to its aspiration for a permanent critique of the present age.

If confinement provided the central experience that troubled Foucault's thought, he concluded quite early that the strongest wall of the contemporary mind's prison was humanism and the figure of man that was at its core. Foucault's thought is probably best known for its proclamation of man's death, its assertion that our understanding of man is but temporary and contingent, destined to "be erased, like a face drawn in sand at the edge of the sea."[16] It was an intuition he had first had in his 1961 study of Kant's anthropology and to which he was faithful up until the appeal in his last works for a renunciation of our modern selves.[17] Humanism represented the incarceration of human beings within a specifically modern system of thought and practice that had become so intimately a part of them that it was no longer experienced as a series of confinements but was embraced as the very substance of being human. The prison that becomes the special target of Foucault's criticism is none other than the modern identity of man himself. This identity is the center of that humanism that is both a particular understanding of human reality and a technology for human development: a truth that is power and a power that exhibits itself as truth.[18] As we take up his writings individually, we shall develop Foucault's specific delineation of humanism as the modern age's most subtle incarceration as well as the essentially antihumanistic operations that characterize his thought. It may be pointed out here that his work moves against three general molds in this confinement: philosophical, political, and ethical.

The philosophical confinement consists in an egocentric illusion in which man himself is regarded as an ahistorical nature and as the privileged object of reflection, and in which his ego is taken as the autonomous source of all thought and meaning.[19] The political confinement consists in the construction of an individuality that serves the project of administering large populations in the interest of making them both more useful and more docile. Under the cloak of its self-professed benevolence, humanism produced institutions such as the prison whose actual functioning did not seem to demythologize the humanistic justifications upon which they rested. The ethical confinement consisted in the elaboration of a particular relationship to the self that incites the desire to identify with the positive figure fabricated by modern power-knowledge relations. Self-formation is reduced to the task of self-subjugation. While all three dimensions of this humanistic confinement are implicitly at work throughout Foucault's writings, a primacy was exercised by one of them at each general stage of his thought. Thus, in the 1960s, it was principally philosophical confinement that he sought to illuminate (chapters 2 through 4 of this work). In the 1970s, his examination of power-knowledge relations focused on political confinement (chapter 5 of this work). In the 1980s, Foucault developed an ethical thinking that would propose a critique of and an alternative to modern self-subjugation (chapter 6 of this work).

Foucault's reflective resistance to all three levels is the most intensive and sustained denunciation of humanism that has yet been put forward. Although the idea of antihumanism has become more familiar in contemporary discussions, it is nevertheless still the case that the notion provides the "most scandalous aspect" of contemporary French thought.[20] While Foucault's antihumanistic critique, and especially his utilization of historical research to advance that critique, is original, there is a French context for his work, and some notice of that context is necessary to ward off preliminary misunderstanding of its meaning.

At eighteen, Foucault left Poitiers for Paris, where French intellectual life had suddenly been shocked into the need to define its own identity and significance. When he entered the Ecole Normale Supérieure, Foucault walked into a climate of widespread desire for social and intellectual renewal.[21] In contrast to the disenchantment with historical knowledge that had followed the First World War as a result of its failure to anticipate or account for the great event that would shatter the foundations of European culture, a passion developed in the generation after 1945 to understand the historical reality that had forced itself so brutally into their lives. The so-called critical approaches to knowledge, value, and history of the neo-Kantianism that had dominated French philosophical thought between the wars suddenly appeared to be so much illusion. The war brought, as Sartre expressed it, a "taste for history," the sense that, well beyond the movement of spirit with which idealists concerned themselves, we were situated amid currents of obscure and dangerous historical forces.[22] To understand them became imperative, and France turned to Hegel for enlightenment.

The writings, translations, and teaching of the major inaugurators of Hegelianism in France, Alexander Kojève and Jean Hyppolite, put forward a unique and fascinating image of the German philosopher and of history understood as conflict and tragedy.[23] While Hyppolite asserted that Hegelianism represented an overcoming of the "refusal of history" that had characterized French philosophy from Descartes to Bergson, it was an overcoming that seemed to open not just a philosophical current but a way of living, a unity of thought and action. Although it was concretized in the very different approaches represented either by the tragic existentialist encounter with history or by the Marxist commitment to world struggle, Hegel's texts disclosed a vision of history that was felt to be adequate to the times, a vision that Descombes has called a "terrorist conception of history."[24] The face of historical change lost its serenity as a smooth process of intellectual and moral advance, and in its place emerged a struggle to the death, typified in the master-slave dialectic upon which Kojève placed such emphasis in his interpretation of Hegel. While the meaning of this struggle might differ between existentialists and Marxists, there was one reality on which they were united: the figure of man was idolized as the central element in the historical process. Both the existentialism and the Marxism of this period were rooted in an anthropological reading of Hegel, and both presented themselves as humanisms in which God was replaced by man, and in which an authentic human existence became an historical possibility.

Mirroring the slave's discovery of the humanity he found crushed by the terror of a master's oppression, as Hegel presented it in his *Phenomenology*, both movements dedicated themselves to the affirmation of man. Whether the specific statement of it were that of the atheist Sartre or the Christian Marcel, existential philosophy was defined as anthropology, and the unity and centrality of the notion of man served as the starting point for thought.[25] The humanistic temper of existentialism was matched in Marxist circles, assisted by the appearance in France of Marx's 1844 manuscripts and the weight they gave to the image of Marx as a philosopher concerned with man and his alienation.[26] Issues of man and authentic humanism became the horizon for the most varied projects of thought: man as an ego whose subjectivity is the source of his individuality and reflective power; man as a being whose alienation and the attempt to overcome it is the principle of his engagement within history.

Neither history nor man sustained this centrality for reflection, and there appeared in the 1960s a sharp turn away from France's postwar faith and a widespread abandonment of its humanistic core. While both existentialists and Marxists had glorified the individual's historical responsibility, the figure of man came to seem peculiarly impotent to make history in a world in which personal intentions and actions appeared so feeble in comparison with the modern age's great social and economic forces, and in which the moral passion of Marxism had culminated in Stalinism and state bureaucracy. Instead of placing the French at the dawn of a novel campaign for freedom from human alienation, the 1944 liberation from the Nazis seemed, in retrospect, to have situated them at a frontier in which the only option was to identify with either Americanism or Communism. Ultimately even this choice would be determined by events and powers beyond them. The disillusionment of postwar hopes was only one of several factors forging an alternative to the humanistic discussions that had proliferated in the years prior to 1960. Humanists themselves had prepared the way for this alternative in their tendency to fragment the concept of man within the many differing perspectives in which he found himself the main character. With some calling for an integral Christian humanism and others speaking up for existentialist or Marxist versions, it was inevitable that the concept of man's identity and character would be far from having a common starting point and a shared conviction. Man became increasingly problematic, and his form less distinct. While Sartre's identification of existentialism as a humanism led him into a long debate about the character of this humanism, Merleau-Ponty's later philosophy moved furthest from the Cartesian and Kantian assumptions regarding subjectivity to which the concept of man was tied. If the sheer multiplicity of anthropological concepts that were discussed by French thinkers, and Merleau-Ponty's powerful interrogation of their assumptions, weakened the hold of the idea of man, certain reinterpretations of major thinkers opened up gaps in the humanistic network through which would rush other objects for thought.

At the same time that an anthropological interpretation of Hegel came to be regarded as fundamentally flawed, Louis Althusser's reading of Marx directly attacked another major philosophical source for the climate of humanism.[27] Althusser argued that Marx's specific contribution to thought broke with the humanistic frame of reference contained in certain of his earlier writings. In his view, Marx's economic texts were discontinuous "with every philosophical anthropology or humanism," and this break was "no secondary detail: it is Marx's scientific discovery."[28] The questioning of man is thrust aside in favor of a science of praxis that analyzes productive forces and their relations within an economic system. Just as Marxist humanists found themselves charged with gross misunderstanding of Marx's thought, the existentialist temper promoted by Sartre was cut off from the Heideggerian source of its inspiration. At least since 1947, with the publication of Heidegger's "Letter on Humanism" to Jean Beaufret, it became clear that an existentialist and humanistic interpretation of his thinking was basically in error.[29] As Heidegger's own philosophy became better known in France, it was evident that his entire project was precisely a critique of the anthropological and Cartesian principles that still operated in existentialism. A more accurate appropriation of Heidegger's thought soon led French thinkers to a serious encounter with Nietzsche, on whom Heidegger had written the most original and provocative commentary. The Nietzsche who appeared on the French scene was the smasher of the idol, man, and proclaimer of the Superman.[30]

Although humanistic existentialism and Marxism never disappeared from French debate, they were eclipsed by new interests that developed in the 1960s. In the position that man and history had occupied, structure emerged as the key concept for thought. Although it was defined differently, depending upon the type of structure under consideration and the specific interests of the examiner, it did generally designate that the intelligibility of experience ought to be sought in an analysis of nonapparent systems.[31] The passionate pursuit of structures that developed at this time rested upon the pioneering work of the linguist Ferdinand de Saussure. Saussure sketched a project for the examination of signs as elements of the system in which they functioned and to which they were subordinate. Language thus is a system possessed of a structure that determines the use of the words that speakers employ. In suggesting this approach to linguistics, Saussure had pointed out that such an analysis was part of a new science, semiology, which treats all social practice as a system of signs. Saussure's linguistic model seemed to provide a unifying perspective on a vast range of diverse activities. As a result, it galvanized the enthusiasm of several major French thinkers, whose similarity of interest grouped them under the banner of structuralism.[32]

Despite the often profound differences among such intellectuals as the Marxist Althusser, the literary critic Roland Barthes, the psychoanalyst Jacques Lacan, and the anthropologist Claude Lévi-Strauss, they did share a search for unconscious structures that would permit explanations that held out the promise of complementing one another as well as transcending categories of an insufficiently scientific character. Among these categories, subjectivity and history attracted the principal critical demolition. Although all the structuralists displaced interest in the individual to a study of the system within which his activity was determined and made coherent, Lacan's radical decentering of the subject caught the temper of an entire intellectual movement. Even one's unconscious, structured in the form of a language, constitutes a discourse that cannot be claimed as one's own. The subject is necessarily dispersed in language, and is always but a "fading thing" whose presence is in a chain of signifiers that exist only for other signifiers.[33] This dispersion of the subject concretized itself, for example, in a type of literary criticism, represented by Barthes, that dispensed with the autonomy of the author. Literary texts proliferate with meanings that cannot be accounted for in terms of the category of an author. The writer is only an element in the functioning both of a system of language and of a social and political order.[34]

When man was driven out of the center of intellectual interest by structuralist approaches, the historical perspective seemed to be exiled along with him. The linguistic model that guided structural analyses was rooted in Saussure's distinction between the synchronic and diachronic, language in its static state as opposed to language in its evolutionary development. The analysis of a system such as language gives priority to the synchronic state, and an understanding of the structure must precede the study of the change from structure to structure. As Saussure pointed out, the linguist "can enter the mind of speakers only by completely suppressing the past. The intervention of history can only falsify his judgment."[35] This concern with the synchronic and static in contrast to the historical became one of the defining features of French intellectual life in the sixties. Lévi-Strauss was its most articulate champion. For him, the great achievement of the linguistic model was to place the "necessary and sufficient" explanation for customs and institutions in those unconscious systems that are necessarily apprehended synchronically.[36] Historical understanding turns away from this possibility of scientific explanation by imposing the construct of a continuous pattern, a pattern that is merely the product of western illusion and ethnocentrism. A structural anthropology would help to demystify the hold historical understanding had on western societies, and demonstrate how the so-called primitive mind and the advanced logical mind are structurally one.[37] It was fitting that Lévi-Strauss's major articulation of his position should include an attack on Sartre's thought. More than any other thinker, Sartre represented the claims of man and history against the structuralist tide. The defender of dialectics was the proponent of human praxis and freedom against those trying to lock human beings within structures. For Sartre, history is the sphere of human action and cannot be treated in the same way as already constituted systems such as myths. The crucial issue is not what has been made of man but how he will respond, how he himself will create.[38]

The various debates that revolved around the issues of humanism and antihumanism, history and system, in the France of the 1960s were ultimately a question of how thinking should proceed. Two fairly well-defined and opposing procedures were put forward as its guide: structuralism and phenomenology. Structuralism, seeking to break with what it regards as the illusion of subjectivity and ego-centricity, is drawn to an analysis of the unconscious structures that account for the identity and character of specific systems. Such systems are self-enclosed, and questions of their reference to a "world" are displaced by considerations of the rules that define the systems and the functioning of their elements. This structural approach necessarily subordinates historical or diachronic reasoning to synchronic analysis: the study of development is harnessed to the comparative description of distinct systems. On the other hand, phenomenology, as a mode of understanding, is attracted to the interpretation of the multiple meanings that emerge out of the interaction between man and the world. Phenomenology explores two poles: that of the conscious meaning-giving of the human subject, and that of the world as given—the "real has to be described, not constructed or formed."[39] The turn to the subject leads into an historical world, for its present life opens on to "temporalities outside my living experience and acquire a social horizon, with the result that my world is expanded to the dimensions of that collective history which my private existence takes up and carries forward."[40]

These conflicts over man, history, and thought formed the background for Michel Foucault's own thinking, and provide a context for certain of his formulations. His own consideration of these topics is important because the issues transcend the French milieu that we have so briefly sketched, and point to developments by which we are all affected. While the term "antihumanism" may bear an unmistakable French accent, it refers to an internationally known phenomenon: the challenge to the modern image of man as the center of the world's intelligibility. Nowhere is this challenge more evident or more heavy with implications than in the sphere of historical thinking. In recent years, there has been a proliferation of various historical approaches that do not concentrate on the role of human action, but rather on that of such objects as disease, sea routes, weather, unconscious structures, geography.[41] Such an historical approach is welcomed by some because it announces the end of ideological interpretations; for others it proclaims a new ideology of fatalism in which human beings are made the playthings of anonymous social, economic, and natural structures, structures that are haughtily indifferent to the claims of free will and human praxis. Because it involves a substantial element of our culture's identity and meaning, this crisis in historical knowledge is bound to evoke many different attempts at resolution. Within such abstract methodological formulations as structuralism and phenomenology are very precise efforts to provide guidance beyond this turning point for historical consciousness. Lévi-Strauss's radical resolution of the crisis was hinted at as early as 1955, when, in *Tristes Tropiques*, he voiced his melancholy at the significance of westernization and development in South America: "from being eternal, it has become historic; from being metaphysical, it has become social." Those prehistoric societies maintain fidelity to a "past conceived of as a timeless model." In their allegiance to this model, Lévi-Strauss sees the wisdom for the West of those cultures he has devoted so much of his life to studying. The highly vaunted historical consciousness of our own culture is only an element of its own myth, and social anthropology finds its greatest mission in making possible a de-historicizing of western thought. Guarding this possibility, anthropology is a discipline that keeps alive a "permanent hope for mankind."[42] Such a structuralist response may be applauded as providential, coming at a time when European nations have been dislodged from the long primacy they exercised in determining the world's destiny. The creation of a system of thought that does not require history and that calls for a release from the pain and responsibility of historical consciousness is a solution that aspires to radical decisiveness. If the ruins of European civilization nourished in Lévi-Strauss an admiration for timeless societies, it was the danger of yielding to this temptation that motivated Edmund Husserl to begin a new philosophizing of history. What had to be saved from the destruction unleashed upon Europe in this century was the Greek invention of a philosophical thinking that was the "first breakthrough to what is essential to humanity as such, its *entelechy*." Man is a "teleological being and an ought-to-be" who finds his destiny in a will to truth, in the endless task of reason's expansion. This task and its agent, man, are essentially historical, and phenomenology's duty is to follow their historical-teleological course. Phenomenology's philosophical thinking of history is at the service of the "West's mission for humanity," of the recovery of the "heroism of reason" it invented, of working out the "concept of Europe as the historical teleology of the infinite goals of reason."[43]

Unable to find destiny in Husserl's Reason and unwilling to seek refuge in

Lévi-Strauss's eternal system, Foucault was obliged to discover his own way of thinking historically. Neither structuralism nor phenomenology showed him the way. His conviction as to our ignorance of those factors generating our world, and his sense of the need to comprehend the difference of our contemporary period, separated him from structuralist approaches. Phenomenology's apotheosis of man's subjectivity and meaning isolated him from Husserl. He came to conclude that both structuralism and phenomenology were inadequate to an analysis of the event, of those ruptures in history that offer possibilities for thought and action discontinuous with those that preceded them. That inadequacy renders them incapable of indicating a route for escape from the historically constructed confinements that so concerned Foucault. We shall see that a major element in his originality is to have created experiments for inquiry that allow one to break out of the limited option of a necessary allegiance to either phenomenology or structuralism. One is enabled to transcend this option by a comprehension of the humanistic problematic and culture from which both lines of questioning ultimately arise.

3. Escape

Many of Foucault's critics accuse him of not only identifying prisons but celebrating them, of creating such a sense of entrapment within systems of ideas and practices that one is left with no scope for personal freedom and cultural change. Although Foucault may have rejected Kant's question of man and the consequent search of his critiques for formal, universal structures, he has certainly not avoided the charge that Goethe leveled at Kant, namely, that he had put the "mind in a cage" and then beckoned it to "look beyond the bars."[44] While confinements are the central experiences that Foucault's work describes, the ardent desire of his thought was to facilitate flight from them. He certainly recognized the cages within which human life and thought are exercised, and he possessed an acute skepticism about those modern windows of knowledge that promised a way out, but that in fact, by not breaking with the logic of confinement, would always remain windows of prisons. The "within" that he shows thought to occupy is the decisive moment for the act of thinking itself, for it to recognize both its prisons and the illusory character of the authorized exits from them. If Foucault is able to imagine the walls of confinement giving way, it is because he envisioned a new horizon for the practice of thought.

The distinct experiments in thinking that Foucault fashioned were meant to indicate through very concrete experiences the powerful movement of escape that thought is. At the same time, however, they are not random experiments, but join together to effect a common dynamism and model of escape. That dynamism and model is an ethics for thought itself. It was only in his last works that Foucault actually proposed a schema for an ethical interrogation of experience; that schema had a long gestation period, however, and represents Foucault's fashioning of his personal relationship to his entire work and the desire that inhabited it. The schema's elements were created by four arts of questioning that were developed in the course of Foucault's long journey of thought. These four modes of interrogation were: (1) What was it necessary to think today, in contrast to the traditional domain of the thought-worthy? What should the substance for thought be? (2) In examining this domain, what sort of understanding should be sought? What mode of subjection should the thinker take up? (3) How should the search for such understanding find its way? What asceticism must it practice on itself in order to be enabled to think differently? (4) What goal is pursued through this definition of substance, mode of subjection, and practice of asceticism? Foucault's exploration of these questions throughout his works succeeded in establishing a broad ethical inquiry into the activity of thought itself. It is an ethics that is neither a general statement of code for thinking nor even primarily an exemplary model for inquiry. Foucault's writings constitute a practice that educates their readers into an ethical responsibility for intellectual inquiry. They put forward not an obligatory conduct but a possible escape from an intellectual milieu unnourished by ethical interrogation. Foucault's practice of his ethics marks paths for a collaborative assumption of new responsibilities.

The domain or substance of Foucault's ethics is made up of the practices giving rise to those issues that entail, implicitly or explicitly, the exercise of moral discernment and decision. Rejecting moral experience as a matter of either response to religious revelation or commitment to an aesthetic task, the modern period articulated moral conduct in the context of true forms of knowledge. Foucault's project makes this modern statement problematic by an examination of the forms of knowledge or discourse that became paramount in informing moral reflection. Such discourses would include those of psychology, medicine, and sexology as well as the human sciences that direct both the cognitive enterprise and the technologies for human improvement. His examination of how these are created as spheres of truth undermines the experience of reality that these true forms of knowledge legitimate as well as the moral perspectives, or absence of them, that they sanction. Foucault's insight into the role our modern forms of knowledge play in determining our experience of reality, and in concealing that determination, is rooted in his own work in psychology and his own appreciation of the power of language. At the same time, the discovery of this domain was facilitated by the great masters of suspicion, Marx, Nietzsche, and Freud. With their rejection of any primary reality to be read, "interpretation has at last become an infinite task."[45] As a result, Foucault was able to focus on the way interpretations of the real were constructed and championed by various forms of knowledge, which operated in relation to both political and personal concerns. Foucault's work is not the enactment of a program laid down by these masters of suspicion, but decisively separates itself from their own interpretations. Unlike Marx, he recognizes no anteriority of practice to theory, and thus gives to these forms of knowledge their relatively autonomous status as historical agents. Unlike Nietzsche, he does not attach himself to the notion of life, but problematizes that position by his analysis of how life as a philosophical hermeneutics is itself constituted in the operations of a modern bio-politics. Unlike Freud, Foucault does not accept the form of human individuality and of relation to self that characterizes psychoanalytic interpretation. His qualified rejection of these three thinkers was the prelude to a delimitation of the realm on which a contemporary ethics could work: an ethical analysis of truths and their relation to the political and personal. His ethical perspective is signaled in his concern with the action of the axes that are investigated: what knowledge does (and not reads), how power constructs (and not represses), how a relationship to the self is invented (and not discovered). In demarcating this realm, he articulated a domain of truth values to be investigated that breaks not only with the salvation values and aesthetic values of ancient culture, but also with the proposed modern alternatives. The forms of knowledge that produce truth replace Marxist analyses of labor; the study of knowledge-power relations replaces a Nietzschean metaphysic of life; the investigation of knowledge-power-subject relations supplants the Freudian reading of the unconscious text. The categories of labor, life, and language, which were for him intrinsic to the modern configuration of knowledge, survived in the fundamental thought of the three major critics of that culture. Thus all three participated in that specific modern failure, the inability to develop a morality.[46] Foucault indicates a way to overcome this failure by constituting thought itself as an action that must be ethically interviewed as the anxious source of the forms of knowledge that inform our reflection, interpret our political situation, and shape our relation to ourselves.

The second element in Foucault's ethics of thought is what he came to call its mode of subjection, the type of enlightenment that is pursued in questioning the ethical domain of thought. Foucault's debate with Kant was central to his appreciation of this element. The first three Foucaultian experiments with thought that we treat here—cathartic, dissonant, dissident—represent Foucault's effort to denature or historicize Kant's great questions on knowledge, obligation, and hope. This effort is made for the sake of restoring an ethical matrix to our choice of intellectual inquiry. Not "What can I know?" but rather, How have my questions been produced? How has the path of my knowing been determined? Not "What ought I to do?" but rather, How have I been situated to experience the real? How have exclusions operated in delineating the realm of obligation for me? Not "What may I hope for?" but rather, What are the struggles in which I am engaged? How have the parameters for my aspirations been defined? The point of such shifts is to free thought from a search for formal structures and place it in an historical field where it must confront the singular, contingent, and arbitrary that operate in what is put forward as universal, necessary, and obligatory. "The point, in brief, is to transform the critique conducted in the form of necessary limitation into a practical critique that takes the form of a possible transgression."[47]

Such transgressions are enacted through an asceticism of methods for directing our inquiries, an asceticism that provides the third element in Foucault's ethics. His methods of historical analysis aim to displace Kant's central question of man and the formal critiques to which it gives rise. In their place he proposes three other directions for the practice of intellectual responsibility, a practice that entails a work we do to ourselves along the axes of discourse, power, and self. There is a shift of focus from what we supposedly do to language to an examination of what language does to us. This line of inquiry stresses our responsibility for the support we lend to the unchallenged dominance of specific discourses, whether this support be shown in our acceptance of fellowships of experts with authoritative control over a discourse, or in our justification of certain institutional patterns for the dissemination of a discourse. Foucault's examination of the prison is a paradigm of how a discourse of institutional reform became an unwilling advocate of central doctrinal elements in the arrangement that it was presumably criticizing. The ascetic elimination of humanistic themes serves to free the critic from the reformist discourse that is itself the product of modern institutions. The strategy of such discourses is to disarm fundamental criticism by creating its own limited categories for the imagining of change. Through his genealogical investigations, Foucault redefines the field of our action: from an arena that is already enunciated in terms of identifiable repressions and specific programs of liberation for overthrowing them to an ever-changing historical space in which power is capable of colonizing the noblest intentions and projects. The analysis of power-knowledge relations presses a series of invitations: to look beyond apparently liberal values to the many social and political strategies with which they merge and within which they might play roles not originally anticipated for them; to be less trusting that current conceptions of freedom and dignity are self-evident and do not bring with them different enslavements. Genealogy is permanent critique in the interest of an endless practice of freedom. Finally, Foucault's methods of ethical interrogation shift the intellectual's duty away from responsibility for the articulation or rationalization of codes of morality based on a human essence to an interrogation of those practices that shape our relations to ourselves. In doing this, his ethics involves an encounter with those forces that determine our desire for certain forms of knowledge and for particular programs of liberation.

The fourth element in Foucault's ethics for thought was its aspiration. He realized that there was never to be a definitive escape from configurations of knowledge-power-self relations, and yet he was unyielding in his conviction that no specific configuration was necessary and unchangeable. His declaration of the death of man was complemented in his last years by a counsel, in the interest of self-development, to get free of those relationships to self that we have inherited as children of western technologies. This counsel reflects his appreciation of the vitality that had graced his own experiments in thinking through his willingness to embrace ever-changing interests. The counsel was also an invitation to the practice of a thought that would be stimulated more by the differences it confronted than by the coherences it found, more by the discontinuities it faced than by the evolutions into which it was directed. For Foucault, there was a special pleasure to be discovered in thinking, whether its mode be cathartic, dissonant, or dissident. That pleasure was an ecstatic experience of transgressing the limits laid down by intellectual disciplines, and rediscovering the mystery of a world and a history that needed to be newly recognized as worthy of thought and as open to artistic transformation. Such a world inspires the willingness to dispossess oneself of the routines of thought and action that eventually become one's identity. He discovered the goal of thought to be a permanent provocation to the forces that war against our creativity. If, as a result, his philosophy is described as an anarchism, it is only because the modern bureaucratization of intellectual life has made it so difficult to practice the freedom that thinking should manifest.[48] Onto the landscape of vast projects of research and evaluation, Foucault introduced an ethics of responsibility for the truths one speaks, for the political relations into which these truths enter, and for those ways of relating to ourselves that make us either conformists to or resisters of those relations. It is a timely ethics that assists in reclaiming thought's moral responsibilities, but also its excitement and pleasure. It is this rare combination of responsibility and pleasure in Foucault's practice of thought that accounts for the appeal of his writings.

CONCLUSION

In one of the numerous tributes accorded Foucault after his death, Edward Said voiced a common sentiment: "What all his readers will surely remember is how in reading him for the first time they felt a particular shock at encountering so incisive and interesting a mind which, with one electrical burst after another, stages ideas with a stylistic flair no other writer of

Foucault's depth and difficulty possessed."[49] What made Foucault's mind so interesting, what accounts for the shock his readers so often experienced, is that his work at least met, if it did not totally satisfy, a widespread yearning for some ethical vista in the practice of thought, for an ethics imposed not from without, but rather elaborated from within thinking itself, an ethics of thought that would disclose a richer and more worldly intelligence than that to which we have become accustomed. Neither the yearning for this ethics nor the extraordinary renown that Foucault achieved in negotiating his way to it is surprising. The moral disaster of our recent wars and the birth of an atomic age have prompted new questions regarding the ways in which power and knowledge interrelate, and have generated strong suspicions about the harmony of a proclaimed progress of intellect and the power of those who consider themselves its guardians. If Foucault's radical interrogation of the human sciences seems particularly auspicious for the liberal societies that have become restless under their sway, his manner of studying power as a productive force seemed illuminating for the citizens of a democracy who were disturbed by the conformist implications of a mass culture. Against our moral wasteland, which the Second World War especially exposed, any easy faith in the concord between advance in the human sciences and moral improvement had become impossible.

While there are numberless disagreements among Foucault's commentators on both significant and minor points in his work, this disagreement has often obscured the very dissimilar levels on which they are reading him. This incongruity of levels has largely prevented the emergence of a meaningful dialogue, or even conflict, among interpretations. More important, it has concealed the extent to which the major critical perspectives on his work have been shaped by Foucault himself. Each of these perspectives reflects a priority that has been granted to one of the four elements in his ethical interrogation, a priority that has usually resulted in the other elements being relegated to the shadows. The fact that critical readings of Foucault mirror his own ethical strategies bears witness to the yearning for an ethics of thought that has emerged from the wreckage of the modern age's aspirations. It is the ethical domain or substance advocated by his thought that has exercised the most appeal for his commentators. The promise of this domain has been grasped along the three distinct axes he described. The knowledge axis became the focal point of the Nietzschean treatments of Alan Sheridan and Gilles Deleuze.[50] While Sheridan places Foucault within the Nietzschean project of subverting regimes of truth, Deleuze complements this by having Nietzsche and Foucault make a common commitment to a vitalism that overcomes man as a truth. From the Marxist perspective of Mark Poster, the importance of Foucault's knowledge axis is its replacing the model of labor as that philosophy's traditional impetus for interpretation.[51] Barry Smart sees Foucault's contribution to Marxism to consist of his analysis of the power axis—specifically, the insight that "it is no longer feasible to conceptualise relations of power, and the associated mechanisms and effects, simply in terms of the state, class struggle, relations of production and capitalist exploitation. Power has to be analyzed in all its diverse forms, in its exercise, rather than solely in terms of the most centralised possible institutional locus."[52] For Jeffrey Minson, the strength of Foucault's work is located on the subject axis, its excavation of liberalism and that system's production of the personal.[53]

It is the second element of Foucault's ethics, its mode of subjection, that attracts the interest of other major commentators. Mark Cousins and Athar Hussain have written critically of Foucault's commitment to a genealogical understanding because its concern with the conditions for the emergence of branches of knowledge entails the neglect of a normative assessment of them. This criticism, however, leads Cousins and Hussain to a rare appreciation of Foucault's archaeological enterprise of analysis.[54] For Hubert Dreyfus and Paul Rabinow, on the other hand, Foucault's turn to genealogy was a propitious development beyond his archaeological approach, enabling him to found a new project of "interpretive analytics" that they claim represents the "most important contemporary effort both to develop a method for the study of human beings and to diagnose the current situation of our society."[55] For Karlis Racevskis, it is the third element of Foucault's ethics, its ascetic project for thinking, that is of greatest interest. His use of Lacan for the interpretation of Foucault stresses the predominantly subversive character of Foucault's undertaking. While a symbolic order is recognized in the modern period, it is reduced to the status of a mere object for colonization by reason. For Racevskis, Foucault's achievement is his challenge to this colonization and the empire of positive knowledge to which it gives rise.[56] Pamela Major-Poetzl also argues for Foucault's ascetic power. She claims that his "primary intention is to demolish our conventional categories of thought and to render unbelievable the science-myths that organize our perception of the past."[57] She argues that Foucault's archaeology exhibits a common imaginative structure with the theoretical work of contemporary physics; indeed, they are isomorphic forms of thought, both of which assume the existence of a fundamental chaos beneath any order. Charles Lemert and Garth Gillan emphasize the potential of Foucault's asceticism for contemporary social theory; it effects a transgression of the various epistemological strategies that seek to separate knowledge from power.[58] Finally, John Rajchman stresses the goal of Foucault's ethics as his angle of interpretation. That goal is an endless "question of freedom," Foucault's effort to "replace an Idealist philosophy of final emancipation with a nominalist philosophy of endless revolt."[59] The self-disengagement and self-invention of Foucault's last period become the paradigm of free inquiry.

This study of Foucault contains many agreements with, as well as explicit and implicit criticism of, all of these interpreters. The purpose in mentioning them at this point is certainly not to do justice to their readings of Foucault. What their different perspectives and interests reveal, however, is a common appetite for a practice of thinking that exhibits the ethical dimension of reason. Foucault's ethics proposes the wisdom of a dispossession, not only of certain systems of thought and action, but also of a muteness before our age's indigenous suffering. If archaeology became a provocative image for thought, it was in part because of the feeling that such a vision at least attempted to deal with the subterranean forces that erupted in our time. Our modern era's claim to knowledge of, and its will to perfect, the human reality have had unexpectedly tragic consequences, consequences that have mocked that claim and will. In their justification of immense technologies for producing a new man, modern philosophical anthropologies seemed to turn against human beings. Whereas the philosopher had once taught, through his own life, how the universal fate of death could be borne, he had come too often in our age to teach the superior wisdom of how to accept the massacre of others. In the name of truth.[60] It is the inexcusable service professional thinkers have rendered to our era's diminishment, confinement, and, indeed, murder of innocent people that stirs a horror in Foucault that occasionally surfaces in the violence of an image or the shrill tone of a formulation. More usually, however, his sense of outrage is detectable only in that incessant shifting of dusty documents into new orderings that can be heard beyond the silence of his written works. His thought is drawn to the study of language because crusades are always preached. A world organized into great campaigns for the liberation and perfection of human life, while prepared for the destruction of countless thousands in the pursuit of that cause, does not simply appear. Such a world is anticipated in great declarations and manifestos; it convinces itself of the value of its goals by the constant repetition of words become so hallowed that they are the pride of every disciplined mind, so forceful that their mere invocation draws forth the zealous roars of populations and armies. The strategy of Foucault's resistance to this evil is an ethics for thought that consists of a series of questions whose pursuit manifests the assumption of an ethical responsibility. The practice of this ethics disputes the solidity of our world and our history, much as a dream or a work of surrealistic literature might. It is thus appropriate that our account of Foucault's winding journey of thought should begin where it does: in a nightmare.

2

◆

From Man
and Psychology to the
Experience of Thought

In a rare personal disclosure, Michel Foucault once stated to an interviewer that he had been pursued since childhood by a nightmare in which a text is put before his eyes, a text he cannot read, or of which he can only decipher a small part.[1] This chapter will be concerned with presenting Foucault's efforts, as they appear in his writings from 1954 to 1966, to arrive at the type of thinking that is demanded if the text of our age's experience is to be deciphered. We seek to record the steps he took, the false paths he explored, the threshold at which he arrived in his attempt to understand. The intellectual journey of these years was not an easy one: although Foucault was trained in psychology, madness was to have the last word; while he was attracted by phenomenology, the nonapparent was to prove itself decisive; in his search for man, the seriousness of the anthropological question disintegrated: desirous of enhancing freedom, he came to testify to the necessary structures within which it is enclosed; a partisan of the scientific, he allies himself in the end with literature. It was a difficult journey but a far from fruitless one, placing him as it did at the threshold of a unique style of thinking, a new way of expressing and achieving freedom. Although the embrace of his thought in this period is broad, an essential deciphering is taking place. It is the question of what a fundamental thinking is. Although he posed it explicitly in 1964 to surrealism, it had already been his question for at least a decade. "Qu'est-ce que c'est que penser, qu'est-ce que c'est que cette expérience extraordinaire de la pensée?"[2] What is this extraordinary experience that we call thinking? As a result of his studies in psychology, medicine, and literature, Michel Foucault was well on his way to the formulation of an original response.

24

1. THE SEARCH FOR TRUE PSYCHOLOGY

Michel Foucault's journey of thought begins in relative tranquility. It knows the contours of the landscape over which it wishes to move, and the destination it has set for itself is within sight. Its field is psychology, and its goal is to endow the psychological enterprise with the intellectual clarity that will enable it to take its place as a genuine science of man. It is, in short, the search for a true psychology. In his journey toward this goal, Foucault is aware of the variety of paths followed by other psychologists and philosophers, but his own direction is set, and the value of those other paths is considered strictly in terms of whether they seem to point the same way he has mapped or get lost in what is less than fundamental. But what is fundamental? What is a true psychology? It is nothing other than thought's pursuit of man, a comprehension of mental illness on the basis of a reflection on man himself.[3] This first section of our chapter traces Foucault's movement along this way of anthropological thinking as it is to be found in 1954 in his first two published works, *Maladie mentale et personnalité (PER)*, and his Introduction to the French translation of Ludwig Binswanger's *Le rêve et l'existence*.

The need for that anthropological thinking in psychology toward which these texts advance arose from Foucault's conviction that the study of mental illness was hampered by the abstract models that dominated research at that time. Although psychology and psychiatry have been among this century's major fields of research, he found their continuing debate over the most basic issues to be an embarrassment for any claims to scientific status. The most glaring example of this failure to attain the level of science was psychology's inability even to define mental illness and psychological health. The principal error responsible for this state of affairs, for having prevented the medicine of mental illness from becoming "rigorously scientific," was the sway exerted over both mental and organic pathology by an abstract "metapathology" that attempted to apply to both identical concepts and methods.[4] An examination of the postulates upon which this metapathology was based led Foucault to conclude that it had failed to establish the psychosomatic unity of man it had desired as the keystone for the organization of psychological research. Metapathology either had articulated only an abstract parallelism between the mental and organic, or had asserted unity to be a fact on the basis of inadmissible and conflicting assumptions.[5] Although the "unity of body and mind is in the order of reality," the unitary pathology of his day had become "purely mythical."[6]

Metapathology had enclosed psychology's reflection on mental illness within a web of abstractions that prompted a forgetfulness of the simple fact that "actual man" is the unity of mind and body.[7] But how is the way to "man himself" to be negotiated? Foucault sees two questions as providing the essential guidance. First, what are the concrete forms that mental illness can take in the psychological life of an individual? Second, what are the conditions that make these forms possible? These are the questions to which his 1954 works seek to respond. As the beginning of that fundamental thinking to which Foucault committed himself in his search for man, they will be our point of departure as well.

A) THE PSYCHOLOGICAL DIMENSIONS OF MENTAL ILLNESS 1: THREE APPROACHES

The strategy Foucault employs in progressing toward a concrete understanding of mental illness is straightforward. Three different psychological approaches are arranged in a dynamic relationship with one another; each of the three methods discloses a valid dimension of man, and yet each of them needs to be complemented by another. In the end, this pursuit of intelligibility requires moving into another sphere of questioning altogether, not as a substitute for the three approaches but as their correction and fulfillment.

i) An Evolutionary Approach The first of the concrete forms that mental illness can assume in the psychological life of the individual is exposed by taking up an "evolutionary" approach.[8] It has become impossible to deny that regression is a major dimension of mental illness.[9] Illness is not only a phenomenon of deficit, but also exhibits a positive dimension consisting of a presentation of forms of conduct that evolutionary development had left behind. Evolution is undone in a logical pattern that could be used to describe its very development. For example, the human capacity for dialogue, which Foucault calls the "supreme form of the evolution of language," is replaced by a monologic tendency in the seriously ill.[10] Connected with this alteration is that frequent loss of mastery over the symbolic world that a mentally ill person displays: words, signs, and gestures are not integrated into a meaningful system but are experienced, threateningly, as existing in themselves.[11] Moreover, in regressive behavior there is the usual abandonment of any social criterion of truth, and its replacement by a more primitive belief system.[12]

Foucault recognizes that the central role given by the evolutionary approach to this element of regression does not entail a commitment to myths of archaic personalities, libido, or psychic force.[13] Nevertheless, he judges that such an evolutionary approach is inadequate for two reasons. First, it loses sight of the specificity and continuing existence of the morbid personality. However ill a patient may be, there is still a "point of coherence," an individual who is organizing himself in the specific manner that is presented to the psychologist.[14] Second, although regressive analysis may describe the orientation of a disease, it fails to discover its actual origin. A view of mental illness strictly in terms of regression and evolution cannot succeed in making of it anything more than a general potentiality for everyone. Although the evolutionary approach identifies a real element in pathology, it needs to be complemented by another form of analysis that might be able to address the questions of "why this or that person is ill, and is ill at this or that moment, why his obsessions have this or that theme, why his delusion involves these demands rather than others."[15]

ii) A Psychological-Historical Approach The analysis of a psychological-historical approach,[16] such as, for example, Freud employs in his case study of "Little Hans," makes possible an understanding of pathological behavior not only as a potentiality of evolution but as the consequence of an individual's specific history.[17] That evolutionary approach that would juxtapose the structures of archaic conduct with present symptoms is supplemented by a perspective of genesis that permits the psychologist to explore the patient's psychological coherence, not in the mode of describing biological phases but in terms of a specific history of conflict that orders the pathology.[18] What is the present meaning of the patient's regression? What is the pattern of his choice of defense mechanisms? Most important, what are the stages of that anxiety that is specifically his, and that locks him into an inability to integrate his past and present, the failure that Foucault asserts to be the essence of pathological behavior.[19]

The alliance of evolutionary and psychological-historical approaches is still insufficient, however, for an adequate understanding of mental illness. While an analysis of individual history facilitates the comprehension of illness as a fact of psychological development, it still does not account for its necessity. How is it possible for one person to surmount the same anxiety-provoking conflicts that push another to flee into pathological behavior? Standing in need of yet another approach to its clarification is that "sort of a priori" of an individual's existence, that "principle and foundation" in a person's constitution that predisposes him to the escape into pathology.[20]

iii) An Existential Approach[21] The method that is called for to make accessible that principle and foundation, the specific "style of anxiety" that gives a meaningful unity to a particular patient's symptoms, is the practice of phenomenological understanding as it is to be found in the works of Jaspers, Minkowski, and Binswanger.[22] In contrast to the objectivity sought in both evolutionary and historical approaches, phenomenological understanding leaps into the "interior of morbid consciousness" and "tries to see the pathological world with the eyes of the patient himself; the truth it seeks is of the order not of objectivity, but of intersubjectivity."[23] This phenomenology of mental illness has a double task: a noetic analysis of the consciousness that the sick patient himself has of his illness, and a noematic analysis of those spatial, temporal, social, and bodily structures that constitute his pathological world.[24] This phenomenological pursuit of the manner in which the patient's existence is organized is more fundamental than that of psychological history. The causality this latter method discloses, the link that might be discovered, for example, between a child's fear and an adolescent's phobias, is possible only because this pathological world that is uncovered in noetic and noematic analysis already exists in the patient: "it is this world that forges the link between cause and effect, the anterior and the ulterior."[25]

Phenomenology shows that the "nucleus" of mental pathology is to be found in a contradictory unity in which a patient abandons an intersubjective world for a private, morbid world, a choice that is also an abandonment of the objective world as representing anything other than an external fate. Thus, mental illness, as explained by phenomenology, is "both a retreat into the worst of subjectivities and a fall into the worst of objectivities."[26] Like the two other approaches to the fact of pathology, phenomenology suggests its own limits and the need for psychology to adopt yet another complementary form of analysis. Phenomenology has penetrated to the most fundamental level of man, his existence, but explores only its subjective dimensions. But if the pathological existence is both a call to and an abandonment of the world, does not the desire to probe the secret of a patient's "enigmatic subjectivity" force the psychologist to question its exterior conditions, the objective world that is the stage on which the choice of an existence in a morbid world takes place?[27] This is the question in which the second part of *Maladie mentale et personnalité* finds its starting point. Before turning to that concluding part, however, we will at this point consider Foucault's more specific examination of human existence in his other 1954 work, the Introduction to *Le rêve et l'existence*. This study describes more fully the level of existence that Foucault holds to be the most fundamental dimension of man: while it is a dimension disclosed by phenomenological analysis, Foucault will maintain that this same form of analysis must be incomplete in its exploration of it.

B) THE PSYCHOLOGICAL DIMENSIONS OF MENTAL ILLNESS 2: HUMAN EXISTENCE AND THE DREAM

Foucault's lengthy introduction to the first French translation of Ludwig Binswanger's "Dream and Existence" is neither a presentation of the Swiss psychiatrist's thought as a whole nor a strict commentary on the essay itself.[28] While Foucault's intention is "only to write in the margin" of the article, his essay is far from marginal in specifying the level on which his anthropological thinking wishes to move.[29] The statement from Kierkegaard that Binswanger chooses as the essay's opening motto—"Above all, let us hold fast onto what it means to be a man"—expresses the common direction that both Binswanger and Foucault have perceived as necessary for a rehabilitation of reflection in the realm of mental pathology.[30] Although it will not be accepted as completely adequate, Binswanger's project of a *Daseinanalyse*, of which "Dream and Existence" is the initial declaration, has made the correct choice as to the major step such reflection must take: a fundamental thinking of what man is. Inspired by Martin Heidegger's phenomenological examination of human existence in *Being and Time*, *Daseinanalyse* is the attempt to give an "absolute privilege" to man as the object for thought.[31] Binswanger maintained that the promise of Heidegger's investigation was to give the psychiatrist a "key by means of which he can, free of the prejudice of any scientific *theory*, ascertain and describe the *phenomena* he investigates in their full phenomenal content and intrinsic context."[32] The first duty for psychiatric work must be a more adequate phenomenological description of mental illness as it is experienced by the patient.

Foucault is in agreement with both Binswanger's attribution of a privileged status to man as the object for reflection and the Heideggerian inspiration for this reflection. In understanding man as "presence to being, existence or *Dasein*," Heidegger and Binswanger have adopted an ontological mode of analysis that operates on a more basic level than is possible for either a speculative philosophical anthropology or a positivistic psychology.[33] This ontological interrogation of human being holds the promise of revealing those essential structures of human existence that are the very conditions of possibility for the appearance of these other levels of questioning.

Although favorable to Binswanger's project, the "Dream and Existence" essay is not approached by Foucault in terms of the general promise to be found in the project of *Daseinanalyse*; far more important is the actual success achieved by the essay in reaching the very meaning of man, regarding which Kierkegaard counseled tenacity. While the privileged status given to human being as object for reflection is correct, it is the essay's choice of the dream as the key to the meaning of human existence that gives it its "major interest" for Foucault. He admires the sheer boldness of the choice: the desire to circumscribe the positive content of existence by having recourse to an examination of an element of human experience that seems least inserted in the world.[34] Although the choice of the dream is bold, the position accorded it as disclosing the essential meaning of human being retrieves the insight of a long occidental tradition concerning the significance of dream experience, a tradition that is popular and literary as well as philosophical and theological.

The first element retrieved is the relationship that is perceived to exist between the dream and transcendence. The power of the imagination revealed in dream experience is recognizable as a specific and irreducible form of knowledge that possesses the capacity for another distinct experience of the truth toward which thought strives.[35] A second thread in the tradition that Binswanger implicitly takes hold of is its view of the dream as a place of more profound communication with reality; this would be the case, for example, within the theological perspective in which the dream served as the vehicle for communicating the will of God to the free subject, and as a clearer insight into the subject's destiny as well as into the nature of the world in which he lived. The dream was for the imagination what grace was to the heart or will.[36] A third theme surfaces in Binswanger's treatment, that of the dream as revealing the soul's inner depths and its own world. The message of this tradition is not that the dream experience is a private world of fantasy, but rather that in the dream, one is exposed to a more fundamental and original manifestation of experience.[37]

Binswanger's reclaiming of these themes in his essay justifies for Foucault his boldness in privileging dream experience. The dream exhibits the essential meaning of human being to be a "radical liberty" (liberté radicale), a movement of existence that is the matrix within which self and world, subject and object make their appearance.[38] The experience of transcendence that is the dream reveals the most fundamental sense of human being to be not the personage who says "I" but the dream itself, within which the human subject is awakened from that drowsy fascination with the objectivity of the world that characterizes his alert consciousness. In its transcendence, the dream lays bare the original movement by which a solitary existence projects itself toward a world that is constituted as the place of its history.[39]

Foucault maintains that Binswanger has indicated that the dream, as with Macbeth, has the power to murder sleep, for on its deepest level, the dream is the meeting of man with his death. This meeting, however, can take two very different forms, that of either anxiety or serenity. In both, the dream accomplishes its ultimate vocation, for "death is the absolute meaning of the dream."[40] How are we to account for these different appearances of death in the dream? Foucault asserts that the dream experience, in revealing the human being as a radical liberty, reveals him as fundamentally an ethical being, capable of either authentic or inauthentic choice of itself.[41] On the more general level, this choice may be described in terms of human being's decision for itself as either a "radical responsibility" in the world or an abandonment of itself to the world as necessity. For an existence that shrinks from the revelation in the dream of its essential freedom, death is the necessity of existence's annihilation; for an existence that takes responsibility for itself as a liberty, death is the serene presence of a life fulfilled.[42] On a more specific level, the choice may be spoken of as a decision for or against the human being's historicity. The movement of existence is disclosed in the dream both as spatial and as a temporal trajectory, oriented to the future. To dream is for the future to be already in the process of making itself; it is the "first moment of freedom freeing itself."[43] While authentic existence is the choice of this open trajectory toward the future, inauthentic existence is to opt for an objective determinism in which the being's original liberty totally alienates itself. It is Binswanger's exploration of this temporal trajectory in specific case studies that gives his thought such major importance: ontological structures are articulated not a priori, but by a concrete reflection that moves to an ontological anthropology.[44]

Foucault restores the context of psychiatric concern within which this concrete reflection operated by attempting to draw its major implication for psychotherapy. In being disposed to accept a patient's sense of determinism as a verification of his own diagnosis and a justification for his view of the disease as an objective process, the psychiatrist forgets the role the patient himself plays in constituting his illness as a natural history.[45] The strength of Binswanger's study of the dream for psychotherapy is to have located that moment in the movement of a patient's life at which pathology emerges not as an external fate but as an issue of authentic and inauthentic existence. The value and concern that normal psychiatric and psychological practice invest in the examination of the sick person's dream experience and the world of images that he inhabits is justified only if the dynamics of human imagination is understood. Foucault maintains that Binswanger's study of the dream has accomplished this by performing what amounts to a transcendental deduction of human imagining, which locates both the subjective moment of pathology and the space for therapeutic intervention. An appreciation of this accomplishment demands a reversal of familiar perspectives.[46]

The privilege that Binswanger gives to dream experience forces a change in the normal perspective within which are seen the relations of dream, imagination, and image. Instead of seeing the dream as a modality of imagination, it must be regarded as the first condition of possibility for the imagination. The imaginary is the action that emerges in the dream as a way of seizing the reality through which and toward which the existence is moving. As a dimension of dream experience, imagining is an action of transcendence that seeks satisfaction in the actual achievement of what is imagined. It is in the development of this action that the place of possible pathology is to be located. The specific images that are created in this movement, and that so fascinate normal psychological analysis, cannot be identified with the imagination itself and need to be viewed not as the fulfillment of the imagination but as its alteration, and indeed its re-nunciation.[47] Images exist in the order of "as if," and it is in the choice to inhabit this order that pathology appears. If, for example, I remember a friend who is absent, the culmination and fulfillment of this imagining is to be found not in the images of my friend that I entertain, but in my renewal of bonds with him, our presence together in our actual meeting. To eliminate this dimension of actuality toward which imagination moves is to frustrate man's liberty by diverting it into a fantasy of desire. Just as an image mimics perception with a quasi presence, so it has the possibility of mimicking liberty with the quasi satisfaction of desire it makes possible. The image thus constitutes a ruse of consciousness to prevent more imagining: "it is the moment of discouragement in the hard labor of the imagining."[48] To reduce the imagination and the dream to a collection of images is a means of suppressing the action of transcendence that they constitute; such a reduction and suppression is a salvage operation by an alert consciousness confronted with the power of dream experience. The Binswangerian perspective throws light upon that decisive point of division at which a human existence may either alienate itself in a subjective pathology or embrace action within an objective history, a history in which it can fulfill the movement of liberty and imagination that constitutes it. Because the imaginary "is the milieu, the 'element' of this choice," the task of psychotherapy is precisely to liberate the imagining of a patient who has chosen to confine himself in a world of images.[49]

In his view of the imagination, Binswanger has achieved the third success of his essay. In addition to projecting an anthropology that is ontologically secure, and arriving at the level of radical liberty that is the essential character of human existence, he has suggested the moment at which existence is faced with the choice between authenticity and inauthenticity, the life of freedom or pathology. As with phenomenology in general, however, Foucault perceives Binswanger's success as less than complete. It is burdened with two limitations, both of which concern the dimension of history. In his concentration on individual consciousness and its structures, especially that of temporality, Binswanger failed to develop, as part of his description of human existence and imagining, its movement toward concrete embodiment in language, art, ethics, that is to say, in the making of history itself. In the life of a liberated imagining, images possess a different significance, no longer designating something but now addressing someone as a potential sharer in the shaping of historical reality. Since a true psychology will guide choice to this ethical involvement in history, the primacy of the dream that Binswanger employed to such good explanatory effect is absolute only for an anthropological knowledge of concrete man in the present age. The surpassing of the primacy exercised by the dream is an ethical task for those who understand that the very meaning of their existence is at stake in the work of making dreams into reality.[50] The second limitation is that, beyond promoting a fuller description of human existence and providing the ultimate goal for a therapy rooted in a true psychology, the historical dimension plays a role in the very constitution of mental illness itself. It is this second limitation, only implicit in his introduction to

Binswanger's essay, that Foucault takes up in the second half of *Maladie mentale et personnalité*.

C) THE ACTUAL CONDITIONS OF MENTAL ILLNESS

Each of the three psychological approaches Foucault examined has made a contribution to fixing pathology in the interior of the personality. The special value of phenomenology, and of Binswanger's work in particular, however, is to have suggested the need for its own completion in a new form of analysis that would take account of the historical. In focusing on that contradiction by which a fall into a private morbid world is also an abandonment to the external world as a fate, phenomenology led Foucault to question that world itself that was experienced as fate. While a study of psychological approaches shows the forms in which mental illness appears, psychology's search for necessity demands that the conditions for these appearances also be demonstrated. His questioning of these conditions has two branches, which determine the substance of each of the last two chapters of *Maladie mentale et personnalité*.[51]

In the first of these chapters, "The Historical Meaning of Mental Alienation," Foucault argues that mental illness cannot be fully understood apart from an awareness of the particular position it occupies in the shifting history of culture. The alienation that marks mental illness is unintelligible unless seen in the context of the modern world's confinement of the mentally ill in institutions established specifically for them, and their consequent estrangement from any normal social intercourse.[52] The retreat to regressive behavior has significance in a culture that has chosen to erect a barrier between its present and its past, in a culture within which there exists a contradiction between the patterns of life in infancy and those of adulthood. The series of pathological conflicts that a psychological history examines, and the patient's choice of a private world with which phenomenological analysis deals, must be related to a study of those omnipresent contradictions that riddle our exploitative and technological age.[53] The bourgeois revolution of the modern period defined man's humanity by a theoretical liberty and an abstract equality, while at the same time it created a social system that effectively suppresses this equality and liberty. The alienation from his own freedom, which characterizes the mentally ill person, is a consequence of the social and historical alienation of the concrete world in which he lives.[54]

In asserting that historical alienation is a condition for psychological alienation, Foucault's approach reflects the reversal of perspectives that he saw in Binswanger. A patient is not alienated because he is mentally ill; rather, he becomes mentally ill because he is already alienated.[55] There is, however, a danger in such an assertion, a danger of which Foucault is aware and to which he turns in his last chapter, "The Psychology of Conflict." Perceiving the historical as a condition for the psychological may endanger that understanding of the specific reality that mental pathology is, and toward which he has been working throughout his book. It is clear that not every individual living within a culture characterized by contradictions becomes sick. Thus, Foucault sees mental illness emerging in the specific zone in which contradiction is experienced in terms only of conflict and not of understanding. And so the actual appearance of mental illness requires two sorts of contradictions: There are the social and historic conditions that reveal psychological conflicts as rooted in the real conditions of a specific milieu; in addition, there are the psychological conditions that transform the normal, conflictive character of experience into a pathological reaction to such conflict.[56]

As if to complement Binswanger's study of the interior personal dimension of human existence's move into sickness, Foucault turns to Pavlov as providing an experimental analysis of the external conflict in which there occurs the transition from the historical conditions of a milieu to the pathological contradiction of a mental illness.[57] In the light of Pavlov's model of stimulation-reaction, sickness can be conceptualized as a form of defense. It is a form of protection, however, that differs from the normal differentiation of reactions that each individual develops in his continuing dialectical confrontation with an environment. Pathology emerges when the conflicts presented by a specific milieu are so contradictory, or when the individual's possibilities of controlling these contradictions are so restricted, that he responds to the situation by, in effect, withdrawing from it; he chooses to enclose himself within a private world from which the stimulation of the historical and social environment he cannot master is banished.[58]

There are several major advantages to be gained in this turning to Pavlov. The functional analysis, which his model of stimulation-response provides, permits psychology to describe pathological activity according to the same processes as normal development exhibits. The defining of pathology does not begin with an a priori distinction between the normal and the abnormal, but develops in relation to the alienation that is the movement into sickness. Second, this alienation is approached not through the categories of psychological aberration, but in the context of the historical moment's unique character in giving rise to an unbearable intensity of social contradictions, or in accounting for the limited possibilities of response available to the ill person. Third, it makes possible a conception of mental illness that successfully transcends any antithesis between mental and organic pathology. Their unity is founded in the functional difficulty of the total, concrete person in his relation to a specific environment.[59]

Foucault's reflection has progressed toward establishing the possibility of a mode of analysis in psychology that would be "genuinely materialistic." He believes that he has made it possible for such an analysis to avoid two equally reductionist errors. The first would consist in a mere identification of social alienation with mental alienation, of psychological conflict with the historical contradictions of the milieu. The proper reality and specific forms of mental pathology are preserved because its appearance is accounted for neither in terms merely of its historical-social conditions of possibility nor in terms only of a difficulty in functioning isolated from those conditions. The second error would consist in linking the desire to reduce pathology with the hope that mental illness will yield, in principle, to a purely physiological mode of analysis and treatment. The importance that Foucault has attributed to the historical, however, ought to turn psychology away from such a dependence upon some future progress in physiological knowledge; the means of achieving a diminishing of pathology is a commitment to the transformation of those conditions of existence within which human alienation develops from possibility to actuality.[60]

While the guidance that therapy receives from this model of materialistic analysis is general, it is also clear. In concluding both *Maladie mentale et personnalité* and his introduction to Binswanger, Foucault points out that there must be a preference for those therapies that offer the mentally ill concrete means of overcoming their situation of conflict, of changing their milieu, of developing a more differentiated response to the conditions of their existence. A true psychology has for its purpose, as does every science of man, a victory over the alienation that has made him a stranger to the reality of liberty that he is, and an outsider to the history that is the stage for his fulfillment.[61]

CONCLUSION

Let us get our bearings. Foucault knows where he has arrived. His work of thinking was placed at the service of psychology in the interests of helping to secure its position among the sciences of man. His way of advancing toward a model of true psychology already gives evidence of a specific style: fundamental thinking means to interrogate the conditions that account for the appearance of a phenomenon. This questioning of conditions, however, is a search not for how they make something possible but for how they account for a phenomenon's necessity. History and the social milieu are the dimensions that must be thought if such necessity is to be discovered. Dealing as it does with the alienation of mental illness, psychological thinking, like all thinking in the sciences of man, is ethically oriented. It aims not only at ever more adequate knowledge of the mentally ill, but also at the transformation of those actual conditions that reflection discovers as decisive in accounting for their alienation.

The anthropology at which Foucault's thinking has arrived is the foundation for this new model of psychology's task. Instead of merely adopting an abstract notion of "personality" in which much of psychology has invested both the "reality and measure" of illness, Foucault believes that he has arrived at a more basic and concrete understanding of man.[62] Fusing the interior depths of a Binswangerian approach with the external worldliness of a Pavlovian perspective, he has found a being whose potentiality to become mentally ill is a revelation of the character of both his self and his world. Possessed of a radical liberty, structured in temporality, he exists in the midst of historical and social forces that have the power either to alienate or to fulfill.

Having only sketched his model of a true psychology, Foucault's arrival at the first destination set for his thought suggested nothing of a journey's end. There was an abundance of new directions to follow and of new places to reach. Would there be additional historical research to supplement the few pages he had devoted to the subject in *Maladie mentale et personnalité*? Would there be a more thorough critique of those social conditions to which he had attributed such responsibility in accounting for mental illness? Would there be an attempt to develop more fully the elements of the concrete anthropology he saw as the need of psychology? The study of madness that was to occupy his thinking for the next several years offered the possibility of satisfying these different interests. It would be false, however, to see his studies in the years immediately after 1954 as merely satisfying random curiosities to supplement what he had already accomplished. Despite the sure and serene tone that colors his first two works, one can sense already a possible insecurity regarding the question of man that is at the heart of his thinking, and a continuing preoccupation with the mode of reflection that ought to be employed in an attempt to understand him. Certainly, a successful fusion of two such different approaches to man as those of Binswanger and Pavlov required, at the very least, a more detailed effort to harmonize them than Foucault gives us. The danger is that the two models stand in a merely abstract coexistence. Foucault's desire to avoid such abstraction accounts for the diversity of perspectives within which he continued to examine man and psychology as he studied madness.[63] He felt there was no other alternative. For the ethically concerned Foucault, "when it concerns man, abstraction is not simply an intellectual error"; such abstraction runs the risk of participating in the creation of a world in which one can no longer recognize his freedom.[64]

2. THE SHAKING OF THE FOUNDATIONS

In his essay on the dream, Binswanger has occasion to speak of a particular type of experience that is characterized by a sense of the ground giving way beneath one's feet, of a loss of footing, with the result that one is left with the feeling of being suspended and hovering. It is an apt description of the effect that his research into the history of madness had upon Foucault and his project of a true psychology. This section will concern itself with that shaking of the foundations for the project we have just presented. The historical investigation to which he turned as a complement for psychological thinking escaped the bounds allotted to it and turned upon its initiator so as to deprive him of the relatively secure position at which he seemed to have arrived in 1954. My account of this undermining treats *Histoire de la folie à l'âge classique* (hereafter *HF*) and the second part of *Maladie mentale et psychologie* (hereafter *PSY*). The desire to deal with them as a unit implies a decision as to how *HF* is best understood.[65]

Binswanger's description of that feeling of loss of firm footing might also be applied to the initial experience of critics in reading *HF*. The respect accorded to its evident richness of insights is generally accompanied by a perplexity with and annoyance at its manner of execution. The reaction of Steven Marcus is representative: "Although his book is organized generally along chronological lines, and although each chapter focuses upon a distinct topic, reading through most of these chapters is like wading through several feet of water: Paragraphs do not follow one another in logical and sometimes even in associative order, great lacunae open up between what are apparently supposed to be consecutive parts of a discussion."[66] There are several reasons for this reaction, not least among them that the abridged version, of which the English edition is a translation, omits too many of the points that help to give a greater coherence to the original edition.[67] More significant than this limitation, however, is the fact that *HF* is neither a usual work of history nor a systematic work of philosophy. Its more than six hundred pages contain reflections and questions that will gain adequate clarity only in later works, if then; they do signal the beginnings of a unique approach to history that remains largely implicit in 1961. Despite this major limitation that *HF* presents to the reader, a central argument running throughout the work becomes quite clear if it is read in the perspective of his earlier project and the transformation of *PER* into *PSY*, a transformation necessitated by his historical studies. This central argument is brought into focus if it is treated as a unit along with the second part of *PSY*, as shall be done here.

Foucault's history of madness does not treat an unchanging object, but a changing experience of a dimension of human existence that he will call madness. While both madness and attitudes toward it stretch as far back as human history, Foucault's attempt to understand its contemporary sense and our own relation to it concentrates on two periods: the classical age (from the middle of the seventeenth century to the third quarter of the eighteenth) and the modern age (from the end of the classical period through the nineteenth century). After considering his account of these two periods, we shall examine the bearing of this history upon Foucault's earlier project.

A) THE HISTORY OF MADNESS

The experience of madness in the classical age takes shape against the background of a major mutation in the preoccupation of western culture. Huizinga had pointed out many years earlier that one of the principal features that distinguished the late medieval period was its sense of the constant presence of death. "No other epoch has laid so much stress as the expiring Middle Ages on the thought of death. An everlasting call of *memento mori* resounds through life."[68] Foucault's history opens with the very different face that the Renaissance puts forward.[69] In place of death, there is now a sudden proliferation of concern with madness, not only in the imaginative experience of painters and writers, but in the everyday world of Renaissance life. Man's anxiety before the nothingness of existence is transformed: "This nothingness is no longer considered an external, final term, both threat and conclusion, it is experienced from within as the continuous and constant form of existence."[70] Although there were attempts to treat certain of its expressions, madness was generally left free to exist in the culture as a phenomenon that was irreducible to other forms of experience. There was emerging, however, even at this point in time, a differentiation of the experience of madness that would prove crucial in the determination of its future history. There was a cosmic or tragic experience of madness, as enshrined, for example in the works of Shakespeare and Cervantes, where it preserves its autonomy and irreducibility. On the other hand, a critical consciousness attempted to encompass madness strictly in terms of some relation it possessed to reason. Foucault's history is an account of the ever-growing distance between these two experiences.

In contrast to the general hospitality extended to madness in the Renaissance, a radical change in attitude develops in the middle of the seventeenth century, at the beginning of the classical age.[71] Throughout Europe there suddenly arise great centers of confinement for a wide variety of different groups. Among the many populations that found themselves enclosed with those thought mad were libertines, those inflicted with venereal disease, prostitutes, blasphemers, homosexuals, defrocked priests, and the disabled poor.[72] Why did these institutions appear, and what common feature did these groups, so diverse to us, share to warrant their common exclusion from society? Although intellectual, political, religious, and economic forces influenced the rise of these institutions,[73] their essential significance is to be found on a moral level, on the level of a peculiar "perception" that opened up and defined a specific "social space" in which the internment of these groups is explicable.[74] As the bourgeois world was constituted, these were the groups that did not work, and the regime of labor to which these houses of confinement subjected them was a practice of moral correction: "men were confined in cities of pure morality, where the law that should reign in all hearts was to be applied without compromise, without concession, in the rigorous forms of physical constraint."[75]

The moral perception from which these institutions of confinement were derived is rooted in the central role attributed by the classical age to choice and freedom as the source of both reasonable and unreasonable conduct. The phenomenon of madness for this age, while ultimately a question not of the integrity of reason but rather of the will, is defined as a "field of experience" ruled by an opposition between reason and unreason (*déraison*), which are physically separated by the institution of confinement.[76] The mad have chosen or are guilty of a self-deception that issues in a blindness to the true order of the world.[77] Other groups found themselves confined with the mad because they were seen to share with them that unreason in the face of which this age of reason felt a shame, one entailing their exclusion from the social landscape.[78] Even within this general cohabitation, however, the mad often found themselves singled out for purposes of exhibition. Whereas other forms of unreason presented only examples of transgression and immorality, and therefore found themselves condemned to a secret confinement, madness, exhibited for others to see, taught the lesson of how degraded man's humanity could become if it were to choose against reason.

> In the Renaissance, madness was present everywhere and mingled with every experience by its images or its dangers. During the classical period, madness was shown, but on the other side of bars; if present, it was at a distance, under the eyes of a reason that no longer felt any relation to it and that would not compromise itself by too close a resemblance. Madness had become a thing to look at: no longer a monster inside oneself, but an animal with strange mechanisms, a bestiality from which man had long since been suppressed.[79]

The inhuman disciplining and brutalization to which the mad were subjected emerged logically from within this perspective.

The classical age's experience of madness as unreason implied a double opposition to reason. Madness was, first of all, an absence of what ought to be present, and thus the practice of confinement adopted in its regard logically expressed the realization that madness was no longer the "sign of another world," but merely the "empty negativity of reason." Second, however, this absence takes the form of a positivity, for madness is something that can be put on exhibit, placed under observation.[80] This is the paradox of the classical experience of madness: a negativity that is absence of reason but that can appear as ordered and logical for the inquiring observer.

"All that madness can say of itself is merely reason, though it is itself the negation of reason. In short, *a rational hold over madness is always possible and necessary, to the very degree that madness is non-reason.*"[81]

Although the classical experience of madness as unreason, and as an absence that confinement merely acknowledged, was to be transformed later, the field of experience that the age of reason constituted in its dealings with madness exercised a decisive influence on that modern period. In contrast to the Renaissance, which always kept the phenomenon of madness within hearing distance, madness now finds itself banished into an almost complete silence: "although one continued to speak of it, it became impossible for it to speak of itself," for the classical age had deprived it of its language.[82] This silence would intensify in the modern period. Within this zone of silence, the classical age's principle of exclusion had also accomplished a positive work of organization. In finding itself enclosed in a homogeneous space with those thought to be socially and sexually deviant, madness began to be "perceived on the social horizon of poverty, of incapacity for work, of inability to integrate with the group," and forged relations with moral and social guilt.[83] The significance of this horizon and the depths of these relations would manifest themselves fully after the institution of internment was transformed into the asylum of the modern age.

Philippe Pinel's removal of the chains from the patients at Bicêtre Hospital is regarded as the beginning of the end of the fear of the mad that had inhibited a fuller rational understanding of mental illness.[84] The replacement of the classical age's world of internment by the institution of the asylum is thought by that history of psychiatry to be the movement toward a humanistic treatment of the mentally ill as well as the advent of psychology as a positive science.[85] Foucault's revisionist interpretation of the significance of the asylum, of the birth of a *perception asilaire* in the postclassical age, is a work of demythologizing this history, and the key to understanding his view of madness in the modern age.[86]

The institution of the asylum was created in the space cleared by a threefold criticism of the classical age's policy of internment. This criticism was political, economic, and rooted in popular fear, rather than philanthropic. In the aftermath of the French Revolution, the institutions of confinement symbolized the repressive tyranny that was being rejected; as institutions, the centers of confinement had shown themselves to be economically unsound; finally, these institutions had become associated in the public mind with the spread of contagious disease.[87] This change of attitude toward confinement did not, however, lead to a proclamation of freedom for the mad. Indeed, the result was quite the reverse. From among those populations with which it had become associated, madness was singled out as still demanding isolation. Distinguished from the other forms of unreason within which it had been embraced by the classical age, madness and the awareness of a need for its continued and particular segregation resulted in the fact that now, "between madness and confinement, a profound relation had been instituted, a link which was almost one of essence."[88] A new tone characterizes the isolation of the asylum. In place of the foreignness that was their stigma in earlier forms of confinement, the mad now find themselves introduced into a program for the production of an "ethical uniformity." By a systematic policy of both greeting with silence their recourse to peculiar behavior and subjecting them to a rigorous moral education in the essential values of family and work, the asylum intensifies the construction of madness as a matter of responsibility and guilt.[89]

As a regime of moral education, the asylum corrected the paradoxical effect that earlier systems of confinement had produced: "The fortresses of confinement functioned as a great, long silent memory; they maintained in the shadows an iconographic power that men might have thought was exorcised; created by the new classical order, they preserved, against it and against time, forbidden figures that could thus be transmitted intact from the sixteenth to the nineteenth century."[90] These forbidden figures are now eliminated in an ambitious program of education.

> Compared to the incessant dialogue of reason and madness during the Renaissance, classical internment had been a silencing. But it was not total: language was engaged in things rather than really suppressed. Confinement, prisons, dungeons, even tortures, engaged in a mute dialogue between reason and unreason—the dialogue of struggle. This dialogue itself was now disengaged; silence was absolute; there was no longer any common language between madness and reason; the language of delirium can be answered only by an absence of language, for delirium is not a fragment of dialogue with reason, it is not language at all.[91]

In this silent world of the asylum, the patient is subject to perpetual objectification and judgment by official representatives of reason whose duty is to bring him to a knowledge of his objective madness, to a remorse for his failure to adopt a reasonable code of behavior.[92] The older instruments of "cure" that had been employed in an earlier period, when there had not been a clear distinction established between the psychological and the physical, are transformed into techniques (cold showers, rotating machines) that are part of a purely moral and punitive strategy.[93] At the heart of this new enterprise of the asylum is the figure of authority: the doctor. His task is one of ethical supervision, and its justification is only disguised by claims to scientific knowledge. In reality, he is but a "thaumaturge for the patient," made possible by the specific structures of the asylum and by his recourse to ancient therapies; for himself, however, legitimation of his power and the position of the patient required a positivistic myth of scientific objectivity, and thus a certain tactic is transformed into the science of psychiatry.[94]

In creating these structures, the birth of the asylum represented the enslavement of the mad to a system in which they were reduced to the status of children, and their behavior confined to a horizon of guilt and wrong-doing. Thus, in fact, Pinel's "liberation" of the insane brought to the mad not freedom, but rather a "gigantic moral imprisonment."[95] This demythologizing of the asylum as a benevolent institution is not a matter of merely antiquarian interest for Foucault.

B) THE HISTORY OF MADNESS AND THE PROJECT OF A TRUE PSYCHOLOGY

The conclusions to which Foucault had been brought as a result of his historical study of madness possessed fatal implications for his project of a true psychology. These implications are most clearly to be seen in the major differences that separate *PER* and *PSY*. Their change of title hints at the substantial alteration in their author's point of view. His earlier work called into question the relation between mental illness and psychology's abstract view of man, as implied in the employment of the category of "personality." His later work is not calling into question an element or a tendency of psychology, but the very field itself, as well as the object that it assumes to authorize its labor, mental illness. The broadening of psychology that he sought in the second half of his 1954 work is abandoned. The chapter dealing with the psychology of conflict in which he had put forward Pavlov's model is totally eliminated, while the part entitled "The Historical Meaning of Mental Alienation" is replaced by a summary of *HF*, and now bears the title "The Historical Constitution of Mental Illness." The two considerations of history serve totally different purposes. While the earlier volume attempted to complement the work of psychology with historical understanding, the latter study shows historical understanding to be far more powerful than the project to which it was to have been made subordinate.

For Foucault, this history of madness since the Renaissance is the story of a trivialization of those powers within human experience, thought, and dream that called into question the accepted identity of man and the wisdom of his reason. In a coherent development from the beginning of the classical age to our own day, these powers, to which Shakespeare and Cervantes bore witness, have been reduced to an affair between a doctor and his subservient patient. Our "scientific understanding" of madness only completes the exile into silence of that profound otherness that is man's freedom, and is a direct result of that historical process in which an increasingly negative appraisal was made of "what had been originally apprehended as the Different, the Insane, Unreason."[96] The frequent absence of confinement's inhuman constraints that distinguishes both the asylum and contemporary psychiatric practice represents not a liberation but rather the fact that madness had already been conquered. *HF* is the account of how that mastery over madness was achieved, and, as such, the history of those forces that made possible the "very appearance of a psychology," for, like the asylum, "psychology became possible in our world only when madness had already been mastered."[97]

Psychology is not rooted in a study of man but in a certain "homo psychologicus," whose alliance with certain historical developments situated man within two fundamental axes: "an external dimension of exclusion and punishment" and "an internal dimension of moral assignation and guilt."[98] This alliance reduced madness to mental illness.

> In the new world of the asylum, in that world of a punishing morality, madness became a fact concerning essentially the human soul, its guilt, and its freedom; it was now inscribed within the dimension of interiority; and by that fact, for the first time in the modern world, madness was to receive psychological status, structure, and signification. But this psychologization was merely the superficial consequence of a more obscure, more deeply embedded operation—an operation by which madness was inserted in the system of moral values and repressions. It was enclosed in a punitive system in which the madman, reduced to the status of a minor, was treated in every way as a child, and in which madness was associated with guilt and wrongdoing. It is hardly surprising, then, that an entire psycho-pathology—beginning with Esquirol, but including our own—should be governed by the three themes that define its problematic: the relations of freedom to the compulsions, the phenomena of regression and the infantile structure of behavior, aggression and guilt. What one discovers under the name of the "psychology" of madness is merely the result of the operations by which one has invested it. None of this psychology would exist without the *moralizing sadism* in which nineteenth-century "philanthropy" enclosed it, under the hypocritical appearances of "liberation."[99]

We have quoted this lengthy passage because it clearly indicates not only the conditions of possibility for any psychiatric diagnosis, but the radical point to which Foucault's historical investigation has led him. The bar of history not only throws out any claims psychology can make regarding a true understanding of man, but also forces Foucault's search for a fundamental understanding of man to move outside of any identification with a psychological project. In a 1962 introduction to a collection of Rousseau's dialogues, Foucault asks whether the Rousseau revealed in these writings is mad. He answers his own question: "It is a psychologist's question. Not mine therefore."[100] But what then are Foucault's questions in the wake of the collapse of his original project?

CONCLUSION

It is clear that those questions that will mark his path from 1962 to 1966 are not posed from the secure place that was Foucault's in 1954. The achievements of *HF* and *PSY* do not represent a point of arrival so much as the beginning of a wandering within territory that will require years of exploration before it can be charted with any degree of certainty. As a result of the studies he has already completed, however, it would be wrong to conceive of this wandering as merely blind. Although the concrete questions of and directions for his thought in the period between *PSY* and *Les mots et les choses* will be developed in the following section, we can already glimpse major dimensions of the general problematic that preoccupies him at this point.

A fundamental understanding of man and his situation cannot be achieved under the aegis of a psychological reflection, for such reflection only reaches man as *homo psychologicus*, as "possessor of internal truth, fleshless, ironical, and positive of all self-consciousness and all possible knowledge."[101] Man's search for a knowledge of himself through psychology rested on the assumption that he was the being who possessed his own truth and could reveal it to knowledge as an object. Such a conception of man demands an impermissible abstraction from the social and historical world of which he is a part, as well as a forgetfulness of that authentic, difficult identity that is his as a relation between reason and unreason. In the same movement in which it took possession of unreason, reason alienated itself.[102] The transformation of madness into mental illness also effected a reduction of man as a thinking being. The realm of the different and indeterminate is considered as foreign to the true character of reason because the essential reduction of thought performed by historical developments from the Renaissance to our own age has been that "reason ceased to be for man an ethic and became a nature."[103] This development in regard to reason is the same with respect to freedom, which is reduced to a power abstracted from history and society, existing as nothing other than a "nature of nature, but in the sense of a secret soul, an inalienable essence of nature."[104] This naturalization of both reason and freedom is a direct consequence of the elimination of that "tragic split" between reason and unreason that is the place of man's identity as a free, thinking being.[105] At the end of this period in the working out of his thought, Foucault's desire is to restore man to that experience of the split, to renew that "great tragic confrontation with madness" that holds the promise of man's recovery of himself as a radical liberty.[106] From his vantage point in 1962, two routes are privileged for achieving the restoration and renewal.

The first route was suggested to Foucault by the fact that in spite of modernity's banishment of madness, there were certain writers through whom its life continued to be present in culture: Hölderlin, Nerval, Roussel,

Artaud, Nietzsche, de Sade.[107] A large part of Foucault's thought in the years ahead will be given over to an exploration of their witness, their language. The second route is to probe the power of historical thinking that was already revealed to him in *HF*. The meaning of man is as tied to history as it is to the relation between reason and unreason.[108] The problem of man in the contemporary age is bound up with the problem of naturalization that has shaped our age's view of reason and freedom as well as its compulsion to transform the misery of society into sicknesses of nature.[109] His antidote to such naturalization has already found a style and a name. Although his approach to historical thinking is far from a defined method at this point, it is a specific style of questioning historical reality. In *HF*, his interrogation of that reality is neither a history of ideas nor a chronicle of discoveries, but a search for the "fundamental structures of the experience," for the "conditions of possibility" that are responsible for the very appearance of a psychology. His interest is with the "series of ruptures, discontinuities, explosions" that lay behind that fundamental structure of experience.[110] At issue is not the identity of a culture but the limits it sets for itself, the movement by which a culture rejects something that will become for it the outside (*l'Extérieur*).[111]

This style has already found its name even if it is without adequate definition. In his pursuit of a way to restore man to the tragic experience of the split between reason and unreason, Foucault has attempted to do an "archaeology" of the silence that replaced a dialogue between madness and reason. His history of that growth of silence is an "archaeology of an alienation." Indeed, at one point he already speaks of his historical questioning as an "archaeology of knowledge" (*l'archéologie du savior*).[112] From where does this term come? Years later, Foucault will point out that he owes the word "archaeology" to Kant, who employed it to designate the investigation of that which renders necessary a certain form of thought.[113] We may speculate, however, that while Kant provided him with its name as well as a major dimension of its approach, archaeology was also an experience for Foucault, an experience of the disruptive power of historical thinking. On this level, archaeology is linked to his work in psychology and to his consideration of Freud. Neurosis represented for Freud a "spontaneous archaeology of the libido" that revealed the radically different stages of its development. Likewise, the investigation of madness had revealed to Foucault those discontinuous levels of historical development in terms of which modernity's silencing of madness and articulation of psychology become comprehensible.[114] Foucault's description of *HF* as a "structural study" should be seen in relation to both of these factors: the Kantian dimension of archaeology as a search for the structural conditions of a knowledge such as psychology and an institution such as the asylum; second, the disclosure to

Foucault of distinct structural levels in his history of madness and its treatment. Archaeology's interest in the notion of structure, however, does not necessarily place it within the structuralist enterprise. Indeed, Foucault will come to reject with vehemence the structuralist label that will be constantly applied by others to his work. As Foucault understands structuralism, it is a rejection that is warranted.[115] In a criticism of Freud, Foucault points out in his Introduction to *Le rêve et l'existence* (hereafter *IRE*) that Freud's approach to the dream never reaches the level that would account for the dream's concrete necessity. The justification for this criticism is Freud's failure to grasp the *structure* of the dream's language.[116]

3. THE EXPERIENCE OF THOUGHT

Only after an experience of fundamental thinking did Foucault face the need to articulate a method for it. In this section we shall be concerned with presenting the experience of thought that preceded the emergence of archaeology of knowledge as a specific method. In his study of the clinic and in his analysis of certain works of contemporary literature, Foucault was brought to a precise understanding of both thought's place and its task. An examination of the basic "science" of medicine, as a foundation for psychology and all the human sciences, and an exploration of the significance language holds for current thought, uncovered a more radical enclosure for knowledge than had been sensed in his earlier work. While human understanding will be seen to exist within certain perceptual codes and within language, this trait of "being within" is not the final conclusion to which he comes as a result of his work from 1962 to 1966. His appreciation of the achievement of his work and that of certain modern writers discloses a particular experience of thought: a "thinking from without" that is the cornerstone of archaeology as a method. For Foucault, thought is empowered not only by its dialogue with madness but also by an encounter with death: death revealed as the text of the body, and death experienced as the invitation for an endless writing.

A) THE BIRTH OF THE CLINIC: A "WITHIN" AND A "WITHOUT"

HF had shown that the recognition that enables one to say "this man is mad" was an act of great complexity, resting upon a long and tangled history.[117] Is it possible that the judgment "this man is sick" reveals a similar complexity and history? *The Birth of the Clinic* (hereafter *NC*) contains Foucault's investigation of those developments that provided the conditions of possibility for the growth of medicine into a clinical science. It is an effort to comprehend the difference of perceptual structures that separates the eighteenth-century doctor's opening question to a patient, "What is the matter with you?" from that of his nineteenth-century successor, "Where does it hurt?"[118] Concerned as it is with a period of only five decades ending in 1816, *NC* is scarcely an exhaustive history of medicine. Nevertheless, its claim will be to have touched an essential moment in its development, the period when clinical medicine was born as an experience. It offers an understanding of the emergence of the clinic—considered as both the teaching hospital and the science of clinical medicine that developed in it—and of the movement that enabled it to become identified "with the *whole* of medical experience."[119]

i) The Clinic: A Traditional Approach As was the case with psychology, our age does not lack an historical account of the development that led to the triumph of modern medicine. Its view is largely that put together at the end of the eighteenth and at the beginning of the nineteenth centuries. While Hippocrates is taken to be the father of medical empiricism, the history of the medicine after him is largely the tale of a field of experience haunted by suspicion and empty metaphysical disputes, of a long, suffocating embrace by philosophy and a concomitant abandonment of observation as its norm.[120] As it did in so many other realms of human life, the Enlightenment broke with this state of tutelage. In casting off the blindness that was foisted upon it by empty philosophical abstractions, the medicine of the modern age redeemed that subterranean history of empirical medicine that had always managed to survive, despite the suzerainty of the western world's traditional theoretical and academic approach. As an early nineteenth-century writer understood: "There have always been doctors who, with the help of that analysis that comes so naturally to the human mind, having deduced from the patient's appearance all the data needed concerning his idiosyncrasy, have been content simply to study the symptoms."[121] While medicine in the modern age is regarded as being in this grand tradition, it represents, nevertheless, an extraordinary progress beyond it. The clinic, as both a knowledge and a practice, provided the opportunity for these hitherto scattered efforts of observant doctors to come together for the opportunity of joint labor and mutual correction, and thus for the creation of a context that makes a science of medicine possible.

The progress of medicine is part of that political, economic, and intellectual liberation of man in modernity, which is our age's conception of itself. Above all, in the establishment of medicine's scientific capabilities, the transition from the speculative world of university lectures to the experimental world of hospital clinics, represented the liberation of the capacity to look with an eye free of prejudice. The "medical humanism" that is the fruit of enlightenment is a "simple, unconceptualized confrontation of a gaze and a face, or a glance and a silent body." The clinic is, as was maintained at the time, scarcely anything more than the "very practice of medicine at the patient's bedside." It is the same story that can be read in the most recent edition of the *Encyclopaedia Britannica.*[122]

This version of the history of modern medicine provokes doubts, if it is examined in closer detail. For Foucault, there are three major difficulties that suggest the need for a new account. First, the early forms of the clinic that existed throughout the eighteenth century, while marginal institutions, were quite different from the type of clinic that dominated the end of the century and to which they were thought to lead. While it was an institution of teaching, it was quite distinct from the hospital, and its role cannot be reduced to an element in a mythic march toward medical empiricism. Its patients were used as examples of a knowledge already possessed, and its function was not to discover but to demonstrate.[123] Secondly, contrary to the accepted history, for a long time the organization of clinical medicine was excluded by the very political liberalism with which it is supposedly in concert. The aim of much of the legislation after the French Revolution was a "dehospitalization" of disease and a restoration of the sick to their family environments as the proper place for free people to regain their health. The partisans of radical freedom, who had closed the universities, were strongly opposed to the appearance of a new class of doctors, who would establish themselves as yet another institution of privileged knowledge. As a study on the free teaching of the sciences and arts stated: "Render to genius all the latitude of power and liberty that it demands; proclaim its inalienable rights; shower public honors and rewards on all useful interpreters of nature wherever they may be found; do not confine in a narrow circle those intellects that seek only to cast their light afar."[124] A third difficulty of the traditional history is with the role it normally allots to pathological anatomy in the development of the new medical spirit. It was—and is—the custom of these histories to see an objective examination of corpses as the critical step medicine had to take for the clinic to appear and for it to achieve a scientific status. In order for it to take this step, so the history runs, medicine had to overcome the prohibitions against anatomy that were set up by religion, traditional morality, and the ancient prejudices of the civilization. This view is mythical, however, because corpses had been available for anatomical purposes for at least a century before the emergence of the clinic. Indeed, for forty years the clinic was uninterested in the knowledge available through autopsies, because its concern was with the history of a pathology and not with its geography.[125]

These three difficulties with the normal historical account indicated to Foucault that the transformation of the preclinical into clinical medicine was a more complex affair than that history had indicated. If the clinic was to be understood, a more fundamental analysis would have to be made.

ii) The Clinic: An Alternative Analysis Apart from these three difficulties, another question arises with regard to that account: Is there not an obvious naiveté in the weight it gives to the idea that the development of the clinic rested so much upon a simple capacity to "look," as if "for the first time for thousands of years, doctors, free at last of theories and chimeras, agreed to approach the object of their experience with the purity of an unprejudiced gaze"?[126] In addition to attesting to the inadequacy of medicine's consciousness of its evolution, this claim for observation suggested to Foucault where the heart of a true explanation might be sought. *NC* is a study of the "medical gaze" (*regard médical*), as its subtitle states, but certainly not with the expectation of discovering the stages of its gradual unveiling as a power that comes to be appreciated only in the age of the clinic. The explanation of the birth of the clinic was to be sought neither in terms of observation alone nor in terms of a theoretical content, which may have been accepted or rejected, but in the "*formal* reorganization *in depth*" of those conditions, hidden to the age in which they were operative, that structure the domain of clinical experience and the style of its perception.[127] Such an explanation is the search for the "concrete a priori" of clinical experience, and Foucault asserts that it is grasped along three axes: spatiality, language, death.[128]

a) SPATIALITY For clinical medicine to have become possible as a mode of perception, it was necessary to establish a form of spatiality different from that which operated in the earlier eighteenth-century classificatory medicine of the clinic. This earlier spatiality was defined in three dimensions: the geography of a disease's relations to other diseases, to a specific patient, and to the social body.[129] The mapping of diseases as distinct species constituted the primary dimension. In order for a doctor to understand which disease was afflicting his patient, it was necessary for his gaze to set aside the accidental features that any particular patient might exhibit and wait for the differentiating essence of the disease to manifest itself. A secondary dimension of spatialization for the pathological relates the species of disease to the particular organism that was afflicted by it, a correlation that resulted in the development of a careful medical attentiveness to the qualitative varieties that displayed themselves in the course of an illness. In the play of these first two forms of spatiality, the individual patient found himself in a paradoxical position. In its search for the species of a disease, this classificatory medicine could be indifferent to the individual as a source of knowledge. By contrast, in its description of qualitative appearances, the individual played a decisive role. In this attention to the individual, the medicine of species opened the way for a fundamental change in the ideal of medical perception. For this change to take place, however, a third form of spatiality, no less essential than the other two, needed to develop its inherent logic. This is the social space of medical institutions and practices.[130]

A medicine of species needed a social space free of those institutions that might threaten the natural course of the disease and the clear appearance of its essence. The treatment of the patient in the natural environment provided by his family was far superior to a confinement in the artificial space of a hospital, where the patient would be exposed to infection by a variety of other types of sickness, an exposure that not only endangered his health but also obscured the true essence of his disease. This medical point of view is analogous to that which characterized the eighteenth century's political and economic conception of the problem of assistance. It was felt that the wealth of hospital foundations should not perpetuate particular institutions, but rather serve a generalized system of assistance for families, with whom the sick would continue to live. The abandonment of the hospital and the execution of such a general plan of assistance entail a social structure, however, that is crucial for the emergence of the clinic. If proper care is to be given to an individual patient, a large involvement by the state is needed to supervise the proper treatment of the sick, who are no longer conveniently grouped in special institutions. Medicine thus becomes a national task aimed at a "generalized vigilance" over the society as a whole, and based upon a collectively controlled structure: "One began to conceive of a generalized presence of doctors whose intersecting gazes form a network and exercise at every point in space, and at the same moment in time, a constant, mobile, differentiated supervision."[131]

This penetration of social space by medical concern was bound up with the heightened political consciousness immediately before and after the revolution. Medicine took on a positive political significance, and the doctor became a political figure in the age's sense of itself as a movement toward freedom. As an example of this significance, Foucault cites this statement of 1792: "Who, then, should denounce tyrants to mankind if not the doctors, who make man their sole study, and who, each day, in the homes of poor and rich, among ordinary citizens and among the highest in the land, in cottage and mansion, contemplate the human miseries that have no other origin but tyranny and slavery?"[132] This positive significance of medicine rested upon a "spontaneous and deeply rooted convergence between the requirements of *political ideology* and those of *medical technology*." Just as medicine needed a space free of hospitals to carry out its task of improving the health of mankind, so the revolution, in its abolition of university faculties and other associations of privilege, attempted to create a social space in which the exercise of liberty by individuals would reveal the pure truth of man and society, as disease would reveal its truth in the environment that was natural to it.[133] The clinic appears within this social space as a solution to certain problems that arose as a result of the revolution's war against the traditional centers of privilege. As an institution, however, the clinic required a restructuring of the theme of "medicine in liberty," which was so essential a dimension of this space.[134]

The clinic was the solution to major problems that had appeared in the wake of the revolution's abolition of medical faculties and hospitals. There was popular dissatisfaction with the number of medical practitioners without training who had appeared on the scene in the wake of this abolition. A general realization developed that a complete elimination of hospitals was not desirable. There was suspicion about the political use to which a total system of assistance might be put, as well as fear of the large number of paupers who were allowed to roam free as a result of this system. The clinic met these problems in a manner economically viable and basically compatible with the period's ideas of freedom. It represented a contract between rich and poor, since, taken care of medically, the poor became objects of "objective interest for science and vital interest for the rich." In its promise of advancing the cause of medical science, the clinic's cost became supportable.[135] While avoiding identification with the reactionary image of guilds and faculties, the clinic could also guarantee the adequate training of those who would administer medical services. In addition, the clinic, from its beginnings, was part of the wider social and political interest generated by medicine in the age of the revolution. It would provide the opportunity for a new type of knowledge in which medicine would theoretically confront the problems of man and society. At its inception, therefore, the clinic was a place for an "encyclopaedic knowledge of man and nature."[136]

b) LANGUAGE AND DEATH The movement from a medicine of species to that of the clinic was, of course, also a matter of medical understanding as well as political consciousness. The importance the clinic was to give to the perceptual field as the foundation for its science and to the gaze (*regard*) in its practice can be accounted for only in terms of the perceptive codes (*codes perceptifs*) in which observation functioned and in which the expectations for it were defined.[137] These codes possessed two major forms: the aleatory structure of the case and the linguistic structure of the sign.[138]

In the medicine of species, it was necessary to determine the qualities of disease, and thus mathematics was specifically rejected as a model for medical investigation.[139] The ideal for observation in eighteenth-century medicine was to approach as far as possible the essential knowledge of the supreme intelligence that had structured the garden of species. At the end of the century, however, the ideal of knowledge was to study the medical field as an open domain of pathological events that could be mastered with probabilistic reasoning. Putting aside the pursuit of essential species underlying the sick individual, medicine now sought a steady accumulation of individual pathological facts; the collective study of numberless cases by multiple observers becomes the norm that replaces the point of view of an

Ideal Observer.[140] This abandonment of a species-quality perspective reflected the common homogeneous space that had been established for medical perception, and that made a mathematical approach reasonable in a way impossible to conceive of earlier. Although the new mathematical reasoning in medicine was explicit, the value and coherence of its claims rested upon an extension of the hospital domain from the fringe to the center of medical experience.

The second model operative in the creation of clinical experience as knowledge, that of the linguistic structure of the sign, remained implicit in the activity of the clinic but was far more coherent as a structure than the mathematical.[141] The medical tradition of the eighteenth century had made a fundamental distinction between symptoms, which manifested the invariable form of the disease, and signs, which merely indicated a process that was not yet understood essentially.[142] With the loss of interest in pathological essences at the end of the century, this distinction collapsed, and the signs are understood to say the thing that is the symptom: beneath a "gaze that is sensitive to difference, simultaneity or succession, and frequency the symptom therefore becomes a sign." The significance of this assumption for medical knowledge is that it places on the "horizon of clinical experience the possibility of an exhaustive, clear and complete reading" of disease.[143] Disease is totally open to observation and discussion. The medical field was no longer to know silent species that might either lend themselves to or hide themselves from medical observation and description. Instead, the reality of disease itself is conceived on the model of language.[144] If political events had been crucial for structuring a homogeneous social space, the presence of mathematical and linguistic models ended medicine's difficult labor with essences and symptoms, and furnished a "domain of clear visibility" for the gaze.[145]

The operation of these two codes makes sense of the role attributed to observation as a power and to the imperative expressed at the time to "make science ocular."[146] Everything could now be seen by the trained, calculating gaze of the doctor, whose field of sight would be enlarged with the steady extension of the hospital's domain. That natural environment that had been thought necessary for the truth of a disease to manifest itself is no longer required. The modifications of a patient's pathology, which the artificial hospital environment might introduce, are now mathematically calculable. What is needed for advance in medical knowledge is a "neutral domain, one that is homogeneous in all its parts and in which comparison is possible and open to any form of pathological event, with no principle of selection or exclusion."[147] As a unification of both hospital and teaching, the clinic is also a forum for speech. That which is seen in the hospital becomes that which is to be spoken for the instruction of others. The clinic is the power of observation and the power of teaching, because the postulate of its organization is that all that is visible is expressible, and that it is wholly visible because wholly expressible. Clinical experience can be symbolized as a "speaking eye" that "would scan the entire hospital field, taking in and gathering together each of the singular events that occurred within it; and as it saw, as it saw ever more and more clearly, it would be turned into speech that states and teaches."[148] Once the mathematical and language models were at work, only one major additional step needed to be taken for the experience of the clinic to attain a coherent definition.

The final and decisive step in the constitution of clinical experience as a complete model for medicine was taken when death itself became visible, when Xavier Bichat (1771–1802) integrated pathological anatomy into clinical thought. A statement made by Bichat in 1801 represents for Foucault "the great break in the history of Western medicine."

> For twenty years, from morning to night, you have taken notes at patients' bedsides on affections of the heart, the lungs, and the gastric viscera, and all is confusion for you in the symptoms which, refusing to yield up their meaning, offer you a succession of incoherent phenomena. Open up a few corpses: you will dissipate at once the darkness that observation alone could not dissipate.[149]

Clinical experience is the anatomo-clinical perception in which the depths of the human being itself are revealed to sight. A modification of the clinic that preceded, it represents an ultimate triumph for the gaze, which now becomes a plurisensorial structure, medically comprehending with the assistance of a probing in touch and hearing as well as in sight.[150]

The major importance of this capacity for even the invisible depths to become visible is twofold. First, death makes possible a conceptually clear definition of the relation between disease and life, a definition toward which the medicine of the period had been moving. Disease is no longer to be thought of as an accident; rather, it becomes the constant encounter between death and life: "It is not because he falls ill that man dies; fundamentally, it is because he may die that man may fall ill."[151] Life, disease, and death now form a conceptual trinity. Second, death makes it possible for knowledge to overcome the Aristotelian prohibition of the application of a scientific discourse to the individual.[152] In death, the subject can become object for science. For Foucault, this ability to have a scientifically structured discourse about the individual is the essential meaning of clinical experience: "that opening up of the concrete individual, for the first time in Western history, to the language of rationality."[153] Although the study of fevers would complement the articulation of this experience, these three dimensions of space, language, and death that Foucault has examined in *NC* represent for him the essential conditions of possibility for modern clinical medicine.[154]

iii) Thought and History In the preface to *NC*, Foucault describes his history of the clinic as a "strange discourse."[155] And indeed it is, when compared with those straightforward accounts of the progress of medicine that have become part of our culture's self-consciousness. The strangeness of his work—and the discourse becomes even stranger at various points after 1963—is rooted in the type of task for a fundamental thinking that is gradually disclosing itself to him. *NC* is the occasion for greater clarity about this task, and thus a decisive step in the development of the archaeological project.

The strangeness of his works on both madness and the clinic reflects the fundamental level of experience that his thinking is attempting to reach. The effort to understand the experience of madness "must try to return, in history, to that zero point in the course of madness at which madness is an undifferentiated experience, a not yet divided experience of division itself."[156] An understanding of clinical experience demands placing thought "at the level of the fundamental *spatialization* and *verbalization* of the pathological, where the loquacious gaze with which the doctor observes the poisonous heart of things is born and communes with itself"; this entails looking beyond medicine's thematic content or logical modalities to the "region where 'things' and 'words' have not yet been separated, and where—at the most fundamental level of language—seeing and saying are still one."[157] Perhaps the best way to clarify this fundamental level of experience is to see the need that is motivating the search for it, and the direction that Foucault envisions for his inquiry at this point.

As a result of his study of madness and the clinic, Foucault has glimpsed the difficult place in which man's thought is located. We exist within codes that structure the "dark, but firm web of our experience." Capacities and perspectives that seem so self-evident, the power of observation, the reality of disease, are not immemorial but temporary experiences that owe their specific character to certain operative structures and codes.[158] This is the "within" in which thought finds itself enclosed. The ability to identify this enclosure, however, implies a certain power to reflect from without upon these parameters of thought. How is this power accounted for? Foucault maintains that we are able to appreciate both the influence and the historical nature of these codes because "we are only just beginning to disentangle" a few of their threads, because "we are only just beginning to detach ourselves" from traditional perceptions.[159] This beginning is a reality "perhaps because a new experience of disease is coming into being that will make possible a historical and critical understanding of the old experience."[160] The "perhaps" of the last sentence indicates the tentativeness of Foucault's judgment on what ultimately makes his own thought possible. Despite this, however, he has reached conclusions regarding the historical situation within which his questions have arisen.

If one of the major values that the study of madness possessed for him was to liberate his thought from enclosure within the crippling assumptions of psychology, *NC* implies a more sobering type of liberation. It is no longer a question only of psychology's inadequacy, but of the status of the contemporary study of man as a whole. Medicine has a "fundamental place in the over-all architecture of the human sciences," a realization that forces thought into the most disquieting of locales.[161] The history of madness had revealed the curious situation of man becoming psychologically knowable only in the face of a constituted mental illness.[162] Now his history of medicine has shown that death is at the limit of the sciences that study the life of man.

> It will no doubt remain a decisive fact about our culture that its first scientific discourse concerning the individual had to pass through this stage of death. Western man could constitute himself within his own eyes as an object of science, he grasped himself within his language, and gave himself, in himself and by himself, a discursive existence, only in the opening created by his own elimination: from the experience of Unreason was born psychology; from the integration of death into medical thought is born a medicine that is given as a science of the individual.[163]

In the light of this development, the importance of medicine for the sciences of man is ontological, for it involves "man's being as an object of positive knowledge."[164] The significance that major figures of medicine have had for philosophy in contemporary intellectual life does not mean that doctors were also philosophers, but that in our culture "medical thought is fully engaged in the philosophical status of man."[165]

Although its necessary location in history raises the most fundamental questions regarding what claims can be made for thought, *NC* is not to be understood as an admission of the impotence of thought. It is true that his study of the clinic has occasioned serious suspicions in Foucault's mind about what is generally regarded as knowledge in contemporary culture, namely, the commitment to commentary: "We are doomed historically to history, to the patient construction of discourses about discourses, and to the task of hearing what has already been said."[166] More specifically, the structures that he sees as accounting for clinical experience and the concept of medicine as a positive science have undermined his earlier sympathy for the phenomenological themes that sustain the enterprise of commentary. The roots of medical positivism suggest

> that with which phenomenology was to oppose it so tenaciously was already present in its underlying structures: the original powers of the

perceived and its correlation with language in the original forms of experience, the organization of objectivity on the basis of sign values, the secretly linguistic character of the datum, the constitutive character of corporal spatiality, the importance of finitude in the relation of man with truth, and in the foundation of this relation, all this was involved in the genesis of positivism. Involved, but forgotten to its advantage.[167] Nevertheless, while promoting a certain sense of suspicion, NC also represents a major advance in Foucault's understanding of fundamental thinking.

At the end of NC, Foucault appreciates the general direction his work must take, and thus the level at which a fundamental thinking must operate. His concern in NC was to "attempt to apply a method in the confused, under-structured and ill structured domain of the history of ideas."[168] He rejects two paths taken by the history of ideas. He calls the first the "aesthetic method," which directed its attention to charting history in terms either of a certain temporality, "geneses, filiations, kinships, influences," or of a certain spatiality, "the spirit of a period, its *Weltanschauung*, its fundamental categories, the organization of its socio-cultural world." The second path he rejects is "psychological method," which has "developed into a certain psychoanalysis of thought."[169] Although his case against these methods is not specifically argued in NC, his distance from them is discernible in what he takes to be the object of his own approach as well as in what he sees that approach opposing. His thought is concerned with determining the "conditions of possibility" of clinical experience, indifferent to the stated intentions of major medical personages as well as to the accepted explanations of medicine's history. "What counts in men's thoughts is not so much that which they have thought, but the not-thought (*non-pensé*) which systematizes them from the outset, thus making them thereafter endlessly accessible to language and open to the task of thinking them again."[170]

The project accomplished in NC is regarded by Foucault as a "structural study" in that it is concerned with the clinic as a "formal structure," the development of which is treated in terms of a "profound structural mutation."[171] His intention was to examine speech (*parole*) apart from the assumption that there is an excess of the signified (*signifié*) over the signifier (*signifiant*).[172] The meaning of a proposition is "defined not by the treasure of intentions that it might contain, revealing and concealing it at the same time, but by the difference which articulates it upon the other real or possible statements, which are contemporary to it or to which it is opposed in the linear series of time."[173] This structural project sets itself in opposition to any historical interrogation guided by a priori imperatives to determine whether an historical event was progressive or reactive, or to consider history as the process of abandoning old theories and accepting new ones, or to attempt to discover some proposed hidden continuity that underlies historical change.[174]

At one point in *NC*, Foucault identifies his mode of analysis as directed to the "discursive structure" (*structure discursive*) of the clinic.[175] This notion of discourse will be subjected to a sustained consideration in the years ahead, and will come to play a far more important and definite role in Foucault's thought. In *NC*, it represents the necessary place for thought, that which is its enclosure. However, as Foucault's own discourse on the clinic already shows, thought is a matter not only of acknowledging confinement, but of the power to articulate the character of that enclosure. In order to appreciate better this other dimension of thought, it is necessary to touch upon those analyses of literature that come to dominate Foucault's attention in the years during which he was occupied with the research for *Les mots et les choses* (hereafter *LMC*).

B) LITERATURE: A "WITHIN" AND A "WITHOUT"

With the major exception of *NC*, almost all of Foucault's published writings from 1962 until the appearance of *LMC* in 1966 are studies of literature. In addition to a book-length examination of Raymond Roussel, there are articles on Hölderlin, Rousseau, Bataille, Mallarmé, de Sade, Robbe-Grillet, Klossowski, Flaubert, Blanchot, Verne, among others, as well as more general analyses of literature. Because it would be impossible to attempt even an inadequate summary of his perceptions of each of these writers as individuals, we will limit ourselves to disengaging those principles regarding thought at which Foucault arrived as a result of these literary investigations.[176] The preoccupation with literature in these years does not represent a new direction in his thought, but rather the development of a continuing interest that came to require more rigorous clarification. From his piece on Binswanger through his writing of the 1980s, Foucault's works give a constant testimony to his regard for the arts in general as well as to literature in particular. The long development that resulted in the reduction of unreason to silence and in the triumph of psychology was seen to have failed only in the case of certain writers and painters, among whom Foucault specifically mentions Goya, van Gogh, de Sade, Hölderlin, Roussel, and Rousseau.[177] His writings of this period address the power of their language in a more thorough and general fashion than he had hitherto attempted.

The most fundamental discovery Foucault made in his reflection on literature was the autonomy that language possessed as the experience of the real. Surrealism has enabled us to understand that it is in the element of language that experience occurs, and that, speaking within language, it is always of language that we speak.[178] For thought, language thus assumes a "sovereign position."[179] In attributing this necessarily linguistic character to experience, Foucault echoes the views of much of twentieth-century French literature. While Raymond Roussel was among the first both to recognize this "autonomy of language" and to develop techniques for communicating its "ontological power," this recognition and development are traits common to the literature that Foucault treats.[180] The significance of this literature is disclosed through a questioning that relates it to madness and death.[181]

The character disclosed by the works he studied showed literature to be a transgression of the limits imposed by western culture upon the life of unreason. Because these literary works violated the exclusions that culminated in the constitution of psychology, a psychological approach to this literature is ruled out.[182] In regarding literature as a transgression against the limit imposed by death, contemporary writing has restored to its rightful place a theme as old as Homer's *Odyssey*. While it is the inevitability of death that "hollows out in the present and in existence the void toward which and from which we speak," it is literature itself that resists this necessity by a speaking without end in an infinite space of possibility.[183] For Foucault, the central significance of literature is that it is an experience of transgression, an experience he envisions as being as important for our thought "as the experience of contradiction was at an earlier time for dialectical thought." Although it is an experience for which the "illumination of its being lies almost entirely in the future," Foucault draws from it the essential implication it possesses for an understanding of the character of thought itself.[184]

Fundamental thinking is a "thinking from without." Although this "*pensée du dehors*" is the title of one of Foucault's articles, it represents the culmination of the intellectual journey in which he had been engaged since 1954.[185] That fundamental thinking must necessarily find itself in a realm of exteriority is, first of all, a recognition of the sovereign place occupied by language. Since it inhabits a world that is linguistic, human reality is rooted in an "I speak" rather than in an "I think."[186] The transition from one to the other reflects a displacement of reality from an interiority that had been considered sovereign for the experience of thought to an exterior realm of language within which man and his thought are now dispersed. This realm of exteriority represents the necessity for thought to operate outside of a strictly Kantian framework.

In 1964 Foucault published the translation of Kant's *Anthropology from a Pragmatic Point of View*, which he had finished three years earlier and which opened with this statement by Kant.

> The aim of every step in the cultural progress which is man's education is to assign this knowledge and skill he has acquired to the world's use. But the most important object in the world to which he can apply them is

man, because man is his own final end. So an understanding of man in terms of his species, as an earthly being endowed with reason, especially deserves to be called *knowledge of the world*, even though man is only one of the creatures in the world.[187]

This Kantian perspective had been made obsolete by the central position that language had come to occupy for Foucault and for contemporary experience. "The being of language only appears in itself with the disappearance of the subject."[188] The strength of Mallarmé's writing, for example, is that man emerges within language, outside of all relation to an anthropology constituted otherwise.[189]

While Kant had attempted a fundamental thinking in terms of a philosophy of limits, he had actually opened the way for a dialectics in which "contradiction and totality" came to be substituted for an interrogation of limits.[190] But it is the questioning of limits that identifies what fundamental thinking for Foucault is. Thought finds itself within the space of a reality that is constituted for it in language and perceptual codes. Nevertheless, thought is precisely the power to transgress these limits, to reflect outside of the structure within which a convergence of historical developments has placed it. At the same time, such thought is not autonomous, for it depends upon operating within a period in which a new structure of experience begins to emerge. In addition, thinking as a thinking from without, as a power of transgression, has itself only been revealed in the wake of the event that is called the "death of God." This event has eliminated that "limit of the Limitless" within which western thought had been confined. For Foucault, the significance of this elimination is not to be understood as restoration to a "limited and positivistic world, but to a world exposed by the experience of its limits, made and unmade by that excess which transgresses it."[191] Archaeology will be identified with the type of thinking that moves in the realm of exteriority and reveals the historically constituted limits for thought, and, in this very act of thinking, transgresses. Archaeology is thus a "thinking from without."

CONCLUSION

While this "thinking from without" is Foucault's formulation of the extraordinary experience designated "thought," his concern in the journey that we have followed in this chapter has not been to arrive at a philosophical definition but at a mode of performance. These first writings have situated the future direction for this action of archaeological thinking within history and language, or better, in a striking image he employed, within the library.[192] The interest of his thinking at this point was not to identify with some particular well-worn path for reflection, to announce a shift from anthropology to ontology or some other established line of inquiry. Rather, it was to begin to order part of the sheer multiplicity of things said at different times and in different ways, a task similar to that of the librarian. But is not the thinker more than a librarian? Are there not grander ambitions to be entertained for a power so extraordinary as thought?

When compared with that first anthropological project for his thought, with that dimension of dream and imagination in which man appeared as a radical liberty and thinking as the prelude for an ethical engagement within history, it is perhaps difficult to stifle a sense of disappointment with this image of the library as the home of thought. Although his later work was to show the resources of the library or archive, we can glimpse, even at this period, a continuing concern on his part with those themes that were present at the beginning of his thinking. Certainly man was no longer describable as a "radical liberty," for his existence within history and language had shown that "man does not begin with liberty but with the limit."[193] Nevertheless, it would be wrong on the basis of this to assume that the image of the library symbolized for him the ultimate imprisonment of the thinker, his permanent exile from those dimensions of imagination and freedom that had once seemed so important for Foucault.

Foucault had not abandoned the issues to which his earlier reflection on liberty was tied. The imaginary is now a "phenomenon of the library," and "is not formed in opposition to reality as its denial or compensation; it grows among signs, from book to book, in the interstice of repetitions and commentaries; it is born and takes shape in the interval between books."[194] The library is the place for thought's freedom.

> Henceforth, the visionary experience arises from the black and white surface of printed signs, from the closed and dusty volume that opens with a flight of forgotten words; fantasies are carefully deployed in the hushed library, with its columns of books, with its titles aligned on shelves to form a tight enclosure, but within confines that also liberate impossible worlds. The imaginary now resides between the book and the lamp. The fantastic is no longer a property of the heart, nor is it found among the incongruities of nature; it evolves from the accuracy of knowledge, and its treasures lie dormant in documents. Dreams are no longer summoned with closed eyes, but in reading; and a true image is now a product of learning.[195]

Foucault's later work was a reading that continued to seek the grounds of the experience for which, by accepting it as reality, we are in part responsible. His pursuit demands the most radical of deaths, the modern conception of man himself. His thesis on Kant had already claimed that Nietzsche's death of God implied the death of man, for the nature of the latter was inseparable from the identity of the former. This was a philosophical claim, however; the archaeological assassination of man is a deed of the human sciences executing the logic of their own knowledge.[196]

3

◆

Cathartic Thinking

INTRODUCTION

Because this chapter will be given over almost exclusively to a consideration of Foucault's *Les mots et les choses* (hereafter *LMC*), it risks complicity with a common tendency to treat the work as isolated from the development that we have just examined.[1] Such isolation threatens the possibility of understanding the text accurately, and is due, in large part, to the very success that greeted its appearance in 1966. If Foucault's earlier writings had been received, at best, with quiet respect, *LMC*'s publication was, as Claude Bonnefoy noted, the "event of the season."[2] The celebrity status that this difficult philosophical volume achieved by having its first printing exhausted within a month has had the unfortunate consequence of distorting *LMC*'s proper place in the body of Foucault's work. It was often consigned to the status of a synthetic statement for archaeological thought. Thus, for example, the absence in *LMC* of the interest in social and political factors, which had been present both in *HF* and *NC*, did not imply, as it would for an effort of synthesis, that these factors were no longer considered significant. *LMC* must be read as one of a series of studies, along with those of madness and clinical medicine, each of which, while related to the others, does not displace them. [3] According to Foucault's own desire, it should be approached as a "workbook," a stage of transition in the development of archaeology.[4]

Although it is not a synthetic statement, *LMC* is a decisive step in the articulation of his thinking. Its goal is to perform, as its subtitle states, an "archaeology of the human sciences." The sciences of psychology, sociology, of the analysis of literature and myth, history, psychoanalysis, and ethnology all require a radical interrogation of their historical identity and conditions of existence. These human sciences delimit the regions within which much of our contemporary reflection moves. Despite the central role they play, the human sciences are, in Foucault's view, too often accorded an uncritical acceptance. Certain temporary modes of reflection and the objects fabricated for them are thought to possess foundations of such rational solidity that they no longer need to be put into question. This state of affairs can only hinder genuine thought, and is rooted in our culture's failure to "pose the problem of the history of its own thought."[5] This failure is the invitation for an archaeology of the human sciences—Foucault's attempt to "uncover the deepest strata of Western culture" for the sake of "restoring to our silent soil its rifts, its instability, its flaws."[6] The central ambition of *LMC* is cathartic, a comprehension and purgation of the conditions that determine contemporary forms of knowledge.[7]

On the one hand, this need for catharsis is personal. An archaeological questioning of the human sciences is an inquiry into the foundations of that sphere of knowledge in which the figure of man is principal focus. It is the sphere in which Foucault's earliest studies formulated themselves. A strictly personal perspective on the cathartic task of *LMC* is far too limited, however. Foucault's work is not a search for a justification of his own earlier choices but an examination of why they were his questions, why he was unable not to ask them, why they are our questions.[8] He is still haunted by the nightmare of a text that cannot be deciphered by the questions that are posed to it. The text is contemporary experience itself, and the interest running through the pages of *LMC* is how this experience can be thought about in a manner adequate to its uniqueness. *LMC* does not provide a definitive answer to this question, but it does advance Foucault's effort to contribute to such an answer. The unity of *LMC*'s diverse investigations is in their confrontation with those "internal conditions of possibility" that account for the style of our contemporary thought, and in their identification of the major obstacle blocking the way to a more adequate thinking of our actuality.[9]

A) THE CONFRONTATION WITH THOUGHT

Foucault tells us that *LMC* was occasioned by his reading of a passage by Jorge Luis Borges referring to a Chinese encyclopaedia in which

animals are divided into: (a) belonging to the Emperor, (b) embalmed, (c) tame, (d) sucking pigs, (e) sirens, (f) fabulous, (g) stray dogs, (h) included in the present classification, (i) frenzied, (j) innumerable, (k) drawn with a very fine camelhair brush, (l) *et cetera*, (m) having just broken the water pitcher, (n) that from a long way off look like flies.[10]

The text indicates the profound difference that exists between this system of ordering and our own ways of organizing the multiplicity of existing things. It also suggests the limits our minds confront in trying to think the coherence of the Chinese definitions, ideas that can only be juxtaposed for us in language.[11] Its order is foreign to our thinking. As inhabitants of different cultures, we find ourselves within different codes, different homes for our thought.

It is a point familiar to us by now. *NC* led Foucault to conclude that we were destined to history, and that our experience was already structured by specific, temporary codes. This involvement with history is also a confinement to language, a confinement that acquires greater force in *LMC*: "we are already before the very least of our words, governed and paralysed by language."[12] The sovereign position that language has come to occupy for our reflection in the contemporary period makes a questioning of it—a constant concern throughout *LMC*—a questioning of thought itself. Any attempt to fathom the nature of the "I think" is a pursuit of the "I speak." Although working with familiar themes, *LMC* is far from a mere repetition of his earlier work, for it explores a different dimension of mind's confinement. While *HF* was an account of the way reason exorcises the otherness of experience in an action of exclusion, *LMC* details the way the multiplicity of experience is ordered into a sameness that authorizes thought to distinguish into kinds and collect into identities. Between the two texts stood the bridge of *NC*, which, in its analysis of disease, encountered both disorder, "the existence of a perilous otherness within the human body," and the experience of regularity and order, disease as a "natural phenomenon with its own constants, resemblances, and types." *LMC* is the last of a trilogy of investigations that have sought to probe those fundamental differences that constitute the "threshold that separates us from Classical thought and constitutes our modernity."[13]

LMC hunts down thought in the context of understanding not how it excludes but how it includes and orders, how it achieves sameness, how thought is always a thinking within. Nevertheless, one of its principal results is ceaselessly to remind us of thought's other dimension: that thinking from without, that bringing into light and consequent distancing from the specific system, that both confines thought and determines its direction at a particular period. *LMC* accomplishes this distancing by making us aware of the development that accounts for the crossroads at which contemporary thought finds itself. This awareness had already been anticipated. We have seen, at the end of *NC*, how Foucault's earlier sympathy for phenomenological themes was undermined by his recognition that they shared a common structure with positivism.[14] As a result of *LMC*, thought will realize why it journeys within modernity's two major paths of reflection: that of hermeneutics or interpretation and that of formalization or the discovery of system.[15] While the relation between these two forms of reflection is, to Foucault's mind, "probably the most fundamental question that can present itself to philosophy," archaeology's task will not be to say "whether this relation is possible, or how it could be provided with a foundation," but rather to grasp the common ground from which these alternatives for thought arise.[16] But this would be to say too little for Foucault's archaeology of the human sciences. *LMC* also undermines, in an explicit and sustained fashion, the principal obstacle blocking the movement of thought into a form of thinking more capable of comprehending the age in which it presently dwells.

B) THE OBSTACLE TO THOUGHT: MAN

Because the anthropological question has been at the center of our century's intellectual preoccupations, Foucault's interest in the topic, from the very earliest of his writings, gives no cause for surprise. The diversity of radically distinct philosophical perspectives in which man assumes heroic status attests, however, to the confusion that cloaks the modern definition of man himself.[17] This confusion was reflected in Foucault's initial difficulties with the investigation into the topic of man. We have already pointed out the awkwardness that characterized his attempt to establish a harmony between such different perspectives on man as those of Binswanger and Pavlov. By 1957 he had already been struck by the paradox of a knowledge of man that developed psychologies of consciousness, love, and intelligence from a point of view rooted in investigations of the unconscious, perversion, and mental weakness.[18] His studies of madness had already forced him to distinguish the question of man from that of "homo psychologicus," who provided a harbor for other voyages of reflection.[19] If *NC* had been the occasion for realizing that the birth of a science of the individual was strangely linked to an integration of death into thought, his interpretation of contemporary literature implied an opposition between the being of language disclosed in literature and the being of the subject.[20]

If Foucault's concern with the issue of man and his difficulty in developing a clear concept or position on anthropology is not surprising, what astounded his readers was the radicalness of the solution to the problem of man that is developed in *LMC*. In place of that one insight with which our age has become perhaps most comfortable in its knowledge of man, his temporality, Foucault claims that he is merely a figure who is temporary. Man is but a "recent invention," a fashion that did not exist before the end of the eighteenth century.[21] Furthermore, he is an invention that is "perhaps nearing its end," and thus we need to question whether we ought "to give up thinking of man, or, to be more strict, to think of this disappearance of man."[22] Imagining such a disappearance for man is as radical as Nietzsche's proclamation of the death of God. Unlike Nietzsche's announcement, however, there is no anxiety to be felt, no weightlessness to be experienced as a result of the death of man; on the contrary, it is "comforting" and a "source of profound relief" that man will disappear from our knowledge. And could there be any other reaction to a disappearance that will enable thinking to awaken a sleep "so deep that thought experiences it paradoxically as vigilance"?[23] Since we still think in that area in which the figure of man exercises sway, anthropology constitutes the "great internal threat to knowledge in our day."[24] This figure of man is the major obstacle to an adequate thinking of contemporary experience.

Of course, because these few paragraphs are only an introduction, the identity of this "man" who is in the process of disappearing, and what significance his absence will have for thought, are far from clear. The thesis of man as a recent invention does lead us, however, to the heart of Foucault's text. If man can disappear, if he truly is less than two centuries old, how did he come to be, and through what developments did he seize domination over thought? These are the questions to which the major part of *LMC* attempts to respond. Before turning to it, however, a few words on the methodology in *LMC* are warranted.

C) METHODOLOGICAL PRENOTE

Since we are attempting to follow Foucault's route as it in fact developed, we shall avoid the temptation to examine *LMC* in terms of the later statement of method contained in *AS*.[25] Nevertheless, *LMC* does contribute to the definition of the archaeological method that made its appearance as a practice in Foucault's earlier writings. The historical periods treated by his archaeology of the human sciences are roughly the same as those examined in *HF*: a classical period appearing in the middle of the seventeenth century and stretching to the modern period at the beginning of the nineteenth century.

Like his earlier studies, *LMC* pursues the "historical *a priori*" that constituted the conditions of possibility for the *existence* of different fields of knowledge in a particular historical period. This archaeological form of analysis is correlative to a level of investigation to which *LMC* gives the name of "episteme." This level is identified as a "middle region" between the empirical orders that provide a culture's positive knowledge and the field of scientific theory and philosophical interpretation that furnishes the general principles for these orders.[26] In *LMC*, archaeology is most frequently defined in opposition to what Foucault calls "doxology." The latter is a history of opinions in which attention is focused on the evident intellectual controversies of the day and the choices made by different individuals and groups with regard to the issues involved in these controversies; the former is concerned with articulating the hidden conditions that account for the specific opinions that clashed in a particular historical period.[27] Thus, for example, in the realm of the analysis of wealth, there are at least two approaches that may be taken to the question of the physiocrats and their opponents.

> The first would be a study of opinions in order to discover who in the eighteenth century was a Physiocrat and who an Antiphysiocrat; what interests were at stake; what were the points and arguments of the polemic; how the struggle for power developed. The other, which takes no account of the persons involved, or their history, consists in defining the conditions on the basis of which it was possible to conceive of both "physiocratic" and "utilitarian" knowledge in interlocking and simultaneous forms. The first analysis would be the province of a doxology. Archaeology can recognize and practice only the second.[28]

We are familiar with the satisfaction that the mind can derive from the approach employed in such a doxology. Recognition of the need to move beyond it arises from a most unfamiliar catharsis.

1. THE BIRTH OF MAN

Man emerges in a modern space of knowledge as the specific being who produces, who lives, and who speaks. He takes on this identity as a result of the three modes of knowledge that become privileged in giving access to him: economics, biology, and philology. If the event of man's birth is to be appreciated and the place he occupies in the modern episteme understood, we must grasp the mode of being these investigations possess and the form of knowledge they sanction.

A) ECONOMICS, BIOLOGY, PHILOLOGY

Although the constitution of economics, biology, and philology is a complex affair, Foucault decides to indicate their general archaeological foundations in terms of the work of three figures: David Ricardo for economics, Georges Cuvier for biology, and Frans Bopp for philology.[29] All three reveal the historical problematic within which the nineteenth century was organizing itself.

Ricardo (1772–1823)[30] In economics, Ricardo showed that all wealth, all value is a product of labor, and therefore must be understood as an accumulation that takes place in a temporal development. Giving rise to labor, economic activity itself, is the situation of scarcity that is man's lot as his numbers increase. The struggle of men as economic creatures is a battle between life and death, and man, *homo oeconomicus*, is the "human being who spends, wears out, and wastes his life in evading the imminence of death."[31] Thus, economics has necessary reference to a view of human reality as naturally finite. Paradoxically, immobilization of history, although of two very different types, results from the relation between this historicity of production and this anthropology of finitude. With Ricardo, a stabilization of population will entail a limit to scarcity itself, while a new mode of distributing wealth will bring an adjustment of needs to labor. With Marx, on the other hand, the growing misery of men will lead to a reversal of the development that is responsible for the distress of the human condition. These three elements—the historical conception of the process of production, the finitude of human existence, and the eventual arrest of history—define for Foucault the new configuration of knowledge that was involved in the constitution of economics: "History, anthropology, and the suspension of development are all linked together in accordance with a figure that defines one of the major networks of nineteenth century thought."[32]

Cuvier (1769–1832)[33] In biology, Foucault chooses Cuvier as the example of the historicity that came to be perceived in the nineteenth century as a fundamental dimension of living beings. This perception was the condition of possibility for the appearance of biology. Cuvier replaced the study of organs in isolation by an examination of the functional relationship that existed among the anatomical structures of organs. In doing so, in focusing attention on the functioning of life, Cuvier sketched a genuinely novel space for thought. Nature, to the extent that it is alive, cannot be reduced to a scale of genera and species. In the multiple functionings that make up the natural world, a history proper to life itself becomes a possibility. "It is no doubt true that in Cuvier's time there did not yet exist a history of living beings such as was to be described by evolutionism; but from the outset the living being is conceived of in terms of the conditions that enable it to have a history."[34] The understanding of nature demands that one penetrate through a natural organism's illusion of being to the great infinite force of life in which it participates but momentarily. Any reality, defined as living, is necessarily besieged on all sides by forces of death that will inevitably triumph. Man is no exception. The fate of death is the spouse of his identity as a living organism.

Bopp (1791–1867)[35] In the case of philology, the work of Bopp indicates the mode of being with which language was invested in the nineteenth century. Language is a reality of sound, and is treatable as a totality of phonetic elements. With this approach, the transformations of language can be examined strictly in terms of themselves, in contrast to any investigation that would need to relate changes to forces and events outside the language itself. Languages thus contain their own principles of evolution. This historicity that traverses language in the nineteenth century was constituted in the same manner as that which came to characterize living beings. Bopp's comparative work in Sanskrit, Persian, Greek, Latin, and German made their internal composition, their structures, transparent, and as a result, interest in chronological continuity among languages was replaced by the perspective that searched for internal historical development in the very formation of a language. The stages in linguistic formation are to be sought not in investigations relating them to historical movements with which they might have been contemporary, or in studies of the imaginative life of men. Instead, language's intelligibility is to be found in the "conditions that properly belong to the phonetic and grammatical forms of which it is constituted."[36]

Foucault's recourse to these transformations represented by the figures of Ricardo, Cuvier, and Bopp leads to two essential claims. The first is the singular quasi-transcendental status that labor, life, and language possess in the nineteenth-century configuration of knowledge. They are transcendental in the sense that they "make possible the objective knowledge of living beings, of the laws of production, and of the forms of language." Outside of knowledge and functioning as conditions of knowledge, these transcendentals have, however, two fundamental differences when compared with those of Kant. Life, labor, and language are situated beyond the objects—they totalize phenomena and express the a priori coherence of the empirical regions that economics, biology, and philology study—but they are also situated with the objects: they provide the empirical regions with a "foundation in the form of a being whose enigmatic reality constitutes, prior to all knowledge, the order and connection of what it has to know." In addition, unlike Kant's, these transcendentals concern the "domain of a posteriori truths and the principles of their synthesis—and not the a priori synthesis of all possible experience."[37] These quasi transcendentals constitute the epistemological space for a positive knowledge of man as the being who labors, lives, and speaks.

The second claim Foucault makes is the constitutive role played by history in this modern episteme. In the economic analysis of production, in the biological analysis of organically structured beings, in the philological analysis of linguistic groups, history is the fundamental mode of being in which the objects for analysis present themselves. Since the beginning of the nineteenth century, history defines the "birthplace of the empirical, that from which, prior to all established chronology, it derives its own being."[38] It is important to recognize, however, that in making this assertion, Foucault is not repeating the view that western knowledge is characterized by an historical consciousness or that in the nineteenth century, man's greater awareness of his own historicity led to a greater critical interest in history itself. The historical constellation that rises up in the perspective of Ricardo, Cuvier, and Bopp is fundamentally different from the consciousness of history with which western culture has been familiar since the time of the Greeks. This was an awareness of history as a single, uniform stream in which all of reality, the human as well as the nonhuman, found itself subject to the same great cycles of ascent and decline.[39] This traditional conception was shattered at the beginning of the nineteenth century, when it was discovered that there existed histories proper to nature, labor, and language. The various ways life adapts to an environment, the modes of development in economic production, the modifications of language—all have their own "internal laws of functioning," whose "chronology unfolds in accordance with a time that refers in the first place to their own particular coherence."[40] This conception sharply distinguishes Foucault's view from more common ways of understanding the nature of nineteenth-century historical consciousness, and marks the place where he sees man appearing in the configuration of the modern episteme.

The historical interest that operates in the study of economics, biology, and philology is not a consequence of a historicity that nineteenth-century man discovers as his own and then adopts as a principle for interpreting the world he inhabits. It is quite the reverse. The historicity discovered as proper to nature, production, and language freed these spheres from an alien chronology. Thus, on one level, nineteenth-century man is dehistoricized: "the human being no longer has any history: or rather, since he speaks, works and lives, he finds himself interwoven in his own being with histories that are neither subordinate to him nor homogeneous with him."[41] However, this dehistorization of human being, this reduction to the rank of passive participation in the movement of histories that are outside of his control, is but one side of a more complex event.

If production, life, and language themselves have their own histories, is there not a historicity that is proper to human life itself? Does not the being who works, who lives and dies, who speaks in language have a "right to a development quite as positive as that of beings and things, one no less autonomous" than theirs?[42] With the awareness of the history within these three empirical domains, human being makes its own claim to history, the character of which will often be sought in the histories of men from the perspectives of their existence within economic laws, of their development as a living species or as cultural totalities.[43] In the nineteenth century, with the appearance of these three empirical domains, something new has occurred: "the order of time is beginning."[44] Contemporaneous with this inauguration is man himself.

B) MAN

In claiming that man has existed only since the eighteenth century, Foucault is asserting that there was "no epistemological consciousness of man as such," no domain that was specifically proper to man before the modern period. "Renaissance 'humanism' and Classical 'rationalism' were indeed able to allot human beings a privileged position in the order of the world but they were not able to conceive of man."[45] This "man" whose birth represents the threshold of our modernity and who continues to hold such sway over our thought is an "empirico-transcendental" doublet, a constitution of human reality as a "being such that knowledge will be attained in him of what renders all knowledge possible." He is both the difficult object of knowledge as well as the sovereign subject of knowing, a "being whose nature (that which determines it, contains it, and has traversed it from the beginning of time) is to know nature and itself, in consequence, as a natural being."[46] His reality is determined by the unique place that has been hollowed out for him by the operation of the three quasi transcendentals.

Man is a figure of finitude, condemned to exist by the sweat of his brow, an organism living under the sentence of death, a process of thinking forced to lodge its thought in the density of language.[47] His essentially finite identity is proclaimed through those domains of knowledge in which he has sought enlightenment. The experience of human reality as "man" is as a living body, an appetite in relation to which value emerges, and as a user of language. The knowledges of biology, economics, and philology are in a state of interminable cross-reference with man's finite nature itself. Paradoxically, this finitude is unstable in that it is sketched within the context of an endlessness.[48] Man's evolution as a species has perhaps not yet terminated; changes in production and the processes of labor are possible vehicles for diminishing alienation; the complex reality of language may yet yield to intelligible systematicization. Thus, finite though he may be, man is nevertheless a figure of hope. This hope, however, inhabits a difficult region, and man finds himself in constant struggle with himself. At the very center of his thinking is a darkness that protects its shadows against the cogito's entrance.

> How can man *be* that life whose web, pulsations, and buried energy constantly exceed the experience that he is immediately given of them? How can he *be* that labour whose laws and demands are imposed upon him like some alien system? How can he be the subject of a language that for thousands of years has been formed without him, a language whose organization escapes him, whose meaning sleeps an almost invincible sleep in the words he momentarily activates by means of discourse, and within which he is obliged, from the very outset, to lodge his speech and thought, as though they were doing no more than animate, for a brief period, one segment of that web of innumerable possibilities?[49]

At the heart of his identity, there is an obscurity to which man bears witness in his search for origins.[50]

Man is always a sedimented being, a figure articulated on the already-begun of labor, life, and language. Not contemporaneous with those regions in which his being appears, existing within histories that have a calendar in which he does not figure, man discovers himself as time, as the figure who is dispersed within alien chronologies and yet who hopes for the dawn that will unite, in a harmonious achievement, his reality with those of production, life, and language. Human being as an historically existing man is thus the holy grail of modern thought: the revelation of his identity and the vehicle for achieving his harmony. This double function accounts for the ambiguity of history itself. History is divided

> into an empirical science of events and that radical mode of being that prescribes their destiny to all empirical beings, to those particular beings that we are. History, as we know, is certainly the most erudite, the most aware, the most conscious, and possibly the most cluttered area of our memory; but it is equally the depths from which all beings emerge into their precarious, glittering existence.[51]

The ambiguity of both history and that empirico-transcendental doublet we call man has not prevented them from becoming the archaeological foundation for modern thought as well as for much of our own. The continuing power of their presence for us can best be appreciated, however, when we see the episteme that preceded man's birth.

2. THE ABSENCE OF MAN

We know the critical turning point at which Foucault arrived as a result of his research in the human sciences. In his study of the classical age's theory of signs and of that period's way of organizing empirical studies, amid the clutter of detailed and conflicting analyses, a most glaring absence betrayed itself: man did not exist at the interior of classical knowledge. In his place there existed a power, belonging to discourse, to represent the order of things.[52] The task of representing the order of things is the vocation of thought in the classical age, and the hallmark that defines its essential difference from the modern episteme.

As Foucault had done in *HF*, his treatment of the classical age's mode of thinking rises up against the background furnished by a brief consideration of the Renaissance.[53] That period's fascination with the figures of microcosm-macrocosm was but a "mere surface effect" of the archaeological level on which all existing realities were recognized as similar to one another. On this level, thought found its fulfillment in bringing to light the resemblances with which creation had been endowed. The activity of mind is to set out on a "quest for everything that might reveal some sort of kinship, attraction, or secretly shared nature" among things.[54] The world is a system of corresponding signs that articulate their meaning for knowledge in the linguistic signs that are analogous to them. The work of language is to make everything speak: "nature and the word can intertwine with one another to infinity, forming, for those who can read it, one vast single text."[55] This necessity, however, that thought identify itself with the search for resemblances made its knowledge extremely precarious.

Resemblance never remains stable within itself; it can be fixed only if it refers back to another similitude, which then, in turn, refers to others; each resemblance, therefore, has value only from the accumulation of all the others, and the whole world must be explored if even the slightest of analogies is to be justified and finally take on the appearance of certainty. It is therefore a knowledge that can, and must, proceed by the infinite accumulation of confirmations all dependent on one another. And for this reason, from its very foundations, this knowledge will be a thing of sand.[56]

It was within this a priori that was set for knowledge in the Renaissance that the idea of microcosm-macrocosm attained its prominence as both the guarantee and limit of that knowledge. It was an epistemic configuration that was only temporary in western culture.

The event that divides the classical episteme from that of the Renaissance was the "dissociation of the sign and resemblance" that took place in the early seventeenth century. Although the madman would continue to seek resemblances everywhere, and the poet seek for the hidden affinities between things, both would be only marginal figures in the classical age. The general life of reason set out on a very different path. No longer moving in a network of corresponding similitudes, the work of reason identified itself not with interpretation but with ordering, with the pursuit of an adequate representation of a world that had suddenly begun to abound with differences among its beings and the signs that represented them.[57]

Thought now aimed at the construction of a taxinomia, a table of identities and differences that would overcome the temporal and necessarily discontinuous representations that we form of the world by means of a spatial arrangement in which the continuum of things could be exhibited: the "establishment of a simultaneous system according to which the representations express their proximity and difference, their adjacency and their separateness—and therefore the network, which, outside chronology, makes patent their kinship and reinstates their relations of order within a permanent area." This goal authorizes two distinct projects for classical thought. The first is the development of a "mathesis," a "universal science of measurement and order"—not a project of universal mathematicization, but rather, a mode of analysis attempting to represent order in terms of a system of signs. The second is the performance of a genetic analysis that sought to account for the way this complex system of signs came to be constituted from a field of specific elements; thought must discover the "ideal genesis of the complexity of things."[58] The goal of an exhaustive reading of the world, displaying itself in a taxinomia and utilizing a mathesis and genetic analysis, defines for Foucault the major features of the classical episteme.[59] This arrangement of knowledge gives rise to new sciences of order in the representation of words (general grammar), in the representation of beings (natural history), and in the representation of the needs to which wealth is related (analysis of wealth). Despite the plurality of these new sciences, the classical field of knowledge in which they came into existence was perfectly homogeneous: "all knowledge, of whatever kind, proceeded to the ordering of its material by the establishment of differences and defined those differences by the establishment of an order."[60]

GENERAL GRAMMAR[61]

Since the task for thought in the classical age is to master representation, the study of language enjoyed a prominent position among its domains of research. As an initial ordering of the representations of the world, language is the fundamental medium by which the beings of the world are known. Enunciated in time, language is nevertheless the ordering of beings in space through the employment of signs that define identities and differences. The classical age's analysis of language, general grammar, is the "study of the verbal order in its relation to the simultaneity that it is its task to represent."[62] Thus it is under the obligation to systematize linguistic signs in terms of a taxonomy. As opposed to the Renaissance's demand for commentary, for texts to interpret other texts in an effort to uncover the hidden meanings of signs, general grammar's approach to discourse is in terms of criticism, the comprehending of how languages accomplish their task of representation. Within the complex epistemological space in which general grammar operates, there is an entity that is both central and privileged, the name: "To name is at the same time to give the verbal representation of a representation, and to place it in a general table." In the status it accords to the name, general grammar reveals that the essential problem raised in the classical episteme is how to discover a *nomenclature* that would be a *taxonomy*.[63]

NATURAL HISTORY[64]

Although natural history is an epistemological formation separate from that of a general grammar, it is organized in a mode that is correlative to the project of a nomenclature that would be a taxonomy. "Natural history is nothing more than the nomination of the visible."[65] Functioning within the space of representation, such nomination was accomplished in natural history by the exercise of two key categories: structure and character. An analysis of an object's elements in terms of their form, quantity, manner of distribution, and magnitudes in relation to one another determines the parameters for what will be seen, and thus produces a structure that can be put into language. In order for this structure to be utilized as more than merely a proper name with a strict individuality, it must become part of a system of characters, "groups of identities selected to represent and distinguish a number of species or a number of genera."[66] In taking this approach to the study of natural beings, natural history entailed the duty of constructing a universal classification or taxonomy within which empirical individuals could come to be represented and known. Once again, Foucault uses the Renaissance as a contrast to this new configuration of knowledge.

In the Renaissance, the identity of natural realities was determined by a knowledge of the positive mark that a creature bore. The criteria for the definition of a group in the animal or plant kingdom were independent of the nature other groups might possess. Thus, one group of animals might be described in terms of a specific hunting habit without any reference to another group that was known by its choice of environment. Within the classical episteme, however, natural history designates only in relation to other possible designations. "To know what properly appertains to one individual is to have before one the classification—or the possibility of classifying—all others. Identity and what marks it are defined by the differences that remain."[67] The natural being is recognized in that it is limited by what can be distinguished from it.

ANALYSIS OF WEALTH[68]

In his treatment of economic affairs, Foucault detects the same radical replacement of the Renaissance's epistemic a priori of resemblance by the classical age's analysis of representation. For the earlier period, metal money functioned as a measure of the value of commodities and as a substitute in trade precisely because it was itself wealth. The precious quality of the material utilized for money determined its intrinsic value as a sign and made it possible to ascertain its equivalence with other goods. The intrinsic value of the precious material was ultimately founded in the order of creation and through the similitudes with which Providence had endowed its work. Creation is a system of correspondences among goods and, as blessings of Divine Intelligence, these goods are, in principle, capable of being exhaustively calculated in terms of their reciprocal value.

Although gold and silver continued to serve as money in the classical age, the epistemic formation in which they operated during that period totally changed the way they and their use were understood. For the classical age, the functioning of metals within a system of exchange and circulation determines their value. The relation between money and gold or silver is an arbitrary one, and not dependent upon a material's intrinsic character. Value proceeds from the relations among things, and the preciousness of metals such as gold and silver is due to their representative function as signs. They continue as the medium for economic exchange because certain material qualities (imperishable, divisible, easily transportable) favor them for endless representation. This perspective on the realm of wealth made it possible for thought in the classical age to develop a table of identities and differences in which a continuity of all the wealth in the world, as elements in a system of exchange, could be represented.[69]

Despite the multiplicity of specific differences among them, general grammar, natural history, and the analysis of wealth share a mutual task and obey a common epistemic formation. They are modes of being through which thought constructs an order of things.

> All wealth is coinable; and it is by this means that it enters into *circulation*—in the same way that any natural being was *characterizable*, and could find its place in an *articulated language*; that any representation was *signifiable* and could find its place, in order to be *known*, in a system of identities and differences.[70]

This manner of ordering things was possible if there was a continuity of being that was transparent to a labor of representation. Such a mission for mind had no need of the man's agency as an empirico-transcendental doublet: "man, as a primary reality with his own density, as the difficult object and sovereign subject of all possible knowledge, has no place" in the classical episteme.[71] This figure of man appears as a requirement of knowledge only after an epistemological rupture that took place in the last years of the eighteenth century, and that was as profound and puzzling as that which divided the Renaissance from the classical age. We do know its fundamental effect, the birth of man, as well as certain events that signaled the approaching end of representation as an episteme.

At the end of the eighteenth century there appears a "sort of behind-the-scenes world even deeper and more dense than representation itself."[72] It is the inability of representation to determine the directions of inquiries that were originally conceived within its embrace that will force thought to begin to look for a way of penetrating beyond the level of representative appearances to the depths that account for them as well as to a figure for whom they can be significant. In the realm of the analysis of wealth, this behind-the-scenes world is introduced by Smith's notion of labor.[73] With labor as an operative category, a table of equivalent values attempts to integrate a component that is heterogeneous to such an ordering. The order of exchange now finds itself in relation to a principle of toil, to an anthropology, in which there is implicit the possibility of a "political economy whose object would no longer be the exchange of wealth (and the interplay of representations which is its basis), but its real production: forms of labour and capital."[74] In the domain of natural history, it is in the category of organic structure that we can glimpse the appearance of a possible new space for thought.[75] When it begins to function as a method of characterizing natural beings, a dimension of invisibility announces itself, one that is irreducible to a classification in which natural beings would be analyzed in terms of the representations we construct of them. More important for knowledge is a certain relation within the natural being, a transition that can be sighted in the growing importance of the categories of the organic and inorganic to classification. The space of biology comes into view. The analysis of the inflectional system of a language plays the same role for general grammar that labor and organic structure played for the other empirical domains.[76] Although originally functioning in the context of a search for the representative values of a language, it begins to suggest that the grammatical structure outside of representation is the dimension that requires exploration, that the definition of a language "is not the way in which it represents representations, but a certain internal architecture, a certain manner of modifying the words themselves in accordance with the grammatical position they take up in relation to one another."[77] It is within this new internal space that there will appear the need to question what makes possible the syntheses of representative appearance, as Kant will come to do, as well as the being of those "never entirely representable representations" that the modern age will call the "force of labour, the energy of life, the power of speech."[78]

Although Foucault mentions certain elements that were crucial in the eclipse of the classical episteme, his sketch is intended neither as an explanation nor as a theory of transition. The rupture that exists between classical and modern epistemes preserves its enigmatic status, while his presentation has achieved its central purpose: the portrayal of the essential difference between an episteme of representation and that of anthropology. What separates general grammar, natural history, and the analysis of wealth from philology, biology, and economics is not a refinement in method or concept but a total transformation in the system of knowing. The life, language, and production of the modern empirical domains did not exist in the classical age, for the figure of man with whom they are in cross-reference was absent. The figure of man made his appearance when words ceased to intersect with representations, and instead of providing that "spontaneous grid for knowledge" that they had in the classical period, they found themselves reduced to the status of being an object for a subject.[79] This objectification, however, carried major implications for the anthropological episteme, which would only come to manifest themselves in the contemporary thought of the human sciences.

3. THE DISAPPEARANCE OF MAN

As man's birth is essentially an affair of knowledge, so will be his disappearance. He will be erased by those same "human sciences" (psychology, sociology, language analysis, psychoanalysis, ethnology) that were formed in the modern episteme as instruments for comprehending him. In his specific consideration of these sciences in *LMC*, Foucault has two objectives: first, to define their essential quality and show how the thinking characteristic of them is due to the place they occupy in the modern episteme; second, to indicate how the logic of their thought ultimately leads to a dissolution of the man they took to be their object.

A) THE PLACE OF THE HUMAN SCIENCES IN THE MODERN EPISTEME[80]

While the human sciences may be spoken of as those branches of knowledge that choose to make man an object of science, such a description runs the risk of misunderstanding the reason for that "invincible impression of haziness, inexactitude, and imprecision left" by almost all of them.[81] The fact that there is such difficulty in the research and analysis of the human sciences is not to be attributed to some extraordinary complexity that man possesses, but rather to the unique position these sciences occupy in the modern configuration of knowledge. If, therefore, the human sciences are to be defined "in their essence," if their "essential property" is to be isolated, they must be understood in the relations they maintain with the three faces of that modern configuration: that of mathematical knowledge, that of philosophical reflection, and that formed by the sciences of biology, economics, and philology.[82] Of these three, mathematics is of least relevance from an archaeological point of view. Although the human sciences undoubtedly have recourse to mathematics, there is nothing specific to them in such utilization. In addition, and more important, for Foucault, the analysis of the epistemic formation that gave rise to the birth of man did not reveal any a priori role exercised by a mathematical advance. Indeed, when this modern formation is contrasted to the classical episteme and the function the latter allotted to the general science of order, man's appearance as an object for study coincides with a comparative "demathematicization" of knowledge.[83]

Since man is an empirico-transcendental doublet, modern philosophical reflection and the sciences of life, labor, and language are the spheres most pertinent for situating the sciences that claim man as their object. Engaged in the analysis of man, the human sciences find themselves in relation to the philosophical thinking that has articulated man's radical finitude and has attempted to unify his being in terms of empirical and transcendental dimensions. As we have pointed out above, modern thought finds itself placed, through its anthropological a priori, in that obscure region where it is obliged to think the identity and sameness of a being who is dispersed among the activities of living, laboring, and speaking. In the figure of man, philosophy attempts to unify the empirical and transcendental, the cogito and the dimension of his being irreducible to it owing to a dispersion in his own temporality and in the histories within which he finds himself situated.[84] Within this difficult zone, philosophical inquiry found its mandate to be both a knowing and a modifying of what is known, "reflection and a transformation of the mode of being of that on which it reflects."[85] Arising in relation to this mode of thought, the human sciences develop their archaeological foundation in a paradoxical accord between positivistic tendencies, in which the object is the sole source of knowledge, and eschatological inclinations, in which the reality of man is to be searched for in the still-to-be-achieved harmony of his being. They appear as a terrain distinguished by both an ideal of value-neutrality and a task of social redemption.[86]

Concerned as they are with man as a living, speaking, and producing being, the human sciences stand in close rapport with those empirical studies that examine these activities. Nevertheless, they cannot be identified with economics, biology, and philology because their object is not man as a nature (as, in fact, living, speaking, and producing) but man as a being who forms representations of these activities. Their mode of analysis extends from man in his specific positivity to "what enables this same being to know (or seek to know) what life is, in what the essence of labour and its laws consist, and in what way he is able to speak."[87] In comparison with the empirical domains as such, the human sciences find themselves more specifically related to the philosophical analysis of finitude, and Foucault ventures to speak of them as developing in the "exteriority of knowledge" what the philosophical accomplished in the interiority of knowledge. They lead economics, biology, and philology back to the analysis that shows "how man, in his being, can be concerned with the things he knows, and know the things that, in positivity, determine his mode of being."[88]

While they cannot be identified, it is also the case, however, that economics, biology, and philology give the human sciences (in this case, sociology, psychology, language analysis) their constituent models; they are constitutive in the strict sense that they "make it possible to create groups of phenomena as so many 'objects' for a possible branch of knowledge; they ensure their connection in the empirical sphere, but they offer them to experience already linked together." Thus, the three models "play the role of 'categories' in the area of knowledge particular to the human sciences."[89] The epistemological regions of the human sciences are covered by the relationships constituted in the operation of these models. While this complex position occupied by the human sciences in the modern episteme already suggests the difficulty of the knowledge they pursue, it is in examining the operation of these models that one appreciates the character of that knowledge. In that examination, the significance this type of knowledge possesses for Foucault emerges in its full threatening and promising reality.

B) THE OPERATION OF THE HUMAN SCIENCES

The architecture and mode of analysis of the human sciences reveal themselves in the operation of the three models provided by the studies of life, production, and language; through this operation are exhibited the principal concepts that "completely cover the entire domain of what can be known about man." Within the sphere of the biological, man is posited as a being who possesses *functions*. He acts in relation to an environment that is physiological, cultural, and social. He is an organism with specific conditions for its continued existence and with an intellectual ability to discern the *norms* that allow him to perform his functions. Within the sphere of the economic, man is posited as a being who is in a state of constant *conflict*. His needs and desires lead him into an opposition with other men, but this contest can be limited by establishing a body of *rules* for social conduct. Within the linguistic sphere, man is posited as a being who is a bearer of *meaning*. His behavior, personal and social, voluntary as well as involuntary, expresses a coherent significance that may be examined as a *system* of signs.[90] These three pairs of concepts constitute a schema of intelligibility for the knowledge articulated in the human sciences. Since all these sciences interlock, the action of these concepts need not be limited exclusively to the particular human science in which a specific pair is rooted.

According to Foucault, this schema offers three advantages for an understanding of the human sciences. First, analysis is provided with a "formal criterion" for clearly distinguishing the levels on which a study is functioning.[91] Second, the schema might facilitate a modern history of the human sciences: on a general level, the succession of Comte, Marx, and Freud would be described as the movement from a biological model through an economic one, which in turn yields to a philological model; on a more specific level, this historical account could be written in relation to the shift that occurs from a thought guided by the first concepts of each constitutive model (function, conflict, signification) to that guided by the second terms (norm, rule, system).[92] The third advantage of the schema is the most important and possesses crucial significance for the claim toward which Foucault's text has been advancing. The human sciences lead thought to the sphere of the unconscious without forcing it from the realm of representation. Each of the pairs of concepts allows for representation to take place (that of signification for language, conflict for need, function for life), while at the same time relating to an unthought (the system that precedes signification, the unthought rule that organizes need, the norm that shows the conditions of possibility for function).[93] Foucault finds in the operation of these concepts the total domain of what can be known about man. These concepts articulate the fundamental arrangement of the modern episteme: they relate the empirical positivities, those "on the basis of which man first detached himself historically as a form of possible knowledge," with the dimensions of finitude that define man's being.[94] The pairs of concepts, therefore, are the very basis on which man is able to present himself to knowledge.

These concepts are utilized by the human sciences within the horizon of unveiling the fundamental conditions for man's reality and knowledge. This project, which Foucault sees as central to the work of these sciences, necessarily ties them to an exploration of the unconscious. The essential nature of the human sciences is constituted by this exploration rather than by a particular object that can be discriminated as man.[95] A human science exists "not wherever man is in question, but wherever there is analysis— within the dimension proper to the unconscious—of norms, rules, and signifying totalities which unveil to consciousness the conditions of its forms and contents."[96] This definition of the human sciences as necessarily related to the unconscious carries with it the major implication Foucault wishes to draw from the investigations in *LMC*. He makes his claim, however, not in reference to the human sciences he has been discussing up to this point (psychology, sociology, language analysis) but in terms of psychoanalyis and ethnology. These may be considered "counter-sciences" in that they return the human sciences to their epistemological foundation, and in doing so, undermine the project of a science of man.[97] Psychoanalysis and ethnology, spanning the entire field of knowledge produced in the human sciences, are movements of thought that bring them to their limits.

Psychoanalysis does not question man but explores the region of unconsciousness that constitutes his limit. Its great themes of Death, Desire, and Law designate the conditions of all knowledge about man. The knowledge of life, its functions and norms, finds its basis in death; desire, as the unthought at the heart of thought, is the foundation for conflicts and rules; law, as language, establishes signification and system.[98] Ethnology, like psychoanalysis, is not concerned with interrogating man; it investigates the historicity of a culture, the specific limits within which a culture defines its relations to life, need, and meaning. It focuses attention on unconscious structures in a society: the norms by which the functions of life are governed, the rules by which its needs are experienced and their satisfaction planned, the systems within which all significant expression takes place.[99] The importance of both psychoanalysis and ethnology for Foucault is that their investigation of the unconscious, both individual and cultural, does not arrive at man or issue in a general theory of him; indeed, in moving to what constitutes his outer limits, they "dissolve" man.[100] Foucault imagines the possibility of these inquiries intersecting in the area where the unconscious itself is considered a certain formal structure. Thus, there would appear a third counter-science, linguistics. This linguistics would be a formal model for both ethnology and psychoanalysis, and thus would cooperate with them in disclosing the limits of an anthropological knowing.[101]

This counter-science of linguistics may be expected to have consequences for contemporary thought even more fundamental than its service to the human sciences. The object status accorded language in the modern episteme implied that language would become intensely problematic: its objectification gave it a new prominence as a field of special study that was concretized, for example, in modern efforts to develop a scientific language and a symbolic logic.[102] Such concentrated study forces thought to confront the enigmatic being of language, and thus to share the preoccupation of contemporary literature. The maturation of the human sciences ultimately leads to a result parallel to that of this contemporary literature: the being of language replaces the figure of man as the major problematic for thought. *LMC* has labored to bring into view the dissolution of man as a logical consequence of the epistemological configuration to which he is central. His displacement by language proceeds from an understanding of anthropology's own conditions of possibility. It is a cathartic understanding that ought to reorient our gaze toward an ocean of other possibilities for thought. We can already sense the powerful pull of its tides for Foucault, even though he does not describe it. The figure of man, who has so fascinated thought, and turned its attention away from the roar of those other possibilities, is disappearing, "like a face drawn in sand at the edge of the sea."[103]

4. THE SITUATION OF AND THE TASK FOR THOUGHT

There is no assurance that those currents that are erasing man, the depths into which thought is entering, do not hide an abyss, a "bottomless sea" that will elude the most careful efforts to chart and navigate it. In order to recognize what course his own thought ought to take, it was necessary for Foucault to comprehend that framework within which we still, to a large extent, continue to think.[104] The complexity of the modern episteme indicates that an adequate appraisal and measure of our modern thought's foundations would require a "quasi-infinite investigation"; as a result, these foundations remain "largely beyond our comprehension." Nevertheless, continuing the efforts of *HF* and *NC*, *LMC* is a major effort to "dominate by fragments" the framework within which we experience and reflect.[105] In terms of our theme, the investigations of *LMC* result in two broad consequences. Foucault has achieved a greater comprehension with respect to the epistemological situation in which his and our thought has functioned, and while archaeology still lacks methodological precision, this comprehension has enabled him to clear the space for a more rigorous statement of a language-centered, deanthropologized reflection on contemporary experience.

A) THE SITUATION OF THOUGHT

The great event that has inaugurated modern thought is the appearance of man and his objectification for scientific research. In his discovery of this appearance and his analysis of its place in the modern episteme, Foucault has received more guidance from nonphilosophers than philosophers.[106] Nevertheless, just as the human sciences are bound up with philosophy, so has Foucault's investigation been, from its very inception. Speaking of the early stages in his study of the human sciences, Foucault remarked on the double obligation under which he saw them laboring: the necessity of discovering a hidden sense, their hermeneutical duty, and the necessity of uncovering structures, their duty of formalization.[107] This double responsibility issues from the modern configuration of knowledge, as well as marking the channels of philosophical thought in which the presuppositions for his own earlier thinking had been formed.

Hermeneutics (or interpretation or exegesis) and formalization (or the discovery of system, or that of invariant structure, or that of networks of simultaneities) constitute the two great paths for thought in the modern period.[108] Developing in relation to the new density that we have seen language to have taken on as a result of its objectification for man, modern thought is archaeologically rooted within these forms of analysis. Since these inquiries represent the essential tasks for thought emerging from the modern episteme, their relation is perhaps the most fundamental question with which a traditional philosophy can be concerned in our day.[109] It is most important to realize, however, that the philosophical question of the relation between these forms of analysis is not Foucault's question, and archaeology's allegiance to one of the methods is neither his interest nor wish.

Foucault has been explicit in his opposition to phenomenology as a guide for archaeological thinking. Its investigation of actual experience (*analyse de vécu*), its pursuit of meaning, its probing of subjectivity—all merely fulfill the demands set by the anthropological framework in which it was born.[110] While there can be no doubt of Foucault's opposition to phenomenology, his relation to structuralism at the time of *LMC* is far more complex and much more likely to be misunderstood. Indeed, the almost universal approach among his critics at this time was to put him in the camp of the structuralists.[111] Although we have already referred to the vehement denunciation of this label that Foucault will come to make, the tendency to identify him with the structuralists at this time is understandable, even if inaccurate. Foucault has written of *HF* and *NC* as structural studies, and his intentions seem at times quite close to those of the structuralists. He remarked that the phenomenological interest in meaning was ended for him by those researches of Lévi-Strauss and Lacan that pointed to the "surface effect" that "meaning" represented when compared to those systems that operate independently of what they relate. In contrast to the generation represented by Sartre and Merleau-Ponty, Foucault admits that he and his generation developed a passion for the concept and the system.[112] In addition, there is the fact that the dissolving of man that Lévi-Strauss considered to be the consequence of his own studies manifested an interest in common with the work of Foucault. Structuralism is a major element of that contemporary thought dedicated to the "uprooting of Anthropology." Like the structuralists, Foucault places the emphasis in his study of history on the synchronic over the diachronic; a history of knowledge "can no longer content itself with following the development of that body of knowledge in a temporal sequence" but must be written "on the basis of what was contemporaneous with it, and certainly not in terms of reciprocal influence, but in terms of conditions and *a prioris* established in time."[113]

Despite the passion for system, however, and the various concerns Foucault shares with the structuralists, the label is inappropriate in light of his understanding of what structuralism attempts to achieve. There is no doubt that his own mode of understanding, to the extent that it grows from the soil of contemporary thought, has relationships to methods that are intrinsic elements in the modern episteme.[114] Nevertheless, from the beginning of his project Foucault has been occupied with an analysis that accounts for the *existence* of the historical reality he is exploring, and in *LMC*, archaeology is still tied to this pursuit of existential necessity as contrasted to formal possibility.[115] In Foucault's mind, this fundamental difference of interests constitutes the irreducible barrier between him and the structuralists. In his studies of discourse, he is seeking "not its laws of construction, as do the structural methods, but its conditions of existence."[116] While structuralists may disagree with Foucault's formulation of their enterprise, there is sufficient clarity in his writings to recognize where he wishes to stand in relation to them in this period. In the context of *LMC* as a work through which Foucault is attempting a catharsis of his own presuppositions, structuralism is a formalization that remains rooted in the anthropological network. It is within this network that "structuralism and phenomenology find, together with the arrangement proper to them, the general space that defines their *common ground*."[117] Archaeology is attempting to move beyond the common ground: "What I am doing is neither a formalization nor an exegesis."[118]

We know the essential step that he has already taken in that attempt to arrive at a new territory for thought. Negatively stated, it is a thinking that aims to be antianthropological, a mode of reflection that will be disengaged from the transcendental-empirical dilemmas that the figure of man represents and within which both positivistic and critical thought in the modern period are still locked. All efforts to think anew are directed at the obstacle of anthropology.[119] Formulated more positively, this antianthropological ambition of *LMC* is a continuation of his earlier struggle in *HF* against the banishment of difference that was represented in the exclusion of the mad and in the birth of the asylum. *LMC* has attempted to show how the modern mind establishes the Same, how anthropology constructed a figure who finds experience only a mirror of his finitude. In contrast, Foucault wishes to chart the course for a diagnostic: "to say that which is the present, to say in what way our present is different and absolutely different from everything else which it is not."[120] For Foucault, the possibility of an adequate thinking of contemporary experience is tied to the ability to think difference. The question that remains, of course, is whether archaeology exhibits such ability.

B) THE TASK FOR THOUGHT

As if to balance their delineation of the frameworks within which thought necessarily functioned, Foucault's earlier works had also pointed to the power of "thinking from without" that made such comprehension possible. In contrast, *LMC* and the passion for system that he proclaimed after its publication left the distinct impression with many that the balance had not been preserved, and indeed, that he no longer desired to preserve it. There was a strong reaction from those those who regarded themselves as partisans of human liberty and historical consciousness. Even if Foucault's critics often placed him in the structuralist camp, their critique was primarily addressed to the implications of the conceptualization of system and episteme that *LMC* had presented.

Foucault's attempt to comprehend our modernity had led him to become an "ideologue of the system." Although it is a fact that our world is governed by technocracy, what necessity led Foucault to canonize such governance by enshrining it, in the functioning of an episteme, at the heart of thought itself, in attempting its methods and furnishing it with an ideological justification that it had hitherto lacked?[121] Sartre maintained that central in this abdication to the present system was Foucault's very refusal of history. *LMC* privileges system and coherence while refusing to speak about modes of transformation and contradictions; the reality of fixed moments overwhelms the sense of passage. He is one of the new Eleatics, denying not sensible movement, but rather historical change.[122]

i) Archaeology and the Thinking of History Foucault himself found the most striking reaction to *LMC* to be the division among its critics between those who claimed it was an assassination of history and those professional historians who accepted it as a work of history.[123] Although *LMC* does continue Foucault's project of thinking history more adequately, it must be acknowledged that suspicion regarding its precise attitude toward history, even to the point of seeing in the work a refusal of history, is not totally without foundation. *LMC* treats historical consciousness as part of the modern anthropological episteme. Although Foucault is discussing only a form of historical awareness, there is never a clear statement as to the role he envisions for historical thought in the wake of man's disappearance. This lack of clear definition is not of crucial significance if the cathartic function of the work is kept in the foreground of our reading of it. *LMC* is a declaration neither of method nor of program, both of which Foucault was unprepared to make in 1966. His silence with respect to the general role for reflection upon history in the work of a deanthropologized reason is grounded in a deep distrust as to the adequacy of such reflection—the historical interpretations that were implicitly or explicitly rejected in *HF* and *NC*—and to the "sacralization" of history that he felt existed among many contemporary intellectuals. While historical inquiry holds a privileged place for archaeology, the latter cannot be identified with the former.[124]

Foucault's enterprise is an archaeology rather than a doxology, that is, it seeks after the a priori, the epistemic level in which a field of experience for knowledge is delimited, the mode of being that characterizes this experience is identified, and the methods and concepts utilized for comprehending it are defined. From this angle, archaeology designates a "domain of research" that explicates the system of knowledge that accounts for the types of theory and practice present at a particular historical period.[125] In its analysis of this domain, archaeology becomes a critique of any historical treatment of knowledge that would necessarily assume an evolutionary perspective. Natural history, the analysis of wealth, and the study of language in the classical period are radically disconnected from the biology, economics, and philology of the modern period. To speak of biology, for example, as existing before the end of the eighteenth century would be anachronistic for the simple reason that "life itself did not exist" as an object for thought.[126] In contrast to the normal historian's interest in continuity, therefore, archaeology orients reflection to discontinuity, to the reality of the "fact that within the space of a few years a culture sometimes ceases to think as it had been thinking up to then and begins to think other things in a new way."[127] One of the major advantages promised by such an archaeological exploration of discontinuity is to challenge the normal ordering of the major steps in the development of a theory. Thus, for example, *LMC* shows that Cuvier and not Lamarck is crucial for understanding the intellectual foundations of modern biology, while in the sphere of economics, Marx and Ricardo emerge as sharing common anthropological assumptions.[128]

In the light of *LMC*, this domain of research and mode of critique can be characterized in its essence as deanthropological thinking. It is a thinking that stands outside of subjectivity and a search for meaning or teleology, that is uninterested in the persons who may have been the vehicle for thought and finds the idea of man useless for its form of research.[129] In place of man, Foucault enshrines the density of things said as the object for historical thinking. Two years after the appearance of *LMC*, he was to define his undertaking in the following manner:

> To determine, in its diverse dimensions, what must have been in Europe, since the seventeenth century, the mode of existence of discourses and particularly of the scientific discourses . . . , in order that the knowledge which is ours today could come to exist, and, in a more precise manner, that knowledge which has taken as its domain this curious object which is man.[130]

We can appreciate in this formulation the unity of *LMC*'s investigations with the cathartic function they served in Foucault's development. The questioning of madness and psychology, of medicine, of the human sciences, of man, of language excavates major dimensions of our culture's thought as well as the fundamental basis of Foucault's own development.

While archaeology preserves its tie for Foucault to the thinking of history, *LMC* leaves major methodological difficulties, which will require future resolution. We mention only the three principal ones. The first is the need for a more precise articulation of the difference between the aesthetic method of historical thinking, the search for a *Weltanschauung* that Foucault has already rejected, and his own analysis of epistemes.[131] The possibility that archaeology might be reducible to a mere variation of this other method finds justification in the strength of this statement in *LMC*: "In any given culture and at any given moment, there is always only one *episteme* that defines the conditions of possibility of all knowledge, whether expressed in a theory or silently invested in a practice."[132] The second major methodological difficulty posed by *LMC* was an absence of an account of how exactly the transformation of one episteme into another takes place. In contrast to the matter of the episteme, Foucault admits clearly that this difficulty exists and that he is not prepared to define, at this point, how such an escape from one system of thought into another occurs; at the same time, he rejects any attempt to account for such a change in terms of such magical notions as influence or crisis.[133] The third principal methodological problem was constituted by the failure to consider the relationships that exist between the level of archaeological networks of knowledge and the level of social-economic institutions and practises. While he had not ignored this latter level—*HF* and *NC* had entered into it—Foucault had become convinced that the connection between the levels was more complex than these works had described. His intention is to arrive at a more adequate formulation of this relationship, one that will be guided by the desire to avoid any anteriority of theory to practice and practice to theory, as well as to preserve the homogeneity of the archaeological field of research as a domain of linguistic events.[134] Although these methodological issues are serious, Foucault's professed antihumanism provoked the strongest criticism of archaeology as a project for thought.

ii) Archaeology and Politics The disappearance of man, rather than revealing a loss or deficiency, must be regarded as the "unfolding of a space in which it is once more possible to think." Foucault turns his back on those who still wish to talk of man and take him as their starting point in attempting to understand experience, historical as well as contemporary.[135] His thesis on the birth and disappearance of man and his definitive rejection of any reflection operating within an anthropological framework gave rise to a very loud controversy. There was, of course, misunderstanding. Thus, in the light of his careful effort to define man as an empirico-transcendental doublet, it was hardly to the point to suggest that Sophocles' ode on man offered a refutation of his thesis. This type of error was warned against by his major commentators.[136] At issue in the debate on whether man's disappearance ought to be welcomed, however, was no mere matter of verbal definition.

Foucault had delineated epistemic systems within which thought functioned necessarily, reduced man to a merely temporary figure of knowledge, and consigned humanistic themes of liberty and the surpassing of alienation to the region of warped reflection. In doing so, he had, as Sartre saw it, abandoned philosophy's task to think the overcoming of those structures that shape man. Foucault had left the impression, as Levinas put it, that there was no place to be found in his thought for indignation and passion.[137] The uneasiness felt in reaction to Foucault's celebration of man's disappearance and his passion for system found its best formulation as an issue for his thought in a question the French journal *Esprit* put to him in 1968.

Doesn't a thought which introduces constraint of the system and discontinuity in the history of the mind remove all basis for a progressive political intervention? Does it not lead to the following dilemma:
　　　—either the acceptance of the system,
　　　—or the appeal to an uncontrolled event, to the irruption of exterior violence which alone is capable of upsetting the system?[138]

Foucault recognized the question as one that "concerned the very core of my work," and while his reply does not fully answer the question or diminish the uneasiness, it does have a double importance.[139] It provided certain methodological clarifications of his earlier works, but since these clarifications were developed at greater length and depth in *AS*, they will be specifically taken up in the next chapter. Second, along with several interviews, his response to *Esprit* marked the beginning of his consideration of what relationship exists between archaeological thinking and political action. In concluding the chapter, we wish to focus on this issue, one that will become increasingly important in his future writings.

In the year of *LMC*'s appearance, Foucault had already pointed out that his critique of anthropological thought or humanism was a "political work."[140] Humanism was an abstraction that failed to appreciate the reduction of reason that had taken place in modernity's silencing of madness and its determination to establish a realm of the same. It is precisely this expulsion of difference that is the meaning of humanism as an ethics and a politics.[141] In attempting to rid himself of this humanism, and thus clear the ground for a thinking of difference, Foucault has welcomed the appearance of discourse as the object of his analysis and accepted the reality of the systems that can be shown to operate in discourse. Such receptivity to the appearance of discourse is a greeting of man's disappearance, although he admits that the fact of this disappearance can only be the source of uneasiness. Compared to a philosophical thinking concerned with themes of existence and destiny and the surpassing of alienation, archaeology is both less charming and less consoling.[142] This does not mean, however, that archaeology is at a disadvantage in its relation to political thought.

The themes that his archaeological research attempts to undermine are not necessary for a theoretical thinking of a progressive politics.[143] In displacing man, continuity, teleology, he is merely making a justified critique of a mode of thought that did not recognize its limits, that had become comfortable with inadequate evolutionist metaphors, and most important, that had become shallow in its dealings with the reality of language, with the concrete power of the experience that is constituted by the "things said." Can there possibly be

> some necessary relationship between a progressive politics and the refusal to recognize in the discourse anything else except a thin transparency which flickers for a moment at the limit of things and of thoughts, then disappears immediately? Can one believe that this politics has any interest in rehashing one more time the theme—I would have thought that the existence and the practice of the revolutionary discourse in Europe for more than 200 years might have been able to free us from it—that words are just air, an exterior whispering, a sound of wings which one hears with difficulty in the seriousness of history and the silence of thought?[144]

In addition to challenging themes that are both unwarranted and useless for accurate political thought, archaeology identifies the need and holds out the promise of being able to explore the political role exercised by the functioning and institutionalizing of scientific discourse in our century. This exploration, by breaking with a simple model of structure and superstructure, will be adequate to the complexity of that discourse.[145] Archaeology's service to a progressive politics will be to promote an understanding of the "historic conditions and the specified rules of a practice"; other conceptualizations of the political realm offer "only ideal necessities, univocal determinations, or the free play of individual initiatives."[146] It is clear that in 1968 Foucault had no general theory of political power; it is equally clear that archaeology is not without implications for a politics that wishes to engage in history in a progressive manner. The issue of political power and its analysis will continue to grow in importance for him in the years ahead.

CONCLUSION

By means of the cathartic thinking operative in *LMC*, Foucault was able to understand the foundations for his interrogation both of man and of language. His performance of an archaeology of the human sciences has cleared a space for a type of thinking that, he hopes, holds the promise of adequacy to our twentieth-century reality as well as of potential political significance for a progressive form of political engagement. The birth of this new space for thought makes its appearance only after a double death, that of God and of his executioner, man, both constituting as they do limits upon the power of thought to think difference, to transgress the order of things. Although he has shown the power of system, his interest remains liberty. It is a liberty that arises only in discourse, and that can be achieved only in relation to the complex systems that control it from the depths. His work is an effort to push the system back, to open rifts where it seems most stable, to prepare for an advent of difference.[147] Beyond that horizon in which history is harmony and continuity, there is already in sight a certain "nondialectical culture" and nondialectical thinking whose birth cries we can at times hear, most especially in the accents of Nietzsche.[148] Foucault regards his own archaeology as only an element of this culture and renewal of thinking. After the catharsis of *LMC*, Foucault was prepared for an attempt to define it methodologically.

4

◆

Dissonant Thinking

INTRODUCTION

Foucault's writings from 1969 to 1971 aim at securing a beachhead in the complex and confusing space for thought that has come into sight after the catharsis effected in *LMC*.[1] To a large extent, this securing is methodological, and *L'archéologie du savoir* (hereafter *AS*) begins to fulfill the promise, made in his preceding book, to address explicitly the problems of method raised by archaeological study.[2] It is only a beginning, however, and Foucault's concern in this period is not to provide an instruction manual for the would-be archaeologist, but to consider some of the theoretical problems, and opportunities, that his earlier investigations have raised. The concrete ways in which archaeological method will be implemented in specific domains is a task for future empirical studies.[3] His methodological declaration is an attempt to portray a thinking that has been liberated from the anthropological theme and that defines its analysis neither as an interpretation nor as a formalization of thinking.[4] *AS* articulates a style that will be adequate to a specific archaeological level of investigation and to the procedures for its interrogation. This methodological formulation will be taken up in the last section of this chapter. It comes last because the statement of archaeological method functions for Foucault within a wider context than that provided by its relations to a review of his earlier works and to the anticipated direction for his future labors.

As method, archaeology is itself an event in thought, and one of Foucault's principal interests during these years is to clarify for himself the precise conditions that account for its emergence. His examination of the human sciences was cathartic, and revealed those foundations for thought that had to be purged. In contrast, his considerations during this period of his earlier works, of the persons from whom he learned, and of the type of historical analyses to which he is indebted, anchor the positive catalysts for his own unique perspective. These considerations will be treated in the second section.

The acknowledgement of debts and the expression of gratitude are often the fruits of an awareness that one is on a correct path that is recognized as one's own. This is certainly the case for the Foucault of these years. Not since his earliest anthropological writings had he been so certain of his project and its importance, not only in terms of its relation to the history of ideas but, what is of more consequence, to thought itself. Archaeology is the promise of a thought adequate to a culture that is awakening from belief in its dialectical intelligibility. Foucault tells us that he was first ripped from that dialectical universe in which he had been living by the experience of music, by listening to those contemporary French representatives of serial and twelve-tone music, Barraqué and Boulez.[5] It is a revealing remark, enabling us to glimpse the fundamental sense of the journey on which his thought has embarked. Arnold Schönberg, the father of the twelve-tone scale, which had educated our modern ear to discord and the absence of a tonal center, defined its essential character as the "emancipation of dissonance."[6] It is a description that captures both Foucault's experience of being lifted from the harmonies of a dialectical universe and the aim of his archaeology. In place of the smooth concord that is imposed on a multiplicity of separate occurrences by the desire for sameness, he wishes to place before the mind a constantly sounding dissonance. His earlier work has cleared the way for this dissonant thinking, which will become the inspiration of the "philosophy of event" emerging in this period as the horizon for archaeology.[7]

1. THE GOAL OF ARCHAEOLOGICAL THINKING

Archaeological thinking aims to make it possible to think difference; it wishes to establish that "we are difference, that our reason is the difference of discourses, our history the difference of times, our selves the difference of masks."[8] The contemporary crisis for thought is that its accepted practice enables us to "avoid the difference of our present."[9] Human reality has been reduced to the modern figure of man, historical reflection has been locked into a chain of evolutionary perspectives, thought has been imprisoned in a search for sameness. Foucault's work has long been struggling, implicitly or explicitly, for an understanding of those factors that account for the difference between actuality and possibility. Since *HF*, he has been aware of the reduction of human reality that comes with the expulsion of difference, an expulsion that is bound up with anthropological thought and humanistic ideology.

While the goal of thinking difference is not surprising, a certain change in the tone of his formulation of program can at times be detected during this period. Since the collapse of his own anthropological project, Foucault had always been rigorously modest in discussing his program.[10] While this self-effacement was sincere, it nevertheless served to obscure his fundamental grappling with the problem of thought itself. In relation to this problem, his various investigations were mere diggings in the major excavation toward which he has been working. His philosophical ambition surfaced more clearly in this period than it ever did before or after. While his earlier work may be only a "slight wedge" slipped into the history of ideas, it is nevertheless acknowledged as a device "permitting the introduction into the very roots of thought, of notions of *chance, discontinuity*, and *materiality*."[11] This ambitious formulation reflects his realization that his probings in the domain of the history of ideas have placed him at the core of the crisis in thought itself. The suppression of difference is bound up with a banishment of the chance, the discontinuous, and the material, a banishment to which our contemporary discourse frequently testifies.

A) THE CONSTRAINTS ON THOUGHT

Since his studies of literature, Foucault has understood that the fate of thought is tied to the status of language; it was an appreciation that increased with his growing political concern. Discourses are not merely winds that pass amid the serious activity of history.[12] To speak is to act, and only if the constraints under which such action operates as a practice are recognized will it be possible to free thinking from an avoidance of difference. This entails confronting our culture's logophobia, its fear of language.

This fear is manifested, first of all, in the fact that discourse operates for us only within a social system that defines the conditions under which it may be employed. Far from appearing within a free field, discourse functions ceremoniously within our society, with specific privileges over it awarded to those who meet certain qualifications, whether of class, education level, or status within a specific group.[13] Internal constraints also exert control over discourse. There is the control exercised by the organization of discourse into disciplines that strictly regulate the construction of new statements. There is the prominence that the principle of commentary enjoys in our culture. The chance element in linguistic events is averted by wedding the production of discourse to the continuous repetition of what has been said in other texts, most especially those heralded as classics. In alliance with this search for sameness is the manner in which the author functions as a device for mastering the multiplicity of linguistic events. Appearing within a specific social system of limitation and law, the author principle promotes the submission of linguistic statements to individuals as legislators of their significance and coherence.[14] Yet another form of constraint is exercised by rules of exclusion and division, not only in the separation between the prohibited and the permitted or between the rational and the mad, but also, which is more important, between the true and the false. Discourses justify themselves in terms of their rapport with "true" discourses, while at the same time they conceal their relations to desire and power.[15]

Twin of that logophobia, which is the historical source of the fundamental division between the true and the false, is the specific form of the will to knowledge that is Plato's legacy to western thought.[16] We are heirs to an ideophilia, a love of an ideal intelligibility that can be separated from appearance, of a sameness that seeks to institute an identity amid multiplicity. Within this philosophical stream, three themes emerge that cooperate with logophobia in denying the specific reality of discourse. The theme of a founding subject reduces language and meaning to mere instruments of a subjectivity that animates the presumed emptiness of words within its objectives. Although seemingly opposed, the theme of originating experience plays an analogous role: the world speaks meanings that our language merely reflects. Finally, the theme of universal mediation offers an omnipresent functioning of meaning, a presumption that makes discourse "no longer much more than the shimmering of a truth about to be born in its own eyes."[17] These constraints and this philosophical heritage suppress the discontinuities, hazardousness, and material reality of discourse, and in doing so, serve as a catalyst for an inquiry such as the history of ideas.

B) THE FREEING OF THOUGHT

In attempting to formulate a perspective that allows for the thinking of difference, Foucault hits upon a striking image, one that captures his project's anti-Platonic bias. Thought must be regarded as a theatrical performance. Inquiry is exposed to a reality that is not solid and natural but empty and dark. The stage of being is not univocal; arising within it are actions that are multiple, "simultaneous, broken into different scenes."[18] Being must be conceived of as the "recurrence of difference," and the duty of thought is to describe and account for the play of these differences.[19] Its goal is to think difference, which is accomplished when it does justice to the event (*l'événement*), when it grasps its distinctive level, frees it from a phenomenological subjugation to a sovereign self, and when it resists the temptation of a philosophy of history to subordinate it to a solidly centered pattern of time.[20] That which obscures the event "obstructs the successful formulation of thought," and so archaeology's destiny is tied to the liberation of the precarious being called event.[21]

If the theater is the image Foucault employs for thought in this period, it is historical study that is privileged in the production of the events that thought needs to consider. Historical study, however, must be guided by a Nietzschean genealogical interest, which Foucault understands not as a search for origins but as an assault upon a traditional history rooted in Platonic viewpoints.[22] Traditional history has teleological ambitions. Its quest for purposes, patterns, and values dissolves the singular event into an ideal continuity. Its field of investigation is constituted by periods that are regarded as noble, ideas that are considered major, and personages who are accorded world-historical status. For Foucault, as for Nietzsche, such history avoids precisely what needs to be captured. Genealogy responds to this need by situating our existence within a host of entangled events, foreign to any particular orientation or end. Inimical to the Platonic passion for identity and memory of ideal being, the genealogical interest commits itself to the historical description of areas considered to be without history: sentiments, love, the body, conscience. Such an interest is for the sake of an "effective history" (*histoire effective*): "History becomes 'effective' to the degree that it introduces discontinuity into our very being—as it divides our emotions, dramatizes our instincts, multiplies our body and sets it against itself."[23] The multiplicities and differences thrown up by history triumph. This anti-Platonic purpose served by the genealogical interest shows itself most clearly in its determination to submit the traditional historian's aim, the search for objective truth, to an interrogation of its place in history: what is the specific configuration of social and intellectual forces within which emerges the will-to-knowledge that sustains such objective inquiry?

Recourse to an historical-genealogical reflection is for the purpose of theatrical thinking. In staging multiple events in their singularities, the desire of such history is to "isolate the different scenes where they engaged in different roles."[24] Nietzsche's genealogical passion is thus intrinsic to the archaeological project, with its goal of thinking difference and confronting the event. While their relationship stands in need of further clarification, Foucault will deny that archaeology is reducible to genealogy. It could not be otherwise. Thinking itself is an event, and Nietzsche's genealogical event occurs in a perspective different from that of Foucault's archaeology event. Unlike those traditional historians who take "unusual pains to erase the elements in their work which reveal their grounding in a particular time and place," both Nietzsche and Foucault recognize that their thinking is essentially perspectival.[25] In addition to complementing the catharsis effected in *LMC*, Foucault's *AS* seeks to clarify the perspective within which his archaeology is being articulated. "Thought must consider the process that forms it and form itself from these considerations."[26]

2. The Situation of Archaeology as an Event

Few thinkers have been as self-conscious as Foucault in understanding their thought as an event tied to a particular time and place, or as determined to grasp its specific conditions of possibility. As we have pointed out in chapter 2, Foucault stresses how all thought is necessarily tied to history, and understands how his own analyses of the histories of madness and clinical medicine were rooted in changes so fundamental and extensive that they can only be grasped in a fragmentary manner. While the investigation of *LMC* constituted an extraordinary advance in comprehending the epistemic foundations of the questions dominating modern intellectual history, Foucault persists in his intense desire to locate his own thought as an event.

Foucault's own sounding of the terrain on which his thought stands is not for him a matter of establishing a hierarchy of influence among the thinkers he had read or known. The notion of influence is far "too magical," and his suspicions of the author function far too great for this task to have offered much of an attraction.[27] The lure of linking him with a particular thinker or a certain school has proved too tempting for many of his commentators to resist.[28] Foucault cannot be identified with a specific school, because he realizes what it means to be a man of the library. It is a nonspecialized library, or rather, a library of many specialties, containing, as it does, erudition in psychology, literature, philosophy, and the histories of science and society. One cannot rank its volumes and shelves on a scale of importance, for "everything must be read, must be studied" in the interest of ordering the materials of knowledge in a manner that is indifferent to its presentation as "written by" or as "part of the work of" such and such an author or tradition.[29] Any critical endeavor to locate Foucault in terms of specific authors and traditions would entail a commitment to be a fellow researcher in his own "quasi-infinite" investigation of the being of our modernity.[30]

With the exception of the few major thinkers who are identified in Foucault's writing, the desire to place him in a lineage of writers and traditions that have influenced him would face an inescapably dizzying number of options. Should his books be arranged in terms of the different periods he has studied, with a special shelf dedicated, as one commentator has urged, to the Renaissance because Foucault's thinking is essentially nostalgic for that period?[31] The suggestion is no more convincing than are attempts to order his sources into categories reflecting different disciplines or into such incorrect divisions as pre- and post-structuralist phases. The best that could be done to organize the numerous events of thought contained in Foucault's library would be to classify them into certain broad areas that reflected something of the specificity of his own thinking. Thus, one might imagine dividing his library into works of literature and works in the positive sciences in order to echo the two conflicting passions that he admits had marked his early intellectual interest.[32] Another possibility would be to separate those volumes that carry special weight for Foucault in pointing to a nondialectical culture: Nietzsche, Heidegger, Russell, and Wittgenstein.[33] Yet another possibility suggests itself: a more precise and extensive division of materials might be achieved by arranging them according to their relation to one of the two major directions along which contemporary thought moves. Thus, in terms of Foucault's understanding of interpretation, we know that Husserl, Heidegger, Merleau-Ponty, and Sartre made the greatest contribution; formalism was learned through the writings of Lévi-Strauss, Lacan, Russell, and Freud.[34]

Each of these orderings, among others, would entail an element of arbitrariness, and involve massive omissions. Hence the wisest course to follow in understanding the foundation for Foucault's own thought as a specific event is to recognize those forces that he has identified as decisive for "what made it possible to say what I did."[35] There are three: specific thinkers, an epistemological mutation in the work of historians, and his earlier researches.

A) THE DEBT TO SPECIFIC THINKERS

The solemnity of Foucault's inaugural lecture at the Collège de France provided him with the opportunity to acknowledge the three contemporary thinkers to whom he felt he owed the greatest debt, and to indicate the contributions each made to his own thought.

i) Georges Dumézil In expressing his respect for Georges Dumézil, Foucault mentions three elements that he derived from the French historians of religion. Dumézil's own researches had pointed to the need for an analysis of discourse distinct from traditional methods of exegesis as well as from those of linguistic formalism. In addition, he made comparison central in treating the functional relations of different discourses. Finally, he pressed on Foucault the desirability of describing the transformations of discourse in terms of their relations to institutions.[36]

In following these approaches, Foucault—and this is the force of Dumézil's contribution—was provided with a concept of structure that was fundamentally different from the general linguistic model utilized by Lévi-Strauss, and one more compatible with his own pursuit of existential necessity. Dumézil was concerned neither with the application of a general model nor with the hypothesis of a common mental structure to account for phenomena. He dedicated his efforts to uncovering common structural principles among texts that were viewed strictly in their specific historical, institutional, and ideological functioning.[37]

ii) Georges Canguilhem The contribution of Canguilhem's work to Foucault's project is taken as crucial both as to what is warned against and the line of investigation it encouraged. He showed that the history of science could avoid the alternative of being either a chronicle of discoveries or an account of those ideas and opinions pertinent to science's genius or effects. Canguilhem set forth for Foucault an historical questioning that approached science as a coherent ensemble from which its theoretical models and conceptual tools could be disengaged.[38]

In this recognition of Canguilhem, Foucault names a primary source for two of his most characteristic ideas. The first is the suspicion, which Canguilhem himself had derived from Bachelard, of science's account of itself as a story of linear progression, and thus the concomitant disposition to deal with the discontinuities evident in the history of science. The historical analysis of a concept must be conducted in relation to its various rules of usage and to the many theoretical contexts in which it functioned.[39] The second is the inclination to explore history not in quest of a total dialectical comprehension but in terms of specific problematics within which there was determined for a specific field of study both the object of its reflection and the manner in which that reflection would be carried out. "We must think problematically rather than question and answer dialectically."[40]

iii) Jean Hyppolite Pride of place in Foucault's statement of debt is reserved for Jean Hyppolite. It was under his direction that Foucault did his thesis study on Kant. In that study, he first glimpsed man as an empirical-transcendental doublet, and thus perceived the dilemma of modern anthropological thought. Foucault's testimony to the impact of Hyppolite, a former teacher and his predecessor at the Collège de France, is not a mere academic formality, although at first glance its expression of indebtedness is puzzling. Hyppolite was the one Frenchman most responsible for bringing Hegel into the center of French intellectual life, and it is precisely this contribution for which Foucault praises him.[41] But such an acknowledgement is puzzling in that Foucault's project is tied to a rejection of the Hegelian desire for totalization and the passion for dialectics. The reduction of difference to nonbeing that is the fruit of dialectical reasoning is precisely the adversary against which Foucault's philosophy of event is struggling.[42] Hyppolite remained a true disciple of Hegel, connecting philosophy to the effort of totalization. But despite this never-wavering Hegelian strain, other dimensions in his teaching of Hegel were, in the end, far more powerful for Foucault.[43]

First of all, Hyppolite forced his students to confront and understand Hegel. Foucault came to realize that without such understanding, it would be impossible to escape Hegel. As with other French thinkers, he experienced the need to "determine the extent to which our anti-Hegelianism is possibly one of his tricks directed against us, at the end of which he stands, motionless, waiting for us."[44] More important, however, in the development of Foucault's specific philosophical style was the fact that the Hegel Hyppolite presented was always a Hegel under interrogation by his philosophical successors. Under this interrogation, Hegel underwent a transformation. A

Hegel questioned by Husserl made philosophy appear no longer as a search for a totality to be found in the movement of a concept but as an "endless task, against the background of an infinite horizon."[45] Battered by Kierkegaard, Hegelian thought was forced into constant connection with the singularity of experience and philosophical generalization linked to continuing contact with nonphilosophical domains. This ceaseless relating of the philosophical and the nonphilosophical was intensified by Fichtean, Marxian, and Bergsonian interrogations that were the hallmarks of Hyppolite's appropriation of Hegel and of Foucault's assimilation of Hyppolite's teaching.

Foucault emphasized in a memorial lecture for Hyppolite that the latter had not identified himself as an historian of philosophy but rather as an historian of philosophical thought.[46] In seeking philosophical thought in the nonphilosophical, Hyppolite attempted to open up a new domain for research: the engagement with a realm underlying both our everyday experience and the activity of the positive sciences.[47] This proved decisive for Foucault's understanding of his own philosophical activity. He speaks of that enterprise not as a study of thought in general, but rather of that which contains thought in a culture.[48] In this perspective, there is a sense in which philosophy, as a specific form of thought rooted in Plato, no longer exists for Foucault. He does not mean that it has disappeared, but rather that it has been disseminated among a wide variety of diverse activities, embracing not only the critical reflection of the scholar but also the work of the revolutionary and the man of politics.[49]

Hegel's integration of history into philosophy is transformed by Hyppolite into a dependence on history, and, through Foucault's reworking of the theme of philosophy's nature, philosophy is wrested from absolutes and transfigured into theater.[50] Through this transformation, philosophy becomes part of the great task of contemporary thought, but it also finds its character in jeopardy. With exposure to the multiplicity of thought contained in the events of culture, there is no guarantee that philosophy will emerge with the commanding presence it once enjoyed in the enterprise of thought. "For Hyppolite, the relationship with Hegel was the scene of an experiment, of a confrontation in which it was never certain that philosophy would come out on top. He never saw the Hegelian system as a reassuring universe; he saw in it the field in which philosophy took the ultimate risk."[51]

Turning now from those thinkers who had a personal impact on Foucault, the one other who must be singled out can scarcely be said to have turned his philosophical thinking away from risk.

iv) Friedrich Nietzsche Although Foucault came to regret the "absolutely privileged, meta-historical" place that Nietzsche seemed to occupy in *LMC*, there is no doubt that more than any other philosopher, it is Nietzsche who haunts Foucault's thought.[52] I have already indicated that the utilization of history by archaeology is explicitly related to a Nietzschean genealogy. Nietzsche, however, did not simply provide a tool for future archaeological thought; he helped create the possibility for it. Foucault mentions three elements of this contribution. First, Nietzsche the philologist cleared an intellectual space for the "enigmatic multiplicity" of language to appear by linking philosophical thought to a "radical reflection upon language."[53] Second, Nietzsche's understanding of the necessary bond between the idea of God and the idea of man led him to appreciate the need to subvert anthropology, a destruction that was prefigured in the image of the superman: the "promise of the superman signifies first and foremost the imminence of the death of man."[54] Finally, Nietzsche's genealogical critique and decentering of the historical development of reason joined forces with these other insights in unfolding a space for a nondialectical thinking to occur. Nietzsche "burned for us, even before we were born, the intermingled promises of the dialectic and anthropology."[55] In attributing this incendiary role to Nietzsche, Foucault elevates him to a unique status. In questioning both anthropology and dialectics, Nietzsche displaces the only other thinkers who might have come to dominate Foucault's thought: an anthropological thinking under the sign of Kant or a historical thinking under that of Hegel.

Perhaps in this displacement and in the special position Nietzsche assumes for Foucault through it, we may still catch sight of the powerful presence and complex impact of Hyppolite. In Foucault's 1961 thesis written under his direction, the Kantian question of what is man finds itself "ended in the response which impugns and disarms it: the superman."[56] As Hyppolite pointed out nine years earlier, this Nietzschean critique of humanism was already anticipated by Hegel.[57] The probing of philosophical thought in culture's diverse activities, the Nietzschean style of thinking that Foucault so esteems, is precisely the risk that Hyppolite saw Hegel taking for philosophy, and upon which he placed such value.[58] For Hyppolite, Hegel's superiority over Kant consisted precisely in the fact that whereas Kant had confined himself to the problem of knowledge in his attempt to discover its conditions, Hegel sought such conditions in the historical situation of man seeking understanding. Hegel's question was "how to *ground* human history and a possible truth, or *reason*, within the development of history."[59] This Hegelian theme of grounding history occasionally surfaces in *HF* and *NC*. In the revision of the latter work that came after the catharsis of *LMC*, the theme is deliberately excised.[60] While it would be reasonable to surmise that Foucault's regard for the historical might have made him receptive to the Hegel whom Hyppolite had forced him to confront, it is Foucault himself who testifies to the fact that Nietzsche's status for him is directly related to the appeal that Hegelian thought had once exercised. "I will only say that I would have remained ideologically historicist and Hegelian, if I had not read Nietzsche."[61] This reading of Nietzsche took place in the early 1950s, and *HF* is already an investigation performed under the influence of Nietzsche.[62] It is clear that Nietzsche's significance for Foucault is in part related to his preservation of strengths exhibited by Hyppolite's Hegel, and the avoidance of a teleological view of historical development. In the light of this relationship, we can perhaps understand why Foucault chose to publish his essay on Nietzsche in the particular volume it appeared: *Hommage à Jean Hyppolite*.

B) EPISTEMOLOGICAL MUTATION

It would be a mistake to overemphasize the responsibility Foucault attributes to these individuals. Far more important in making possible the archaeological mode of thinking is an "epistemological mutation"; this *mutation épistemologique* sabotages modern thought's fidelity to the central role of the subject and its attachment to a humanistic view of history.[63] Foucault specifies two aspects of this mutation. The first is a century-long operation of decentering the sovereignty of the subject. It is represented in Marx's analysis of the relations of production and in the function he gives to economic determination and class struggle.[64] Nietzschean genealogy cooperates in this decentering by its rejection of history as a search for origins.[65] Furthermore, with the development of the human sciences comes the inevitable displacement of the subject, because, according to psychoanalysis, linguistics, and ethnology, the subject is inadequate to account for the unconscious, for the systematic forms of language and the hidden rules that guide action.[66]

The second aspect of this epistemological mutation lies in the actual work of current historical research. Here, however, we seem to be faced with a conflict between two very different directions in that research. On the one hand, we have a prominence given to the existence of discontinuities, which is reflected in the analyses of Bachelard, Canguilhem, and Althusser, among others. Their studies force one to establish limits instead of tracing a line of continuous development, and to define the specificity of the many different, irreducible transformations involved in historical change.[67] While Foucault had obviously been marked by this stream of thought, he had been no less affected by that larger group of historians who dedicated their efforts not to discontinuities but to a presentation of that "submerged" history of stable, long-term structures of which Braudel's account of the Mediterranean world serves as a model.[68] Within the long-term perspective, change is almost imperceptible. Beneath what seem to be significant alterations, we find the history of great continuities of geography, sea routes, and agriculture. *AS* was published forty years after Lucien Febvre and Marc Bloch founded

Annales d'histoire économique et sociale, which initiated this long-range perspective on historical development. Foucault paid tribute to many of the most prominent historians associated with this approach as creators of a "new adventure" for historical thought.[69] The *Annales* movement had been so successful that most other styles of historical research declined in France, and a lack of real debate pervaded that country's discussions on historiography.[70]

Foucault brought a new vigor to the debate. He maintained that the opposition between historians concerned with stable structures and historians of literature and science, who emphasize the discontinuous, was but a "surface effect" of a more fundamental accord.[71] Both movements placed the document at the center of their questioning. Instead of the elision of the document that traditional history accomplishes by treating it as a trace, as something to be interpreted to get at the real object of history, current historians, whether occupied with discontinuities or with structures, transform documents into monuments. These historians no longer regard documents as inert materials but as a historical reality that must be ordered into series so that their unities and relations may be grasped.[72] Foucault saw several major consequences resulting from the monumentality of the document. There is the realization that the order or series within which historical phenomena are to be examined must be constituted, while traditional history involved itself with defining events that were regarded as already having their place within an accepted series. In establishing the different levels at which series may be organized as well as the limits and fluctuations of long-term trends, the structural historian is also concerned with discontinuities, not regarded as obstacles to accurate history but rather as necessary elements of that history, if the continuities themselves are to be grasped and specified. In addition, the need to be specific in constituting series and in relating the different orderings thus constituted place both groups in opposition to the project of a total history seeking the overall unity of a civilization or period. Such a philosophical total history rests on presuppositions—a homogeneity of relations between historical phenomena and the assumption of a single principle of cohesion common to an entire epoch—that the acceptance of different modes of ordering events rejects. Finally, the methodological problems imposed by the monumentality of the document places both groups in the same camp against any philosophy that aspired to the disclosure of a teleology in historical development.[73]

By asserting this fundamental accord between these two spheres of historical work, Foucault annexed the great analyses of the *Annales* school to his own archaeological enterprise of focusing thought upon the event and upon difference. It is an extraordinary feat in that this school often thought of its work as standing in opposition to a history of the short term, to a history of the event that was regarded as "capricious and deceptive," "ephemeral," the "headlines of the past."[74] Foucault undermined this opposition by showing that in its very concern with such phenomena as parish registers and price lists, the individuality of an event is highlighted. Historians concerned with structure enlarge the field of events by their analyses of new layers of documentation, evidence that was once thought insignificant, and by their definition of new orders within which this documentary evidence may be placed. They turn thought into event.[75] Their contribution is no longer a search of the same, but rather a new way of apprehending the event—the exception that is thrown into prominence by the discovery of structures—and an intensified interest in difference. Foucault thus accounts for the inclination of this school to study such areas as sorcery, popular literature, and feasts, the world of the peasant.[76] In effecting this displacement, Foucault has restored the original hopes of Bloch himself, who envisioned the new objects and methods he proposed for history leading to an enhanced sense of difference.[77] Through his point of view on the actual achievement of the *Annales* school, Foucault enlisted this century's most creative historical work in the campaign against those approaches that see in history but a "place of rest, certainly, reconciliation, a place of tranquillized sleep."[78]

C) EARLIER RESEARCHES

As a specific project for thought, archaeology finds its most concrete foundation neither in certain teachers nor in general epistemological mutation, but rather in the various studies that Foucault had already published. "The ground on which it rests is the one that it has itself discovered."[79] As a distinct mode of thought, archaeology is definable as a method of analysis freed from the anthropological theme. Thus, its "historical possibility" was dependent upon the discovery in his works of the constraints upon thought forged by humanism and anthropology.[80] In his scattered remarks regarding the bearing of the earlier work on the creation of that historical possibility, Foucault restricts himself to *HF, NC,* and *LMC,* while passing over in silence his first two publications, those of his own anthropological period (*IRE, PER*). His attitude toward the three studies upon which he does comment is of a dual nature. While cognizant of the contribution they made to opening up a mode of thinking, he is equally aware of their limitations. They can only be described as a "very imperfect sketch" of a formal archaeology of knowledge because they had not sufficiently broken free from the humanistic network of our contemporary thought.[81] This admission is not at all new, for Foucault had already acknowledged how much his earlier work had been tied to the framework of our epoch's knowledge.[82]

What distinguishes the Foucault of 1969, however, is that he sees far more clearly how that anthropological framework actually functioned in his writing. First of all, even if the cogito had been called into question by his history of madness, an anonymous subjectivity had persisted, a subjectivity that manifested itself in his utilization of such categories as experience, perception, and the gaze (*regard*).[83] Second, he had been confused in formulating the level that his thought was aiming to uncover. If there was a phenomenological tinge to his desire in *HF* to arrive at that "zero point in the course of madness at which madness is an undifferentiated experience," *NC* seemed at times to embrace the alternative of identifying with a study of structures that threatened to submerge archaeology's interest in specificity.[84] In his 1972 revision of *NC*, one of the major items corrected is his earlier recourse to structural terms.[85] Finally, as a result of these confusions, *LMC* may have given the impression that its analyses were aimed at cultural totalities, which was indeed the case, as we have already seen in speaking of the notion of the episteme.[86] A more precise methodological formulation of archaeology was required if the pluralism of systems and discontinuities, which he claimed to be among the major fruits of his research, was to be clearly appreciated.[87]

Although *HF, NC,* and *LMC* can only be regarded as imperfect sketches, the formulations of *AS* do not necessitate any fundamental rejection of these studies. If one of the major successes achieved by contemporary approaches to history was to exhibit the multiplicity of series into which documents and events could be ordered, Foucault's own work had already forced him into the realization of how this responsibility for creating an order could not be denied. In advancing toward the point where the traditional neutralization of discourse as event could be avoided and the options for archaeology's "controlled decisions" about how best to order discourse could appear, Foucault regards his choice of fields of study to have been a fortunate one.[88] Areas such as psychology, medicine, and the various human sciences provided discourses with complex series of relations, and yet, relatively unformalized as they were, their investigation did not become a matter of studying formal models.[89] The privilege given to these areas as archaeological orderings of discourse was, however, strictly provisional. *HF* had shown a double futility. Discourse could not be organized in terms of accepted disciplines, for the rationality of psychology was embedded in a whole set of social and economic relations.[90] In addition, as psychology showed, the specificity and coherence of a discourse could not lie in the analysis of a particular object, for one of the major achievements of Foucault's history of madness was to dissolve madness itself as a permanent and unique phenomenon.[91] If the coherence of a discourse was not located in its relation to such an object, *NC* made it evident that there was no key to be found in understanding the organization in terms of a certain procedure of descriptive analysis shared by a specific professional group in a society. Clinical medicine's corpus of knowledge was no less involved with institutional needs, ethical choices, and general philosophical hypotheses than was the study of madness.[92] Finally, *LMC* had indicated the flaw of those accepted organizations of discourse that rested upon the hypotheses of a permanence of concepts or of an identity and persistence of themes.[93]

The loss of madness as an object, of clinical medicine as a science of observation, and of the human sciences as progressive insight into the human phenomena were accomplishments that, in undermining standard organizations of discourse, cleared the way for discourse to appear in new relations. Thus, a more precise formulation was possible for the level of discursive analysis that archaeology had reached.

3. ARCHAEOLOGY AS METHOD

In seeking to do justice to archaeology as an event, there is a danger of misrepresenting Foucault's attitude at this time. More than at any other period, in his writings from 1969 to 1971 he is preoccupied with the proximate foundations for his thought and with the accomplishments and failures of his earlier researches. However, his wish to grasp archaeology as an event and to become more secure about the place in which it occurs is not rooted in a desire to fortify some already achieved insights, but rather in the new obligation to provide a methodological formulation for his thought. His review of the past is oriented to the future. He is attempting to develop a language for a thinking adequate to the event. Foucault is leaving behind the secure situation of vague philosophical counsel for the much more exposed position of a defined conduct. As a beginning, Foucault worries that the result of his effort, which we here summarize in four distinct steps, may only be the creation of a "bizarre machinery."[94] Such self-doubt is common to beginnings that commence with conversions.

A) ESTABLISHMENT OF A FIELD OF EFFECTIVE SIGNS: THE STATEMENT

Conceived of as a mode of acting, the technical term "statement" (*énoncé*) designates the medium for archaeological thinking, the very air that sustains its vitality. Like air, however, it is overfamiliar, and unlike air, it is not transparent; for both reasons, in order for it to become obvious, to be recognized in itself, a definite conversion (*conversion*) of viewpoint and attitude is required.[95] This conversion holds as central a place for the archaeologist as the reduction does for the phenomenologist; however, it serves an opposite purpose. Where the phenomenological reduction suspends questions of existence as data for consciousness, the archaeological shift in attitude is performed for the very sake of confronting the dimension of existence, of grasping a series of signs, as actually operating and not as mere possibilities. The stating of signs seizes a place that had been unoccupied, and it is toward this action of eruption into discourse that the archaeological attitude aims to develop a receptivity; discourse must be "treated as and when it occurs."[96] Constituting a readiness for this existence quality of discourse, for its dimension as statement, entails both a negative moment of suspension and a positive moment of attentiveness.

First of all, the archaeologist suspends the normal syntheses that are taken for granted in confronting discourse. Foucault's listing of these syntheses is extensive. Discourse must not be accepted against a background of permanence and continuity, which is created by approaching it as if it were an element in a tradition, or as an item in an evolution. We must refrain from categorizing the events of a discourse into genres of literature, philosophy, science, and so forth. Furthermore, just as the author is a function meriting suspicion, the grouping of signs into the unities of a book or a work needs to be challenged. The frontiers of both lack precision as a way of ordering discourse, and their presumed importance rests upon decisions and viewpoints that demand the justification that only a theory can furnish. The suspension of these habitual syntheses need not imply definitive rejections. Yet their self-evidence does function as an obstacle to a fresh encounter with discourse as a field of dispersed events, as raw material for a host of different possible groupings.[97] Once these discursive events have been set free for notice and ordering, a second element of suspension must be applied for the archaeological point of view to take shape. These events possess only a precarious hold upon life, and must be sheltered from those two major modes of modern reflection that threaten to make them parasites. The cluster of hermeneutical questions that rapidly arise to organize discourse must be restrained. We need to attach ourselves to the surface of discourse, not to treat it as a veil for a supposed origin hidden beneath what is manifest. Such attachment bars any concern with who was speaking, with a meaning some consciousness might have wished its spoken or written words to convey, with some unsaid that the imagination glimpses instead of what is in fact there. The alternative impulse to perform a linguistic analysis must also be placed under restraint. No refuge is to be sought in an attempt to determine the rules of a language system, for such rules would authorize an infinite number of linguistic performances rather than the actual ones that confront us.[98]

These moments of suspension are one side of an attentiveness specific to the archaeological attitude. Its curiosity is aimed at the rarity (*rareté*) of what is said, at the fact that within the wealth of rule and vocabulary language provides, relatively few things are actually stated. The archaeological attitude embraces an interest in the exteriority (*extériorité*) of those signs that do come into existence. The life of an event in the space of discourse possesses a relative autonomy in its transformations and relations with other discursive events. As matter for description, it is independent of the intentions and temporality of the consciousness that was the vehicle for its appearance. Such autonomy does not imply, however, an existence apart from the place where or the status from which it is enunciated; on the contrary, it is the idea of consciousness that is responsible for indifference to the historical and social situation of discourse. Finally, archaeology is attentive to the numerous ways in which the accumulation (*cumul*) of discursive events occurs. Why are some and not others preserved by certain institutions and practices? How are they combined together to present a claim to unity? What are the unique ways of accumulation that form different types of system as, for example, in codes of law or canons of religious texts?[99]

These moments of suspension and this attentiveness to rarity, exteriority, and accumulation permit the appearance of a level of interrogation of discourse that is specific to the archaeologist. The level is composed not of discrete atomic units but of specific existential functions exercised by what is said.[100] Foucault holds that there are four criteria that may be utilized for the identification of this enunciative level of discourse, in which signs take on the life of a statement. They are distinguishable but closely related criteria, and are the fruit of his earlier investigations. First is the desired relation between the statement and what is stated in it. Reflecting the approach he learned to adopt in examining assertions about madness, a statement's "referential" (*référentiel*) is not sought in some relation to a permanent object but in the existential rules and conditions that account for the definition and delimitation of the phenomenon described.[101] Second, a statement must always betray the specific place and status from which it is spoken. The medical statement, for example, as statement, is not the vehicle for the communication of medical understanding, but rather a signal as to the existing system of relationships (of knowledge, of institution, of society) in which such a statement is made.[102] Third, for some sentence or proposition to be regarded as a statement, it must be situated in the specific field in which it relates to other formulations and in which it plays a particular role. No statement can be considered neutral, for it is always in relation to a network of coexisting statements in connection to which it takes on a certain force and effectiveness.[103] Finally, a statement is defined by a materiality that is not primarily a question of its character as substantial or of its spatio-temporal location, but rather of its capacity to be repeated. To do justice to this "repeatable materiality," statements are identified as institutional phenomena. By functioning within institutions, formulations take on the efficacy of a statement, whether that efficacy limits what else can be said or permits new forms of discourse.[104]

Foucault defines the statement as a particular modality of existential functioning exercised by signs and specified through the four criteria. The line of questioning arising from these criteria distinguishes the unique quality of the statement and prevents its reduction to the nature of a sentence or a proposition.[105] Avoiding hermeneutical and formalistic approaches, its description will address this level of effective functioning that signs take on as phenomena of social and historical existence. While this perspective avoids conceiving of the statement as an atomic unit, it also opens out into a need to define the wider systems within which such effectiveness takes place. This requires the fashioning of the notion of discursive formation (*formation discursive*).

B) ESTABLISHMENT OF A DISCURSIVE FORMATION

That the statement is distinguishable from other verbal formulations does not imply its isolation: it is always part of a system of statements to which Foucault gives the name "discursive formation." While these formations may be defined as "groups of statements," and discourses as the "group of statements that belong to a single system of formation," they are not unified on the basis of either grammatical similarity or psychologically based connections. They are the product of a single discursive practice (*pratique discursive*), which accounts for their existence as statements and the relationship existing among them as statements.[106] The practice of discourse is a "violence" done to things, not by virtue of men's ideas nor through the grammatical systems of language, but by a set of rules that determine what can be stated at a particular time and how these statements are related to others.[107] Discursive practice must be understood as a "body of anonymous historical rules, always determined in the time and space that have defined a given period, and for a given social, economic, geographical, or linguistic area, the conditions" for the operation of statements.[108] Statements belong to a single discursive formation because they have the same rules of formation (*règles de formation*). One of the critical tasks of *AS* is to bring these rules of formation into prominence as the sphere in which archaeological thinking takes place.

The first set of rules requiring archaeological study are those that account for the formation of the objects with which a discourse is concerned. *HF*, more than any of his other researches, led Foucault to recognize the existence of these rules and appreciate the role they played. A discourse such as the psychopathology utilized in the nineteenth-century asylum involved the unification of very diverse phenomena into categories of mental illness, and forged treatments out of such differing perspectives as medicine and religion. Its understanding demanded an analysis of those rules that enables a coherence to be thought within this diversity. *AS* exposes the goals of such an analysis in more exact terms than had been possible earlier. An analysis of rules of formation will establish the surfaces of emergence for an object such as mental illness, illustrating how the interrelationship of different communities, different types of knowledge, and various social practices cooperated in delineating a particular field. It will also identify what principles were attributed to authority in determining the nature of an object, as well as the relations that existed among such different authorities as those attached to religious, political, and scientific institutions. An understanding of these sets of rules should account for the specific ways in which the objects of a discourse were divided up and classified, for those grids of specification through which certain dimensions of phenomena become discernible.[109]

Reflecting the importance Foucault saw at work in the status accorded to different figures in the birth of clinical medicine (the changing roles played by the academic professor, the hospital doctor, and the government health official), a second series of rules needs to be considered in charting the parameters of a particular discourse. These are the rules for the "formation of subjective positions."[110] What position must a spokesman occupy for a statement to be considered a statement of a particular type? What role does the institutional site of this spokesman play in molding the character of the statement itself? What relations determine the hierarchy of statuses involved in the actual formation of a discourse?[111]

A third class of rules consists of those responsible for the formation of the concepts that operate in a particular discourse. This class was suggested to Foucault by his study of the complex interaction of conflicting concepts in *LMC*. This interaction was irreducible to a simple architecture that would coherently embrace general grammar, natural history, the analysis of wealth, economics, philology, and biology. How are the statements of a particular discourse ordered, and what criteria are developed for establishing types of dependence among them? What rules define statements as conceptually related, and what rules define a fundamentally different conceptual framework? How are statements organized for utilization in varying frames of reference?[112]

These questions dealing with the formation of concepts lead to a fourth demarcation of the rules of discursive practice: those that account for the formation of strategies, the principles circumscribing what theories and themes are possible for a discourse at a particular period. What rules determine that there will be either an incompatibility between theories occupied with the same general field, or merely alternative possibilities? What relations exist between the themes of a specific discursive formation and those governing nondiscursive practices of the same period?[113]

The direction for inquiry that proceeds from these four questionings of the field of dispersed statements, released by the archaeological conversion in attitude, allows the field to be divided by a series of controlled decisions constituting specific, analyzable discourses. A discursive formation emerges as the object of archaeological investigation once the rules of the formation of objects, subjective positions, concepts, and strategies are understood to be of the same type and relation. When a single system of formation is established for a specified group of statements, we have arrived at a discourse's historical a priori (*l'a priori historique*). The four sets of rules that make up this a priori function not as a criterion for the "validity of judgment," but as a "condition of reality for statements."[114] This a priori is itself subject to transformations, with shifts in its various sets of rules, and thus it ought not to be conceived of as a formal structure that in addition has a history.[115] Rather than having histories, these discursive systems are the creatures of history, a situation that archaeological thought makes manifest.

Foucault's major methodological accomplishment in defining the statement, discursive formation, and their establishment as the special domain of archaeological thinking is his precise formulation of the level at which such thinking must operate. The plane of "undifferentiated experience" on which *HF*'s archaeology wished to operate yielded in *NC* a "region," beyond any thematic content, where "'things' and 'words' have not yet been separated." In *LMC*, this became a "middle region" different both from a culture's empirical orderings of knowledge and from the philosophical interpretations of those orderings, a distinction that permitted archaeology to be distinguished from doxology.[116] By means of the rules of discursive practice, he has now defined a "preconceptual level" and a "positive unconsciousness" for our thought that is nevertheless decipherable on the surface of discourse as the rules forming what is said and how it is said.[117] While a doxology of the history of ideas had been opposed to an archaeological study, their different objects may now be described in terms of two different levels for thought: fields of cognition (*connaissance*) and fields of knowledge (*savoir*). While the former is the conscious, accumulated understanding of the world as an object to be understood, *savoir* designates the level of discursive practices, those "conditions that are necessary in a particular period for this or that type of object to be given to *connaissance* and for this or that enunciation to be formulated."[118]

In elaborating and specifying the level of investigation proper to archaeology, Foucault has not wished to narrow the domain with which it is rightfully concerned. The discursive relations that the archaeologist treats are distinguishable from two other types that at first glance might suggest such a narrowing. Discursive relations are neither external nor internal. Rather, in their formation of objects and their ordinance of position, concepts, and strategies, they are at the "limit of discourse."[119] They must be thought of as the meeting point of discourse with the nondiscursive domains of institutions, political events, and economic processes.[120] The discursive practice that he has attempted to define is not put forward to "guarantee the sovereign, sole independence of discourse," for such a result would strike at the heart of the archaeological project, namely, the establishment of the conditions for the reality of statements.[121] The life of discourse is caught up with the nondiscursive in two complementary ways. On the one hand, the nondiscursive cannot be regarded as simply a zone of heterogeneous institutions, practices, and events, a zone more fundamental than and unrelated to the discursive practices that assist and define the connections within that realm.[122] The apprehension of and reflection on the nondiscursive is by way of the discursive. On the other hand, while discursive formations possess a measure of autonomy, they are not historically independent. Although it would be simplistic to treat the nondiscursive as causes of specific discourses, it would be equally fallacious not to see them related to the conditions for the emergence and functioning of these discourses. While the concrete elaboration of these relations is beyond the limits of a general description of method, it is nevertheless clear that archaeological thinking, as Foucault charts its course at his point, is under the imperative to uncover the "particular level in which history can give place to definite types of discourse, which have their own type of historicity, and which are related to a whole set of various historicities."[123]

In bringing to light this *savoir* dimension of thought as accounting for the different enterprises of cognition, and in asserting that this dimension is bound up with social and political practices, Foucault has carved out of the mass of spoken events a precise level for thought's action, the "archive" (*l'archive*). The archive is the "general horizon" within which archaeological work must be performed.[124] It is composed of extensive systems of discursive practices that not only determine the appearance of a particular formation but also differentiate "discourses in their multiple existence" and specify them in "their own duration."[125] Beyond the specific practices and relations available to any particular archaeological investigation, an almost infinitely complex set of relations could still be established. Thus, the archive can be spoken of as the "general system" for the formation and tranformation of statements.[126] As a horizon, however, the archive can never be described exhaustively. Its character emerges only in the fragments disclosed by specific descriptions of different discursive formations and the relationships among them. As an analysis within this horizon of the events of discursive statements and of the historical a prioris responsible for their groupings, archaeology may be defined as the description of "discourses as practices specified in the element of the archive."[127] With this impossibly dense definition, Foucault wishes to indicate two limits. First, the notion of archive entails that the archaeologist always examines a dimension of *savoir* from which he is, at least to some extent, intellectually distant; enjoying such a distance, he may approach the discursive formation of his study as an archivist approaches historical documents. Second, the archaeologist's research takes place in a domain of such complexity that all of his discoveries are tentative, subject to reorderings in the light of new problematics. While Foucault's establishment of a field of statements and of the types of rule that constitute a discursive formation give a general sense of his project, archaeology is itself a practice. It is best characterized by the analytic route it lays down for dealing with the strange objects it has constituted.

C) THE DIRECTIONS FOR INTERROGATION

By the time of *AS*, Foucault had concluded that the concerns of archaeology were radically distinct from the project of a history of ideas with which he had been willing to associate himself earlier.[128] The reasons that led him to this judgment on the necessity of divorcing archaeology from the history of ideas are not difficult to perceive. In attempting to formulate his own method with greater precision, he developed a profound aversion to the anarchy of the latter field: its lack of clear object, its willingness to adopt heterogeneous methods, its general failure to achieve any measure of rigor.[129] In addition, Foucault had come to recognize that his project of thinking the event through a thinking stirred to encounter with chance, materiality, and the discontinuous was in fundamental conflict with any approach oriented to the study of ideas. Archaeology stood opposed to this study's search for origins, to its effort to establish their lines of continuity, to its desire for a totalization of history. As a result, the archaeological program, which Foucault advances in 1969, is held to be an "abandonment of the history of ideas, a systematic rejection of its postulates and procedures, an attempt to practice a quite different history of what men have said."[130] This abandonment and rejection permeate the four directions that he lays out for archaeological thinking, each of which is deliberately enunciated as running at cross-purposes with a form of questioning characteristic of the history of ideas.

i) Regularities One of the devices by which anthropological thinking continues to exert its pressure on contemporary thought is revealed in those attempts to reduce the specific existence of discourse to a movement of subjective life, to read what is said in terms of creative contributions as opposed to standard and everyday functioning.[131] This anthropological shackle is evident in the tendency of the history of ideas to treat all discourse as a domain with only two values. Does the particular object of study represent something new in the field of thought, or does it still function within the old pattern? Is the discourse of so-and-so truly original or simply another formulation of what has been known traditionally? Is it merely ordinary, or does it possess the seeds of deviancy?

Underlying these questions is a view of history and a methodological presupposition. History is seen as a field combining the weight of inertia with moments of enlightenment that break free of everyday banality. Thus we have the images of a Middle Ages stretched between the pillars of classical and Renaissance creation, or of a night of authority dispelled by the light of the Age of Reason. While an approach to history in terms of original-banal dichotomies would seem to imply the concession of a certain importance to specific events, that would be merely a first impression, for in this approach it contained the search for a pattern of continuities. Documents are ransacked to discover anticipations and echoes. In foisting an analysis upon thought according to a pattern of old-new, the history of ideas presupposes that "one can establish a sort of single, great series in which every formulation would assume a date in accordance with homogeneous chronological guidelines."[132] Guided by such an assumption, an absolute privilege is accorded to chronological priority as the measure of the original against the repetitive. This results in the avoidance of what constitutes a resemblance between statements.

After the archaeological conversion, there is neither a banal statement nor a single great series. Each statement effects the violence of a discursive practice. The task is to establish it as part of a particular discursive formation, a task made especially difficult by the fact that two verbal formulations, even though identical, need not be of the same discursive practice. While there is no single great series within which each statement would find a proper place for itself, regularities of statements are produced within specific discursive formations. Such regularities are not set off against irregularities of other statements. Not accepting any difference in nature between creative and imitative statements, archaeological analysis attempts to show an enunciative homogeneity (*homogénéité énonciative*) among statements, which are regarded as unrelated when considered apart from the discursive practice that accounts for them.[133] Once such a common character has been established for a field of statements, a tree of enunciative derivation (*dérivation énonciative*) may be grasped. This tree would exhibit those statements that are more extensive in the actual application of specific rules of formation and those that limit and localize the extension of this formation, for example, specializing in an articulation of its conceptual structure in place of its field of objects. Through these operations, regularities take the position for the archaeologist that originality held for the historian of ideas.

ii) Contradictions The second major imperative under which Foucault places an archaeological thinking is a commitment to the description of contradictions.[134] The commitment runs counter to the guiding heuristic principle followed by historians of ideas, namely, that the discourse to be analyzed is coherent, and that beneath apparent irregularities, there lies a more fundamental, hidden principle of unity. This principle of coherence finds an array of techniques for melting stubborn contradictions: an ideal architecture of system to organize a bewildering host of different researches; an affective rather than a rational movement of meaning; the coherence provided by an historical figure's biography, or the character of a period, or the type of society. This passion for coherence at any cost assumes two different faces, each of which is actually only one side of the same prejudice. Either the contradictions remaining after analysis are minor, certain defects and mistakes, or one contradiction is selected as the fundamental source from which all other contradictions flow.

In rejecting the heuristic principle of coherence, archaeological thinking stands against the recognition of contradiction either as a mere appearance to be overcome or as a single founding principle to be discovered. Contradictions are to be described as events with their own specific reality. They must be grasped in accordance with their differences in type, level, and function. While an embarrassing wealth of contradictions is available for any recital, the archaeologist is not concerned with those that exist within particular assertions of a discourse or those between different discourses. His concern is with those that are intrinsic to the discourse itself, those that, unknown to the discourse's practitioners, betray different ways of forming statements within a single discourse. The diverse elements that make up a discursive practice lead the archaeologist to identify different levels of contradiction. Have the objects of statements that are intrinsically opposed been formed by different rules? Is there a divergence in the roles allotted to the subjective positions? Is there incompatibility of concept formation? What theoretical exclusions are entailed in the specific discursive formation? These types and levels of contradiction function differently. While some represent additional development within a formation, others involve a reorganization of the discourse itself. Still others function to limit the discourse's field of application. Although discursive formations may be considered groups of statements, archaeology's commitment to the accurate description of contradictions prevents a view of discourse as a simple text, a creation of some mind gifted with genius, or of some period or temper of the times. Rather, discourse is a "space of multiple dissensions," alive with the play of oppositions.[135] Turning away from the idea of inhabiting a terrain populated with creations, each in search of its Book of Genesis, archaeological thinking chooses to live in the space of events and their multiple contradictions.

iii) Comparisons Like all forms of thinking, archaeology involves comparative operations.[136] The point of this comparing is, however, quite dissimilar from that in the history of ideas. The latter employs comparison, whether it be of ideas, implicit postulates, principles, or models, in order to highlight a certain unity of culture, mentality, or period. Archaeology's comparisons serve an opposite purpose: not to unite but to divide up the diversity of separate formations into different figures. It is always a limited, regional study attending to a certain number of specific discursive formations. Foucault regards as irrelevant those criticisms that assert that his studies omit significant discourses from the periods in question.[137] Those omissions are intrinsic to the archaeological effort to individualize discursive formations. Archaeology confines its analysis to specific interdiscursive relations and to the similarities and differences that appear within their rules of formation. Such a comparative undertaking entails a number of distinct operations.

First, it identifies isomorphisms between elements in different discursive formations that may proceed from similar discursive rules. Second, it shows how these rules share or do not share the same model according to which they find application. Third, it illustrates how different concepts may occupy similar positions despite the fact that they are formulated in discourses with heterogeneous histories. This would be the uncovering of archaeological isotopia. Fourth, it indicates archaeological shifts in notions, how a single notion may function in different discourses to describe radically distinct elements. Finally, comparison is employed to establish correlations, relations of subordination or complementarity, both between and within discursive formations.

As in the analysis of discursive formations, comparative study always takes the relations between discursive formations and nondiscursive practices as its field for treatment. Such a choice is interested neither in symbolic analysis, examining the discursive and the nondiscursive as mirroring a similar meaning, nor in casual analysis, the presentation of the discursive as determined by the social, political, or economic. In seeking to portray the specific forms of emergence and articulation of a practice as discursive in its relation to nondiscursive events, archaeology is concerned with neither contexts of motivation nor shared common meanings.

iv) Transformations The fourth imperative of archaeological interrogation is the exposition of the transformations that occur in one or several discursive practices.[138] Foucault's characterization of this dimension of archaeology is intended both to juxtapose the accounting for transformations with the theme of change utilized by historians of ideas, and to reply to those critics who had accused him in his earlier work of freezing history into static, synchronic levels.[139] By refusing to reduce differences, archaeology nurtures an instinctive hostility to the tendency in the history of ideas that eliminates difference by placing events within the perspective of a complete continuity leading to the achievement of an ideal goal. Archaeology endeavors to give content to the empty notion of change by inspecting different types of transformation. What exactly were the transformations that took place in the sphere of interdiscursive relations as well as the intradiscursive relations and rules of a practice? In this precise defining of transformations, archaeology parts company with those synchronic histories that discern some common structure in a part of history and an absolute rupture between such historical periods.

While the archaeologist does not accept chronological succession as the way to view historical transformations, the decision to subordinate such succession does not represent an indifference to historical temporality. It is taken in order to reach the temporality of the discursive formation itself. Such temporalities are multiple, and their identities are dependent upon the level of event under investigation. One temporality is unique to the actual appearance of statements and to the action of discursive rules. Another temporality may be traced in the derivations of certain rules in a specific formation from others of the same formation. An additional temporality appears in the replacement of one discursive practice by another. Foucault separates himself from the perspective of chronological development adopted in the history of ideas because he rejects two models for conceiving of succession: the model of a stream of consciousness in which the present is disregarded in the flood of past and future impressions, and the linear model of speech according to which events follow one another without coinciding or superimposing themselves upon one another. Discourse for the archaeologist can be conceptualized neither as a language nor as the product of a speaking subject. In describing transformations, archaeological research attempts to be faithful to the uniqueness of a discursive practice that has its own forms of succession and sequence, its own temporality.

While more devoted to discontinuities and ruptures than is the history of ideas, archaeology wants to avoid the danger of falling into the trap of a *Weltanschauung* approach, with its inclination to speak of single ruptures traversing an entire culture or age. "The idea of a single break suddenly, at a given moment, dividing all discursive formations, interrupting them in a single moment and reconstituting them in accordance with the same rules— such an idea cannot be sustained."[140] Archaeology is concerned not only with the task of dispersing discontinuities among the different levels and functions in which they occur, but also with the effort to acknowledge those very continuities that a knowledge of discontinuity brings to light. Ruptures are always individualized, and are discernible only in terms of transformations that deal with the specific rules of a particular practice.[141]

To his definition of the statement and his establishment of discursive practice as an object, Foucault has now added general directions for archaeological thinking to pursue. Together, these three areas form a project that is radically distinct from that of a history of ideas, and is largely defined in terms of an opposition to it. There remains one further aspect to this general definition of archaeological method that Foucault presents at this time: the areas to which it may be applied.

D) THE FIELDS OF APPLICATION

Pluralism has been one of the most characteristic traits of Foucault's thinking from its beginnings. He has delighted in crossing frontiers that seemed relatively well defined. His work in psychology entailed no renunciation of historical or literary studies; his research in medicine brought no abandonment of economic or social reflections. Despite this long-standing catholicity of interest, the actual domains he has examined with care— psychology, medicine, and the areas treated in *LMC*—suggest that archaeology has a close connection to fields that are proto- or quasi-scientific. In formulating archaeology as a method, Foucault felt the need to consider whether it was in fact restricted to those areas within which his analysis had already operated.[142]

One of the major methodological clarifications of *AS* concerns the nature of the episteme. Earlier the notion of the episteme found itself in an ambiguous position. On the one hand, it served as a specific configuration of knowledge, the system of relations that could be articulated, as existing, for example, among the discourses of general grammar, natural history, and the analysis of wealth in the classical age. On the other hand, the episteme also seemed to designate the more general horizon for archaeology itself, as, for example, when he refers to the episteme of western culture or when he states that there is only one episteme that determines the conditions of possibility for knowledge (*savoir*) at a particular time.[143] In *AS*, however, defining archaeology in terms of an archive, which serves as a general horizon, enables the specific identity of the episteme to be established.[144]

To grasp his clarification of the episteme, one must recognize that several distinct emergences of a discursive formation can be delineated.[145] One of these emergences designates the point at which a discursive practice becomes positively distinct in its individuality and autonomy, the moment at which a group of statements forms a single system. This point is what Foucault calls a discourse's threshold of positivity (*seuil de positivité*). There is also a threshold of epistemologization possible for such a formation (*seuil d'epis-témologisation*). Within a specific practice, a subgroup of statements is given the responsibility for validating principles of coherence or is allotted the privilege of serving as the dominant model according to which all the statements of a practice ought to be formed. A threshold of scientificity (*seuil de scientificité*) marks the stage at which a discourse not only obeys its archaeological rules of formation but also explicitly defines formal criteria for the construction of propositions. Finally, a threshold of formalization (*seuil de la formalisation*) is achieved when a discourse can be ordered into a formal system of axioms. In taking note of these various thresholds, it is important to realize that from the archaeological point of view, they do not constitute final and exclusive divisions. Furthermore, they cannot be understood in terms of a chronological succession that would map some orthogenesis of reason. The level of *savoir* does not disappear when a threshold is crossed, and the emergence of a discursive practice that is historically simultaneous with its form as a science is certainly possible.[146]

Despite the encouragement that this schema of thresholds might give to a chronological point of view, Foucault risks this danger for the merit it possesses in distinguishing archaeology from other investigations. While the history of mathematics would be the exemplar for a study of the level of formalization, there is also an epistemological history of the sciences, of which Bachelard and Canguilhem have provided models, that studies the refining of concepts that is contained in the constitution of a domain regarded as scientific. In contrast to these two perspectives, archaeological analysis is concerned with that moment when discursive practices define their epistemological figures in terms of the possibility of their taking on scientific status.[147] This level of investigation with its specific connections to other levels may be designated as the archaeological investigation of the episteme, of the "total set of relations that unite, at a given period, the discursive practices that give rise· to epistemological figures, sciences and possibly formalized systems."[148] The episteme is inextricably linked as a technical concept in archaeology to those relations that are involved with the ways in which epistemological configurations, areas of scientific status and formal systems, are tied to an ensemble of discursive practices. Thus, scientific domains for historical study must be distinguished from the archaeological territories that constitute the *savoir* for their systems of cognition.

Archaeology, however, is not bound to the domain of the scientific or the quasi-scientific because, as Foucault now sees, there is no intrinsic necessity for it to be tied to an analysis of the episteme. While his studies have in fact concerned themselves with epistemic domains, Foucault recognizes that archaeological analysis might be applied to other spheres without reference to the epistemic. Sexuality, painting, and politics are the three possibilities mentioned specifically in *AS*.[149] Archaeology could examine each of them in terms of their epistemic configurations, their orientation to the sciences. Thus an archaeologist could investigate, for example, in the case of sexuality, the biology and psychology of sexuality as a specific discursive practice. However, sexuality can also be investigated, archaeologically, in terms of its ethical configuration. Separate from its connection to discourses that claim scientific status, an examination of other relations (prohibitions, transgressions, and so on) would show sexuality as a particular discursive practice that is ethical. Likewise, one could analyze archaeologically discursive practices for both political knowledge, in terms of its concrete struggles, tactics, and decisions, and painting, in terms of its processes and techniques.

These are only hints of other forms of archaeological study, but Foucault's intention in imagining them at this point seems clear. Some commentators have asserted that there was a reduced role for the episteme in AS's definition of method. They claim that this constituted a fundamental shift in Foucault's thinking, perhaps even the emergence of a Foucault II.[150] It seems evident to us, however, that what has actually taken place is the refinement of a category that had been ambiguous in LMC, but that was seized on much too quickly by many students of his archaeology of the human sciences as the fundamental notion of Foucault's thought.[151] Neither the episteme nor LMC ever warranted the unique status that they were given—by others—as the heart of archaeology. His refinement of the notion of the episteme furnished the theoretical clarity for other domains to be archaeologically investigated.

CONCLUSION

Foucault has situated thought within the archive because, like the library, it is there that a unique mode of thinking may take place. Among those "entangled and confused parchments," those documents that have been "scratched over and recopied many times," we are able to confront what we have avoided: the material, discontinuous, and hazardous reality of those spoken and written things from which we snatch our various fields of cognition.[152] The archive is the site where we can once again be shocked by the overwhelming multiplicity of what there is to know, by the staggering number of possibilities by which we can arrange what has been enunciated, by the force of the various systems that determined what was to be said and preserved as well as what was to be excluded and destroyed. Those who enter that obscure region of the archivist with the desire to understand the present will have customary ideas blotted out. Instead of wondering about who might have created a specific document or a collection of them, about how these assorted items can be linked together to form a continuous, smooth pattern of meaning, the history of an idea perhaps, we are faced with more pressing questions. What are the systems of inclusion and exclusion that account for the existence of these documents out of the vast domain of what could have been said or preserved? What regularities can be deciphered from among this mass of statements? Into what series can they be ordered so as to assist us in understanding the specific historical configuration in which they appeared?

These are the archaeologist's questions, and they are posed in contrast to the history of ideas and the western fascination with the world of ideas that is its source. The four major categories of the historian of ideas—meaning, originality, unity, creation—are displaced, in the archive's dim illumination, by the interests of the archaeologist: the statement's conditions of existence, the series into which it can be placed, its character as event.[153] Foucault delights in the archive as the home for archaeological thinking because the archive is the repository of relentlessly active events, the historical a priori of what can be apprehended. Even though we may be unconscious of its functioning, these events disclose the *savoir*, the knowledge in which our fields of cognition appear. The task for archaeology is to bring various chambers of this archive into the light of day.

The writings that we have examined in this chapter have attempted to secure archaeology's potential for fulfilling this task. Foucault has responded to the three major methodological difficulties for his enterprise that were mentioned in the preceding chapter.[154] By refining the notion of the episteme, his analysis is no longer open to the charge that archaeology is a description of *Weltanschauungen*. By specifying the elements that constitute a discursive formation and the directions for inquiry into it, he offers a wealth of concrete points at which transformations may be located and at which they are to be examined. Finally, he has pledged archaeology to an analysis of the relations between the spheres of discourse and those of the social-economic. It is this pledge, however, that constituted the single claim from these years that produced the most criticism from his commentators. In spite of his intentions, has Foucault, in the end, written a declaration of independence for discourse? Does his distinction between the discursive and the nondiscursive result merely in "juxtaposition," as one critic judged, or in "blind" differentiation, as another charged?[155]

The issue is not minor. Without effective treatment of the social and political conditions within which discourse appears and functions, archaeology will fail to reach the dimension of existential necessity. In addition, in its critique of humanism, archaeology has identified itself as a political work. Humanism's categories "dissolve the event." In struggling precisely for a mode of thought adequate to the event, archaeology is a program for fostering a receptivity to the radical breaks and transformations that may be introduced into history by events.[156] It is a political struggle against a form of enslavement, for humanism represents a philosophy of self-subjugation: it speaks of soul—"ruling the body, but subjected to God"; it proclaims the power of consciousness—"sovereign in a context of judgment, but subjected to the necessities of truth"; it heralds the individual—"a titular control of personal rights subjected to the laws of nature and society"; it professes its solicitude for basic freedom—"sovereign within, but accepting the demands of an outside world and 'aligned with destiny.'"[157] In combating this humanism, dissonant thought must be considered a thinking for politics, a sphere that is of crucial importance for the Foucault of 1971: "the essence of our life consists, after all, of the political functioning of the society in which we find ourselves."[158]

Neither Foucault's personal interest in the political realm nor his project's stated ambitions, however, preserves archaeology from the charge of merely juxtaposing the discursive and the political. It is discourse itself that accomplishes this. Our culture's logophobia and its systems of control indicate that our discourse is not only a matter of manifesting desire; it constitutes an object of desire itself. Like all other products of practices, discourse may become the goal of desire and the object of a struggle for political power: a statement "allows or prevents the realization of a desire, serves or resists various interests, participates in challenge or struggle and becomes a theme of appropriation or rivalry."[159] From the moment of its existence, the statement is caught up in a political struggle—a struggle involving the discursive as well as the nondiscursive.

The themes that archaeology brings to political thought will be distinctive. Archaeology is not interested in formulating a theory of justice or ensuring the rights of human nature. Rather, its concern is with today's "real political task": the analysis of those institutions, especially institutions that produce knowledge, that appear to be neutral in the political struggle while in fact they entail a constant exercise of political violence.[160] In the years after his inaugural lecture at the Collège de France, Foucault's dissonant thinking is in combat with this violence. That combat will lead him to complement an archaeological analysis of discursive formations with a genealogical investigation of the historical field in which they operate. Archaeology will remain, however, essential to Foucault's form of critique.

5

◆

Dissident Thinking

INTRODUCTION

Although Foucault's writings from 1972 to 1979 presented great quantity and diversity, there is no mystery as to their fundamental concern.[1] A cursory glance at the topics that interested him in those years might lead the observer to suppose that Foucault had only fulfilled the program he anticipated in *AS*: studies of painting, politics, and sexuality.[2] While it is true that his writings might be divided up and distributed according to these categories, such an exposition would overlook the specific characteristic that defines the Foucault of this period. Politics was not merely one area of study among others, but the passionate interest underlying all the work of those years as well as the development in his methodological thinking that occurred during them.[3] The Collège de France, the institution that served as Foucault's "theater," as he called it in his inaugural lecture, has long provided a stage for dissident drama.[4] It was appropriate, then, that such a site should be the place for Foucault's elaboration of his work as a dissident thinking, a challenge to contemporary forms of the distribution and practice of power in our society and to the types of understanding that conceal the grounds for these forms. His dissident thinking was no less cathartic or dissonant, but its excavation of foundations and its exposure to event were now allied to explicitly political tasks. This was accomplished not only in a general struggle with humanism but through quite particular campaigns against adversaries with faces, whether they were the harsh visages of correction officers or the sympathetic countenances of medical and psychological staffs.

The first section of this chapter will deal with Foucault's analysis of our contemporary political situation as it is described in his examination of the prison and his initial 1976 study of sexuality. While engaged in these, he did not cease to reflect upon the conduct of thought itself and its practice in political criticism. This reflection, however, was not to furnish dissidence

121

with an "ideological base" or to define a systematic form for it; rather, he wanted to "give it instruments."[5] This chapter's second section will treat the development of his thinking and method into instruments for a political thought. The key to understanding both this development and the precise form his study of politics took is found in the nature of a crucial political assumption that was Foucault's prior to 1972. While his general comments regarding politics have been touched upon,[6] his most significant presupposition regarding the political realm was a conception of how power operated. The clearest formulation of his assumption is the consideration in *L'ordre du discours* (hereafter *OD*) of our culture's logophobia in the face of discourse. Whether through rules of exclusion or principles of limitation and constraint, discourse is conceived of as controlled and forced into submission by a power that functions repressively.[7] Foucault's recognition of this assumption and his evaluation of its basic inadequacy for a study of power in modern society provide the most characteristic traits of his political analysis. His earlier conviction that the present order in political society made it impossible to envision alternatives that would be free of its principles indicated the need for a study of politics.[8] When Foucault embarked upon a sustained critique of that order, such a study became a necessity if his dissident thinking was not to be merely a maneuver within the system from which it wished to dissent.

1. TOWARD AN UNDERSTANDING OF CONTEMPORARY POLITICS

Since at least 1963, Foucault had been struck by a peculiar tone in our modern value discussions, namely, the prestige they accord to medical discourse.[9] Politics is not a sphere isolated from the cultural transition represented by the shift from a debate conducted largely in the religious language of salvation to one preoccupied with health. One cannot fail to notice the privileged role that a whole cluster of issues revolving around the quality of life theme has had in the modern age: contemporary controversies on such matters as rights to health care, to one's own body, to a sanitary environment are characteristic of modern politics in general.[10] That such topics have become common in the chambers of government is determined, according to Foucault, by the ways power operates in our society and by the manner in which knowledge articulates our society's conception of itself and its needs. Both *Surveiller et punir* (hereafter *SP*) and *La volonté de savoir* (hereafter *VS*) are attempts to uncover the functioning of the form of knowledge and the type of power that constitute the parameters of our political thought and action. Foucault's choice of the prison and sexuality as his routes into this functioning is a brilliant one. In having the character of our political condition emerge, on the one hand, from an institution that seems to be on the periphery of society, and on the other hand, from a dimension that is regarded as interior and intimate, he fashions an insight that, traversing all the divisions of public and private, social and personal, makes untenable any disassociation of personal and political existence.

The foundation of contemporary politics is found in what Foucault calls "bio-politics" (*bio-politique*), a politics of life fabricated by the knowledge and power operative in the modern age. The members of western societies have been constituted as a population preoccupied with its biological life and engaged in a political conduct dedicated to the administration of that life. His studies on the prison and sexuality treat two dimensions as crucial for the emergence of this bio-politics: one concerned with the disciplining of the human body and the other addressing the health of the social body as a whole. Although these two dimensions are inseparable in his understanding of contemporary politics, the following two sections—the carceral archipelago and the birth of bio-politics—respect both their distinction and the calendar of their presentation by Foucault.

A) THE CARCERAL ARCHIPELAGO

A thinking adequate to the political must build upon a comprehension of the actual workings of power. Where ought the desire for such comprehension begin to probe? Foucault's choice of the prison as the place to study the action and character of power seems logical. As he pointed out in his conversation with Gilles Deleuze in March 1972, prisons hold a fascination because in them we are able to see the "most frenzied manifestation of power imaginable"; in the prison, power's "brutal tyranny" does not conceal itself.[11] A month later, Foucault made his first visit to a prison, and toured the facility in Attica, New York, only a half year after its bloody riot. In an interview following his visit, he told John Simon that such an institution could not really be reduced to its negative functions: "its cost, its importance, the care that one takes in administering it, the justifications that one tries to give for it seem to indicate that it possesses positive functions."[12] The dates of these two conversations are stressed because I believe that here, more than at any other point in Foucault's development, we have an exact chronological index for a decisive transition in viewpoint. His study of the prison might have become a history of yet another form of exclusion such as he had explored in *HF*. Instead, as his remarks after the visit to Attica already suggest, his study of the prison will aim to understand a type of power that cannot be reduced to its tyrannical exercise of confining and excluding; his objective will be to decipher the workings of a power that perhaps might still manifest itself most clearly in prison, but that operates throughout the whole of society. The prison will point to the carceral network that touches us all to the extent that we are exposed to disciplines. Not far from the dust of the documents that yield a history of the prison are the sounds of the prison revolts that have swept our time. While occasionally directed against the tyranny of specific wardens or guards, these voices of protest are most frequently shouts against the prison as such, against model prisons and the doctors, psychiatrists, and educators who help to make it function more "humanely."[13] In putting forward his account of the prison, Foucault continues his history of the present; it is a study of a specific modern form of power, and of a political impotence that prisoners are not alone in raging against.

i) The Prison Although extensive recourse to the institution of imprisonment is a phenomenon only of the last century and a half, the prison has won an extraordinary status in that it is judged both a failure and yet irreplaceable.[14] If there is a single reason for its tenacity as an institution, for its continuing capacity to be regarded as a self-evident solution, it is perhaps that the prison is considered an improvement, a more humane response to criminal activity than the systems of punishment that preceded it. For a society that envisions its political order in the context of a social contract, there is an intrinsic reasonableness to a punishment that deprives a criminal of the liberty that is the fruit of the contract. In addition, this deprivation of liberty is grounded in the noblest sentiments of those reformers who expressed the widespread repugnance for torture that was felt at the end of the eighteenth and the beginning of the nineteenth centuries. As Beccaria, one of the most prominent of the eighteenth-century reformers, expressed it: "Who does not shudder with horror when reading in history of so many terrible and useless torments, invented and coldly applied by monsters who took upon themselves the name of sage?"[15] How could the prison not be considered an advance in a period of enlightenment that judged the punishments of earlier times as the "barbarity of centuries" and as proof of the "feeble influence of reason and religion" in a preenlightened era?[16] Although a crime may violate the social contract, the criminal's humanity still ought to be respected; the prison is born in the midst of cries from the heart in defense of this humanity.

As Foucault so dramatically illustrates in the contrast between a public torture of 1757 and the regulated day of a young prisoner eighty years later, the scene that opens *SP*, there is a fundamental difference between a monarch's punishing revenge and the prison's timetable. The issue, for Foucault and for thought, however, is to ascertain in what this difference consists. Is it actually a result of the "progress of ideas and the improvement of morals" that the nineteenth century claimed?[17] Foucault's study of the prison attempts to see it differently, tries to grasp another history that, once made to speak, will drown out the constant chant of progress and improvement that provides one of the principal pillars of the prison's acceptability.

It is striking that the critique of the prison system is almost simultaneous with the prison's historical appearance and does not find itself in the chronology one might expect: the establishment of the prison, which would then be followed by a recognition of its failures, and in turn the creation of a reform movement. Instead, criticism of the prison appears at the same time as the institution itself and forms a critique that continues to be repeated in almost the same terms today. In reality, the prison does not lead to a reduction in the rate of crime; it is plagued with recidivism; if one has not gone into prison a hardened criminal, it seems to be the institution guaranteed to produce such a character; it fosters a milieu of crime and breeds a population rarely reabsorbed by society; it is a cruel economic disaster for the convict's family.[18] If this nineteenth-century critique of the prison looks familiar to us, so does that century's call for prison reform. The goal of the prison penalty is reformation and social rehabilitation for the criminal (the principle of correction); there is a need for a prison's inmates to be distributed according to the character of their crimes as well as their age, their attitudes, and their progress in rehabilitation (principle of classification); penalties need to correspond to the individuality of the crime and the criminal (principle of the modulation of penalties); prison labor is an integral element not of punishment but of reform (principle of work as obligation and right); rehabilitation demands that provision be made for the inmate's education (the principle of penitentiary education); the prison must be staffed by individuals who possess the specialized knowledge, the moral qualities, and the technical abilities that are expected of educators (principle of the technical supervision of detention); finally, assistance must be provided to criminals after their detention in order to continue promoting their rehabilitation (the principle of auxiliary institutions).[19] These principles, which Foucault calls the "seven universal maxims of the good 'penitential condition,'" have monotonously dominated discussion of prison reform for the last hundred and fifty years.[20] Quite apart from the questions raised by their constant repetition, their character points to an inescapable conclusion for Foucault.

The principles regarding the prison that reformers have rallied around for so long show that the institution of prison cannot be simply regarded as a form of punishment that is a mere juridical deprivation of liberty. From the moment of its historical appearance, the prison not only deprived of liberty in the context of making amends under the law, but linked with this penalty a technical project, the very transformation of those who were entrusted to the prison institution. Only this goal of transformation is capable of furnishing an explanation for the series of practices that functioned in the prison and for the debates that revolved around it as an institution. The minute regimentation of the day's time and activity, the constant supervision, the obligation to work, the whole panoply of methods utilized to promote an ethical and religious consciousness and bring the prisoners to a regret for the past, the desire to keep the sentence indefinite so that the length of the prison stay could be synchronized with the prisoner's growth—these practices were not matters of security but tools for the transformation of conduct and consciousness at which detention aimed. The question of how these various practices could be orchestrated, what mixture of isolation and group work should be introduced, what elements in such competing models as the reformatories in Philadelphia and Auburn should be combined—these were the concerns dominating the penal debate of the early nineteenth century.[21] This pressing need to transform behavior as well as deprive of liberty, this mutation of a cry from the heart into the rigor of the prison system requires, for its explication, a more precise understanding of when and where the reform movement entered the historical stage.

Foucault locates the desire to reform the modes of punishment at a point where two different struggles intersect.[22] The first of these was the struggle against the power of the sovereign. The manifestation of royal power that torture represented needed to be resisted not so much because the cruelty of the king had become unbearable but because the distribution of power in the society had become unacceptable. What primarily interests Foucault in this struggle, however, is not the drama of king versus people at the time of the French Revolution, but the nature of the new economy of power that was seen as desirable. The aversion to royal justice that was felt in the late eighteenth century was aimed at the irregularity of such justice, its constant tendency to be exercised arbitrarily and in contradictory ways. The desire of the period was for a system of justice that would be consistent and, most important, that would permeate the society in place of the unpredictable acts of royal intervention and revenge. One of the essential objectives of reform was to make the workings of justice regular, "not to punish less but to punish better."[23] Foucault finds the roots of this aversion and desire in yet another struggle, not against the superpower of the king, but rather against the infrapower of the illegalities that flourished in a monarchy but that had become intolerable. There are many reasons for the growth of this intolerance toward areas of conduct to which the king might be indifferent or with which he might be only occasionally concerned: the development of a capitalist society, the simultaneous diminishment of violent crimes and augmentation of crimes against property, the emergence of the capability to develop a police apparatus.[24] If these struggles against king and illegalities locate the birthplace of reform, its character and tone can be specified more fully by another, not unrelated, factor.

Foucault puts the discourse that counseled moderation in the application of punishment in relation to the discourse of a society theorizing itself in terms of a social contract and the power unleashed by such theorizing.

Instead of offending the sovereign majesty, the criminal now chooses to be the enemy of society as a whole; instead of the sovereign's vengeance, the right to punish is now connected to the defense of society itself, and criminal wrongdoing, an attack upon society itself, gives society the right to oppose such acts in its entirety. "The malefactor has been saved from a threat that is by its very nature excessive, but he is exposed to a penalty that seems to be without bounds."[25] The reformist cry from the heart is, unknowingly, a response to this new terrible power, but its call for the humanization and moderation of punishment is a calculated one. There is a demand for a type of punishment that takes into consideration the new punishing authority, the members of society itself. Punishment must be approached in terms of its utility, and the penalty for a crime must be considered not only in relation to the crime itself but more important, to its possible repetition. What had been thought of within the monarchical system as an effect of a punishment's public spectacle now becomes a principle of its very constitution and functioning. Punishment is advanced as a sign that will serve as an obstacle. The prison and its disciplinary codes appear within this concept of punishment as a semio-technique.

Instead of the tortured body of the criminal serving as an example for others, it is now necessary to be more rigorous: establishing a chain of ideas along which the thought of a crime's advantage will be connected to the certain knowledge of the punishment that will necessarily follow a crime's commission. The art of punishment must embrace a system of clearly defined crimes with which specific punishments will be associated. A new dawn for penal justice has arrived, along with an explosion of modern criminal codes: Russia in 1769, Prussia in 1780, Pennsylvania and Tuscany in 1786, Austria in 1788, and France in 1791, 1808, and 1810. Crime and punishment now function within a great educative enterprise. An eighteenth-century text captures the sense of this new politics of punishment: "A stupid despot may constrain his slaves with iron chains; but a true politician binds them even more strongly by the chain of their own ideas"; it may be the case that "despair and time eat away the bonds of iron and steel, but they are powerless against the habitual union of ideas, they can only tighten it still more; and on the soft fibres of the brain is founded the unshakeable base of the soundest of Empires."[26]

The actual prison institution that did appear, however, is not reducible to an effect or embodiment of this reformist discourse. Two facts prevent such a facile reduction, and suggest the tangled factors in terms of which the prison must be understood. First, the common recourse to detention as punishment for almost all crimes that developed in this period contradicted one of the major objectives of the reformers. In order to root out monarchical arbitrariness and enhance a penalty's educative value, the reformers wanted to weave a tapestry of different punishments whose diverse characters would correspond to the various types of crime. Within this multiformity, the criminal would be brought to an appreciation of how he himself is responsible for the punishment he suffers. This value was lost in the imposition of detention as an almost universal response to the violation of law.[27] Second, while the reformers placed their emphasis upon the forming of a connection of ideas, and envisioned punishment as directed to the criminal's soul in contrast to monarchical law's interest in the body, the prison institution was quite different. The arsenal of punitive techniques—systems of work, timetables, isolation, and so forth—that was in fact used by prisons functioned as a coercion of the body. While on the theoretical level of social contract, the reformers saw rehabilitation in relation to the restoration of the criminal as a juridical subject, the prisons seemed to develop a quite different goal: not the restoration of a juridical subject as a fit party to the social contract, but the production of an "obedient subject, the individual subjected to habits, rules, orders, an authority that is exercised continually around him and upon him, and which he must allow to function automatically in him."[28] The common employment of penal detention and the coercive character it took on must be accounted for not in terms of the reformist semio-technique with which it was historically contemporary, but in connection to a specific technology of power that aimed at the training of an obedient subject. In delimiting this technology, Foucault uncovers another level in the archaeology of the prison, a level that has long been hidden by the reformist discourse cloaking the prison's origin.

ii) The Disciplinary Society As a historical event, the birth of the prison is tied to several other processes taking place at the same time. While Foucault is not indifferent to the economic and social aspects of these processes, his study of the different threads that come together to constitute the milieu in which the prison is institutionalized aims primarily at defining the specific level of political technology that must be appreciated if the prison's sudden appearance and rapid deployment is to be understood. As a route of access to this specific level, Foucault chooses an idea that Jeremy Bentham had formulated in the late eighteenth century as an architectural model for a host of institutions, including the prison. Bentham's "panopticon" serves as an eloquent image of the intersection of the prison institution with the political technology of the general society, and which demonstrates the goals of this technology.

The panopticon was a structure that arranged a series of adjacent cells around an open space that had in its center a tower within which an official could keep the inmates of the cells under constant surveillance while he himself would not be observed. The novelty claimed by the panopticon was that the inhabitants of the cells could never be sure when they were being observed at any particular moment, and thus it achieved the effect of an anonymous, perpetual observation with only slight expenditure of man-power.[29] For the normal historian of ideas, Bentham's architectural figure and its popularity might be seized on to characterize the power of an idea whose time had come. It was hailed as the "intelligence of discipline in stone" and as an event in the "history of the human mind."[30] Why was it considered such an event, and why had its time come? Foucault's answer is that the panopticon appeared at a period during which a disciplinary society and the instruments capable of operating it were in the process of formation. The late eighteenth century witnessed many dreams of a perfect society. While historians of ideas usually place their emphasis on those dreamed by the philosophers and jurists of the period, Foucault chooses to examine the military vision of perfection. This is the age in which national armies appear for the first time, and it is perhaps more than a coincidence that the source for Bentham's idea of the panopticon was his brother's account of a visit to the Ecole Militaire in Paris.[31] While philosophers were discussing the state of nature, rights, social contract, and a general will, the military was involved with the construction of a great military machine and the elaboration of techniques of discipline by which bodies could be trained to become docile instruments in its functioning. A new anatomy of the body and a new force of technology were being assembled.

Discipline is the major means for the production of peace and order within a society, and the best guarantee of their preservation. Discipline is not an abstract value but a mechanism in which different powers are placed in relation to one another in order to produce a certain type of human conduct. Perhaps in earlier times a soldier's suitability was announced through the possession of natural qualities such as strength, bearing, and so forth; in the modern period, suitability could be constructed through a procedure of military training. The feasibility of producing a soldier fit for the machine in which he will function is linked to the operation of four distinct powers. A "cellular" power was required, one that would distribute the individual members of groups into manipulable series. Individuals are to be located in specific spaces defined in terms of rankings and possible transitions from rank to rank. The functioning of an "organic" power was also needed. The body had to be mastered, and its movements and opera-tions mapped and ordered. Through a rigorous definition of the body's proper movements, a system of training could be established to provide guidance for precise and regulated exercise of the body. Third, there is a "genetic" power that operates by determining the stages through which the trained body must pass to achieve the specific ability demanded of it; the disciplining of the body is put within a movement of time that never reaches its limit. Finally, there is a "combinatory power" that subjects the body to a precise system of commands that are articulated in relation to the variety of roles required in a multisegmented machine.[32]

These powers of discipline and the practices they require—the drawing up of tables, the prescribing of movements and exercises, the tactics for making combinations—are made to function successfully through a simple instrumental technology of three major components. Whether the space in which individuals find themselves distributed is that of a military camp, a working-class housing project, or a school, a constant hierarchical observation is taking place. The architectural composition of such space, while less corporeal than the power of the torturer, is more subtly physical. Second, these spaces are illuminated by the constant appearance of judgments on the observance or nonobservance of norms. Rewards and penalties are ingredients of this continually pronounced normalizing judgment. Finally, the examination concretizes and combines these two other techniques: the success of training and the individual's progress are evaluated.[33] The powers and technology of discipline represent neither enslavement (bodies are not appropriated) nor asceticism (renunciation is not its goal), but something quite distinct. Discipline aims at a difficult objective: the greater utility of the body through the same processes that make it more docile. A political anatomy of the body attempts to increase its force, to make it more useful, and at the same time to diminish its political force by making it more obedient. In sum, "it dissociates power from the body" and establishes in the body a "link between an increased aptitude and an increased domination."[34]

Although our description of these powers and this technology has followed that of Foucault, in which the specter of the army forms its background, military organization is only an example of the type of power that has permeated modern society and that Foucault wishes to throw into relief. This power must be thought of as positive and productive of the style of a society's institutions and of its forms of knowledge. The panopticon is an image of both, and it is revealing that Bentham could propose its architectural figure for a host of institutions, not only prisons but also schools, factories, asylums, and poorhouses.[35] In contrast to the manner of exercising power that sought to confine and exclude, that displayed its strength in a negative functioning, disciplinary power aspires to an exercise of coercion that is positive, continuous, and subtle; its goal is a system of surveillance so automatic, so generalized, so spread throughout the social body, so light and rapid, so taken for granted that it is experienced not as a sovereign's repression but as the natural result of each individual's striving for effective performance. The practices of discipline swarm through society's institutions with the paradoxical result that discipline appears deinstitutionalized. In any case, it is a power that cannot be identified with any particular institution because it is the fabric of all of them. Disciplinary power appears in the wise choices of an enlightened age that can no longer tolerate the irrational and arbitrary powers of sovereignty and that, in its construction of capitalism, has stumbled upon a device that maximizes a body's utility while depoliticizing it.[36]

The functioning of this disciplinary power when theories of punishment were under discussion established the conditions for the birth of prisons even though reformers thought they were laying the foundations for something else. At first glance, the prison institution seemed a hopeless confusion of models. Is it an army, a factory, a school, a justice-producing machine, a laboratory? In reality, it reflects the disciplinary society that had already constructed a prison form prior to its use in the penal system. Within a disciplinary society, a new approach will be adopted toward the strange reality of the criminal as imagined in this age. No longer a violator of royal majesty, he is the monster who puts himself outside the social compact with his fellow citizens. Nevertheless, he is not beyond redemption, which is effected not by a superstitious restoration of a monarch's majesty but by a salvific, rehabilitative knowledge. The criminal is less to be punished than he is to be known, which is now made possible thanks to a technology of hierarchical observation, normalizing judgment, and a process of examining.[37] This technology permits the knower to probe the singularity of the criminal; the prison is the place of the case, of a careful biographical knowledge that makes rehabilitation a possibility. An individual's specific criminal acts are far less important than a knowledge of the dynamics in his life that led to them and that provide the key to the type of treatment he requires. The multiple models and practices followed in a prison, monotonously decried within the same system of thought and power that produces them in the first place, are not the random actions of incoherent elements. They simply manifest the logical workings of a disciplinary society. Within such a society, it cannot be surprising that "prisons resemble factories, schools, barracks, hospitals, which all resemble prisons."[38]

Such resemblance ought to disturb one of our everyday convictions, namely, that the penal machine operates only in the distance, away from us, a conviction that a whole literature of crime has buttressed.[39] Foucault's probing of the disciplinary society began to throw light on the factors responsible for a similarity of style among the institutions in our society. His study of the prison indicates that we are far from being outside the penal institution, for we are not outsiders to the functioning of the power-knowledge relations that form the foundations not only for the prison but also for our contemporary political life and thought. One of the major accomplishments of *SP* is to permit a glimpse into those foundations.

The carceral archipelago is a landscape in which power functions in a unique way. While it may have its occasional tyrants and repressive out-bursts, it is a territory characterized by the multiplicity of small powers that come together to constitute a disciplinary power. This suggests that power must be thought of differently than is usual; it is not possessed but exercised. It appears not in those rituals of force associated with the absolute monarch, but in the visibility of a light and facile functioning.[40] Most important, power must be thought of positively: "We must cease once and for all to describe the effects of power in negative terms: it 'excludes,' it 'represses,' it 'censors,' it 'abstracts,' it 'masks,' it 'conceals.'"[41] In reality, power must be approached in terms of its productive capacity; this production is nowhere more heavy with implications for Foucault than in the sphere of knowledge.

The most important of the institutions operative in our political field are those manifesting the interrelationship of power and knowledge. In exhibit-ing the direct complicity of power and knowledge with one another, they force an abandonment of the tradition that dichotomized interested and disinterested knowledge, that taught that knowledge was in part the achieve-ment of withdrawal from power.[42] Few institutions provide such a clear case of this complicity as does the prison. The role of specialized knowledge—psychiatrists, psychologists, geneticists, criminologists—has raised the most profoundly disturbing problems for a judicial apparatus that is supposedly concerned with the enforcement of law.[43] The problems faced by judges in a liberal society, however, are only minor indications of knowledge's capacity to fabricate domains of objects and legislate the modes of cognition required for approaching them. Foucault's point goes far beyond asserting the indisputable fact that a discipline such as criminology must be understood in terms of the institution within which it functions. The study of the prison has led to yet another perspective on his perennial concern with the consti-tution of man himself. In *SP*, it is man's character as an individual that specifically attracts his attention. While it might be argued that the concep-tion of man as a unique individual is connected to the social contract model, which confers upon him the status of an abstract juridical figure, Foucault suggests that the view of man as an atom of society owes more to the specific technology of discipline that functioned in the eighteenth century. Individu-ality is tied to the field of comparison constituted by discipline and within which a differentiation and hierarchy of abilities is established.[44] The opera-tion of the powers and technology of a disciplinary society constitutes perhaps the most fundamental level from which the "man of modern humanism was born."[45] It is not only the criminal who becomes an object to be known during the modern period but human reality itself, in the figure of man: "Knowable man (soul, individuality, consciousness, conduct, what-ever it is called) is the object-effect" of a disciplinary society.[46] Criminology owes its existence to the same conditions that account for the emergence of the human sciences in general.

Although the study of the prison represents only a segment of the investigation required to illuminate the night in which our political conflicts occur, Foucault nevertheless feels that it permits an identification of the decisive political issue in contemporary political thought. The problem is one of normalization, the functioning of norms in contemporary practice and thought. Modern society has witnessed a proliferation of techniques that have made the growth of an extensive power possible. At the heart of this disciplinary society is the norm: "We are in the society of the teacher-judge, the doctor-judge, the educator-judge, the 'social-worker'-judge; it is on them that the universal reign of the normative is based; and each individual, wherever he may find himself, subjects to it his body, his gestures, his behavior, his aptitudes, his achievements."[47] Probing the norm's roots and the mechanism of its operation gives the key for understanding the most puzzling of political events: not only that the power to judge and punish has been naturalized and legitimated in our society, but rather that such immense powers have been so readily accepted and tolerated.[48] Like the penal condition itself, this power of normalization is not exterior to us; in the carceral archipelago, it penetrates the depths of what we consider most internal and intimate, our sexuality.

B) THE BIRTH OF BIO-POLITICS

In 1976 Foucault published the first of an announced six-volume study on the history of sexuality. Following immediately after his investigation of the prison, with its direct political implications, such a project may seem at first to represent a shift away from politics. This, however, is not the case, and at the core of his work on sexuality is the political issue of power.[49] In order to understand the connection between the investigation of the prison and that of sexuality, one must keep in mind the fundamental organizing principle that Foucault discovered as operating in the disciplinary society, namely, the norm. The notion of the norm, not to be identified with the external imposition of a law, is rooted in the idea that there is a principle of correct functioning for a specific organism, a principle established on the basis of a recognized knowledge.[50] In writing a history of sexuality, Foucault's interest is not to account for different patterns of sexual conduct but to probe the foundations that tie sexuality, with its many accepted norms, to knowledge and the power to normalize.[51] Although the first volume was only an introduction and was described as tentative, Foucault did announce it as an "overview" of the planned history as a whole. He had already postulated that the fundamental form of power necessary for understanding the operation of the norm, and thus the functioning of that society in which contemporary politics is conducted, is life: "A normalizing society is the historical outcome of a technology of power centered on life."[52] The importance of sexuality as a domain of a politically interested research is due to its key place at the intersection of the two axes along which this technology and bio-politics developed. In delineating his history of sexuality, Foucault reconnoitered the parameters of our political order and thought.

i) The History of Sexuality: An Overview Foucault's own history of sexuality defines itself by contrast to a historical view with which we are all familiar, we Victorians or post-Victorians, depending on the value system with which we prefer to identify.[53] According to this common historical reckoning, a movement of increased prohibition began in the seventeenth century and culminated in the repressive Victorian Age. There was a new silence to be observed, a modesty of word about matters that ought to be strictly private. This restraint was at its greatest when the topic was children's sexuality, and most especially, when their actions seemed to suggest that the age's firm conviction as to their absence of sexual feelings was not totally justified. In addition to restrictions on discourse, a new control was exercised over sexual conduct in the modern period; sex was confined to the parents' bedroom and the marital duties of adults. Finally, the rule of silence joined rigid codes of sexual behavior to create a sea of ignorance from which a clear-headed understanding of the most fundamental of human drives rarely surfaced. Western societies passed through two centuries of sexual repression involving an "injunction to silence, an affirmation of non-existence, and by implication, an admission that there was nothing to say about such things, nothing to see and nothing to know."[54] Fortunately, however, according to the repressive account, this is past history—at least for some. The overcoming of fear and the growth of psychological knowledge, of which Freud was only a timid anticipation, has led to a greater toleration of sex and a reduction in penal sanctions on different forms of sexual expression.

Foucault's own look at the historical record indicates that the three tenets of this history of sexuality are all fundamentally inaccurate. Although new rules of propriety might have been introduced into discussions of sexual themes, there has been an undeniable explosion of discourse about sex during the modern period, when suppression was supposed to have been the dominant fact.[55] The Counter-Reformation's intensification and extension of confessional practice throughout its domains was a sign of the new injunction under which modern Europeans found themselves: sex must be spoken of. Of course, for centuries, monks, who knew how the unexamined temptation could be fatal for a life aiming at perfection, had striven to put their desires into words and analyze the character of these desires in excruciating detail; what was novel in the seventeenth century and after, however, was that so many others felt compelled to do the same. While the many studies on sexual concerns published during this period might open with their author's apologies for the need to enter into detail on these matters, what is important about such moralism is that it was so obviously an obstacle to be overcome. In addition to the sheer multiplicity of discourses on sex, the number of institutional sites for these discourses proliferated. While ecclesiastical bodies had long made sex and its regulation their cause, they acquired new associates: governments and their police apparatus begin to concern themselves with illegitimacy and the population implications of sexual activity; doctors and educators involve themselves with the management of adolescent sex. In place of that unified deliberation on sex and its sins that medieval Christianity had conducted, the modern age scattered its discourses and its experts on sexuality: they seem to be everywhere, in "demography, biology, medicine, psychiatry, psychology, ethics, pedagogy, and political criticism."[56]

Contrary to the accepted account of restricted sexual behavior, Foucault asserts that the explosion of discourses about sex was also an explosion of unorthodox sexualities, or at least of interest in and talk about them.[57] The three explicit codes that governed sexual activity up until the end of the eighteenth century—canonical law, Christian pastoral teaching, and civil law—were all centered on matrimonial relations and their careful regulation. In the eighteenth and nineteenth centuries, there is a displacement of interest. While monogamous couples won greater privacy, a passionate inquisitiveness was unleashed on sexual domains that had escaped careful scrutiny in the earlier dispensation; four were regarded as particularly rich for analysis. The woman's body, first of all; there took place what Foucault describes as a hysterization of women's bodies: a conceptualization in which these bodies were regarded as saturated with sexuality, in which they were constituted as objects for medical intervention owing to their intrinsic disposition for pathological development, and in which they were crucial for analysis of the social body because of their central link to family and fertility. Second, children's sex became a matter for pedagogical concern: an alliance of doctors, families, and educators was charged with responsibility for the development of a sexuality that was potentially correct, but that could become abnormal if those unnatural activities to which most children seemed inclined were allowed. Third, there was a socialization of procreative behavior in that economic and political questions began to be asked about fertility and the responsibility of couples to society as a whole. Fourth, perverse pleasure became a subject for psychiatry, which sought to isolate the sexual instinct, to comprehend the distortions to which it was subject, and to develop techniques for a regime of correction. In this modern preoccupation with sex, there thus emerged four privileged objects of knowledge: "The hysterical woman, the masturbating child, the Malthusian couple, and the perverse adult."[58]

Foucault asserted that a third devastating difficulty confronts the common view. Far from entering into a sea of ignorance, modern society has been the first to embark upon a project, vast in its conception, of mastering the truth of sexuality, of constituting a *scientia sexualis*.[59] One can only be puzzled by the attribution of ignorance to the Victorian Age when one recalls that it was in precisely this period that theories of racism were formulated in terms of scientific study in biology and medicine, that categories were articulated for the sexualities of children, women, and the abnormal, that a science of demography was constituted, and that through it the state involved itself with a range of issues regarding reproductive life that had rarely been dealt with before. Other cultures had contented themselves with an *ars erotica*, in which knowledge of the various sexual pleasures was transmitted by masters of eroticism; modern western societies were determined to achieve a scientific comprehension, solidly founded upon minute details of a vast population speaking the truth about its sexual behavior. While this search for the truth of sex may have been anticipated in medieval confessional practice, the differences separating them are more significant. Speaking of sex is no longer an affair between priest and penitent, but is involved with a widespread network of new questions and new forms of evidence. There is the constant murmur of conversation between children and parents, students and teachers, patients and psychiatrists, criminals and criminologists. The confession of sexual sin is replaced by detailed examinations, by the construction of autobiographical accounts, by the assembling of dossiers that not only state the forms of behavior but also reconstruct its milieu, the "thoughts that recapitulated it, the obsessions that accompanied it, the images, desires, modulations and quality of the pleasure that animated it."[60] All these minute observations are then ordered into a system aspiring to scientific status: techniques for the guidance of speech and the solicitation of information needed clinical codification; the significance of detailed observation rested upon the postulate of sexuality as a general and diffuse causality that revealed the key to the most varied forms of behavior; the formulation of systems of interpretation were required to recover a behavior's sexual character, one that by its very nature tried to stay hidden; finally, observations needed to be integrated within a scientific and medical knowledge that effected a therapeutic healing.

Perhaps there is to be found in the project of a *scientia sexualis* a new type of *ars erotica*, the sheer pleasure western society derives from seeking the truth of sex, from detailing sexual behavior, from having desire's secrets torn from it. Rather than being ignorant, we moderns explore a knowledge that never seems to lose its fascination, speaking the truth of a sex that will reveal the truth of our human character. This paradoxical pursuit of knowledge defines the style of modernity's relation to the sphere of sexuality: "What is peculiar to modern societies, in fact, is not that they consigned sex to a shadow existence, but that they dedicated themselves to speaking of it *ad infinitum*, while exploiting it as *the* secret."[61]

These three historical monuments—the proliferation of discourse concerning sex, the preoccupation with different forms of sexuality, the pursuit of a science of sexuality—destroyed the story of modern western culture as fundamentally repressive and sketched the issues with which Foucault intended his history to be concerned. Sexuality was to be regarded neither as some natural given that the power of church and state attempted to check nor as some reality that knowledge has striven to uncover. Sexuality was itself a historical construct, a product of the way power and knowledge function.[62] Foucault did not hesitate to emphasize his radical perspective. He is not offering a history of those ideas that were formulated in the course of the centuries in order to comprehend a reality that may be called sex. There is no sex-in-itself. It is rather an object constituted in the deployment of a sexuality that occurs only within a specific configuration of knowledge and power: "We must not place sex on the side of reality, and sexuality on that of confused ideas and illusions; sexuality is a very real historical formation; it is what gave rise to the notion of sex, as a speculative element necessary to its operation."[63]

The major directions Foucault intended for the history of this formation could already be grasped in the introductory volume and in the titles proposed for the following five. In the projected second volume, *La chair et le corps (Flesh and Body)*, Foucault proposed to follow Christianity's establishment of discursive existence for a sexuality centered on the notion of flesh. Succeeding volumes would take up each of the major nineteenth-century developments that he had already touched upon. Volume 3, *La croisade des enfants (The Children's Crusade)*, would treat of the way children were sexualized and how their sexual behavior became a major concern for education. Volume 4, *La femme, la mère et l'hystérique (Woman, Mother, and Hysteric)*, would study the sexualization of the woman's body, the concepts of pathology that arose in relation to that sexualization, and the insertion of that body into a perspective that invested it with significance for social policy. Volume 5, *Les pervers (Perverts)*, would study the isolation of the sexual instinct, the definition of its normal and abnormal functioning, and the corrective technology envisioned to deal with the latter. Volume 6, *Population et races (Population and Races)*, would examine how the sexual domain became an object for ever-increasing state concern and intervention, the emergence of eugenics and theories of race in the contemporary configuration of knowledge, and most important, the constitution of society's members as a "population" warranting such concern, intervention, and conceptualization.[64]

This history of sexuality would follow a chronology, or rather chronologies, different from the popular account of sexuality. One chronology would concern the techniques by which sex was spoken of, analyzed, and integrated into a discourse that aspired to science. Foucault had already sighted two especially productive moments in this development: the middle of the sixteenth century, when precise procedures for the examination of conscience were articulated, and the beginning of the nineteenth century, when medical technologies of sex appeared. A second chronology would trace the diffusion and application of these techniques among the lower classes. In this calendar, not the same as might be found to apply to the privileged classes, three points marked themselves: the end of the eighteenth century, with the issue of birth control; the early nineteenth century, when the conventional family's organization was regarded as fundamental for successful political control and economic regulation; and the end of the nineteenth century, when juridical and medical controls were developed for the protection of society and race.[65]

Although VS was only an outline for a much larger project, there is no doubt about the issue that was central to his history of sexuality. Whether taken up with children, women, perverts, or the population as a whole, modern sexuality's development reveals the functioning of a power that cannot be reduced to repression. While Foucault would not deny that repression does, in fact, occur in the sphere of sexuality, it is certainly not modernity's major theme. Its intelligibility demands that such repression be put back into the more general economy of the specific power characterizing our period, the power centered on life, bio-power.

ii) Bio-Politics Foucault's overview of the history of sexuality already indicated that any analytic of power adequate to modernity must dispense with the representation of it within the juridical model of law that has been common in western discussion. This model conceives of power as working only in a negative manner, as prohibiting and limiting desire or action. Power is regarded as manifesting itself in the legislator's articulation of rule and law, and as performing successfully because it threatens punishment. Its mode of operation is perceived as uniform with power relations (for example, parent-child, teacher-student, doctor-patient) existing only as variations on the theme of lawgiver on one side and obedient subject on the other. In the end, this model leads to the imagining of power as a monotonous, easily decipherable reality that is fundamentally incapable of inventiveness and craftiness. This juridical image is totally inadequate to the task of charting the maneuverings of power in the area of sexuality. What is striking about modern discourses on children's sexuality is not the barriers against certain forms of sexual behavior they constructed, but the many opportunities for intervention in the life and education of children they helped to make possible, and the many authorities who were constituted as responsible agents for such intervention. The manner in which perversions were specified and personality types established, the ways medicine came to involve itself with questions of sexual pleasure—these were the forms of power that Foucault felt demanded study, rather than the series of prohibitions existing in a culture at a particular moment.[66]

Although *VS* suggested the type of relations that required greater scrutiny, Foucault's alternative model for their analysis was far from adequate definition. What it ought not to be was more precise.[67] The power operative in a disciplinary society will not find successful formulation if its nature is approached as a group of institutions that dominate a society through the imposition of rule. Power is scattered amid a multiplicity of relations that entail some form of force; these relations of force, however, are difficult to situate within a particular institution, for they are caught up within a process of constant conflict and transformation that robs any institutional site of a claim to permanent possession and control. These relations of force must not be regarded as a superstructure concealing more fundamental relationships, whether economic or intellectual, but as immanent in these and as having a directly productive role in their constitution. Foucault envisioned a "strategic model" for the analysis of power as a replacement for the juridical model.[68] Such a model would look beyond the promulgated law to the unstated objective that is being served. An interest in prohibitions would yield to a consideration of the tactical efficacy of the relations that are actually in force. Rather than probing seemingly dominant institutions, the strategic model's concern would be with the ever-changing field of forces where a power is exercised but not possessed.

Although the strategic model was but a sketch, the reasons for needing it are quite definite. The power that creates and sustains a disciplinary society is not monarchical . Although the sovereign has been driven from his throne, our notion of power is still his vassal. Both *SP* and *VS* labored to uncover a new dispensation of power. Thus, Foucault draws an example from the sphere of punishment in order to emphasize the unity of his two investigations, and as a vivid illustration of the difference between the modern and premodern exercise of power.[69] The monarch's right to decide between life and death for his subjects operated within the context of a privilege to seize life or let it continue. Despite the conditions within which it had to function, the right to take life symbolized sovereign power. The modern period has seen a decline in recourse to capital punishment because the power unique to this period is a power charged with the administration and fostering of life itself; within this context, execution offends the justification for the very exercise of power. Thus, for such extreme punishment to be justified at all, theories of punishment must place their emphasis not so much on the crime as on the character of the individual who committed it and the need to protect society from him: "One had the right to kill those who represented a kind of biological danger to others."[70] This difference between a power that manifests itself in the taking of life and one that is exercised in the fostering of life marks the frontier between the premodern and the modern. Modernity is announced in the advent of a bio-politics, in the fact that "methods of power and knowledge assumed responsibility for the life processes and undertook to control and modify them."[71] Bio-politics designates those forces that "brought life and its mechanisms into the realm of explicit calculations and made knowledge-power an agent of transformation of human life."[72]

As the position the sovereign occupied in western politics disintegrated, a new strategy for the functioning of society emerged. Its task was no longer to guarantee obedience to a personal will but to generate an allegiance to society itself, and to secure the conditions for its smooth functioning. Nothing less than a general power over life was required, a power that was assembled in two distinct movements: the development of a control over the body, an "anatomo-politics" of the human body in which systems of discipline functioned; second, the elaboration of regulatory controls for the population of a society as a whole. In constituting this bio-politics of the population, the discourses that dealt with sexuality played a decisive role. In 1976 Foucault had already anticipated that one of the volumes of his history would have to treat modern discourses on population, for they signal the new form of power operative in the modern period. Whether the discourses were concerned with a population's labor capacity, health, or wealth, it was life itself that was being considered, life understood as the "basic needs, man's concrete essence, the realization of his potential, a plentitude of the possible."[73] These two distinct streams—the anatomo-politics of the human body and the bio-politics of populations—come together in the nineteenth century to solidify the foundations for a disciplinary society. A power that assumes responsibility for life needs to establish norms for life's functioning and for its correct development. This power demands vast enterprises of knowledge that aim to uncover the patterns along which life was destined by nature to flourish, and that assist in the creation of policy for a society that desires the full realization of its potential.

It is within the field created by the functioning of this bio-power that the issues that cluster around the quality-of-life theme arise, and that medical discourse assumes political standing. Bio-politics permits us to understand how movements could appear that make sexual repression the object of a critique that is advanced as political. Sex as a political issue was made possible because it is located at the pivot of the two dimensions along which this power of life developed; it is involved both with the disciplining of the body and with considerations relating to the control of populations. For the modern period, sex "was a means of access both to the life of the body and the life of the species."[74] The notion of a political-sexual critique is consistent with the system of power within which it operates, and such a critique cooperates in blocking a comprehension of the actual mechanisms of power in our society. To take repression, specifically sexual repression, as the fundamental form in which power acts creates the illusion that in merely speaking about it, in violating taboo, one is challenging power. The very concept of sex as naturally given serves this illusion; an object is defined in such a manner that constituted along with it is both the possibility of its repression and the chance to win freedom by rising against this force of prohibition. The "irony" of modernity's discourses on sex and its repression consists in "having us believe that our 'liberation' is in the balance."[75] Here Foucault finds the beginning of an answer to his question of how it was possible for generations to tolerate the formation of a disciplinary society. Power is acceptable only when the most substantial part of it is hidden. For it to function throughout a society, power must hide its pervasiveness beneath a web of identifiable repressions. For those caught within its grasp, would such pervasive power be acceptable "if they did not see it as a mere limit placed on their desire, leaving a measure of freedom—however slight—intact? Power as a pure limit set on freedom is, at least in our society, the general form of its acceptability."[76]

This capacity of power to conceal itself cannot cloak the tragedy of the implications contained in Foucault's examination of its functioning. While liberals have fought to extend rights and Marxists have denounced the injustice of capitalism, a political technology, acting in the interests of a better administration of life, has produced a politics that places man's "existence as a living being in question."[77] The very period that proclaimed pride in having overthrown the tyranny of monarchy, that engaged in an endless clamor for reform, that is confident in the virtues of its humanistic faith—this period's politics created a landscape dominated by history's bloodiest wars. What comparison is possible between a sovereign's authority to take a life and a power that, in the interest of protecting a society's quality of life, can plan, as well as develop the means for its implementation, a policy of mutually assured destruction? Such a policy is neither an aberration of the fundamental principles of modern politics nor an abandonment of our age's humanism in favor of a more primitive right to kill; it is but the other side of a power that is "situated and exercised at the level of life, the species, the race, and the large-scale phenomena of population."[78] The bio-political project of administering and optimizing life closes its circle with the pro-duction of the Bomb. "The atomic situation is now at the end point of this process: the power to expose a whole population to death is the underside of a power to guarantee an individual's continued existence."[79] The solace that might have been expected from being able to gaze at scaffolds empty of the victims of a tyrant's vengeance has been stolen from us by the noose that has tightened around each of our own necks.

2. THINKING AS AN INSTRUMENT FOR POLITICS

That noose is loosened by breaking with the type of thinking that has led to its fashioning, and by a mode of political action that dissents from those practices of normalization that have made us all potential victims. A prere-quisite for this break is the recognition that human being and thought inhabit the domain of knowledge-power relations (*savoir-pouvoir*), a reali-zation that is in opposition to traditional humanism. In the light of SP and VS, man—that invention of recent date—continued to gain sharper focus. By means of that web of techniques of discipline and methods of knowing that exists in modern society, by those minute steps of training through which the body was made into a fit instrument, and by those stages of examining the mind's growth, the "man of modern humanism was born."[80] The same humanism that has invested such energy in developing a science of man has foisted upon us the illusion that power is essentially repressive; in doing so, it has led us into the dead end of regarding the pursuit and exercise of power as blinding the faculty of thought.[81]

Humanism maintains its position as Foucault's major opponent because it blocks the effort to think differently about the relations between knowledge and power. His weapon against this humanism continues to be a form of thinking that exposes human being to those dissonant series of events that subvert our normal philosophical and historical understanding. Foucault's thought and the action it motivates may be approached as two distinguish-able elements. The next part of this section will look at his understanding of thought in terms of that strategic model within which Foucault is articulat-ing it, a model that is of the greatest consequence for understanding the development of his style of thinking after AS's statement of method. In the region of power-knowledge relations, thinking finds itself allied with a political engagement, with a practice of dissent; the last part of this chapter will be given over to a consideration of Foucault's own political dissent.

A) THE DEVELOPMENT OF FOUCAULT'S THINKING AND METHOD

In their consideration of the studies he published in the 1970s, there was a rare measure of agreement among Foucault's commentators: his writing was judged to be clearer, his organization of material more controlled, his assertions and arguments more precise. This welcome accorded his style and mode of presentation was, however, one of the few points of consensus among those who evaluated such works as *SP* and *VS*. On other issues, there were those radical disagreements, even on the most basic points, that characterized the interpretation of Foucault throughout his career. As far as one of these basic points is concerned, the question of the relationship between his earlier statement of archaeological method in *AS* and his work while at the Collège de France, we hear contradictory voices. On one hand, the work is regarded as an application, without significant change, of the method presented in the last chapter; on the other hand, there is the chorus of those who claim that his more recent work represents a break with archaeology itself and the initiation of a radically new project.[82] There is no reason to make the relationship between archaeology and genealogy an enigmatic one. Doubtless Foucault's work at the Collège is not an exact mirror of that which preceded it. *AS* had already stated his intention to turn archaeology toward different areas. Thus, he had already anticipated investigations that would be oriented not to the episteme but to sexuality in terms of an ethics, painting in terms of its practice, political knowledge in terms of concrete political struggles, decisions, and behavior.[83] These are, of course, the three areas that became his focus after the statement of method. To judge that his actual analyses in these areas represent an abandonment of archaeological method is untenable. Certainly there is no slavish point-by-point correspondence between the schema of archaeology, as sketched in *AS*, and the presentation of the births of the prison and of bio-politics. At the same time, archaeology's respect for the relative autonomy of discursive formations persists in Foucault's discrimination of both the reformist discourse in the debate over prisons and the *scientia sexualis* that operates in bio-politics. Nevertheless, there had been a major development in Foucault's thinking and method since its 1969 formulation. This development furnishes some justification for those who recognize that there has been change in Foucault's thought, even as they misinterpret it as a rupture with and an abandonment of archaeology.

The investigations of the prison and of sexuality extended his thinking and produced a major new category for its theoretical formulation. This extension and production entailed the enunciation of new rules for inquiry, but rules that are *complementary* to those that were enunciated in *AS*. The inability to see this complementarity is rooted in a failure to appreciate the two principal factors that account for the differences separating *AS* from the theoretical formulations involved in his political analysis: the change of domain for analysis, and the shift in the planes on which his thought is expressing itself. In order to grasp Foucault's development, it is necessary to recall the major methodological difficulty that was without final resolution in *AS*, and to realize the effect that the study of power had on his own thought. In the last chapter, I emphasized the importance of Foucault's pledge to analyze the relations between the spheres of discourse and of the nondiscursive. If the discursive was merely to be juxtaposed with social, economic, and political practice, archaeology would be unable to aspire to that existential necessity for the formation of a discursive practice that it puts forward as its ultimate objective. In addition to this explanatory goal, Foucault had already indicated that discourse was not existentially independent of the political struggles in which it functioned as an object of desire. Thus, even while conceding a certain autonomy to discourse as the object of its examination, archaeology was committed to a more thorough explication of the relations between the discursive and the nondiscursive than had been possible in 1969. Foucault's description, at that time, of these relations as situated at the limit of discourse lacked adequate precision. The recourse to what he identifies as a genealogical study does not represent a privileging of the nondiscursive over the discursive.[84] Foucault's style of thinking has long had the objective of permitting him to "avoid every problem of the anteriority of theory to practice and the inverse."[85] To the extent that Foucault is read through the old glasses of the theory-practice debate, his turning to genealogy would entail the rejection of archaeology's form of analysis. Freed from these spectacles, one is able to appreciate the complementarity between archaeology and genealogy in Foucault's effort to "resituate the production of true and false at the heart of historical analysis and political critique."[86] While archaeology attempts to do justice to the specific production of forms of rationality and truth, the intricate links between these discourses of knowledge and political practices cannot be grasped in terms of univocal relations to institutions conceived as simple forces of prohibition or approval. Genealogy's task is to grasp the complex functioning of these discourses within the deployment of an historical field in which the interaction of the discursive and nondiscursive produce an outcome quite different from the logical development of either taken separately. In a 1978 interview, Foucault reiterated the two complementary directions for his work: "My general theme isn't society but the discourse of true and false, by which I mean the correlative formation of domains and objects and the verifiable, falsifiable discourses that bear on them: and it's not just their formation that interests me, but the effects in the real to which they are linked."[87]

An additional obstacle to an accurate reading of the relationship between archaeology and genealogy is that his thought is working itself out on a different plane from that of his methodological statement for an archaeology of knowledge.

In his earlier formulation of method, the history of ideas served a role analogous to his previous notion of power. Thus archaeology defined its interests in discontinuity, in the statement's conditions of existence, in the procedures for its ordering, in the event, and so forth by way of an opposition to a history of ideas whose categories repressed these dimensions. Archaeology was the liberation of themes that had been excluded and silenced. What is new in Foucault's thinking as a result of discovering the need for a strategic as opposed to a repressive analysis of power is that the operation of his own thought is functioning strategically. *AS* represented a definite culmination in Foucault's statement of his style of thought and its methodological implications, a statement that presented itself over against a definite force of domination, the history of ideas. Such works as *SP* and *VS*, on the contrary, reflect a mode of thinking that is functioning strategically, probing different lines of attack on a space more complex than discourse itself. This strategic thinking is looking less for a single path or method at this time than a series of tactical approaches to a continually shifting field of knowledge-power relations. Methodological formulation is very much subordinate to these strategic considerations. There is no incompatibility between these planes of strategic thinking and methodological formulation, but that one recognize their difference is necessary for an adequate analysis of Foucault's later thought. The notion of the *dispositif*, the major methodological novelty introduced since *AS*, permits us to see how closely linked the two planes are.

The importance of the concept of the *dispositif* may be easily overlooked by anyone who reads *SP* or *VS* in their English versions, since it is translated by several different terms. Its proper meaning is conveyed by the term "deployment," which captures the military connotation Foucault intended in its usage. The *dispositif* is a concept that proceeds from the strategic model of thought according to which Foucault's own thinking is operating. Methodologically, it is pressed into service in order to define a level for investigation that is more general than that of either discourse or the nondiscursive field. Thus, the *dispositif* is a heterogeneous ensemble of discourses, institutions, architectural arrangements, administrative procedures, and so forth. In his examination of this ensemble, the genealogist attempts to describe certain relations that are established among these elements at a given moment by the need to respond to a specific historical urgency. Finally, Foucault identifies two stages in the actual genesis of a deployment. Initially, there is the fashioning of an objective strategy to meet the specific crisis. Following the creation of this strategy, a second moment occurs that is proper to the deployment as such, and that characterizes it as long as it continues to be a deployment: the *dispositif* becomes the place for a double process. One is a process of "functional overdetermination" (*surdétermination fonctionelle*), in which the strategy's negative and positive consequences, whether desired or not, effect harmonious or contradictory relationships between the various elements that make up the field under examination, and evoke adjustments among the elements. The second process is one of "strategic filling" (*remplissement stratégique*), which specifically identifies the proliferation of unanticipated consequences produced by the objective strategy that has been adopted.[88] Although this is a rather abstract statement, the study of the prison first betrayed the concrete relations that the *dispositif* wishes to exhibit. The penal realm is an ensemble of extremely disparate elements: it is constituted not only by the discourses of political revolutionaries, psychologists, judges, legislators, doctors, but also by the architectural forms of prison construction as well as the system of daily order and discipline practiced within prisons. We have seen how this heterogeneous collection emerged from a project of humanistic reform and as a political response to tyrannical authority to become a tyrannizing force leading to that catalogue of abuses that has been bemoaned for over a century.

The studies of the prison and of sexuality suggested the methodological efficacy of the *dispositif*, its ability coherently to approach power-knowledge relations on a level that embraces both the discursive and the nondiscursive. Its implementation with a refined archaeological investigation was a task for future studies. Its introduction does not entail, however, any surrender of the archaeological tools that have already been developed. More important for archaeology as a method than any restatements of previous concepts are the new complementary rules that extend its capabilities. While knowledge and power are united in discourse, discourse itself always functions as part of an historical deployment. In order to establish the relations that make up this deployment, a certain conversion is necessary. Beyond the obvious presence of institutions that are seen as powerful and of discourses that are identified with knowledge claims, power-knowledge relations must be grasped in their complex essential functioning. That these relations appear demands a suspension of certain attitudes toward both knowledge and power. With respect to knowledge, any opposition between what is considered "interested" and what is thought of as "disinterested" is cast aside; knowledge conceived of as the fruit of individual consciousness is put out of play. With respect to power, the juridical and repressive model of its functioning is disregarded. This suspension is but the condition of possibility for a sphere of power-knowledge relations to appear. Once this possibility is established, it must be protected, as was the field of discursive statements, from two modes of organizing it: dialectical and semiotic approaches must be rejected, for they would demolish the specific character of knowledge-power relations as events that are produced by chance interactions as much as by intended objectives, and that are insubordinate to any meaning.[89] The intelligibility of these relations is to be sought in the strategic action of a nonrepressive power, the establishment within such a strategy of a specific form of knowledge, and the unanticipated consequences of this action and knowledge.

In examination of this power-knowledge sphere, the first concern must be with the discursive fact itself. Why is an object field being created to be put into discourse? Who is doing the speaking? What positions and viewpoints do the speakers occupy? Which institutions prompt speech, and which store up what is said?[90] In the analysis of this discursive fact, Foucault suggests four rules that ought to be put into play. The first is that of immanence (*règle d'immanence*): no exteriority is conceded to the relationship between types of knowledge and strategies of power. Second, thought must be guided by rules of continual variations (*règles des variations continues*): the domain of power and knowledge is not one of easily identifiable institutions and static distributions, but of relations that are in a constant state of transformation. The third principle to be followed by archaeological description is the recognition of a double conditioning (*règle du double conditionnement*): no a priori discontinuity is accepted as existing between the general strategy of a deployment and the many concrete relations and specific tactics that occur in the same deployment. But while there is no rigid dichotomy between a microscopic and macroscopic level in a deployment, it cannot be approached as constituting a simple homogeneity, as if tactics were always merely the expression of a general strategy. This rule counsels an approach to the strategy and tactics of a *dispositif* as constantly conditioning one another. Finally, there is the rule of the tactical polyvalence of discourses (*règle de la polyvalence tactique des discours*): discourses cannot be approached in terms of a simple division between those that embody power and those that seem to struggle against power. Discourses must be understood as elements in an unstable process within which their strategic and tactical uses change. Discourses must thus be studied in terms of their tactical efficacy—the service they render to a precise reciprocal effect of power and knowledge—as well as of their integration within a more general strategy.[91]

While this concept of the *dispositif* and the different lines of questioning Foucault has put forward, more as "cautionary prescriptions" than "methodological imperatives" for its analysis, are totally consistent with archaeological method, they do clearly illustrate the paradigm by which Foucault's own thinking is now guided.[92] Thought, whose major duty since Kant had been largely envisioned as a reflection on time, is now thrust onto a spatial field of battle in which knowledge-power relations are conspicuous.[93] Foucault's thinking is a specific strategy that responds to a particular historical urgency. On the modern terrain of a functioning bio-power, thinking considered as a strategic action is more than a striking image. The omnipresent, although not omnipotent, operation of this power has determined that thought has no secure haven to which it can retreat as an escape from combat. Even fathoming the hidden currents that feed his own thought, Foucault began a consideration of those discourses on war and strategy with which his own thinking had chosen to associate itself.[94] His uncertainty at this point as to those currents did not keep him from entering the conflict. On that political field of battle in which the issue at stake is nothing other than life or death, Foucault's thought continued the attack against its old adversary, humanism.

B) THINKING IN POLITICS

Foucault chose to identify himself as an intellectual, and he was certainly correct in saying that his readers would smile if he were to try to deny that status.[95] He would also be the last to deny that the concrete shape of this identity and the nature of the intellectual's engagement in politics is formed by the specific historical epoch in which he finds himself. The contemporary participant in politics finds himself in much the same situation as were the early Christians when the Second Coming did not occur with the imminence that had been expected. We perhaps live in that in-between period separating revolutions.[96] The importance of twentieth-century revolutions for thought and politics is rooted in that space of possibility the French Revolution created. It is no accident that so many of Foucault's analyses revolved around this historical irruption. For him, it was the political event par excellence, for it provided a glimpse into the profound depths of possibility for radical change: the institutions within which history had placed men were subject to revolt.[97] Perhaps it might even be said, as was maintained in a study conducted under Foucault's supervision, that the continuing presence of the French Revolution in political thought and memory is due to the fact that "the *event* as such arose" from it, and that in it was announced the "assured revelation that no one was safe from the event, not even the tyrant." "Everything could henceforth happen, since *it* had happened."[98] In any case, the revolution's fundamental challenge to the order of things left modernity with a question that still worries or heartens it: Will it reappear? Foucault stands within that question in a spirit of doubt: unsure as to whether it will occur again, uncertain, in the light of twentieth-century experience, as to whether its occurrence would even be desirable, and yet absolutely confident that it inaugurated a new possibility for thought and life within whose shadow every serious politics dwells.[99]

More than a few might be troubled by Foucault's likening of our political condition to that of the early Christian era. For a long time the failure of the Second Coming to occur as anticipated bore major responsibility for a withdrawal from political concern and for a passivity in the face of history. How could it have been otherwise, if the focus of the age emphasized the awaiting of an event over which man himself had no control? Foucault's comparison might be appropriate in a way that he himself had not intended. The same questions might be put to him as were posed after the appearance of *LMC*.[100] Have these studies conspired with his earlier work to undermine the possibility of human action changing the reality it finds? Whereas his notion of epistemic systems had once prompted doubts about the political efficacy of his thought, it was now his perspective on power and its functioning that generated suspicion. Just as archaeological thinking was divested of the target that the history of ideas had provided, so political movements were deprived of that clear opponent against which they struggled. Those movements that defined themselves in terms of the struggle against the power of the state or against the powers of a specific class seems to be antiquated. In the modern period, there is no king, no center of power to function as a magnet for revolt, only a vast network of diverse elements that have various natures and function at different levels.[101] While the notion of a transgression against a prohibitive power may be attractive and galvanizing—as it had been for Foucault in the past—the present deployment of power does not permit a conception of its overthrow as obeying a law of all or nothing.[102] There is "no single locus of great Refusal, no soul of revolt, source of all rebellions, or pure law of the revolutionary."[103] Against whom, or against which constitution, does one revolt when the complex system of power-knowledge within which we exist has neither a great man nor any particular group of individuals that is consciously responsible for putting the system into operation and for maintaining its functioning?[104]

Foucault does not evade the *possible* implications of the type of society that his analysis shows modernity to have fabricated. Bio-power may well maintain its hegemony, and the questions of common concern that emerge within its system may simply involve its smoother functioning. Such questions will be responded to not by political debate but by the increasing intervention of experts for whom general political discussion on such issues has become anachronistic. In the light of our contemporary deployment of power, Foucault did not avoid considering whether politics itself is threatened with extinction, that we are "perhaps experiencing the end of politics."[105] And yet Foucault's imagining of this very real possibility is but a dimension of a critical hope. When he was censured in the past for having locked men into discourses and rules over which they had no control, Foucault argued that, far from wanting to make a prisoner of human being, his aim was to comprehend what needed to be changed and how such transformation could be enacted. While it is true that he deprived the "sovereignty of the subject of the exclusive and instantaneous right" to effect such transformation—which is only an obvious acknowledgement of the situation—the point of his studies was to master the rules in regard to which human creativity could operate.[106] He had wanted to demonstrate how fragile an epoch's order of things actually is so as to "show up, transform and reverse the systems which quietly order us about."[107]

Foucault's analysis of power led to a similar form of response. One always exists within a specific deployment of power, and to nurture a wish to be outside of power is merely to cultivate a private fantasy. At the same time, this is not to say that one is trapped by the specific distribution of power within which one finds oneself.[108] In fact, Foucault felt that his analysis of power had given hope regarding resistance to it. The other side of power's pervasiveness is precisely the omnipresence of the resistance it discovers. No ruse of reason can guarantee ultimate triumph to the system of power that is at work, and its adversaries are as scattered, as multiple, and as heterogeneous as power itself. The opposition to power is the twin of its birth, an opposition that is constituted, with different intensities at various times, of "mobile and transitory points of resistance, producing cleavages in a society that shift about, fracturing unities and effecting regroupings, furrowing across individuals themselves, cutting them up and remolding them, marking off irredicible regions in them, in their bodies and minds."[109] Power cannot be considered a massive, irresistible force, since so many within a specific society, so much within a particular individual, have to cooperate for it to function and its objectives to be realized. As "soon as there is a power relation, there is a possibility of resistance. We can never be ensnared by power: we can always modify its grip in determinate conditions and according to a precise strategy."[110] The political function of the intellectual is tied to this task of modification.

To be a politically concerned intellectual is to act as an historian, to assist one's society in grasping the long perspective on its formation, to locate where the hold of power is especially strong as well as where it is particularly fragile.[111] Foucault's interest is in the political efficacy of this historical knowledge. At the same time, however, he wants to break with those conceptions of the intellectual modeled after the Jewish prophet, the Greek wise man, the Roman legislator, and the Marxist revolutionary. Those models make of the intellectual a conscience for mankind or a consciousness of its universality.[112] In place of such a "universal intellectual," Foucault envisions a "specific intellectual" who refrains from any absolute claim to truth and justice and who is deeply involved in mastering the specific power dynamics of the particular institution within which he labors. The capacity of the intellectual to pose any realistic threat to the smooth functioning of power does not rest in that general discourse of which he is capable and of which Voltaire was a prototypic spokesman. Rather, it rests in the actual knowledge at his disposal, the superior understanding he possesses of such institutions as the hospital, the asylum, or the university, and thus his greater capability to pose questions to them.[113] Foucault's own work suggests an obvious association with this image of the specific intellectual. He has been concerned with the type of knowing in particular institutions and with the how of power's functioning within his knowledge and these institutions. He does not offer a general theory of power, nor a discourse that revolves around such abstract notions as justice or the proletariat.[114] During these years, Foucault characterized his work as the study of the political production of truth.[115] Lest that sound too general, however, we should note the two directions his political labor took.

i) The Combat with Truth The question of truth was not a new one for Foucault. In his inaugural lecture at the Collège de France, he announced his intention to study our culture's will to truth.[116] In the context of power as repression, which was dominant in Foucault's understanding at the time, the true-false division was considered the lynchpin for the other systems of exclusion he mentioned: the disjunction between prohibited and permitted speech and the mad and the sensible were finding themselves more and more anchored, in the contemporary period, in the firm foundation of a true discourse in relation to which other divisions required justification.[117] Thus, when Foucault opened his first course at the Collège, he placed his teaching in the context of initiating a series of analyses that would gradually form a "morphology of the will to knowledge."[118] In that series, sexuality provided the most dramatic example of the central place that the category of truth has taken on for us. Not only is there the need to discover and proclaim the truth of sexuality, but truth itself is perceived as possessing almost magical powers: "Spoken in time, to the proper party, and by the person who was both the bearer of it and the one responsible for it, the truth healed."[119]

This insatiable need to speak the truth, and the thaumaturgic effects connected with such speech, is not only an affair of sexual discourse. While it may be traced to perspectives unleashed by the Greeks, it has taken on a particular urgency in our present situation; in a disciplinary society, it is in the search for truth that a whole technology of examinations sutures those techniques of an observing hierarchy that are the sinews of such a society. Whether the place of its specific application be the school, the army, or the hospital, the examining function transforms the individual into an object for description, into an individual case, a reality whose truth can be grasped; thus, it constitutes one of the principal conditions for the establishment of the human sciences.[120] The form of penal investigation employed in this society provides a good example of the nature and impact of the pursuit of truth in the political sphere. In the Middle Ages the inquiry into a crime followed an inquisitorial model, a central element of which was a correlation between degrees of suspicion and degrees of punishment. Such a model did not follow a dualistic system of truth and falsity, but a principle of continuous gradation between levels of guilt and levels of punishment. This model of investigation has been replaced in the modern period by one that patterns itself on empirical research, and that is ruled by a principle of truth or falsity. The facts of a crime must appear with the certainty of a mathematical truth.[121] In the search for such certainty, the model itself allots special privileges to those discourses that put themselves forward as scientifically true. The interest of Foucault and his 1972 seminar in the study of a nineteenth-century parricide is due to the importance he saw in this over-riding concern with truth, a shift to which the case of Pierre Rivière gives eloquent illustration.[122] The memoir Pierre wrote regarding his crime fits into a realm of discourse, quite common to the period, that was defined by the production of tales of monstrous crimes. This memoir took on extraor-dinary interest for the period because it was the battleground of psychiatric interpretation at a time when psychiatry was beginning to aspire to scientific status. The intervention of medical expertise in Rivière's judicial process and the analysis of his memoir in terms of truth and falsity signaled a new area of power for discourses that claimed to be scientific.[123]

This area of power is cleared by a search for certainty. One can no longer be content with a determination as to whether a crime has been committed and what laws have been transgressed; one must also understand the act itself. Does it belong to the field of psychotic action, is it a fabrication of fantasy, is it the consequence of perversion? No longer is it simply a matter of establishing who committed the crime; the causal process that produced it must also be determined. Are we dealing with an issue of environment or heredity, an effect of consciousness or unconsciousness? Knowing the law is insufficient when there is a knowledge of act and man available to guide the measures that should be taken toward the criminal and on the basis of which his rehabilitation may be achieved.[124] In this relentless pursuit of truth, a wedge is driven into the judicial process that has never ceased to weaken its coherence. The scientific discourses that fill the courtroom proliferate, and the "master of justice is no longer the master of its truth."[125]

The confrontation among experts in the courtroom is merely the dramatic illustration of a much more extensive movement within contemporary society as a whole: the depoliticization of political processes by our search for truth and the discourses born of it. While the state racisms that grew in the soil of biological and historical truth constitute the most sobering reminder for modernity of the possible implications of this search, the political force of truth cannot be isolated in the peculiar excess of a specific policy.[126] The search for truth forms the central dynamic of government operation today, whether the society be Marxist or liberal, whether the specific point of discussion be an economic policy or an educational and health program. The ensemble of discourses on truth determine which alternatives for a society's conduct will be articulated, and which opportunities will be conceded to political action and human intervention. Because what is at stake in the operation of these discourses is nothing less than the capacity to influence human decision regarding life and death, the battle over the status of truth engaged Foucault's political energy. It is a conflict not over which truths are to be discovered, accepted, or rejected, but over truth itself, truth understood as the "ensemble of rules according to which the true and the false are separated and specific effects of power attached to the true."[127] The general field of this conflict is defined by the fact that in contemporary society, truth is tied to scientific discourse, to the institutions that produce such discourse, to the few apparatuses by which it is transmitted. Since "truth is a thing of this world," and is not the "child of protracted solitude" or the "privilege of those who have succeeded in liberating themselves," it is in the world, in the force of common action, in the alliance with the unfree that Foucault battled.[128]

ii) The Practice of Dissent In a situation in which political judgment finds itself increasingly constrained by discourses of truth, a progressive politics is defined by the challenges it poses to those discourses that have hegemony in the present day. As a work of dissent, its ultimate objective is the repoliticization of our social life.[129] Foucault's own practice of dissent embraced a wide domain of issues. In his writings are to be found a general critique of the way education is conducted and the specific denunciation of particular educational politics; he censured power's tendency to hide behind a wall of secrecy and forced the recourse to torture into the public light; while involving himself with those who wish to communicate knowledge regarding the brutal consequences of imperialistic policies, he took up the advocate's role on behalf of particular individuals who had been unjustly treated.[130] Although these various interventions reflect Foucault's conviction that the specific individuals and the exact actions through which a more general strategy of power operates must be identified and accused in the public forum, they give the impression of that occasional dissent that is common among liberal intellectuals.[131] Their mere enumeration does not capture the much more characteristic style of dissent in which Foucault engaged. He saw the special duty of the contemporary intellectual to be in a form of dissent arising from mastery of a specific institution and from the knowledge of the intricate manner in which its power operates, a knowledge that only a participant can have.[132] Following his conception of the role of the intellectual, Foucault committed most of his energies to two strategies of power: the penal and the medical.

Foucault's long involvement with the plight of prisoners in France led him to conduct a program of public education regarding the prisons through both his individual writings and his work with a group that disseminated basic information on the prisons and their inmates (*GIP, Groupe d'Information sur les Prisons*). In addition to its denunciation of specific abuses perpetrated by political authorities and by the agents of the human sciences who function within the prisons, his program of public education attempted to repoliticize the prisons.[133] Through his study of the prison's history, Foucault had become aware of the older system of public punishment as an ambiguous ritual. While the public execution manifested the absolute authority of the monarch, it also provided the occasion for local rebellion, when particular sentences were unpopular, as well as the opportunity for generating a class solidarity.[134] When punishment was put behind walls and out of society's sight, these dangerous possibilities of political response to punishment were eliminated. The political efficacy of the prison cannot be reduced, however, to this merely negative advantage; more important, the prison constitutes a population whose very existence fragments an economically exploited class of society and justifies the maintenance of a powerful police apparatus.[135]

The prison recruits a group from society that, while engaged in forms of illegality that pose no fundamental threat to the operation of power within that society, does successfully manage to intimidate the economically oppressed, and fosters the perception among them that their interests are in conflict with those of the prison population. A measure of the success the prison achieves in this regard lies in the difficulty of imagining a popular revolt in our own day making one of its first tasks, as did revolts of the nineteenth century, the liberation of those in prison.[136] The common tendency of political prisoners to want sharply to distinguish their "crimes" from those of common criminals testifies to the genius of our modern carceral system at depoliticizing crime.[137] The inquiries and publications of the *Groupe d'Information sur les Prisons*, of which Foucault was a co-founder, sought to integrate the prisons into a political struggle. In its studies of their actual operations, even in model prisons, and of the crimes and suicides committed within them, it has tried to make that information available to the general public in order to demythologize the humanistic claims to which these institutions appealed. In addition, the *GIP* served as a vehicle for communicating to prisoners themselves the reality of political support in the wider society for their challenge to mistreatment.[138]

Just as *SP* had shown that society could not regard itself as outside the workings of disciplinary power in its prisons, so its political fate is not independent of the depoliticization that has ravaged those institutions. The second major focus of Foucault's engagement in politics was on the role of medicine in our society. The unholy alliance among the forces of medicine, psychiatry, and police power, which we have become accustomed to see operating in the Soviet Union, is not confined to Communist countries.[139]

While Foucault wrote the occasional piece identifying a specific abuse of power, his principal interest was to examine the foundations of the medical hegemony constituted through the action of bio-power.[140] Unlike such figures as Thomas Szasz, who place great weight upon the actual conspiracy of medical and governmental authorities, Foucault's emphasis was archaeological: the study of those categories that emerge in modernity to promote the power of normalization.[141] Thus, the birth of a politics of health as a depoliticization of social space became the major subject of two cooperative studies conducted under his supervision. The 1976 *Généalogie des équipements de normalisation* continues the examinations of *NC* by exploring the conditions of possibility for, and the specific character of, the important place the hospital has acquired in the modern period.[142] The 1977 *Politiques de l'habitat (1800–1850)* investigates the appearance of medical categories as decisive elements in the enunciation of a housing policy, both governmental and architectural, and in the formulation of plans for urban construction.[143] As in his work with prisoners, Foucault found that the formation of an informational group could serve as a major tool for challenging medical power and for repoliticizing questions inscribed in the domain of scientific knowledge. Founded in 1972 with Foucault's participation, the *Groupe Information Santé (GIS)* attempted to challenge what it saw as a medical confiscation of health care knowledge and issues through both the dissemination of essential information and the challenge to specific policies.[144] Its objective was to link health to the wider social struggle.

As a result of his work in both *GIP* and *GIS*, Foucault became convinced of the efficacy of the specific, limited struggles with which these groups had identified themselves. Although there was always the danger of manipulation by political parties and labor unions in these limited critiques, he took heart from two developments: the appearance in our day of major prison rebellions, which he felt were encouraged by the prisoners' knowledge of the political support that existed outside of the prison, and the fundamental calling into question of psychiatric knowledge and authority that has become commonplace.[145]

This involvement in fundamental criticism both of the prison and of the functioning of medical psychiatric knowledge defines Foucault neither as a utopian calling for the immediate elimination of the prison as such nor as a theoretician of the antipsychiatry movement. The development of adequate policies for both these areas would take place only after the type of analyses with which he was absorbed had been done, and after the grip current penal and medical viewpoints have on our society had loosened. In other words, the articulation of intelligent policy rests upon a repoliticizing of the domains to which such policy is directed.[146]

In his struggle to repoliticize issues seized by knowledge as its privileged realm, Foucault followed one fundamental principle in his dissent, which proceeded from his very approach to history. His historical writings ignored the idea of a hero, which has served as a device to explain change apart from the millions of unknowns who are responsible for that change. Likewise, his political dissent aimed at developing instruments to give a voice to those who are overlooked, to those who are in prison, to those who bear the burden of our modern health politics, to those who do the hard labor of western societies, and to those who suffer from the imperialistic policies of these nations. Both *GIP* and *GIS* were instruments for generating this voice and providing it with the audience that was its due.[147] Gilles Deleuze considers them one of Foucault's major contributions to the contemporary climate of politics: he resisted the "indignity of speaking for others."[148] While Foucault's work was a forceful reminder of this indignity, he was interested in the so-called marginal groups of society not for the sake of generating a sense of identification, of furnishing his readers with a "sign of belonging" to the "good side."[149] His political dissent and his fabrication of instruments for others to speak was aimed at a culture that had been so deafened by its humanistic discourses as to be oblivious of the fact that its own intelligibility, the way it thinks and the power through which it acts, is tied to the victims that this power and knowledge have produced. The sufferings inflicted upon human beings in the twentieth century have too often led intellectuals to return to the great texts, to see Stalinism as an error of Marxism, and to regard capitalism as requiring new models of social contract. Rejecting such returns, Foucault counseled a willingness to listen to the victims of that modernity, even if they have "only their tortures to recount."[150] It is in the shock delivered to humanistic pretense by the voice of this suffering that an opening for a different future may be created.

CONCLUSION

Foucault's understanding of his own contribution to that future was secure at this point. In looking back on the route along which his thought had moved, he judged the principal interest of his work since *HF* to have been the question of power and its relation to the production of discourses claiming the status of truth.[151] *HF*'s study of psychology and the birth of the asylum had prepared him to appreciate the mechanisms of power, an issue finding explicit formulation in his response to the student revolts of 1968, and his work with prisoners.[152] His thinking was now so closely tied to an analysis of the political production of truth that Foucault tended to regard it as having always been his problem. He felt that its delay in becoming a precise problematic for his thought in the 1950's was owing to the Marxism of his intellectual milieu. This Marxism failed to give intellectual access to a serious study of medicine and psychiatry, a failure that was perhaps not unrelated to Stalinism's own political use of psychiatry and the reluctance among those sympathetic to the Communist Party to probe areas of potential damage to its cause.[153] In any case, the obligation for Foucault's thought at this period was clear: a persevering dissent from those humanistic myths that cloak the relationship of knowledge and power, that obscure the problem of a politics of truth, and thus limit thought and action.

Just as the task of dissident thinking entails labor in the archive, the painfully patient work of probing documents and throwing light on writings that had been left in dark corners, so dissident action is most often a slow-moving struggle on behalf of concealed groups such as prisoners.[154] While Foucault chose his place in this struggle, his engagement reflected another dimension of political possibility. Just as the French Revolution and its disclosure of the event formed a backdrop for our modern politics, so a new revolution always remains a possibility for our age. Foucault had suggested in *VS* that the scattered resistances to which the exercise of power always gives rise could come together and produce a radical rupture in political affairs. Such a fusion of resistances in our society would be the other side of that institutional integration of power relationships upon which the state rests.[155] Foucault saw the major task of political thought and struggle as strategic: the discovery of where power is weakest and resistance most fruitful. Such strategic action recognizes its limit in the event, the ever-present chance of an unexpected occurrence shattering the normal patterns of political development, and thus overthrowing the strategies selected as responses to them.[156] When such events erupt in history, Foucault's thought offers no ideological plot to diminish the agony of human choice confronted with events that remind men that human time has the form of a history and not of an evolution.[157] Although his expectation of possible radical historical ruptures diminished in the years before his death, he never abandoned his belief in the value of dissident thinking and acting.

6

◆

Ecstatic Thinking

In June 1984, after years of delay, Foucault released two new volumes in his series on the history of sexuality: *The Use of Pleasure* and *The Care of the Self*. Within days of their appearance in the bookstores, their author died suddenly on June 25th in Paris. There was genuine and widespread grief over the premature departure of a philosopher who had stimulated so many to the pleasures and obligations of thought.[1] When his readers turned to a consideration of the last chapters they would have from Foucault, they encountered works that were for many as unexpected as his death. Even for those who had carefully followed his development in the eight years since *VS*, Foucault's final works suggested a rupture as much as an evolution. Although they were published as studies in the history of sexuality, their perspective was concerned less with sexuality than with the "desiring man" who comes to recognize himself as a subject of desire.[2] While the studies contained detailed analyses of the sexual domain, their interest is in how sexual desire was problematized as an issue for moral conduct. It is this notion of problematization that structures the relationship between archaeology and genealogy for Foucault in this period. Archaeology examines the forms of problematization through which something can be thought as an issue for moral reflection; genealogy studies the wider system of practices out of which such problematizations emerge.[3] If in Foucault's last works he wished to preserve both archaeology and genealogy as methodological directions for thought, it was also clear that they introduced another dimension to the domain of experience that was to be questioned. That dimension is the modality of one's relationship to oneself, the ways we have of fashioning our subjectivity and its attachment to any objectification of the human. Inquiry into the process of creating this relation to the self, this process of subjectivization, must be distinguished from the notion of modern subjectivity. While the latter is the determination of the self as objective and is only the interior side of modern man, Foucault's subjectivization is a

158

process at work in different cultures and need not take a modern form. On the level of historical investigation, this axis of subjectivization complements his earlier axes of truth and power.[4] On the level of Foucault's own philosophical project, this focus on freedom completes his archaeological and genealogical directions and culminates his experiments with thought by sketching an ethical interrogation that manifests the free, ethical activity of thought. It is a freedom that Foucault still defined in opposition to modern humanism; in addition to its intellectual and political confinements, there was also a moral confinement, for, as Foucault had realized many years earlier, it was in humanism that "reason ceased to be for man an ethic and became a nature."[5]

In his 1963 examination of the novelist Raymond Roussel, Foucault had been fascinated by Roussel's last gesture, the legacy of a posthumous volume in which he supposedly explained the techniques and aims of his obscure prose. In fact, Roussel's last work was far less the unveiling of a secret than the disclosure of the "underground force from which his language springs."[6] In the light of our first chapter's claims, Foucault's last works impart an analogous lesson. Foucault came to the project and categories of his final thought only by way of his previous efforts and the underground force of their movement toward an ethics of thought. The last works identify the elements in that ethics that his earlier interrogations had chiseled out. The schema he proposes for ethical analysis—ethical substance, mode of subjection, asceticism, goal—mirror the experiments in thinking that map his journey of thought. In his examination of ancient and Christian cultures, Foucault also made a personal statement of his relationship to his entire work and of the desire that implicitly guided it to the project of an ethics for thought. The achievements of his work disclose themselves through his schema: the discovery of a domain that was worthy of thought, the commitment to the search for a very precise form of intelligibility, the elaboration of an ascetics for the methodological exercise of thought, and finally, in those last writings that are encompassed by the silence of death, the declaration of an ethical goal of dispossession.

The last experience of thought that Foucault elaborated as an escape from the prison of humanism was an ecstatic thinking, a characterization that may be understood provisionally as a designation for two transitions. First, it acknowledges a double movement of his thought in his last works: a transition to issues both of ethical subjectivity and of individual conduct, as well as a transfer of research from the modern period to the classical and early Christian eras. The occasion for this shift was his study of Christian experience. The first section of this chapter, "On Christian Experience," focuses on the context and content of this study, which would have been the substance of the announced fourth volume in his history of sexuality,

Confessions of the Flesh. Respecting Foucault's own wishes, this unfinished volume will never appear. A brief review of his understanding of Christianity will give a clearer insight into why Foucault's final work evolved in the way it did. The second and more important dimension constituting Foucault's ecstatic thinking is his effort to pass beyond the modern mode of being a subject. This movement will be the focal point for our other two sections. "The Politics of Ourselves" delineates Foucault's archaeology of the Freudian hermeneutical subject; this Freudian subject exemplified the modern form of relating to the self. This archaeology was the precondition for the ecstatic thinking that will be explicitly treated in our last section. It explores the experience of thinking that makes comprehensible the strange maxim at which Foucault's path concluded, his counsel to get free of oneself.

It is the unusual character of both ecstatic thinking and its maxim that accounts for some of the harsh responses that have marked the reception of Foucault's last writings. Two recent voices may be cited as representative of this large chorus of critics. Maria Daraki writes of his study on Greek ethics: "It is not a question of 'errors' of scholarship. Foucault is a hard-working and well-informed writer. It is, rather, a question of this tragic blindness the Greeks called *Ate* which takes hold of a man like a *daimon*. Foucault's *daimon* is a fantasm of dominating narcissism which demands the sacrifice of all facts." Richard Wolin argues that "Foucault's position ultimately becomes indistinguishable from that of a narcissistic child who deems 'maturity' in all its form simply repressive."[7] What are we to make of such a style of criticism? Having wondered for several years about the violent reactions Foucault evokes, I have come to conclude that his work, especially its last stage, exposed an especially sensitive area of contemporary consciousness, not only its reluctance to think differently, but more important, its sacralization of the modern experience of the self. This experience functions as a refuge from a world and a history that are grasped as fatally determined. Foucault's uncovering of the early processes from which the experience of the self derives, and his call to abandon that experience, affronted not only a philosophical position but a love, a self-love, that survives in a culture that has lost its way intellectually, politically, and morally. The charges of narcissism against a thinker who proclaims the need for a freedom from our current relations to the self are a subterfuge meant to conceal a narcissistic attachment to an experience of the person, which Foucault's entire work attempted to subvert. If his earlier declaration of the "death of man" was tolerable, it is because it was directed at forces that could still be considered as somehow extrinsic to the self; the ecstatic renunciation of the modern relation to the self, which is announced in Foucault's last writings, was unacceptable because all too many in his audience have only that relation as an imagined last barrier to nihilism.

1. ON CHRISTIAN EXPERIENCE

While there had been scattered remarks on Christian themes in his earlier studies, it was only with his investigation of normalization and sexuality that Christian experience became an explicit focus of Foucault's work. At first this focus was totally subordinated to other interests. His 1975 course at the Collège, which was a transition from the study of the prison, sought to grasp how the general domain of abnormality was opened up for a psychiatric understanding. Foucault laid the responsibility for this development on the articulation of sexuality as a dimension within all abnormality, and, most important, on the necessity for each individual to avow a sexual identity. His effort to analyze the conditions accounting for the appearance of this obligatory avowal of sexuality encouraged him to study the Christian practice of confession. Confession was a topic that Ivan Illich had once recommended to him for examination, and that Foucault had mentioned in his inaugural address at the Collège in the context of a possible investigation of its role in the functioning of the "taboo system" involved with the language of sexuality.[8] Neither his 1975 course nor the first volume of his history of sexuality entailed a turning from modernity itself as Foucault's field of interest. His initial examination of confession concentrated on its practice after the Council of Trent (1545–1563), and the expansion of this "millennial yoke of confession" to ever-larger numbers of relationships in the period after the Reformation.[9] Despite this modern perspective, Foucault came to the insight that would motivate a more intense study of Christian writers, and ultimately of ethical self-formation: "Now we must ask what happened in the sixteenth century. The period which is characterized not by the beginning of a dechristianisation but by the beginning of a christianisation-in-depth."[10]

It was a very circuitous route that led him to an investigation of early Christianity's experience of the subject, a route barely suggested by Foucault's own accounts.[11] As I have already indicated, Foucault first sketched the plan of a multi-volume history of sexuality in the context of an analysis of modern bio-politics, which designated those forces that "brought life and its mechanisms into the realm of explicit calculations and made knowledge-power an agent of transformation of human life."[12] In the emergence of this bio-politics, sexuality was a crucial domain because it was located at the pivot of the two axes along which Foucault saw the power over life developing: access to both the individual body and the social body.[13] The titles of the projected volumes in the series on sexuality indicated the direction he intended to pursue in exploring the constitution of modern "sexuality."[14] In the years immediately following the publication of the history of sexuality's introductory volume, Foucault's research roamed across a field of topics closely related to the issues of the projected last volume, *Population and Races*. This projected study was to examine both how the sexual domain became an object for ever-increasing state intervention and the emergence of eugenics and theories of race in the contemporary configuration of knowledge. In 1976 he taught a course on the appearance of a discourse on war and how it functioned as an analysis of social relations; in 1978 and 1979, he presented courses on the genesis of a political rationality that placed the notion of population and the mechanisms to assure its regulation at the center of its concern, and he conducted seminars on the theory of police science and on the juridical thought of the nineteenth century.[15] Despite the variety, however, a special concern took shape that oriented Foucault's approach to the study of Christianity. He became preoccupied with the problematic of governance that appeared in the sixteenth century and that showed itself in the development and dissemination of discourses on personal conduct, on the art of directing souls, and on the manner of educating children. This intensified Foucault's exploration of the crisis of the Reformation and Counter-Reformation, which provoked in that period an anxiety over the matter of governance by putting in "question the manner in which one is to be spiritually ruled and led on this earth to achieve eternal salvation."[16] The exploration of the knowledge-power relations involved in governance directed him to an analysis of the Christian pastorate, and thus to a confrontation with the ethical formation critical to its way of obtaining knowledge and exercising power.

The first major statement of the results of his research in premodern Christian experience came with his course "On the Governance of the Living," which he presented in 1980. The prelude for this course was his series of two lectures at Stanford University in late 1979, and its discoveries were refined in later courses, lectures, and publications.[17] Foucault's reading of the Christian experience was selective, but it was decisive in expanding his horizon beyond modernity, and especially beyond power-knowledge relations, to include subjectivity. In his 1980 course, Foucault presented this new regime against the background of an opening meditation on Sophocles's *Oedipus*, in which he followed the objective construction of the king's true identity by the authorized voices of others, voices that terminated the search for truth. Christianity put forward a far different search, one that embraced different forms of power, knowledge, and relation to self. It is the continuing vitality of variations on each of these that justifies Foucault's claim of a "christianisation-in-depth" throughout the modern period.

A) POWER

Christian experience represents the development of a new form of individualizing power, that of the pastorate, which has its roots in the Hebraic image of God and his deputed King as shepherds. This power is productive, not repressive. Exercising authority over a flock of dispersed individuals rather than a land, the shepherd has the duty to guide his charges to salvation by continuously watching over them and by a permanent concern with their well-being as individuals. Christianity intensifies this concern by having the pastors assume a responsibility for all the good and evil done by those to whom they are accountable and whose actions reflect upon their quality as shepherds.[18] Paramount in the exercise of this pastoral power is a virtue of obedience in the subject, a virtue that becomes an end in itself. "It is a permanent state; the sheep must permanently submit to their pastors: *subditi*. As Saint Benedict says, monks do not live according to their own free will; their wish is to be under the abbot's command."[19] Such obedience is the necessary antidote to the condition of the human being after Adam's Fall. With the Fall, the original subordination that human nature accorded to soul and will was lost, and the human being became a figure of revolt not only against God but also against himself. This situation was graphically illustrated in the lawlessness of the sexual yearnings.

> The famous gesture of Adam covering his genitals with a fig leaf is, according to Augustine, not due to the simple fact that Adam was ashamed of their presence, but to the fact that his sexual organs were moving by themselves without his consent. Sex in erection is the image of man revolted against God. The arrogance of sex is the punishment and consequence of the arrogance of man. His uncontrolled sex is exactly the same as what he himself has been toward God—a rebel.[20]

This seditious sexuality signals the need for a struggle with one's self, and permanent obedience is essential to this struggle. The obedience that is intrinsic to the exercise and responsibilities of pastoral power involves specific forms of knowledge and of subjectivity.

B) KNOWLEDGE

In order to fulfill the responsibility of directing souls to their salvation, the pastor must understand the truth, not just the general truths of faith but the specific truths of each person's soul. For Foucault, Christianity is unique in the major truth obligations that are imposed upon its followers. In addition to accepting moral and dogmatic truths, they must also become excavators of their own personal truth: "Everyone in Christianity has the duty to explore who he is, what is happening within himself, the faults he may have committed, the temptations to which he is exposed."[21] Perhaps the most dramatic illustration of this obligation to discover and manifest one's truth took place in those liturgical ceremonies in which the early Christians would avow their state as sinners, and then take on the status of public penitents.[22] Less dramatic but more enduring was the search for truth served by those practices of examination of conscience and confession that Christianity first developed in monastic life. This search entailed a permanent struggle with the Evil One, who "hides behind seeming likenesses of oneself" and whose mode of action in the person is error.[23] The Christian campaign for self-knowledge was not developed directly in the interest of controlling sexual conduct, but rather for the sake of a deepened awareness of one's interior life. "Cassian is interested in the movements of the body and the mind, images, feelings, memories, faces in dreams, the spontaneous movements of thoughts, the consenting (or refusing) will, waking and sleeping."[24] Foucault was fond of citing three comparisons that Cassian employed to portray the process of spiritual self-scrutiny. It is compared with the work of a miller who must sort out the good and bad grains before admitting them to the millstone of thought; another likens it to the responsibility of a centurion who must evaluate his soldiers in order to assign them to their proper tasks; finally, one must be like a money changer who studies the coins presented to him in order to judge those that are authentic from those that are not.[25] All of these affirm the rigorous self-analysis to which Christian practice was committed, as well as anticipating modern recourse to a hermeneutics of suspicion. In addition, this endless task of self-doubt is accompanied by regular confessions to another, for verbalization of thoughts is another level of sorting out the good thoughts from those that are evil, namely, those that seek to hide from the light of public expression.[26] Through its examination of conscience and confession, Christianity fashions a technology of the self that enabled people to transform themselves.[27] The principal product of this technology was a unique form of subjectivity.

C) SUBJECTIVITY

Within Christianity, there has taken place an interiorization or subjectivization of the human being, an event that Foucault locates as the outcome of two processes. The first is the constitution of the self as a hermeneutical reality, namely, the recognition that there is a truth in the subject, that the soul is the place where this truth resides, and that true discourses can be articulated concerning it.[28] The Christian self is an obscure text demanding permanent interpretation through ever more sophisticated practices of attentiveness, concern, decipherment, and verbalization. The second process is both paradoxical and yet essential for appreciating the unique mode of Christian subjectivity. The deciphering of one's soul is but one dimension of the subjectivity that relates the self to the self. While it involves an "indeterminate objectivization of the self by the self-indeterminate in the sense that one must be forever extending as far as possible the range of one's thoughts, however insignificant and innocent they may appear to be," the point of such objectivization is not to assemble a progressive knowledge of oneself for the sake of achieving the self-mastery that classical pagan thought advanced as an ideal.[29] The purpose of the Christian hermeneutic of the self is to foster renunciation of the self who has been objectified. The individual's relation to the self imitates both the baptismal turning from the old self to a new-found otherness, as well as the ceremony of public penance that was depicted as a form of martyrdom proclaiming the symbolic death of the old self. The continual mortification entailed by a permanent hermeneutic and renunciation of the self makes of that symbolic death an everyday event. All truth about the self is tied to the sacrifice of that same self, and the Christian experience of subjectivity declares itself most clearly in the sounds of a rupture with oneself, of an admission that "I am not who I am."[30] This capacity for self-renunciation was built from the ascetic power with regard to oneself that was generated by a practice of obedience, and from the skepticism with respect to one's knowledge of oneself that was created by hermeneutical self-analysis. Foucault's interpretation of Christian experience and his recognition of these two processes decisively shaped the major themes and interests of his last work: first, his project of a historical ontology of ourselves with its genealogy of the man of desire; second, his vision of a contemporary philosophical ethos. These form the substances of our next two sections.

2. THE POLITICS OF OURSELVES

In Foucault's first volume of the history of sexuality, with its recognition of bio-politics, he already recognized the key role that sexuality exercises in the modern deployment of power-knowledge. The most graphic example he gave of how this power operated for an individual was found in the memoirs of a nineteenth-century hermaphrodite, Herculine Barbin, a document Foucault published in 1978 and on which he wrote an essay two years later.[31] Upon her birth in 1838, Barbin was baptized as a girl and lived with that status for the next twenty years. Then she found herself subjected to new and precise categories of a single, true sexual identity, with the result that a civil court decreed a change of gender status and of name for her; on June 22, 1860, Mademoiselle Herculine became Monsieur Abel. Although the local newspapers carried sensational reports on the reaction of her small town to the shocking transformation of its schoolmistress, they were generally sympathetic to her plight for, as the papers pointed out, she had "lived piously and modestly until today in ignorance of herself."[32] Despite the sympathy, it can hardly come as a surprise that eight years later, his-her corpse was discovered, a suicide, or rather, to Foucault's mind, the victim of a new passion for the truth of sexual identity.

And yet not totally new. In the light of his study of Christianity, Foucault saw that Barbin's fate was tied to a "demonic" transformation of that Christian pastorship whose elements are "life, death, truth, obedience, individuals, self-identity."[33] Far from diminishing with the decline of its ecclesiastical institutionalization, pastoral power spread and multiplied within the modern state, which may itself be understood as a "new form of pastoral power."[34] Although its aims may have become worldly, the effect of state power is to mold a precise kind of individuality with which one's desire is incited to identify. If sexuality is most often the "seismograph" of that identity, it is because the legacy of the Christian technology of the self is to have linked "sexuality, subjectivity and truth" together as the terrain for self-discovery.[35] Foucault's realization of that triad's existence had two immediate effects on the way he articulated his own project. First, he particularized political struggle in terms of what he called a "politics of ourselves."[36] In addition to resistance against forms of domination and types of exploitation, politics necessarily entails combat with a pastoral power that "categorizes the individual, marks him by his own individuality, attaches him to his own identity, imposes a law of truth on him which he must recognize," and that "makes individuals subjects." Because of the pastoral functioning of state power, present political struggles must "revolve around the question: Who are we? They are a refusal of these abstractions, of economic and ideological state violence that ignores who we are individually, and also a refusal of a scientific or administrative inquisition which determines who one is." If one side of this resistance is to "refuse what we are," the other side is to invent, and not discover, who we are by promoting "new forms of subjectivity."[37] The second effect on Foucault's articulation of the project derives from the first. It is because he conceives of the political issue as a politics of ourselves that the practice of ethics becomes central to his last work, an ethics "understood as the elaboration of a form of relation to self that enables an individual to fashion himself into a subject of ethical conduct."[38] It does not represent an abandonment of his interest in politics, but rather is an effort to get at a form of becoming a subject that would furnish the source of an effective resistance to a specific and widespread type of power. This is why he was able to speak of his final concerns in terms of "politics as an ethics."[39] The prelude to the practice of an ethics that is politically effective is a defamiliarization of the "desiring man" who lies at the root of our willingness to identity with the form of individual subjectivity constructed for us in the modern period. Thus, one of the central enterprises of the second and third volumes in his history of sexuality was to "investigate how individuals were led to practice, on themselves and on others, a hermeneutics of desire," and to "analyze the practices by which individuals were led to focus their attention on themselves, to decipher, recognize, and acknowledge themselves as subjects of desire, bringing into play between themselves and themselves a certain relationship that allows them to discover, in desire, the truth of their being, be it natural or fallen."[40]

Such a project is an "historical ontology of ourselves," an investigation of how we have been fashioned as ethical subjects. While the domain of such a study is ethics, its aim is to sustain a form of resistance to newly recognized political forces.[41]

The significance and form of Foucault's history of the man of desire are best grasped if the history is understood in the context of its contribution to his "archaeology of psychoanalysis"; the objective of this latter project was to undermine modern anthropology and the notion of the self that was one of its firmest supports and expressions.[42] Freud's understanding is a model of this notion, and thus becomes the principal target of Foucault's effort to render the self freshly problematic. The failure to recognize the confrontation with Freud that is taking place in Foucault's last works has often prevented commentators from appreciating his intentions and organization in these writings, most especially with regard to their central history of the man of desire. Foucault's dialogue with Freud and psychoanalysis continued throughout his career; a brief account of it entails returning to points made in earlier chapters. In the context of his treatment of the way madness was reduced to the empty, inauthentic speech of mental illness in the modern asylum and in psychiatry, Foucault nevertheless acknowledges Freud's greatest achievement. Freud's work brought the "violence of a return," for in place of the asylum's cult of observation, he returned to madness at the level of its language, so radically different from everyday speech. He was the "first to undertake the radical erasure of the division between . . . the normal and the pathological, the comprehensible and the communicable, the significant and the non-significant." Freud's accomplishment, and thus his "scandal" for psychology and psychiatry, was his challenge to their anthropology, their grasp of human being as a "homo psychologicus" who was positive in his self-consciousness.[43] In the first volume of his later history of sexuality, Foucault paid tribute to the opposition that psychoanalysis maintained against the "political and institutional effects of the perversion-heredity-degenerescence system" that was allied with a state-directed racism.[44] Despite these achievements, however, Freud and psychoanalysis remain exemplary of the system from which Foucault sought escape. Taking Foucault's own mention of Sophocles' *Oedipus* in his 1980 course as a clue, I wish to indicate how his history of the man of desire is the last stage in his subversion of the psychoanalytic vision of the person.

Freud's interpretation of the play is familiar. For him, Oedipus's search for the truth "can be likened to the work of a psychoanalysis." One relentlessly pursues the truth of one's identity, which is hidden far from one's conscious awareness and shows itself as tied to the dimension of desire and sexuality. The story possesses perennial appeal because we recognize ourselves in Oedipus. As Freud points out: "His destiny moves us—because the oracle laid the same curse upon us before our birth as upon him."[45] Perhaps the myth would attract Foucault because it portrays so well the major domains of his own work: an analysis of the branches of knowledge through which we are constructed as knowable and from which we derive the paths for fleeing self-ignorance; an examination of the power relations generated with this knowledge and of the systems of dependence to which we become subject in seeking our truth; finally, a study of how subjectivity became intimately associated with both truth and sexuality, how the discovery of one's true sex is the discovery of one's true self. In Foucault's earlier writing, the archaeology of psychoanalysis involved an identification of its general power-knowledge relations, especially its relationship to a medical model and its notion of the unconscious; in the first volume of his history of sexuality, it entailed a critique of the place psychoanalysis occupies in the modern deployment of sexuality; finally, his history of the man of desire excavates the relationship of the self to the self that operates in Freudian thought. I shall briefly touch on the first two stages.

While Freud admitted that psychoanalysis "had its origin on medical soil," he had hoped that it could be transplanted.[46] Foucault's *Birth of the Clinic* indicated, however, that modern readings of the person are tied to a medical perception. The work argued that clinical medicine was the first science of the individual. Integral to this science was the role of death as constitutive of one's individuality and unique intelligibility, a status that was the precondition for the extraordinary importance given by historians to pathological anatomy in the development of a science of medicine. Death and disease broke away from metaphysical understanding and became essential elements in the identity of the person. The idea of a disease attacking life and destroying it is replaced by the concept that death is embodied in the living bodies of individuals. It is not because diseases attack him that man dies; it is because he will die that he is susceptible to disease. Developed here was the crucially significant notion of a "pathological life" that can be carefully charted and analyzed in terms of an *individual's* existence. But death is the essential truth of human life, and any inquiry into the meaning of individual life will necessarily meet the medical perception that holds up to man the "face of his finitude," but that also promises to exorcise it through certain techniques.[47] The medical component is clear in questions of sexuality, but if Foucault is correct, all knowledge of the modern finite, bound-to-death self is oriented, by its very object, to aim at a truth that aspires to function as cure. This would explain why Freud, who could demystify so many of the asylum's major structures—its constant silence, observation, condemnation—could not eliminate the place occupied by the doctor, upon whom these transformed structures were concentrated: the trained observer whose silence is judgment. It is the very knowledge of our finite, individual selves that invites a medical paradigm and accounts for the fact that in our culture, Freud and medical thought have come to take on philosophical significance.[48] The controversies that swirl around the relationship between medicine and psychoanalysis are native and permanent to Freudian thought to the extent of its modernity. Foucault's *Order of Things* extended his archaeology of psychoanalysis by indicating the foundations for the specific character of the unconscious that is at the core of psychoanalytic self-knowledge. Psychoanalysis occupies a central position in modern thought because it explores, but is also defined by, an opaqueness or unconsciousness generated by modern knowledge's dispersion of man within processes of life, labor, and language. All of these possess histories alien to and independent of man. The themes of Death, Desire, and Law, in which one's psychoanalytic search for intelligibility take place, are born together with and remain dependent upon modern knowledge's drawing of man in those great colors of life, labor, speech. In exploring these psychoanalytic themes, western culture is brought back to the foundations for its anthropological knowledge, and thus, as Foucault points out, "pivots on the work of Freud, though without, for all that, leaving its fundamental arrangement."[49]

The central role sexuality plays in the psychoanalytic image of the person is the next major element indicating the coherence of Freudian thought with the modern network of knowledge-power. Psychoanalysis is in alliance with the modern period's threefold sexual production: the creation of sexuality as a reality, especially the sexualization of children's experience; the constitution of a *scientia sexualis* based on global study of the population and analytic study of the individual; and the privileging of sexuality as the access to the truth of human identity. The "cultural vigor" of psychoanalysis is at the "junction of these two ideas—that we must not deceive ourselves concerning our sex, and that our sex harbors what is most true in ourselves."[50] Despite its greater subtlety, psychoanalysis operates within the modern regime of sexuality, and even intensifies it. It gives support to the conception of sex as a stubborn drive, constantly at war with repressive powers; psychoanalysis, therefore, obscures the positive function of power as productive of what we take the sexual realm and its themes to be. And for Foucault, this is the case, whether the psychoanalytic approach is conducted according to a theory of instincts or in terms of how the law itself constitutes the nature of sexual desire. In addition, psychoanalysis unifies the system of the family with the modern sphere of sexuality by placing the incest desire at the center of the individual's sexual life. Freud cooperates in constituting the family as a privileged target for political governance in that it is transformed into the "germ of all the misfortunes of sex." Finally, psychoanalysis provides one of the most striking examples in the modern transformation of pastoral power. It has taken over the techniques of confessional practice, and thus places the individual under the obligation of manifesting truth to another in a situation of dependence and through the action of speech, which is invested with a special virtue of verification.[51]

The greatest support for the psychoanalytic project is provided by a special relationship that the self takes up with itself, namely, that sexuality is the index of one's subjectivity, of one's true self. The kinship of subjectivity-truth-sexuality is the lynchpin of Freudian thought. The capacity of sexual desires and deeds to become the most revealing signs of our truest, deepest selves is dependent upon a long historical formation through which we were created as subjects in a special relation to both truth and sex. I have already indicated that their actual historical fusion is, for Foucault, a legacy of Christian experience. That experience, however, is the last of the three moments in early western culture's constitution of this kinship. Foucault's final two volumes study the first two moments in the construction of western subjectivity, the cultures of classical Greece and the later Graeco-Roman period. The initial interrogation of the "man of desire" grew from the soil of Greek ethics. The central problematic of this pre-Platonic ethic was the proper use of pleasures so that one could achieve the mastery over oneself that made one fit to be a free citizen and worthy to exercise authority over others. Each of the great arts of Greek conduct of the self involved with sexual matters—dietetics, economics, and erotics—was characterized by a program of moderation. Dietetics directed a moderation that recognized the special anxiety provoked by the use of sexual pleasures, pleasures that were experienced as perilous because they entailed violence to the body and encounter with death as well as the transmission of life. Economics guided a man's training in self-mastery by regulating his conduct with his wife in the interest of the hierarchical structure appropriate to the sphere of the household.[52] Foucault exposes the earliest pre-history of modern subjectivity in his consideration of erotics, the Greek art of love.

At the center of this art was the special relationship in that culture between the older male, who was an active participant in the city, and the young male who was still dependent upon others for his educational formation. While sexual relations between the two were fully accepted, this acceptance was not at all a simple matter, and Foucault points to much evidence that indicates a persistent uneasiness about the relationship: an oscillation between what was thought natural and unnatural; a clear reticence in speaking about these sexual relations as well as a reluctance to concede that the younger male might experience pleasure through them; the relationship was also explicitly subordinated to the nonsexual friendship that should be its eventual outcome.[53] The complexity of Greek erotics is partially due to the fact that unlike dietetics and economics, in which a man's moderation was rooted in his relationship to himself, the love between the older and younger male implied a moderation by both, and the alliance of these moderations in a mutual respect for the other's freedom. The principal source of the relationship's complexity, and of the elaborate courtship practice and moral reflection that surrounded it, was what Foucault describes as the problem of the "antinomy of the boy" in the Greek ethics of the use of pleasure.[54]

While adolescent boys were recognized as legitimate objects of pleasure, their youth was also a period of trial during which they learned the dishonor of conducting themselves passively. The adolescent free male was expected to train himself to assume his freedom through an exercise of self-control in order to prove his capacity to govern others. Sexual relations were conceived in terms of the fundamental act of penetration, and so were regarded as exhibiting a polarity between positively valued active and negatively viewed passive forms of conduct. Inasmuch as there was an isomorphism between sexual and political relations, the youth's training in the conduct appropriate for a free, active citizen was morally at variance with any relationship that would make him a passive object of pleasure: "But while the boy, because of his peculiar charm, could be a prey that men might pursue without causing a scandal or a problem, one had to keep in mind that the day would come when he would have to be a man, to exercise powers and responsibilities, so that obviously he could then no longer be an object of pleasure—but then, to what extent could he *have been* such an object?"[55]

It is clear that the moral preoccupation of the Greeks with this relationship interrogated neither the nature nor the subject of the desire that inclined an individual to the relationship. The movement to that form of questioning came only with the Socratic-Platonic reflection on love itself, which endeavored to resolve the problematic of the antinomy of the boy. The ethics of the use of pleasure involved a form of knowledge that guided a person's moderation, either in terms of a structural form of knowledge, which declared the supremacy of reason over desire, or in terms of an instrumental form of knowledge that gave practical directions for using pleasure. With Plato, however, a third form of knowledge is introduced, the "need to know oneself in order to practice virtue and subdue the desires." Foucault calls this the "ontological recognition of the self by the self," which represents a new rapport between truth and the self.[56] What creates this rapport and the displacement of the moral problematic of male courtship by a preoccupation with truth and the effort to achieve it is a series of philosophical transformations, to which Plato's *Symposium* and *Phaedrus* give witness. There is a transformation of the earlier culture's deontological question about what is proper conduct by an ontological investigation into the very nature and origin of love. Questions about the one who is loved are replaced by those that inquire about the one who loves and what he knows about the being of love. A second transformation is from a concern with the honor of the boy to the issue of the lover's love for the truth, which enables him to distinguish the good from the bad forms of love. Third, there is a shift from the difficult moral problem posed by a dissymmetry of partners to the notion of a convergence in a true love that transcends and draws them toward each other: "unlike what occurs in the art of courtship, the 'dialectic of love' in this case calls for two movements exactly alike on the part of the two lovers; the love is the same for both of them, since it is the motion which carries them toward truth."[57] Finally, inasmuch as eros is drawn to the true, it is the one who has moved farthest along the road to truth who becomes the central figure in the love relationship. A dramatic reversal takes place: the master of truth comes to take the place of the lover, and the love of the master, as in the relationship of youths to Socrates, becomes dominant over the previous concern with the virtue of the boy.

While this philosophical erotics emerged from the problematic of the earlier Greek ethics, it also signals a major step beyond it. The soul's effort to progress in truth and love demands a novel interrogation about the being of its desire and about the true being that is the object of that desire. With his erotics, Plato broke the ground for the development of an inquiry into desiring man that would lead in time to the Christian hermeneutics of the self. Foucault briefly studied the transition to the latter in the third volume of his history of sexuality, the formation of a culture of the self in the reflections of the moralists, philosophers, and doctors in the first two centuries of our era.

This epoch sees major transitions in each of the Greek arts of self-conduct that Foucault examined. Roman dietetics operates within a context of increased medical concern with the body's pleasures, not merely with respect to the possibility of their immoderate use, but also in their very nature. This tendency to pathologization emphasizes the particular danger that one's self could be carried along passively by the demands of the body and the extravagance of desire in general. In economics, the relationships between men and women take on a greater reciprocity, and new emphases are placed on one's duties to others. In erotics, there is a transfer to marriage of the traits that had been restricted to the friendship among males.[58] What is most significant for Foucault in the period of the empire, however, is the context for these transitions: that culture's intensification of the self's interest in its relation to itself, and the establishment of the theme of "care of the self" at the center of moral preoccupation. The emergence of what

Foucault calls the Roman "culture of the self" is rooted in the obligation its citizens felt themselves under to define new relations with the self. They felt the pressure of this obligation for two principal reasons. First, the greater prevalence and significance of marriage as an institution required an elaboration of the self in the new context of affective relations between the sexes. More important was a new problematization of political activity. There was a need for the Roman citizen to clarify more fully his understanding of himself, for that self was challenged by an historically unparalled multiplicity of potential identities and conflicts created by imperial offices held, powers exercised, and responsibilities shouldered.[59]

The care of the self that responded to this new sense of the fragility of the individual was not just a vague concern but entailed an ensemble of diverse occupations and exercises directed to a more exact grasp of the self. The programs for the scrutiny of consciousness, methodical meditation on and written articulation of the self, developed in such movements as the Epicureans and Stoics, were aimed at the reinforcement of the rational self-control that promised a perfect government of the self, and thus wise social conduct.[60] For Foucault, these practices, establishing a Roman government of the self, may be thought of as a sort of "permanent political relationship between self and self," or a "politics of themselves."[61] While the technology generated by a care of the self served the interests of self-mastery, it also testified to a new pleasure that the culture found in the very experience of the self. Concern with it was a "privilege-duty, a gift-obligation."[62] Despite the intensification of self-examination, however, Roman culture did not issue in a need for a hermeneutics of the self, because it did not fashion the self as an obscure text that required deciphering. Its interest was not in the discovery of the hidden and the unspoken, but rather with a constitution of the self according to a set of rational principles that are apprehended as rules for personal conduct. The techniques of self-examination and self-expression in this culture of the self aimed at a collection of principles that have been forgotten, and that, through meditation, have the power to transform the self so as to make it a more efficient administrator of the self.[63] Nevertheless, this form of care of the self was a transition from the unique relation of the self to truth in Greek experience to the later Christian hermeneutics of the self. This hermeneutics brought to a culmination the earliest development of the western man of desire whose reality was taken over by the modern period and forms the model for its quest of self-knowledge.

Freud's interpretation of Oedipus exemplifies that model of self-knowledge. Having solved the riddle of the Sphinx with the answer "man," Oedipus remains ignorant of his own identity. It is an ignorance that can be erased, however, for there exists a knowledge that will tell him who he is, once he assumes responsibility to seek his secret self, to become a subject to the truth by dependence upon a master of truth. The program for self-knowledge, embraced as a vehicle for discovering one's uniqueness, becomes a mere reenactment of the power-knowledge-subjectivity relations in modern culture. A quest for freedom gets diverted into a series of illusory liberations from repression. Although Foucault never presented the long history that led from antiquity and early Christianity to the modern subject, it is important to realize that along with its appropriation of an earlier technology of the self, the modern age also fundamentally changed the relation to the subject that that other age produced. Foucault's work already indicated the necessity for such a difference, because the earlier self is related to a sexual domain that cannot be identified with modern sexuality. The experience of love's pleasures or the self's desires, with both their dangers and illuminations, is radically distinct from the view of sexuality as a stubborn drive, forced to confront real or imaginary repressions. For Foucault, there were also two especially significant distortions for the subject. As opposed to both the Greek and Roman periods, the modern subject was fashioned in isolation from ethical and aesthetic concerns; truth itself becomes the uncontested ruler of human life. This tyranny of the scientific was strengthened by modernity's rejection of the cardinal element in Christian asceticism. Christian practices involved a renunciation of the self who was articulated. For the Christian, the truths of the self were always precarious, for they always related to the soul's continual conflict with the evil within itself. There could be no firm allegiance to a positive self, for there was no truth about the self that could not be utilized by the False One as a device for misleading and ensnaring the soul. Thus, the Christian always practiced a renunciation of the self who was articulated, a renunciation that mirrored, as I pointed out, the death to the self in baptism or martyrdom. The aim of modern knowledge and technologies of the self, however, is to foster the emergence of a positive self; one recognizes and attaches oneself to a self made available through the categories of psychological and psycho-analytic science, and through the normative disciplines consistent with them. Thus, as was the case with Oedipus, we become victims of our own self-knowledge. For Foucault, this is an event of supreme political importance, because this victimization fashions the potentially transgressive dimension of the person into but another element of the disciplinary matrix that *SP* had described as the carceral archipelago. If the struggle with this modern power-knowledge-subjectivity formation is a politics of our selves, the key campaign in that struggle will be a new mode of fashioning an ethical way of being a self.

3. ECSTATIC THINKING

Although it was only in his last writings that Foucault dealt explicitly with ethics, the ethical interest was decisive for his thought, from his first work thirty years earlier. I have already indicated this origin: in commenting on Binswanger's notion of the dream, Foucault claimed that dreams exhibit the essential meaning of human being to be a "radical liberty," the movement of existence that is the matrix within which self and world, subject and object make their appearance. Dream experience cannot be separated from its ethical content: "not because it may uncover secret inclinations, inadmissible desires, not because it may release the whole flock of instincts," but because it "restores the movement of freedom in its authentic meaning, showing how it establishes itself or alienates itself, how it constitutes itself as radical responsibility in the world, or how it forgets itself and abandons itself to its plunge into causality."[64] He evaluated psychology as a human science in terms of whether it achieved the proper goal of promoting the ill person's victory over the alienation that had made him a stranger to the reality of liberty, which he essentially is, and an outsider to the historical drama that is the stage for human fulfillment.[65] Foucault preserves his ethical interest through his other writings by restoring to the historical field what modernity had proclaimed as natural, and by approaching power and knowledge in terms not of what they are but rather of what they do. In examining the force of knowledge-power relations, Foucault came to appreciate that the description of the human being as a radical liberty was incorrect, because "man does not begin with liberty but with the limit."[66] He also appreciated that such a recognition need not lead to an abandonment of ethics itself, because the encounter with those limits created the opportunity for their transgression, for an ecstacy in both thought and action.

While Foucault's study of sexuality, and of Christianity in particular, opened up the domain of ethics for explicit consideration, two events in the political realm motivated a concentration on ethics, events that were more significant for him than the election of a French Socialist government in 1981. The first was the Iranian Revolution of 1978–79. His initially sympathetic view of it and its creators evoked sharp criticism in many French circles when the overthrow of the Shah was followed by new executions and oppressions. In reply to this criticism, Foucault refused to dismiss the moral achievement of the revolution when the political order inaugurated a new terror. He described his ethics as "antistrategic," as not reducible to the question of political success: "In the end, there is no explanation for the man who revolts. His action is necessarily a tearing that breaks the thread of history and its long chains of reasons so that a man can genuinely give preference to the risk of death over the certitude of having to obey."[67] This specific discrimination of the ethical was promoted by the emergence of the Solidarity movement in Poland, where Foucault had lived in 1958 and whose fortunes he followed closely in the years after. The suppression of the movement and the weak response of western governments to it encouraged him to recognize the political necessity for an ethics:

> If we raise the question of Poland in strictly political terms, it is clear that we can quickly reach the point of saying that there's nothing we can do. We can't dispatch a team of paratroopers, and we can't send armored cars to liberate Warsaw. I think that, politically, we have to recognize this, but I think that we also agree that, for ethical reasons, we have to raise the problem of Poland in the form of a nonacceptance of what is happening there, and a nonacceptance of the passivity of our own governments. I think that this attitude is an ethical one, but it is also political; it does not consist in saying merely, "I protest," but in making of that attitude a political phenomenon that is as substantial as possible, and one which those who govern, here or there, will sooner or later be obliged to take into account.[68]

Foucault's own treatment of ethical life aimed to have a similar impact on those discourses that govern our approaches to good and evil.

The schema he proposes for an analysis of ethical life mirrors the strangeness and effect of the passage from Borges on the Chinese definition of animals that opened *The Order of Things*: it wishes to shatter "all the familiar landmarks of my thought—*our* thought, the thought that bears the stamp of our age and our geography—breaking up all the ordered surfaces and all the planes with which we are accustomed to tame the wild profusion of existing things."[69] Foucault's model for an analysis of ethics in terms of the four distinct levels of ethical substance, mode of subjection, ethical work, and telos was foreshadowed by his delineation of the Christian pastorate's transformation of Hebraic themes of power.[70] It was provoked, however, by his realization that a history of moral codes or of the ways they were followed would not reach the more subtle level on which individuals fashion themselves as subjects of moral conduct, and thus as desirous of a certain code and of conformity to it. On the level of codes, western moralities betrayed an overwhelming similarity. The differences among them were disclosed by interrogating other levels of moral experience: What is regarded as the prime material of moral conduct (determination of ethical substance)? How does an individual establish his relation to a rule of conduct (mode of subjection)? What specific transformation of oneself is invited by an ethical commitment (ethical work)? At what mode of being does the ethical subject aim (telos)?[71] The posing of these questions to ancient and Christian experience uncovered a rich array of differences and modifications in each of the areas. The questions enabled Foucault himself to establish a distance from modernity's problematizing of morality in terms of a subject of knowledge dependent on science.[72] He was able to turn to ethics as the field of a liberty forming itself as a subjectivization, that is, a "process in which the individual delimits that part of himself that will form the object of his moral practice, defines his position relative to the precept he will follow, and decides on a certain mode of being that will serve as his moral goal. And this requires him to act upon himself, to monitor, test, improve, and transform himself."[73]

The task of self-formation that Foucault puts forward has a specificity that reflects his own commitments as an intellectual. He is not seeking a general form of morality applicable to all, but rather developing a particular style that emerges from the history of his own freedom and thought.[74] Although his ethics extracts significant elements from both classical and Christian moralities, this recourse represents neither an idealization of nor a return to the premodern. The elements he derives from earlier periods are integrated into a uniquely personal context, Foucault's effort to articulate himself as a moral thinker. In his last years, Foucault became more comfortable than he had been in the past with the profession of philosophy, and he proposed that his entire work be approached in terms of its ambition to be a philosophical ethos, a philosophy-as-life, a way of acting in the contemporary world that manifests both a way of belonging to it and a task within in.[75] This ethos is exhibited most prominently in the philosopher's mode of thinking, and a striking feature of Foucault's last period is the amount of attention he gives to a meditation on thought itself.[76] I believe that these meditations were initially prompted by a harsh challenge to the worth of his efforts. Hadn't works as such *Discipline and Punish* (*SP*), he was asked, had an anaesthetic effect on prison reformers, because there was an implacable logic to his critique that left no possible room for initiative? More generally, is it really important to think? Does criticism by intellectuals clear up anything?[77] Foucault's replies seek to redirect our expectations for thought away from either merely instrumental or grandly totalizing viewpoints on it. Thought should be subordinated neither to a government's social agenda, that "sacralization of the social," which has often turned thinking into a function of administration, nor to the ambition that demands of it a "subversion of all codes" or "overturning of all contemporary culture."[78] At the same time, he defends the achievements of his type of criticism: "I'll answer the claim that 'it did nothing.' There are hundreds and thousands of people who have worked toward the emergence of a certain number of problems, which today are actually being posed. To say that this did nothing is altogether wrong. Do you think that twenty years ago the problems of the relation between mental illness and psychological normality, the problem of the prison, the problem of medical power, the problem of the relations between the sexes, etc. , . . . were being posed as they are posed today?"[79] Complementary to this defense is a new effort by Foucault to integrate his historical researches with the issue of the subject who must act, who is incited by that research to transform the real. This effort is reflected in his vision of thought as an essentially ethical activity: "Thought is freedom in relation to what one does, the motion by which one detaches oneself from it, establishes it as an object, and reflects on it as a problem."[80]

Foucault's ethics is the practice of an intellectual freedom that may be described as an ecstatic thinking or a worldly mysticism. Religious mystics had created a domain for an experience of revelation that was free of the need to follow the theologically sanctioned routes for encounter with supernatural reality. Foucault's work has opened up a domain for the practice of a freedom that stands outside the humanistic program for the conduct of human life and inquiry in history. Although it may seem strange to employ the model of mysticism for Foucault's thought, it is not an arbitrary imposition on my part. The severe techniques he developed in his archaeological and genealogical methods of questioning, as ways of breaking the spell humanism had placed on the modern mind, reintroduced into the contemporary landscape of thought that negative theology that had "prowled the borderlands of Christianity" for a millennium.[81] Although Foucault never elaborated the analogy, negative theology was one of the few styles with which he explicitly compared his own thought.[82] His choice of the comparison is illuminating. It points first of all to Foucault's own experience of a fundamental personal conflict in his earlier intellectual interests as a "religious problem."[83] On the one hand, he was passionately involved in the new literary work of such writers as Georges Bataille and Maurice Blanchot, which for him displaced interest from a narrative of man to the being of the language within which images of the human are fashioned.[84] On the other hand, Foucault says he was attracted to the structuralist analysis carried out by the anthropologist Claude Lévi-Strauss and the historian of religion Georges Dumézil, both of whom dispersed human reality among cultural structures. That Foucault considers the religious problem as the common denominator for both interests indicates that all four thinkers, although in very different ways, unleashed styles of reflection and forms of experience that overturned for him the accepted natural identity of man. Foucault's negative theology is a critique not of the conceptualizations employed for God but of that modern figure of finite man whose identity was put forward as capturing the essence of human being. Nevertheless, Foucault's critical thinking is best described as a negative theology, rather than a negative anthropology, for its flight from man is an escape from yet another conceptualization of the Absolute. The project of modernity was an absolutization of man, the passion to be, as

Sartre saw, the *"Ens causa sui,* which religions call God."[85] Foucault explicitly recognized that Sartre's anthropology reflected a nineteenth-century portrayal of man as an incarnated God.[86] Foucault's negative theology is a subversion of that faith, an aim that permits us to appreciate its recourse to historical inquiry as a privileged mode of thought for him. Parallel to the death of God was an absolutization of man. Claiming a firm knowledge of this figure, humanism made humanity's happiness its ultimate goal, and human perfection its permanent project. The place for humanism's actualization, however, was not the order of the supernatural but rather that of the historical. In history, purpose and progress could be found and man's victory and beatitude achieved. Uniting the development of modern thought and practice, the order of time became the Sacred History of Man. The religion of the God Humanity, with its priesthood of scientific experts as advanced in Comte's positivist philosophy, is an integral element not only of that philosophy but of the logic of the modern age itself.[87] Faced with a sacred history constituted by man's revelation to himself of his ever-advancing perfection, Foucault has attempted to demythologize the historical reality in which the modern identity of man and the sources of his humanistic knowledges are lodged. That demythologization required more than an act of will; it demanded the ascetic methods for achieving a thought free of anthropology that Foucault developed, most especially in *The Archaeology of Knowledge.* In the light of his last works, it is clear that this asceticism served a greater liberation.

The negative theology that characterized the asceticism of Foucault's methods was a prelude to his conception of the philosophical life itself. He embraced Kant's definition of Enlightenment as an *Ausgang,* an exit or way out, because it corresponded to the central concern of his own work, the need to escape those prisons of thought and action that shape our politics, our ethics, our relations to ourselves.[88] Embracing an ecstatic experiment beyond Kant, his last writings declare the need to escape our inherited relation to the self, a declaration that complements and intensifies his earlier announcement of the "death of man." "What can be the ethic of an intellectual—I accept the title of intellectual which seems at present to nauseate some people—if not that: to render oneself permanently capable of getting free of oneself." The motivation for his last works is identified as a special curiosity, the curiosity that "enables one to get free of oneself."[89] How is this desire to be understood? I believe that it must be approached on two levels. To appreciate either, one must dismiss the type of interpretation that asserts that Foucault's last works are a rehabilitation of the "Nietzschean distinction between the life-affirming character of pagan cultures over against the life-negating essence of the Judeo-Christian tradition." Within this perspective, Christian "self-renunciation" would be identified with "self-debasement."[90] Foucault saw more deeply. He recognized that in addition to code-oriented moralities, Christianity had developed ethics-oriented moralities, which were related to the "exercise of a personal liberty."[91] That liberty was paradoxical because it combined a care of the self with a sacrifice of the self: "Christian culture has developed the idea that if you want to take care of yourself in the right way you have to sacrifice yourself."[92] In Christianity, this sacrifice or mortification of the self reflected that dying to self in baptism and penance that was mentioned earlier. Foucault's desire to be free of the self presents a similar type of paradox.

On one level, it points back to his analysis of Christian hermeneutics. While he gave up its project of seeking a hidden self, he also appreciated the "great richness" of the ascetical moment of self-renunciation.[93] His regard for this self-denial was due to his understanding of how positive knowledge of the self often entails the obligation to identify oneself with the figure of that knowledge. He had long appreciated that the self could become a prison: "I am no doubt not the only one who writes in order to have no face."[94] On this level, Foucault's call for a renunciation of the self is basically the slogan of a program for freedom as a thinker, a commitment to the task of permanent criticism. But there is another, more profound and interesting, level on which Foucault's desire should be understood. It derives from his personal experience, especially as it was shaped through his reading of Bataille and Blanchot. Both saw that Nietzsche's death of God did not provide that "mandate for a redefinition of man," but rather revealed a negativity without rest, which was created by the absence of absolute boundaries.[95] Bataille proclaimed that a morality after God's death was a morality that is "not centered on the guarantee of social and individual life given us by the 'main precepts' but on mystical passion leading man to die to himself in order to inherit eternal life. What it condemns is the dragging weight of attachment to the self, in the guise of pride and mediocrity and self-satisfaction."[96] In the epoch after the death of man, there is a similar need for the mystical passion of an ecstatic transcendence of the self that seeks to set itself as a natural reality in the place of the Absent Absolute. Thought and life achieve ecstasy through a series of critiques that aim not at an Absolute Emancipation but rather at experimental transgressions of the self. Foucault insisted on the necessity for developing new forms of relating to the self, and he exhibited one. Perhaps it was most clearly expressed in the context of revolt: "It is through revolt that subjectivity (not that of great men but that of whomever) introduces itself into history and gives it the breath of life. A delinquent puts his life into the balance against absurd punishments; a madman can no longer accept confinement and the forfeiture of his rights; a people refuses the regime which oppresses it."[97] This breath of life or force of resistance, this Foucaultian spirituality, bears witness to the capacity for an ecstatic transcendence of any history that asserts its necessity. It also testifies to Foucault's subversion of any philosophical ideal of contemplative self-possession, and its replacement by a dispossession. The relation to the self is defined in terms of its worldly sources and its operations within the historical field. Such a relationship demands a task of stylization.

Despite Foucault's efforts to avoid such misinterpretations, his use of the notion of stylization, of an aesthetics of existence, has been taken as a sign of his allegiance to a Greek morality or to an amoral aestheticism. Thus, he is accused of elevating the quest for beauty in life over all other intellectual and moral virtues, with the result that the "*self* rather than the *world* and its inhabitants becomes the central focus of aesthetic enhancement." And so, it is claimed, "Foucault's standpoint favors either an attitude of narcissistic self-absorption or one of outwardly directed, aggressive self-aggrandizement."⁹⁸ Foucault's actual work achieves something very different. Rather than promoting a self-absorption, Foucault deprives the self of any illusion that it can become a sanctuary separated from the world. Just as his earlier work showed the radical dependence of the life of the mind on specific power-knowledge relations, so his last studies indicated how the classical moral experience of the self was shaped from medical, economic, and erotic problematizations. Foucault's notion of self-formation is always presented in the context of a struggle for freedom within an historical situation. It is why he refers to the subject as an "agonism," a "permanent provocation" to the knowledge, power, and subjectivizations that operate on us.⁹⁹ This agonistic self is "not the decontextualized self of inwardness, but a self that becomes autonomous" only through a struggle with and a stylizing or adaptation of those concrete possibilities that present themselves as invitations for a practice of liberty.¹⁰⁰ Foucault's employment of aesthetic terms points to the power this agonism has for an ecstatic art, for leaving itself behind in transgressing the prisons of a particular historical determination, and for creating a new relation to event and, thus, self.

The need for this new relation gains a very concrete shape when it is viewed on the horizon of Foucault's subversion of Freud's story of the soul. Behind his probing of the hermeneutics of desire that rests upon the triad of truth-sexuality-subjectivity is the specter that human existence will continue to understand itself as a struggle of life versus death, eros against thanatos. As he suggested in the last section of *VS*, "Right of Death and Power over Life," ours souls have been fashioned as a mirror of that contemporary political terrain in which massacres are vital, in which there is a right to kill those who are perceived as representing a biological danger, in which political choice is governed by the sole option between survival or suicide. If *SP* showed that philosophical thought must struggle with the power-knowledge relations that would transform the human soul and existence into a mechanism, Foucault's history of sexuality points to the ethical task of detaching ourselves from those forces that would subordinate human existence (the Greek "bios," which Foucault employs) to biological life (the Greek "zoë"). His "aesthetics of existence" would be in resistance to a "science of life." To speak of human existence as a work of art is to remove it from the domain of the scientifically knowable and free us from the obligation of deciphering ourselves as a system of timeless functions that are subject to corresponding norms. For Foucault such deciphering would constitute, of course, a psychological approach. But psychology itself emerges from biological science and its determination of human existence as an organism, as life. If human being is under the obligation to discover its true self as a sexual reality, it is because sexuality is identified with the natural force of life itself. But as Foucault showed in *LMC*, the replacement of a natural history by a science of biology pledged our lives to history and struggle, to a fraternity with death. In place of the priority given by classical nature to the stable kingdom of discrete plants, modern knowledge of life has been captured by the energy of animality. Life is articulated as a murderous evolutionary force. The binding of personal identity and organic life immerses that identity within the flow of blood, which is a sign of life but also an index of that life's fragility. Life bleeds, and thus the confession of sexual identity avows not only life but its permanent war with death. With Freud, this morbid law of biological life became our psychic tale. Human existence and civilization is the contest between the drives of life and death (*Eros und Tod, Lebenstrieb und Destruktionstrieb*). When Foucault's genealogy of the man of desire is approached as the continuation of his excavation of Freud's story of the soul, then Foucault's ecstatic thinking is a transgression, a moving beyond the battle between life and death that bio-power has made our psychic and political landscape. Nietzsche's "beyond good and evil" yields to Foucault's historically specific aspiration of beyond life and death.

This ecstasy would be misunderstood if it were seen as a Nietzschean leap beyond common morality into an elitist superhuman status. In this interpretation, Foucault's work would terminate in a splendid solitude, foreign to any form of human solidarity and sense of common fate.[101] Foucault's ethical and political solidarity in the cause of human rights is well known.[102] It was carried through in both his life and his theory. Unlike Nietzsche, Foucault identified with the weak and the vanquished, the mentally ill and the deviant, with the lives of such infamous people as Pierre Rivière and Herculine Barbin, in whose accounts "one feels, under words polished like stone, the relentlessness and the ruin."[103] This identification motivated the movement of his thought toward an ever-expanding embrace of otherness, an expansion that is the condition for any community of moral action. Rather than replacing intellectual and moral values, Foucault's aesthetics of existence wishes to place at the center of both thought and action the imaginative creativity that has been exiled to the exclusive practice of art. For him, the formation of oneself as a thinker and a moral agent, which develops only through historical struggles, must be understood as the creation of a work of art rather than the execution of a program. The energy of that work of art is an ecstasy, a transcendence of man and self that culminates not in a Nietzschean Superman but in the recognition that in leaving God and man behind, we do not stand in need of a substitute for them.[104] Twenty years before his death, Foucault had tied the quest for liberty to research in the library: "Henceforth, the visionary experience arises from the black and white surface of printed signs, from the closed and dusty volume that opens with a flight of forgotten words." He claimed that the "fantastic is no longer a property of heart, nor is it found among the incongruities of nature; it evolves from the accuracy of knowledge, and its treasures lie dormant in documents."[105] Such a vision was equally distant from those who dreamed of a Total Enlightenment and from those who despaired of any sense. In an analogous way, his last writings acknowledge our impatience for liberty and our passion for ecstasy, but direct these not to the pursuit of some messianic future but to an engagement with the numberless potential transgressions of those forces that war against our self-creation and our solidarity.

CONCLUSION

It is far too early to predict what the ultimate effect of Foucault's work and his ethics of thought will be. Whatever weight his achievement carries for the future, his thought will always be understood in the context of the historical period that evoked his particular anxiety and his unique voice. It was Foucault's fate to have lived at the end of the epoch that witnessed the catastrophic outcome of modern efforts to transform human beings according to a technology deduced from kinds of knowledge claiming the status of truth. Although his studies investigated diverse issues, his ethical project had as its center a "history of truth," a fierce interrogation of that particular regime of truth under which we have lived and died for too long.[106] It was fitting, then, that the theme of Foucault's last courses and seminars was the practice of telling the truth (*parrhesia*) in ancient experience. His final research sought to indicate that the various forms of truth-telling that our culture has developed—philosophical, moral, scientific, political—were concrete responses to historical problematics. In his desire to problematize the truth-teller's role, Foucault asked: "Who is able to tell the truth? What are the moral, the ethical, and the spiritual conditions which entitle someone to present himself as, and to be considered as, a truth-teller? About what topics is it important to tell the truth? . . . What are the consequences of telling the truth? . . . What is the relation between the activity of truth-telling and the exercise of power?"[107] These questions remain as the echo of a long journey of thought. For his readers, they have impact of a force of flight, of which we now have "only its traces, the traces of what escapes."[108] What endures is a powerful realization: his thought makes his readers acutely aware of their ethical responsibility, as seekers or claimants of truth, to appreciate the sources and consequences of such claims. Foucault showed us in fresh ways how to doubt the order of things, and why such doubt must be practiced. He taught us to recognize that the articulation of a domain in terms of the true and the false is no less significant and dangerous in its implications than was the appearance of discourses that defined the holy and the profane, the saved and the damned, the good and the wicked.

Foucault's ethics of thought will be seen to respond to a sense of cultural crisis that emerged from the tragedies of the twentieth century and from the dread of what contemporary knowledge-power-self relations might yet make possible. Whatever conclusions his future readers may draw, Foucault's thought made it more difficult for those who shared his time and interests to think unhistorically, nonpolitically, a-ethically, that is, irresponsibly. Perhaps, as has been charged, his thought is "not a shout of joy."[109] But, it should be asked, when did that become the standard for evaluating a thinker? As far as Foucault's work is concerned, we will have to be satisfied with hearing a voice that suffered with some of the victims, not only those of obvious captivities but also of modern liberties and their programs. It was a thought that struggled impatiently for new practices of freedom. Ultimately, it was a cry of spirit.

APPENDIX 1:

Comparison of *Maladie mentale et personnalité* (1954) and *Maladie mentale et psychologie* (1962)

The differences made in transforming *PER* into *PSY* are crucial to my interpretation of the first major stage in the development of Foucault's thought as it is presented in chapter 2. I am therefore including here (1) a juxtaposition of the tables of contents, and (2) the texts of the major changes in the first part of the two works. Although the second parts are the more important, their almost total difference would demand including the complete texts of both.

1. TABLE OF CONTENTS

PER	*PSY*
Introduction	Introduction
1. Médecine mentale et médicine organique	1. Médecine mentale et médecine organique
Part I: Les dimensions psychologiques de la maladie	Part I: Les dimensions psychologiques de la maladie
2. La maladie et l'évolution	2. La maladie et l'évolution
3. La maladie et l'histoire individuelle	3. La maladie et l'histoire individuelle
4. La maladie et l'existence	4. La maladie et l'existence
Part II: Les conditions réelles de la maladie	Part II: Folie et culture
Introduction	Introduction
5. Le sens historique de l'aliénation mentale	5. La constitution historique de la maladie mentale
6. La psychologie du conflit	6. La folie, structure globale

2. MAJOR CHANGES IN PART 1

A) *PER*: "Nous voudrions montrer que la racine de la pathologie mentale ne doit pas être dans une spéculation sur une quelconque 'metapathologie,' mais seulement dans une réflexion sur l'homme lui-même" (p. 2).

A) *PSY*: "Nous voudrions montrer que la racine de la pathologie mentale ne doit pas être cherchée dans une quelconque 'metapathologie,' mais dans un certain rapport, historiquement situé, de l'homme à l'homme fou et à l'homme vrai" (p. 2).

(The importance that this change represents is at the heart of my argument in the second section of chapter 2, "The Shaking of the Foundations.")

B) *PER*: "Toutefois un bilan rapide est nécessaire, à la fois pour rappeler comment se sont constituées toutes les psychopathologies, traditionnelles ou récentes, et pour montrer de quels postulats la médecine mentale doit se libérer pour devenir rigoureusement scientifique" (p. 2).

B) *PSY*: "Cependant un bilan rapide est nécessaire, à la fois pour rappeler comment se sont constituées les psychopathologies traditionnelles ou récentes, et pour montrer de quels préalables la médecine mentale doit être consciente pour trouver une rigueur nouvelle" (p. 2).

(The notion of scientific rigor is dropped because of the conclusions reached by *HF*.)

C) *PER*: "La pathologie mentale doit s'affranchir de tous les postulats abstraits d'une 'métapathologie': l'unité assurée par celle-ci entre les diverses formes de maladie n'est jamais que factice; c'est l'homme réel qui porte leur unité de fait" (p. 16).

C) *PSY*: "La pathologie mentale doit s'affranchir de tous les postulats d'une 'métapathologie': l'unité assurée par celle-ci entre les diverses formes de maladie n'est jamais que factice; c'est-à-dire qu'elle relève d'un fait historique, auquel déjà nous échappons" (p. 16).

(History has become central to Foucault's argument.)

D) *PER*: "Il faut donc, en faisant crédit à l'homme lui-même, et non pas aux abstractions sur la maladie, analyser la spécificité de la maladie mentale, rechercher les formes concrètes qu'elle peut prendre dans la vie psychologique d'un individu; puis déterminer les conditions qui ont rendu possibles ces divers aspects, et restituer l'ensemble du système causal qui les a fondés.

"A ces deux séries de questions cherchent à répondre les deux parties de cet ouvrage:
1) Les dimensions psychologiques de la maladie;
2) Les conditions réelles de la maladie" (pp. 16–17).

D) *PSY*: "Il faut donc, en faisant crédit à l'homme lui-même, et non pas aux abstractions sur la maladie, analyser la spécificité de la maladie mentale, rechercher les formes concrètes que la psychologie a pu lui assigner; puis déterminer les conditions qui ont rendu possible cet étrange statut de la folie, maladie mentale irréductible à toute maladie.

"A ces questions cherchent à répondre les deux parties de cet ouvrage:
1) Les dimension psychologiques de la maladie mentale;
2) La psychopathologie comme fait de civilisation" (pp. 16–17).

(The differences of the D passages proceed from the conclusions reached by *HF* as I have stated them in chapter 2, in "The Shaking of the Foundations.")

E) *PER*: "Mais c'est peut-être toucher là un des paradoxes de la maladie mentale qui contraignent à de nouvelles formes d'analyses: si cette subjectivité de l'insensé est, en même temps, vocation et abandon au monde, n'est-ce pas au monde lui-même qu'il faut demander le secret de cette subjectivité énigmatique? Après en avoir exploré les dimensions extérieures, n'est-on pas amené forcément à considérer ses conditions extérieures et objectives?" (p. 69).

(The "extérieures" that I have underlined is obviously a misprint and should read: "intérieures.")

E) *PSY:* "Mais c'est peut-être toucher là un des paradoxes de la maladie mentale qui contraignent à de nouvelles formes d'analyse: si cette subjectivité de l'insensé est, en même temps, vocation et abandon au monde, n'est-ce pas au monde lui-même qu'il faut demander le secret de son énigmatique statut? N'y a-t-il pas dans la maladie tout un noyau de significations qui relève du domaine où elle est apparue—et tout d'abord ce simple fait qu'elle y est cernée comme maladie?" (p. 69).

(A change that is accounted for in my argument in chapter 2, in "The Shaking of the Foundations.")

APPENDIX 2:

Note on the Two Editions of *Naissance de la clinique* (1963 and 1972)

The revisions Foucault made in the second edition of *NC* range from the stylistic to the substantial. In this appendix I wish to present several passages as representative examples of the major alterations that Foucault felt desirable. Example 1 illustrates a point I have made in chapter 4, in "The Debt to Specific Thinkers," with respect to the lingering attraction Hyppolite's *Hegel* exercised for Foucault as late as 1963. Example 2 shows the desire on Foucault's part to desubjectivize the language he had employed, a revision to which I called attention in chapter 4, in "Earlier Researches." Examples 4 and 5 illustrate the introduction by Foucault of the *savoir-connaissance* distinction, and the greater precision with respect to discursive formation that resulted from *AS*. They were referred to in chapter 4, in "Archaeology as Method." In No. 6 below, I list the pages on which additional revisions appear, not including stylistic or other very minor changes.

1. EXAMPLE 1
   A) *NC*, 1963, p. xv
      "Une fois pour toutes, ce livre n'est pas écrit pour une médecine contre une autre, ou contre la médecine pour une absence de médecine. Ici, comme ailleurs, il s'agit d'une étude structurale qui essaie de déchiffrer dans l'épaisseur de l'historique les conditions de l'histoire elle-même."
   B) *NC*, 1972, p. xv
      "Une fois pour toutes, ce livre n'est pas écrit pour une médecine contre une autre, ou contre la médecine pour une absence de médecine. Ici, comme ailleurs, il s'agit d'une étude qui essaie de dégager dans l'épaisseur du discours les conditions de son histoire."

2. EXAMPLE 2
   A) *NC*, 1963 p. 88
      La clinique est probablement la première tentative, depuis la Renaissance, pour fonder une science sur le seul champ perceptif et une pratique sur le seul exercice du regard. Il y a eu sans doute, de Descartes à Monge, et auparavant chez les peintres et les architectes, une réflexion sur l'espase visible; mais il s'agissait de fixer une géométrie de la visibilité, c'est-à-dire de situer les phénomènes relevant de la perception à l'intérieur d'un domaine sans regard; les formes intelligibles fondaient les formes perçues dans un étalement qui les supprimait. La clinique n'est pas une dioptrique du corps; elle réside dans un regard auquel elle n'échappe pas. Elle suppose, sans l'interroger, la visibilité de la maladie, comme une structure commune où le regard et la chose vue, l'un en face de l'autre, trouvent leur place.

En fait, cette visibilité suppose le regard et l'objet liés par nature et par origine. En un cercle qu'il ne faut pas chercher à rompre, c'est le regard médical qui ouvre le secret de la maladie, et c'est cette visibilité qui rend la maladie pénétrable à la perception. L'altération du champ est de plein droit modification dans le regard et par le regard. Ce n'est donc pas la conception de la maladie qui a d'abord changé, puis la manière de la reconnaître; ce n'est pas non plus le système signalétique qui a été modifié puis la théorie; mais tout ensemble et plus profondément le rapport de la maladie à ce regard auquel elle s'offre et qu'en même temps elle constitue. Pas de partage à faire entre théorie et expérience, ou méthodes et résultats; il faut lire les structures profondes de la visibilité où le champ et le regard sont liés l'un à l'autre par des *codes perceptifs*; nous les étudierons dans ce chapitre sous leurs deux formes majeures: la structure linguistique du signe, et celle aléatoire du cas.

B) *NC*, 1972 pp. 88–89

La clinique n'est sans doute pas la première tentative pour ordonner une science à l'exercice et aux décisions du regard. L'histoire naturelle s'était proposé, depuis la seconde moitié de XVIIe siècle, l'analyse et la classification des êtres naturels selon leurs caractères visibles. Tout ce "trésor" de savoir que l'Antiquité et le Moyen Age avaient accumulé—et où il était question des vertus des plantes, des pouvoirs des animaux, des correspondances et des sympathies secrètes—tout cela était tombé depuis Ray dans le marges du savoir des naturalistes. Restaient à connaître en revanche les "structures," c'est-à-dire les formes, les dispositions spatiales, le nombre et la taille des éléments: l'histoire naturelle se donnait pour tâche de les repérer, de les transcrire dans le discours, de les conserver, confronter et combiner, pour permettre d'une part de déterminer les voisinages, les parentés des êtres vivants (donc l'unité de la création) et d'autre part de reconnaître rapidement n'importe quel individu (donc sa place singulière dans la création).

La clinique demande autant au regard que l'histoire naturelle. Autant et jusqu'à certain point la même chose: voir, isoler des traits, reconnaître ceux qui sont identiques et ceux qui sont différents, les regrouper, les classer par espèces ou familles. Le modèle naturaliste auquel la médecine s'est pour une part soumise au XVIIIe siècle reste actif. Le vieux rêve de Boissier de Sauvages, être le Linné des maladies, n'est pas encore tout à fait oublié au XIXe siècle: les médecins continueront à herborisor longtemps dans le champ du pathologique. Mais le regard médical s'organise, en outre, sur un mode nouveau. D'abord, il n'est plus simplement le regard de n'importe quel observateur, mais celui d'un médecin supporté et justifié par une institution, celui d'un médecin qui a pouvoir de décision et d'intervention. Ensuite, c'est un regard qui n'est pas lié par la grille étroite de la structure (forme, disposition, nombre, grandeur) mais qui peut et doit saisir les couleurs, les variations, les infimes anomalies, se tenant toujours aux aguets de déviant. Enfin, c'est un regard qui ne se contente pas de constater ce qui évidemment se donne à voir; il doit permettre de dessiner les chances et les risques; il est calculateur.

Il serait inexact sans doute de voir dans la médecine clinique de la fin du XVIIIe siècle un simple retour à la pureté d'un regard longtemps alourdi de fausses connaissances. Il ne s'agit même pas simplement d'un déplacement de ce regard, ou d'une plus fine application de ses capacités. De nouveaux objets vont se donner au savoir médical dans la mesure où et en même temps que le sujet connaissant se réorganise, se modifie et se met à fonctionner sur un mode nouveau. Ce n'est donc pas la conception de la maladie qui a d'abord changé, puis la manière de la reconnaître; ce n'est pas non plus le système signalétique qui a été modifié puis la théorie; mais tout ensemble et plus profondément le rapport de la maladie à ce regard auquel elle s'offre et qu'en même temps elle constitue. A ce niveau, pas de partage à faire entre théorie et expérience, ou méthodes et résultats; il faut lire les structures profondes de la visibilité où le champ et le regard sont liés l'un à l'autre par des *codes de savoir*; nous les étudierons dans ce chapitre sous leurs deux formes majeures: la structure linguistique du signe, et celle, aléatoire, du cas.

3. EXAMPLE 3

A) *NC*, 1963, p. xiii

N'est-il pas possible de faire une analyse structurale du signifié qui échapperait à la fatalité du commentaire en laissant en leur adéquation d'origine signifié et signifiant? Il faudrait alors traiter les éléments sémantiques, non pas comme des noyaux autonomes de significations multiples, mais comme des segments fonctionnels, formant système de proche en proche. Le sens d'une proposition ne serait pas défini par le trésor d'intentions qu'elle contiendrait, le révélant et le réservant à la fois, mais par la différence qui l'articule sur les autres énoncés réels et possibles, qui lui sont contemporains ou auxquels elle s'oppose dans la série linéaire du temps. Alors apparaîtrait la forme systématique du signifié.

B) *NC*, 1972, p. xiii

N'est-il pas possible de faire une analyse des discours qui échapperait à la fatalité du commentaire en ne supposant nul reste, nul excès en ce qui a été dit, mais le seul fait de son apparition historique? Il faudrait alors traiter les faits de discours, non pas comme des noyaux autonomes de significations multiples, mais comme des événements et des segments fonctionnels, formant système de proche en proche. Le sens d'un énoncé ne serait pas défini par le trésor d'intentions qu'il contiendrait le révélant et le réservant à la fois, mais par la différence qui l'articule sur les autres énoncés réels et possibles qui lui sont contemporains ou auxquels il s'oppose dans la série linéaire du temps. Alors apparaîtrait l'histoire systématique des discours.

4. EXAMPLE 4

A) *NC*, 1963, p. 51

C'est que, si les théories de la médecine s'étaient beaucoup modifiées depuis un demi-siècle, ses structures n'avaient point changé. Le principe des perceptions individuelles et concrètes n'était pas dégagé de l'espace nosologique qui en avait le premier formulé l'exigence; et le thème d'une conscience médicale, collective et normative, s'exprimait encore dans le langage d'une médecine des climats et des lieux. Les paysages de naissance n'étaient pas oubliés; et toutes les idées nouvelles gravitaient, dans le vide, autour d'une figure qui était cernée de l'extérieur, mais n'avait pas atteint son statut positif. Seule une mutation structurale profonde pouvait équilibrer la médecine autour de l'expérience clinique.

B) *NC*, 1972, p. 51

C'est que si les théories médicales s'étaient beaucoup modifiées depuis un demi-siècle, si de nouvelles observations avaient été faites en grand nombre, le type d'objet auquel s'adressait la médecine était resté le même; la position du sujet connaissant et percevant était restée la même; les concepts se formaient selon les mêmes règles. Ou plutôt tout l'ensemble du savoir médical obéissait à deux types de régularité: l'un, c'était celui des perceptions individuelles et concrètes quadrillé selon le tableau nosologique des espèces morbides; l'autre c'était celui de l'enregistrement continu, global et quantitatif d'une médecine des climats et des lieux.

Toute la réorganisation pédagogique et technique de la médecine achoppait à cause d'une lacune centrale: l'absence d'un modèle nouveau, cohérent et unitaire pour la formation des objets, des perceptions et des concepts médicaux. L'unité politique et scientifique de l'institution médicale impliquait pour être realisée cette mutation en profondeur. Or, chez les réformateurs de la Révolution, cette unité n'était effectuée que sous la forme de thèmes théoriques qui regroupaient après coup des éléments de savoir déjà constitués.

5. EXAMPLE 5

A) *NC*, 1963, p. 138

Il faut laisser aux phénoménologies le soin de décrire en termes de rencontre, de distance, ou de compréhension les avatars du couple médecin-malade. A prendre les choses dans leur sévérité structurale, il n'y a eu ni mariage ni couple; mais constitution d'une expérience où le regard du médecin est devenue l'élément décisif de l'espace pathologique et son armature interne. Au niveau originaire s'est nouée la figure complexe qu'une psychologie, même en profondeur, n'est guère capable de maîtriser; depuis l'anatomie pathologique, le médecin et le malade ne sont plus deux éléments corrélatifs et extérieurs, comme le sujet et l'objet, le regardant et le regardé, l'oeil et la surface; leur contact n'est possible que sur le fond d'une structure où le médical et le pathologique s'appartiennent, de l'intérieur, dans la plénitude de l'organisme. Le scalpel n'est que le luisant, métallique et provisoire symbole de cette appartenance. Il ne porte plus cette valeur d'effraction que le XVIIIe siècle encore ressentait si vivement; médecine et chirurgie ne sont plus qu'une seule et même chose au moment où le déchiffrement des symptômes s'ajuste à la lecture des lésions. Le cadavre ouvert et extériorisé, c'est la vérité intérieure de la maladie, c'est la profondeur étalée du rapport médecin-malade.

Il faut maintenant entrer un peu dans le détail et faire l'inventaire des moments principaux de cette nouvelle perception.

B) *NC*, 1972, p. 139 (Note: It should be pointed out that these two paragraphs are only part of what Foucault substitutes for the 1963 passage.)

Mais c'est là sans doute projet sur l'histoire une vielle théorie de la connaissance dont on connaît depuis bien longtemps les effets et les méfaits. Une analyse historique un peu précise révèle au-delà de ces ajustements un tout autre principe de transformation: il porte solidairement sur le type d'objets à connaître, sur le quadrillage qui le fait apparaître, l'isole et découpe les éléments pertinents pour un savoir possible, sur la position que le sujet doit occuper pour les repérer, sur les médiations instrumentales qui lui permettent de s'en saisir, sur les modalités d'enregistrement et de mémoire qu'il doit mettre en oeuvre, sur les formes de conceptualisation qu'il doit pratiquer et qui le qualifient comme sujet d'une connaissance légitime. Ce qui est modifié donnant lieu à la médecine anatomo-clinique, ce n'est donc pas la simple surface de contact entre le sujet connaissant et l'objet connu; c'est la disposition plus générale du savoir qui détermine les positions réciproques et le jeu mutuel de celui qui doit connaître et de ce qui est à connaître. L'accès du regard médical à l'intérieur de corps malade n'est pas la continuation d'un mouvement d'approche qui se serait développé plus ou moins régulièrement depuis le jour où le regard, à peine savant, du premier médecin s'est porté de loin sur le corps du premier patient; c'est le résultat d'une refonte au niveau du savoir lui-même, et non pas au niveau des connaissances accumulées, affinées, approfondies, ajustées.

Qu'il s'agisse d'un événement qui atteint la disposition du savoir, la preuve s'en trouve dans le fait que les connaissances dans l'ordre de la médecine anatomo-clinique ne se forment pas sur le même mode et selon les mêmes règles que dans la pure et simple clinique. Il ne s'agit pas du même jeu, un peu plus perfectionné, mais d'un autre jeu. Voici quelques-unes de ces règles nouvelles.

6. OTHER MAJOR CHANGES

1) *NC*, 1963
   a) xiv–xv
   b) 35–37
   c) 53
   d) 61–62
   e) 138
   f) 197–201
2) *NC*, 1972
   a) xiv–xv
   b) 35–37
   c) 53
   d) 61–62
   e) 138–39
   f) 199–203

Notes

CHAPTER 1

1. "La force de fuir" was originally written as a preface to the catalogue for the Maeght Gallery's 1973 exhibit of Rebeyrolle's *Prisoners,* and appeared in *Derrière le miroir* 202 (March 1973): 1–8. It has been reprinted in *Rebeyrolle: Peintures 1968–1978* (Paris: Maeght, 1979). In citing Foucault, I will normally refer to the work's first appearance; when an English translation exists, reference to it will follow the French, accompanied by the abbreviation ET. When there are several versions of the same work, my citation will be to the version marked by an asterisk in the complete bibliography at the end of this book.
2. John Boswell, "How the Greeks Viewed Sex," review of the English translation of *L'usage des plaisirs* (Paris: Gallimard, 1984) (*The Use of Pleasure,* trans. Robert Hurley [New York: Pantheon, 1985]), in *The Boston Sunday Globe* (October 20, 1985): B36; Clifford Geertz, "Stir Crazy," *The New York Review of Books* (January 26, 1978): 3; Devereaux Kennedy, "Michel Foucault," *Theory and Society* 8 (September 1979): 269.
3. As examples, see Hayden White, "Michel Foucault," and John Sturrock's Introduction, both in Sturrock's edited collection *Structuralism and Since: From Lévi-Strauss to Derrida* (Oxford: Oxford University Press, 1979), pp. 81, 16.
4. Geertz, "Stir Crazy," 3; Edward Said, "Michel Foucault as an Intellectual Imagination," *Boundary* 1 (1972): 1.
5. "Non au sexe roi," an interview conducted by Bernard-Henri Lévy, *Le Nouvel Observateur* 644 (March 12, 1977): 130 (ET: "Power and Sex: An Interview with Michel Foucault," trans. David Parent, *Telos* 32 [Summer 1977]: 161).
6. *L'archéologie du savoir* (Paris: Gallimard, 1969) 28 (ET: *The Archaeology of Knowledge,* trans. A. M. Sheridan-Smith [New York: Harper Colophon, 1976] 17).
7. "La force de fuir," p. 63.
8. See Immanuel Kant, "What Is Enlightenment?" in Kant, *On History,* ed. Lewis White Beck (Indianapolis: Bobbs-Merrill, 1963), pp. 3, 9.
9. G. Dez, *Regards sur l'histoire de Poitiers* (Poitiers: Oudin, 1966), p. 5.
10. "Michel Foucault: An Interview," conducted by Stephen Riggins on June 22, 1982, in *Ethos* 1, 2 (Autumn 1983): 5.
11. "Intervista a Michel Foucault," a June 1976 interview conducted by Alessandro Fontana and Pasquale Pasquino, in *Microfisica del Potere* (Torino: Einaudi, 1977), p. 5 (ET: "Truth and Power," trans. Colin Gordon [New York: Pantheon, 1980], pp. 110–11).

12. Riggins, p. 4. On the Foucault of these years, see the memoirs by Jean Piel, "Foucault à Uppsala," *Critique* 471–72 (August–September 1986): 748–52, and by Etienne Burin des Roziers, "Une rencontre à Varsovie," *Le débat* 41 (September–November 1986): 132–36.

13. Foucault, "What Is Enlightenment?" (1984), in *The Foucault Reader*, ed. Paul Rabinow (New York: Pantheon, 1984), p. 41.

14. Ibid., p. 42.

15. Foucault, Introduction to Georges Canguilhem, *On the Normal and the Pathological*, trans. Carolyn Fawcett (Boston: Reidel, 1978), p. xii.

16. *Les mots et les choses: une archéologie des sciences humaines* (Paris: Gallimard, 1966), p. 398 (ET: *The Order of Things: An Archaeology of the Human Sciences* [New York: Pantheon, 1971], p. 387).

17. Foucault, *Thèse complémentaire* for the doctorat ès lettres, University of Paris, vol. 1 (1961), pp. 127–28.

18. Following Foucault, the term "man" will be employed in this study to designate the specifically modern concept of the person, originating philosophically in Descartes and articulated most fully in Kant. The term "human being" is meant to be a broader notion, transcending modernity's image and fabrication of man.

19. On antihumanism as a philosophical critique, see the excellent essay by Reiner Schürmann, "Anti-Humanism, Reflections of the Turn Towards the Post-Modern Epoch," *Man and World* 12 (1979): 161–67.

20. Frederic Jameson, *The Prison House of Language* (Princeton: Princeton University Press, 1972), p. 139. As an example of recent discussion of the notion, see Kate Soper, *Humanism and Anti-Humanism* (La Salle, Illinois: Open Court, 1986).

21. For a recollection of Foucault as a student in Paris, see Maurice Pinguet, "Les années d'apprentissage," *Le débat* 41 (September–November 1986): 122–31.

22. J. P. Sartre, *Situations II: Qu'est-ce que la littérature* (Paris: Gallimard, 1948), pp. 241–42.

23. Mark Poster's "The Hegel Renaissance: Toward a Philosophical Anthropology," the first chapter of his *Existential Marxism in Postwar France: From Sartre to Althusser* (Princeton: Princeton University Press, 1975), pp. 3–35, provides an excellent introduction to the Hegel who appeared in France through the efforts of Kojève and Hyppolite. I return to Hyppolite in more detail in chapter 4, section 2, "The Situation of Archaeology as an Event," where I discuss Foucault's acknowledgement of his sources.

24. Vincent Descombes, *Modern French Philosophy* (Cambridge: Cambridge University Press, 1980), p. 14. As examples of the "terroristic" image history took on, see Maurice Merleau-Ponty, *Humanism and Terror* (Boston: Beacon Press, 1969, original edition 1947) esp. pp. xiii–xlvii, and Jean-Paul Sartre, *Critique of Dialectical Reason* (London: NLB, 1976, original edition, 1960), pp. 428–44.

25. See Descombes, pp. 27–32; Poster, *Existential Marxism*, pp. 26–28, and Jacques Derrida, "The Ends of Man," *Philosophy and Phenomenological Research* 30 (1969–1970): 34–37. For short statements of existential humanism, see Sartre, *Existentialism and Humanism* (London: Eyre Methuen, 1973, original edition 1946). As an example of Marcel's Christian existentialism, see his *Homo Viator* (Chicago: Regnery, 1951, original edition 1944).

26. See Poster, "The Rediscovery of Marx and the Concept of Alienation," *Existential Marxism*, pp. 36–71.

27. On Hegel, see Derrida, pp. 36–37. On Althusser, see his *For Marx* (New York:

Vintage, 1970) and *Lenin and Philosophy* (New York: Monthly Review Press, 1971). On Althusser's specific relation to Foucault, see chapter 4, n. 40.

28. Althusser, "Marxism and Humanism," *For Marx*, p. 227.

29. "Letter on Humanism," in Martin Heidegger, *Basic Writings*, ed. David Farrell Krell (New York: Harper and Row, 1977), pp. 190–242. For interpretations, see Derrida, pp. 37–38; Schürmann, pp. 165–66; Paul Ricoeur, "Heidegger and the Question of the Subject," *The Conflict of Interpretations*, ed. Don Ihde (Evanston: Northwestern University Press, 1974), pp. 223–35; William Richardson, *Heidegger: Through Phenomenology to Thought* (The Hague: Nijhoff, 1967), pp. 530–61.

30. For details of French translations and interpretations of Nietzsche, see Michel Haar, "Nietzsche," in *Encyclopédie de la Pléiade: Histoire de la philosophie 3*, ed. Yvon Belaval (Paris: Gallimard, 1974), pp. 306–53, and the collection of essays edited by David Allison, *The New Nietzsche: Contemporary Styles of Interpretation* (New York: Delta, 1977). With specific reference to Foucault, we return to Nietzsche in chapter 4, in "The Debt to Specific Thinkers."

31. See Jean Piaget's *Structuralism* (New York: Harper-Colophon, 1970), pp. 3–16, for an attempt to generalize the notion.

32. Saussure's *Course in General Linguistics* (New York: McGraw Hill, 1959) is the necessary starting point for understanding the structuralist movement and method. The introductory literature on structuralism is now vast. In addition to Piaget's work, cited in n. 31, see Roland Barthes, *Elements of Semiology* (Boston: Beacon Press, 1970); Pierre Guiraud, *Semiology* (Boston: Routledge and Kegan Paul, 1975); *Introduction to Structuralism*, ed. Michael Lane (New York: Basic, 1970); *The Structuralists*, ed. Richard and Fernande DeGeorge (New York: Anchor, 1972); John Sturrock, *Structuralism and Since*; and Edith Kurzweil, *The Age of Structuralism: Lévi-Strauss to Foucault* (New York: Columbia University Press, 1980).

33. Jacques Lacan, "Of Structure as an Inmixing of an Otherness Prerequisite to any Subject Whatsoever," in *The Structuralist Controversy*, ed. Richard Macksey and Eugenio Donato (Baltimore: The Johns Hopkins Press, 1972), p. 194. On Lacan, see Malcolm Bowie's fine essay "Jacques Lacan" in Sturrock, pp. 116–53, esp. 134–38; Stuart Schneiderman, *Jacqes Lacan: The Death of an Intellectual Hero* (Cambridge: Harvard University Press, 1983); and John P. Muller and William J. Richardson, *Lacan and Language: A Reader's Guide to Ecrits* (New York: International Universities Press, 1982).

34. See the excellent essay on Barthes by John Sturrock in his *Structuralism and Since*, pp. 52–80.

35. *Course in General Linguistics*, 81. For an introduction to Saussure's work in particular, see Jonathan Culler, *Ferdinand de Saussure* (New York: Penguin, 1977).

36. Claude Lévi-Strauss, *Structural Anthropology* 1 (New York: Basic Books, 1963), p. 21; see also p. 33.

37. Claude Lévi-Strauss, *The Savage Mind* (Chicago: University of Chicago Press, 1966), esp. pp. 245–69.

38. Lévi-Strauss's major statement is the chapter of *The Savage Mind* entitled "History and Dialectic," his response to Sartre's *Critique of Dialectical Reason*. For Sartre's own reaction, see his interview "Jean-Paul Sartre répond" in *L'Arc* 30 (1966): 87–96. For an analysis of the debate, see Hugh Silverman, "Sartre and the Structuralists," *International Philosophical Quarterly* 18 (September 1978): 341–58.

39. Maurice Merleau-Ponty, *Phenomenology of Perception* (New York: Humanities Press, 1962), p. x.

40. Ibid., p. 433.

41. A good introduction to these various approaches is provided by the collection of essays from the 1975 Vanderbilt University Centennial Symposium, edited by Charles Delzell and published as *The Future of History* (Nashville: Vanderbilt University Press, 1977).

42. Claude Lévi-Strauss, *Tristes Tropiques* (New York: Atheneum, 1975), p. 74; Lévi-Strauss, *The Savage Mind*, p. 236; Lévi-Strauss, *The Scope of Anthropology* (London: Cape, 1967), p. 49.

43. Edmund Husserl, *The Crisis of European Sciences and Transcendental Phenomenology* (Evanston: Northwestern University Press, 1970), pp. 15, 341, 299. For an understanding of this historical turn in Husserl's later thought, see James Morrison, "Husserl's *Crisis*: Reflections on the Relationship of Philosophy and History," *Philosophy and Phenomenological Research* 37 (March 1977): 312–30, and Ludwig Landgrebe, "Phenomenology as Transcendental Theory of History," in *Husserl: Expositions and Appraisals*, ed. Frederick Elliston and Peter McCormick (South Bend, Indiana: University of Notre Dame Press, 1977), esp. pp. 106–7 and 112–13. A comparison between Foucault and Husserl is directly taken up by Bernard Flynn in "Michel Foucault and the Husserlian Problematic of a Transcendental Philosophy of History," *Philosophy Today* (Fall 1978): 224–38.

44. Cited in Michael Ermath, *Wilhelm Dilthey: The Critique of Historical Reason* (Chicago: University of Chicago Press, 1978), p. 48.

45. Foucault, "Nietzsche, Freud, Marx," *Cahiers de Royaumont* 6: *Nietzsche* (Paris: Editions de Minuit, 1967), p. 187 (ET: "Nietzsche, Freud, Marx," trans. Jon Anderson and Gary Hentzi, in *Critical Texts* 3, 2 [Winter 1986]: 3).

46. *LMC*, p. 339 (ET, p. 328).

47. Kant, "What Is Enlightenment?", p. 45.

48. On Foucault as an anarchist, see Reiner Schürmann, "'What Can I Do?' in an Archaeological-Genealogical History," *The Journal of Philosophy* (October 1985): 540–47. On the problem of the bureaucratization of intellectual life, there is, of course, an enormous literature. Recent studies that have treated the problem are Paul Bové, *Intellectuals in Power: A Genealogy of Critical Humanism* (New York: Columbia University Press, 1986); *Social Science as Moral Inquiry*, ed. Norma Haan (New York: Columbia University Press, 1983); *The Authority of Experts: Studies in History and Theory*, ed. Thomas L. Haskell (Bloomington: Indiana University Press, 1984).

49. Edward Said, "Michel Foucault," *Raritan* 4, 2 (Fall 1984): 9.

50. Alan Sheridan, *Michel Foucault: The Will to Truth* (New York: Tavistock-Methuen, 1980); Gilles Deleuze, *Foucault* (Paris: Editions de Minuit, 1986).

51. Mark Poster, *Foucault, Marxism and History: Mode of Production versus Mode of Information* (New York: Blackwell, Polity Press, 1984).

52. Barry Smart, *Foucault, Marxism and Critique* (Boston: Routledge and Kegan Paul, 1983), p. 107. Also see Smart's *Michel Foucault* (New York: Tavistock, Methuen, 1985).

53. Jeffrey Minson, *Genealogies of Morals: Nietzsche, Foucault, Donzelot and the Eccentricity of Ethics* (New York: St. Martin's Press, 1985).

54. Mark Cousins and Athar Hussain, *Michel Foucault* (New York: St. Martin's Press, 1985).

55. Hubert Dreyfus and Paul Rabinow, *Michel Foucault: Beyond Structuralism and Hermeneutics*, 2d ed. (Chicago: University of Chicago Press, 1983), p. xvii.
56. Karlis Racevskis, *Michel Foucault and the Subversion of Intellect* (Ithaca: Cornell University Press, 1983).
57. Pamela Major-Poetzl, *Michel Foucault's Archaeology of Western Culture: Toward a New Science of History* (Chapel Hill: University of North Carolina Press, 1983), pp. 199–200.
58. Charles Lemert and Garth Gillan, *Michel Foucault: Social Theory as Transgression* (New York: Columbia University Press, 1982).
59. John Rajchman, *Michel Foucault: The Freedom of Philosophy* (New York: Columbia University Press, 1985), pp. 124, 93.
60. See Foucault, "La grande colère des faits," *Faut-il brûler les nouveaux philosophes?* (Paris: Nouvelles Editions Oswald, 1978), pp. 65–66.

CHAPTER 2

1. "Deuxième entretien" with Michel Foucault in Raymond Bellour, *Le livre des autres* (Paris: Editions de l'Herne, 1971), pp. 201–2. (This interview dates from 1967 and was originally published in *Lettres Françaises* 1187 [June 15, 1967]: 6–9).
2. "Débat sur le roman," directed by Michel Foucault, *Tel Quel* 17 (Spring 1965): 13.
3. Michel Foucault, *Maladie mentale et personnalité* (Paris: Presses Universitaires de France, 1954), pp. 110, 2, 6, 10. (Hereafter *PER*.) This work and Foucault's Introduction to Ludwig Binswanger, *Le rêve et l'existence*, trans. from the German by Jacqueline Verdeaux (Paris: Desclée De Brower, 1954), pp. 9–128 (hereafter *IRE*) (ET: "Dream, Imagination, and Existence," trans. Forrest Williams, *Review of Existential Psychology and Psychiatry* 19 [1984–85]: 29–78) are the two items treated in this section. In order to understand Foucault's development, it is most important to note that the so-called second edition of *PER* is a radical revision of the 1954 work and bears a new title, *Maladie mentale et psychologie* (1962, same press, hereafter *PSY*). There are significant changes made in the first part of *PER*, and the second part is totally replaced in *PSY*. Thus I shall treat them as two separate works, with *PSY* to be taken up in the second section of this chapter. There is an English translation by Alan Sheridan of *PSY: Mental Illness and Psychology* (New York: Harper and Row, 1976), and reference to this translation in this section (hereafter ET) will be made only when I have actually used his translation of a line or passage that is the same in both editions, or when the point I am making in the text refers in general to a section of *PER* that is in large part carried over to *PSY* and their differences on the point made is unimportant. For an account of the differences, see section 2 of this chapter, "The Shaking of the Foundations," and Appendix 1.
4. *PER*, pp. 1–2.
5. Foucault's examination of the metapathology is given in the introductory chapter that precedes the two-part division of *PER* in which are contained the positive arguments of the book. Briefly stated, the examination asserts that the similarity to organic pathology of the conceptual structure that operated in the defining of mental illness in the late nineteenth and early twentieth centuries was rooted in two postulates regarding the nature of illness. There was an "essential-

ist" postulate, which held illness to be an essence, "a specific entity that can be mapped by the symptoms that manifest it," and a "naturalist" postulate that attempted to organize illness along the lines of a botanical species, as, for example, Kraepelin did in his use of *dementia praecox*. These two postulates failed to establish anything more than an abstract parallelism between the mental and the organic, and so the problem of psychosomatic totality required a different metapathological solution. The strategy of this new approach was to stress the notion of totality, and abandoning the essentialist prejudice, it perceived illness, organic or psychological, as something that concerns the total situation of an individual in his world. Between pathological physiology and pathological psychology, however, there are operative different procedures of abstraction, different conceptualizations of the normal and the pathological, and finally, different forms of understanding the relation between individual and environment. (*PER*, pp. 2–16).

6. *PER*, p. 12 (ET, p. 12).
7. *PER*, p. 16.
8. *PER*, pp. 19–35.
9. *PER*, p. 23 (ET, p. 19).
10. *PER*, p. 28 (ET, p. 23).
11. *PER*, pp. 28–29 (ET, pp. 23–24).
12. *PER*, pp. 28–32 (ET, pp. 23–26).
13. *PER*, pp. 29–30 (ET, pp. 24–26).
14. *PER*, pp. 32–34 (ET, pp. 26–28).
15. *PER*, p. 34 (ET, p. 28).
16. *PER*, pp. 36–52.
17. Sigmund Freud, "Analysis of a Phobia in a Five-Year-Old Boy," *The Standard Edition of the Complete Psychological Works of Sigmund Freud* 10 (London: Hogarth, 1955), pp. 3–149.
18. *PER*, pp. 51–52 (ET, pp. 41–42).
19. *PER*, p. 51 (ET, p. 41).
20. *PER*, p. 52 (ET, p. 42).
21. *PER*, pp. 53–69 (ET, pp. 44–57).
22. Helpful material on Jaspers and Minkowski can be found in Herbert Spiegelberg, *Phenomenology in Psychology and Psychiatry: A Historical Introduction* (Evanston, Ill.: Northwestern University Press, 1972). Binswanger is mentioned more fully in n. 28 below.
23. *PER*, p. 54 (ET, p. 45).
24. *PER*, pp. 56–67 (ET, pp. 46–55).
25. *PER*, p. 68 (ET, p. 55).
26. *PER*, p. 69 (ET, p. 56).
27. *PER*, pp. 68–69.
28. Ludwig Binswanger (1881–1966) was born and worked for most of his life in Kreuzlingen, Switzerland. His training was in medicine and psychiatry; for almost forty years, he was director of the Bellevue Sanitarium in Kreuzlingen. The school of *Daseinanalyse* or existential psychiatry, of which he is considered the founder, is an extensive effort to relate the phenomenological movement of Husserl and Heidegger to the practice of both psychiatry and Freudian psychoanalysis. Two useful introductions to his thought are Spiegelberg's *Phenomenology in Psychology and Psychiatry*, 193–232, and Jacob Needleman, "A Critical Introduction to Ludwig Binswanger's Existential Psychoanalysis," which serves

as the introduction to *Being-in-the-World: Selected Papers of Ludwig Binswanger*, trans. J. Needleman (New York: Basic Books, 1963), pp. 9–145. This volume contains an English translation of the essay Foucault is introducing: "Dream and Existence," pp. 222–48, which was reissued with the English translation of Foucault's essay (see n. 3 above), pp. 81–105.

29. *IRE*, p. 14 (ET, p. 33).
30. *IRE*, p. 131 (ET, p. 81). The translation is that of W. Lowrie from Kierkegaard's *Concluding Unscientific Postscript* (Princeton, N.J.: Princeton University Press), p. 177.
31. *IRE*, p. 10 (ET, p. 31). Binswanger's own understanding of his relation to Heidegger is best seen in his essay "Heidegger's Analytic of Existence and Its Meaning for Psychiatry," *Being-in-the-World*, pp. 206–21; Martin Heidegger, *Being and Time* (New York: Harper and Row, 1962).
32. Binswanger, "Heidegger's Analytic of Existence," p. 206.
33. *IRE*, pp. 10–11, 105, 124–25 (ET, pp. 31–32, 66, 73–74).
34. *IRE*, p. 15 (ET, p. 33).
35. *IRE*, pp. 47–48 (ET, p. 45).
36. *IRE*, p. 50 (ET, p. 46).
37. *IRE*, pp. 59–63 (ET, pp. 49–51).
38. *IRE*, p. 64 (ET, p. 51).
39. *IRE*, pp. 85, 63–64 (ET, pp. 59, 51).
40. *IRE*, pp. 71, 74 (ET, pp. 54, 55).
41. *IRE*, pp. 65–66, 104 (ET, pp. 52, 66).
42. *IRE*, pp. 66, 72–73 (ET, pp. 52, 54–55).
43. *IRE*, p. 83 (ET, p. 58).
44. *IRE*, p. 105 (ET, p. 66).
45. *IRE*, p. 104 (ET, p. 66).
46. *IRE*, p. 106 (ET, pp. 66–67).
47. *IRE*, pp. 106, 117 (ET, pp. 66, 70–71).
48. *IRE*, pp. 117–119 (ET, pp. 71–72).
49. *IRE*, pp. 127, 121–22 (ET, pp. 75, 72–73).
50. *IRE*, pp. 125–27 (ET, pp. 74–75).
51. *PER*, p. 71.
52. *PER*, pp. 76–83.
53. *PER*, pp. 84–89.
54. *PER*, p. 104.
55. *PER*, p. 103.
56. *PER*, pp. 91–92.
57. *PER*, p. 92.
58. *PER*, pp. 92–102.
59. *PER*, pp. 94, 104–6.
60. *PER*, pp. 106–7. An unmistakably Marxist tone is suggested by Foucault's turning to Pavlov and by his desire for a materialistic psychology. In fact, he was a member of the French Communist Party for a while as a student, and was influenced by the Marxist milieu in which he did his studies. (See his remarks both to Pierre El Kabbach, "Foucault répond à Sartre," *La Quinzaine Littéraire* 46 (March 1–15, 1968): 21, and to Fontana and Pasquino, pp. 3–5). For a discussion of Foucault's attitude toward the Communist Party, see the memoir by Maurice Pinguet, "Les années d'apprentissage," *Le débat* 41 (September–November 1986): 122–31. During his time as a member of the Party, Foucault

wrote several pieces under pseudonyms, pieces that cannot be located. (See Walter Seitter, "Michel Foucault—Von der Subversion des Wissens," in his collection of MF's writings, *Von der Subversion des Wissens* ([Frankfurt: Ullstein, 1978], p. 169).

61. *PER*, pp. 109–110; *IRE*, pp. 127–28 (ET, pp. 74–75).
62. *PER*, p. 10 (ET, p. 8).
63. The diversity appears in three items from this period. In 1957 Foucault published "La recherche scientifique et la psychologie" in *Des chercheurs français s'interrogent*, ed. Jean-Edouard Morère (Paris: Presses Universitaires de France, 1957), pp. 171–201. This article, critical of the positive scientific model with which psychology has sought identification, questioned the constitution of psychology as a field for scientific research. The work has double interest. It is receptive to the challenge posed by psychoanalysis to psychology's alliance with positivism. In addition, psychology, with its myth of impartial observation, is compared unfavorably with history, which is under constant critique by actual history, a form of criticism that psychology lacks. In 1958 MF assisted Daniel Rocher in the French translation of Viktor von Weizsaecker's major work *Gestaltkreis* (1939): *Le cycle de la structure*, with a preface by Henry Ey (Paris: Desclée, 1958). Weizsaecker's work attempted to integrate the notion of subjectivity with biology and physiology, and thus construct a coherent medical anthropology. Such a model was required if understanding was to be adequate to the phenomenon of human illness, a crisis not only for man's organic dimension but for his very identity as a subject. A third perspective is to be found in MF's unpublished thesis on Kant's *Anthropologie*, in which Foucault explored the relationship between Kant's critique of pure reason and his twenty-five years of anthropological teaching: *Thèse complémentaire* for the University of Paris under the direction of Jean Hyppolite, 1961. The thesis is an introduction to and translation, with notes, of Immanuel Kant's *Anthropologie in pragmatischer Hinsicht*. While the translation itself, which comprised the second volume of the thesis, was published as *Anthropologie du point de vue pragmatique* (Paris: Vrin, 1964), Foucault's introduction to it is available only in typescript at the library of the Sorbonne, Paris. (Future reference will be to *Thèse complémentaire*, which will always mean this introductory volume.) In his study, Foucault was fascinated by Kant's constant oscillation between transcendental and empirical perspectives, and the paradoxical identity for man that issued from them. It was an oscillation that would take on great importance in Foucault's later work (see Chapter 3 of my study).
64. *PER*, p. 110.
65. Binswanger, "Dream and Existence," pp. 222–25. *Folie et déraison: Histoire de la folie à l'âge classique* (Paris: Plon, 1961); abridged ed. *Histoire de la folie* (Paris: Union Generale d'Editions, 1964). Reissued as *Histoire de la folie à l'âge classique* (Paris: Gallimard, 1972) with a different preface and two appendices, "La folie, l'absence d'oeuvre" (*La Table Ronde*, May 1964) and "Mon corps, ce papier, ce feu" (*Paideia*, September 1971). My references will be to the 1978 Gallimard edition of the text, issued in the TEL collection (hereafter *HF*), and specific references to the Préface will be to that of 1961 unless otherwise specified. The English translation by Richard Howard, *Madness and Civilization* (New York: Mentor, 1967) is of the drastically abridged edition of 1964 with some additional material from the original. *HF* was the occasion for the first of the many interviews Foucault has given. See "La folie n'existe que dans une

société," a discussion with Jean-Paul Weber, *Le Monde* 5135 (July 22, 1961): 9.

66. Steven Marcus, "In Praise of Folly" (a review of *Madness and Civilization*), *The New York Review of Books* 7, no. 8 (November 17, 1966): 36. For a similar type of response, see Peter Gay, "Chains and Couches," *Commentary* 40, 4 (October 1965): 93–96.
67. We can only hope that an English translation of the original *HF* will be made. The omissions in the abridgement include sentences, passages, and entire sections of the original work.
68. J. Huizinga, *The Waning of the Middle Ages* (New York: Anchor Books, 1954), p. 138.
69. *HF*, pp. 13–55.
70. *HF*, p. 27 (ET, p. 25).
71. *HF*, pp. 56–91.
72. *HF*, pp. 96, 116; *PSY* p. 80 (ET, p. 67).
73. *HF*, p. 87 (ET, p. 59).
74. *HF*, pp. 116–17.
75. *HF*, p. 87 (ET, p. 59).
76. *HF*, pp. 151, 121.
77. *HF*, pp. 258–60 (ET, pp. 91–92).
78. *HF*, pp. 159–61 (ET, pp. 62–64).
79. *HF*, p. 163 (ET, p. 66); cf. *HF*, pp. 162–73 (ET, pp. 65–75).
80. *HF*, pp. 267–68 (ET, pp. 99–100); *HF*, pp. 200, 202.
81. *HF*, p. 261 (ET, p. 93).
82. *PSY*, p. 82 (ET, p. 69).
83. *HF*, p. 90 (ET, p. 61); *HF*, p. 97; *PSY*, p. 82 (ET, p. 69).
84. See the treatment of Pinel in G. Alexander and Sheldon Selesnick, *The History of Psychiatry: An Evaluation of Psychiatric Thought and Practice from Prehistoric Times to the Present* (New York: Harper and Row, 1966), pp. 114–20, 132; and William Sahakian, "History of Psychology," *The New Encyclopaedia Britannica* 15 (Chicago: Encyclopaedia Britannica, 1975, 15th ed.), p. 155.
85. *PSY*, p. 84 (ET, p. 70); *HF*, p. 418 (ET, p. 182).
86. *HF*, p. 411.
87. *HF*, pp. 418–21 (ET, pp. 182–85); *HF*, pp. 430–31 (ET, pp. 188–89); *HF*, pp. 375–78 (ET, pp. 165–68).
88. *HF*, p. 422 (ET, p. 185).
89. *HF*, pp. 513–15 (ET, pp. 207–9).
90. *HF*, pp. 380–81 (ET, p. 170).
91. *HF*, p. 517 (ET, p. 210).
92. *HF*, pp. 519–23 (ET, pp. 213–16).
93. *HF*, pp. 327–60 (ET, pp. 133–62); *PSY*, pp. 85–86 (ET, pp. 71–72).
94. *HF*, p. 528 (ET, p. 221).
95. *PSY*, p. 87 (ET, p. 73); *HF*, p. 530 (ET, p. 223).
96. *PSY*, p. 92 (ET, p. 78).
97. *HF*, p. 548; *PSY*, p. 104 (ET, p. 87).
98. *PSY*, p. 88 (ET, p. 73).
99. *PSY*, pp. 86–87 (ET, pp. 72–73). Jean Esquirol (1772–1840), referred to in this text, was a student of Pinel and is regarded as the founder of French psychiatry.
100. Michel Foucault, Introduction to *Rousseau juge de Jean-Jacques: Dialogues* (Paris: Colin, 1962), pp. xxiii–xxiv.
101. *PSY*, p. 103 (ET, p. 87).

102. *HF*, p. 366.
103. *PSY*, p. 103 (ET, p. 87).
104. Ibid.
105. *PSY*, p. 104 (ET, p. 88).
106. *PSY*, p. 89 (ET, p. 75).
107. *PSY*, p. 89 (ET, pp. 74–75), *PSY*, p. 104 (ET, p. 88); *HF*, pp. 549–57 (ET, pp. 224–31).
108. This conclusion is reflected in two slight changes Foucault makes in *PSY* of the *PER* text. Whereas in *PER* the root of mental pathology was to be sought "only in a reflection on man himself," it is now to be searched for in a "certain relation, historically situated, of man to the madman and the true man" (*PER*, p. 2; *PSY*, p. 2). Whereas it was asserted in *PER* that the unity of the various forms of illness was to be found in the "actual man who carried their factual unity," *PSY* identifies the unity as belonging to an "historical fact that is already beyond our grasp" (*PER*, p. 15; *PSY*, p. 16).
109. *HF*, p. 93.
110. *HF*, p. 548; Préface to *HF*, p. ix; *HF*, p. 415.
111. Préface to *HF*, p. iii.
112. Préface to *HF*, p. ii (ET, p. x); *HF*, pp. 94, 265.
113. In an exchange with George Steiner (MF, "Monstrosities in Criticism," *Diacritics* 1, 1 [Fall, 1971]: 60), Foucault points out that the term archaeology had its source in Kant's work on progress in metaphysics. The passage to which Foucault is probably referring is the following: "Eine philosophische Geschichte der Philosophie ist selber nicht historisch oder empirisch sondern rational d.i. a priori möglich. Denn ob sie gleich Facta der Vernunft aufstellt so entlehnt sie solche nicht von der Geschichtserzählung sondern sie zieht sie aus der Natur der menschlichen Vernunft als philosophische Archäologie" (Immanuel Kant, *Welches sind die wirklichen Fortschritte, die die Metaphysik seit Leibnitzens und Wolfs Zeiten in Deutschland gemacht hat?* in *Gesammelte Schriften*, edition of the Prussian Academy of the Sciences, vol. 20 [Berlin: Walter de Gruyter, 1942], p. 341).
114. *PER*, p. 26: *PSY*, p. 26 (ET, p. 21). In the article cited in n. 113, Foucault specifically rejects the linking of the term "archaeology" to Freud ("Monstrosities in Criticism," p. 60). However, this does not rule out my speculation.
115. Foucault's later explicit denunciation of a structuralist interpretation of his work will be taken up in the following chapter (see in chapter 3, "The Situation of Thought"). Already in 1961, he had identified an influence that was to shape both his view of structuralism's objectives and his understanding of the structure with which his archaeology was concerned. This was the work of the historian of religions, Georges Dumézil. See his interview with Jean-Paul Weber, "La folie n'existe que dans une société," *Le Monde* (July 22, 1961): 9. In chapter 4 of this work, Dumézil will be specifically mentioned in the context of the debt to his work that Foucault acknowledged in his inaugural lecture at the Collège de France.
116. *IRE*, pp. 21–22 (ET, pp. 35–36).
117. *PSY*, p. 93 (ET, p. 78).
118. *Naissance de la clinique* (hereafter *NC*) (Paris: Presses Universitaires de France, 1963), p. xv (2d ed., p. xiv) (ET, p. xviii). Although less extreme than was the case with *PER* and *PSY*, *NC* presents similar difficulties in that many subtle changes were made in the second edition of the work, which was published in

1972 (the third and fourth editions are identical to the second). The changes in 1972 will be taken up later, when their significance will be clear as a result of the development in Foucault's thought. In citing *NC* in the notes, my principle has been to give the page references to both texts when there has been no change or when the change is without theoretical importance. The third item in the entry will be to the English translation (*The Birth of the Clinic*, trans. A. M. Sheridan Smith, New York: Vintage, 1973) when I have actually used it in the body of my text or when it is an exact translation of the first edition. I have resorted to these limits because of the peculiar difficulty that this translation poses. Although it largely follows the second edition, especially in critical changes, this is not always the case, and Smith sometimes employs the first edition or even combines the two editions in a single sentence. Whatever the reasons for this (no explanation is given), it does require great caution in employing the translation.

119. *NC*, p. 63 (ET, p. 62).
120. *NC*, pp. 51–57 (ET, pp. 52–57).
121. J. B. Regnault, *Considérations sur l'état de la médicine* (Paris, 1819), p. 10. Cited in *NC*, p. 55 (55) (ET, p. 56).
122. *NC*, p. xi (xi) (ET, p. xiv–xv); Selle, *Introduction à l'étude de la nature* (French trans., Paris: Year III [1794–95], p. 229), cited in *NC*, p. 104 (105) (ET, p. 104); cf. Douglas James Guthrie, "History of Medicine," *The New Encyclopaedia Britannica* (Chicago: Encyclopaedia Britannica, 1975, 15th ed.), p. 830.
123. *NC*, pp. 56–62.
124. *NC*, p. 43 (43) (ET, p. 44); Fourcroy, *Rapport sur l'enseignement libre des sciences et des arts* (Paris: Year II [1793–94], p. 2. Cited in *NC*, p. 49 (49) (ET, p. 49).
125. *NC*, pp. 125–27 (125–27) (ET, pp. 124–26).
126. *NC*, p. 197 (199) (ET, p. 195).
127. *NC*, p. x (x) (ET, p. xiv).
128. *NC*, p. xi (xi) (ET, p. xv).
129. *NC*, pp. 2–14 (2–14) (ET, pp. 4–16).
130. *NC*, pp. 14–19 (14–19) (ET, pp. 16–20).
131. *NC*, pp. 30–31 (30–31) (ET, p. 31).
132. Lanthenas, *De l'influence de la liberté sur la santé* (Paris, 1792), p. 8. Cited in *NC*, p. 34 (34) (ET, p. 33).
133. *NC*, pp. 37–38, 51.
134. *NC*, p. 68 (68) (ET, p. 69).
135. *NC*, pp. 68–86 (68–86) (ET, pp. 69–85).
136. *NC*, p. 72.
137. *NC*, p. 88.
138. *NC*, pp. 87–123 (87–123) (ET, pp. 88–123).
139. *NC*, p. 12 (ET, p. 13).
140. *NC*, pp. 31, 102 (31, 102) (ET, pp. 31, 102).
141. *NC*, pp. 97–98 (97–98) (ET, p. 98).
142. *NC*, pp. 89–90 (89–90) (ET, pp. 90–91).
143. *NC*, pp. 93–94 (93–94) (ET, p. 94).
144. *NC*, p. 95 (96) (ET, p. 96).
145. *NC*, p. 105 (105) (ET, p. 105).
146. *NC*, p. 88 (88) (ET, p. 88).
147. *NC*, pp. 109–10 (109–10) (ET, p. 109).

148. *NC*, p. 115 (115) (ET, p. 114).
149. *NC*, p. 148 (149) (ET, p. 146).
150. *NC*, pp. 139–40, 160–61, 164–66 (140–41, 162–63, 166–68) (ET, pp. 138–39, 159–60, 163–64).
151. *NC*, pp. 156–60 (158–62) (ET, pp. 155–59).
152. *NC*, pp. 172–73 (174–75) (ET, pp. 170–71).
153. *NC*, p. xi (xi) (ET, p. xiv).
154. *NC*, pp. 175–96, 198 (177–98, 200) (ET, pp. 174–94, 196).
155. *NC*, p. xi (xi) (ET, p. xv).
156. Préface to *HF*, p. i (ET, p. ix).
157. *NC*, pp. vii–viii (vii–viii) (ET, pp. xi–xii).
158. *NC*, pp. 201, 1–2 (203, 1–2) (ET, pp. 199, 3–4).
159. *NC*, pp. 201, 1 (203, 1) (ET, pp. 199, 3).
160. *NC*, p. xi (xi) (ET, p. xv).
161. *NC*, pp. 199–200, 201 (ET, pp. 197–98).
162. Cf. *HF*, pp. 538–40, 545.
163. *NC*, p. 199 (ET, p. 197).
164. *NC*, p. 199 (201) (ET, p. 197).
165. *NC*, p. 200 (202) (ET, p. 198).
166. *NC*, p. xii (xii) (ET, p. xvi).
167. *NC*, p. 201 (203) (ET, p. 199).
168. *NC*, p. 197 (199) (ET, p. 195).
169. *NC*, pp. xiii–xiv (xiii) (ET, p. xvii).
170. *NC*, p. xv.
171. *NC*, pp. xiv, 51.
172. *NC*, pp. xii–xiii.
173. *NC*, pp. xiii (ET, p. xvii).
174. *NC*, pp. 68–69, viii, 55 (68–9, viii, 55) (ET, pp. 69, xii, 56–57).
175. *NC*, p. 51.
176. Certain points made in Foucault's writings between *PSY* and *LMC* have more specific relevance to the latter, and thus will be mentioned in chapter 3. Although I am drawing on all the writings to 1966 in this section, Foucault's approach to literature is already fairly well defined by 1963 (see "Préface à la transgression" and "Le langage à l'infini"). Thus it warrants being taken up in the context of his thinking at the time of *NC*. These are the major literary writings from 1962 to 1966: "Le 'non' du père," *Critique* 1978 (March 1962): 195–209 (ET: "The Father's 'No'" in *Language, Counter-Memory, Practice*, ed. Donald Bouchard (Ithaca, N.Y.: Cornell University Press, 1977, pp. 68–86); "Un si cruel savoir," *Critique* 182 (July 1962): 597–611; *Raymond Roussel* (Paris: Gallimard, 1963) (ET: *Death and the Labyrinth: The World of Raymond Roussel*, trans. Charles Ruas [New York: Doubleday, 1986]); "Préface à la transgression," *Critique* 195–96 (August, September 1963): 751–69 (ET: "A Preface to Transgression," in *Language, Counter-Memory, Practice*, pp. 53–67); "Distance, aspect, origine," *Critique* 198 (November 1963): 931–45; "La prose d'Acteon," *La Nouvelle Revue Française* 135 (March 1964): 444–59; "Débat sur le roman," directed by MF, and "Débat sur la poésie," in which he participated, both in *Tel Quel* 17 (Spring 1964): 12–54, 69–82; "Le langage de l'espace," *Critique* 203 (April 1964): 378–82; "La folie, l'absence d'oeuvre"; "Le Mallarmé de J. P. Richard," *Annales* (September––October 1964): 996–1004; "La bibliothèque fantastique," the preface to Gus-

tave Flaubert, *La tentation de Saint Antoine* (Paris: Le Livre de Poche, 1971, originally written in 1964), pp. 7–33 (ET: "Fantasia of the Library," in *Language, Counter-Memory, Practice,* pp. 87–109; "La pensée du dehors," *Critique* 229 (June 1966): 523–46.

177. *HF,* pp. 530, 549–57 (ET, pp. 223–31); *PSY,* p. 89 (ET, p. 88).
178. "Débat sur le roman," pp. 13, 45.
179. "Le 'non' du père," p. 208 (ET, p. 86).
180. *Raymond Roussel* (hereafter *RR*), pp. 197, 39 (ET, pp. 152, 27).
181. "Le 'non' du père," p. 201 (ET, p. 80).
182. "La folie, l'absence d'oeuvre," p. 577; "Le 'non' du père," p. 197 (ET, p. 71); Introduction to *Rousseau,* pp. xxiii–xxiv.
183. "Le langage à l'infini," pp. 44–46 (ET, pp. 53–57). This questioning of literature in terms of its relation to death is the perspective in Maurice Blanchot's literary analysis. Foucault later identifies Blanchot as the person who has "made possible all discourse on literature" ("Deuxième entretien avec Michel Foucault," *Le livre des autres,* p. 198). Blanchot paid him the tribute of a later study: *Michel Foucault tel que je l'imagine* (Montpellier: Editions Fata Morgana, 1986).
184. "Préface à la transgression," p. 754 (ET, p. 33).
185. "La pensée du dehors," *Critique* 229 (June 1966): 523–46. This "thinking from without" becomes the key for Deleuze's interpretation of the whole of Foucault's work. See his *Foucault* (Paris: Editions de Minuit, 1986).
186. Ibid, p. 525.
187. Immanuel Kant, *Anthropologie du point du vue pragmatique* (Paris: Vrin, 1964, 1970), p. 10. English translation from the German, *Anthropologie in Pragmatischer Hinsicht*—with introduction and notes by Mary J. Gregor, *Anthropology from a Pragmatic Point of View* (The Hague: Martinus Nijhoff, 1974), p. 3.
188. "La pensée du dehors," p. 525.
189. "Le Mallarmé de J. P. Richard," p. 1004. Already in his *Thèse complémentaire,* pp. 100–101, Foucault had noted that Kant's consideration of language in the *Anthropology* should have entailed the displacement of man by language, an implication that Kant obviously did not draw. Kant properly represents the decisive turn in modern thought toward anthropology. See MF's interview with A. Badiou, "Philosophie et psychologie," in *Dossiers pédagogiques de la radio-télévision scolaire* 10 (February 15–27, 1965): 65.
190. "Préface à la transgression," pp. 757–62 (ET, pp. 38–44).
191. Ibid., pp. 753–54 (ET, p. 32).
192. "La bibliothèque fantastique," and "Le langage à l'infini," pp. 52–53 (ET, pp. 66–67).
193. "La folie, l'absence d'oeuvre," p. 578.
194. "La bibliothèque fantastique," p. 10 (ET, p. 91).
195. Ibid., p. 10 (ET, p. 90).
196. *Thèse complémentaire,* pp. 127–28.

CHAPTER 3

1. The chronological slice of Foucault's work treated in this chapter is 1966 to 1968. The major items from these years are: *Les mots et les choses: une archéologie des sciences humaines* (Paris: Gallimard, 1966, hereafter *LMC*) (ET: *The Order of*

Things: An Archaeology of the Human Sciences [New York: Pantheon, 1970]);
"Entretien" with Raymond Bellour, *Le livre des autres* (Paris: Editions de
l'Herne, 1971), pp. 135–44 (originally published in 1966); "Entretien" with
Madeline Chapsal, *La Quinzaine Littéraire* 5 (May 15, 1966): 14–15;
"L'homme, est-il mort? Un entretien avec Michel Foucault," conducted by
Claude Bonnefoy, *Arts et loisirs* 38 (June 15, 1966), pp. 8–9; "Deuxième
entretien" with Raymond Bellour, *Le livre des autres* (Paris: Editions de
l'Herne, 1971), pp. 189–207 (originally published in 1967); "Conversazione con
Michel Foucault," an interview conducted by P. Caruso and published in his
Conversazioni con Lévi-Strauss, Foucault, Lacan (Milano: U. Musia and Co.,
1969), pp. 91–131 (originally published in 1967); "Ceci n'est pas une pipe," *Les
cahiers du chemin* (January 15, 1968): 79–105 (ET: "Ceci n'est pas une pipe,"
trans. Richard Howard, *October* 1 [Spring 1976]: 6–21); "Réponse à une
question," *Esprit* 371 (May 1968): 850–74 (ET: "History, Discourse and Discontinuity," trans. Anthony Nazzaro, in *Psychological Man*, ed. Robert Boyers
(New York: Harper Colophon, 1975), pp. 208–31; "Réponse au cercle d'épistémologie," *Cahiers pour l'analyse* 9: *Généalogie des sciences* (Summer 1968): 9–40
(ET: "On the Archaeology of the Sciences," *Theoretical Practice* 3–4 [Autumn
1971]: 108–27).
2. "L'homme, est-il mort?", p. 8.
3. See Bellour, "Deuxième entretien," pp. 195–96; "Réponse à une question,"
    p. 851 (ET, p. 209).
4. See Caruso, p. 93. Foucault stresses again the transitional quality of the work in
    his later conversation with Sergio Rouanet and J. G. Merquior, "Entrevista com
    Michel Foucault," *O homem e o discurso* (Rio de Janeiro: Edicoes Tempo
    Brasileiro, 1971), p. 25.
5. Bellour, "Entretien," p. 144.
6. *LMC*, p. 16 (ET, p. xxiv).
7. Michel Serres has earlier identified *HF* as having the virtue of a "catharsis
    épistémologique" in his *Hermes I: La Communication* (Paris: Editions de
    Minuit, 1968), p. 189.
8. *LMC*, p. 318 (ET, p. 307).
9. *LMC*, p. 288 (ET, p. 275).
10. *LMC*, p. 7 (ET, p. xv).
11. *LMC*, p. 8 (ET, pp. xvi–xvii).
12. See above, in chapter 2, "The Birth of the Clinic, Thought and History" and
    "Literature"; *LMC*, p. 311 (ET, p. 298).
13. *LMC*, pp. 15–16 (ET, p. xxiv).
14. See *NC*, p. 201 (203) (ET, p. 199).
15. *LMC*, pp. 220, 312 (ET, pp. 207, 298–99); Bellour, "Entretien," p. 140.
16. *LMC*, p. 220 (ET, p. 207).
17. See especially Derrida, pp. 31–44.
18. "La recherche scientifique et la psychologie," *Des chercheurs français s'interro-
    gent*, p. 194; the same point made in this 1957 essay is stated later in *HF*, p. 545.
19. See above, in chapter 2, "The History of Madness and the Project of a True
    Psychology," and "La folie, l'absence d'oeuvre," *HF*, p. 576.
20. See above, in chapter 2, "The Birth of the Clinic, Thought and History" and
    "Literature."
21. *LMC*, pp. 15, 319 (ET, pp. xxiii, 308).
22. *LMC*, pp. 398, 397 (ET, pp. 387, 386).

23. *LMC*, pp. 15, 352 (ET, pp. xxiii, 341). This welcoming of man's disappearance will force Foucault, as it had Heidegger earlier, to try to show why opposition to man and humanism does not entail a defense of the inhuman. I touch upon the beginning of Foucault's response in "The Situation of and the Task for Thought" in this chapter; for Heidegger's defense, see his "Letter on Humanism," in Martin Heidegger, *Basic Writings*, ed. David Farrell Krell (New York: Harper and Row, 1977), pp. 193–242.
24. *LMC*, pp. 396, 359 (ET, pp. 384, 348).
25. In "The Situation of and the Task for Thought," below, I do touch on the question of method that developed after *LMC*.
26. *LMC*, pp. 11–13, 221 (ET, pp. xx–xxi, 208).
27. *LMC*, p. 89 (ET, p. 75).
28. *LMC*, p. 214 (ET, p. 200).
29. Although I have followed in my text the general principle of not anticipating his future development, it should be pointed out that Foucault came to regret having used the names of Ricardo, Cuvier, and Bopp, since he intended to refer to a *transformation* that can be found in the works of those he names, and not primarily to the authors. It should be understood as "la transformation Ricardo," and so forth. (See the discussion following a 1969 presentation by Foucault, "La situation de Cuvier dans l'histoire de la biologie," *Revue d'histoire des sciences et de leurs applications* 23, 1 [January–March 1970]: 88.) As an accurate indication of his thought at the time of *LMC*, Foucault's caution seems totally in order. In *NC*, he had already stated: "What counts in men's thoughts is not so much that which they have thought, but the non-thought which systematizes them from the outset, thus making them thereafter endlessly accessible to language and open to the task of thinking them again" (*NC*, p. xv). (Although the second edition is slightly different, Foucault's point on this matter remains the same, *NC*, 2d, p. xv [ET, p. xix]).
30. *LMC*, pp. 265–75 (ET, pp. 253–63).
31. *LMC*, p. 269 (ET, p. 257).
32. *LMC*, p. 274 (ET, p. 262).
33. *LMC*, pp. 275–92 (ET, pp. 263–79).
34. *LMC*, p. 288 (ET, p. 276).
35. *LMC*, pp. 292–307 (ET, pp. 280–94).
36. *LMC*, p. 379 (ET, p. 368).
37. *LMC*, p. 257 (ET, p. 244). Foucault will speak of the three as "transcendantaux" as well as "quasi-transcendantaux" (cf. *LMC*, p. 262 [ET, p. 250]).
38. *LMC*, p. 231 (ET, p. 219).
39. *LMC*, p. 379 (ET, p. 367).
40. *LMC*, p. 379 (ET, pp. 367–68).
41. *LMC*, p. 380 (ET, pp. 368–69).
42. *LMC*, p. 381 (ET, p. 369).
43. *LMC*, p. 382 (ET, p. 370).
44. *LMC*, p. 306 (ET, p. 293).
45. *LMC*, pp. 320, 329 (ET, pp. 309, 318).
46. *LMC*, pp. 329, 321 (ET, pp. 318, 310).
47. *LMC*, pp. 323–29 (ET, pp. 312–18).
48. *LMC*, p. 325 (ET, p. 314).
49. *LMC*, p. 334 (ET, p. 23).
50. *LMC*, pp. 339–46 (ET, pp. 328–35).

51. *LMC*, p. 231 (ET, p. 219).
52. Bellour, "Entretien," p. 141.
53. *LMC*, pp. 32–59 (ET, pp. 17–45).
54. *LMC*, pp. 46, 69 (ET, pp. 31, 55).
55. *LMC*, p. 49 (ET, p. 34).
56. *LMC*, p. 45 (ET, p. 30).
57. *LMC*, pp. 77, 60–91 (ET, pp. 63, 46–77).
58. *LMC*, pp. 87–88, 70–71, 76 (ET, pp. 73, 56–57, 62).
59. *LMC*, p. 89 (ET, p. 74).
60. *LMC*, pp. 71, 222, 357 (ET, pp. 57, 209, 346).
61. *LMC*, pp. 92–136 (ET, pp. 78–124).
62. *LMC*, pp. 309, 97 (ET, pp. 296, 83).
63. *LMC*, pp. 132, 220 (ET, pp. 116, 208).
64. *LMC*, pp. 137–76 (ET, pp. 125–65).
65. *LMC*, p. 144 (ET, p. 132).
66. *LMC*, p. 202 (ET, p. 189).
67. *LMC*, p. 157 (ET, pp. 144–45).
68. *LMC*, pp. 177–225 (ET, pp. 166–200).
69. *LMC*, pp. 187–88 (ET, p. 176). The citation included by Foucault in this passage is from Scipion de Grammont, *Le Denier royal, traité curieux de l'or et de l'argent* (Paris, 1620), pp. 46–47.
70. *LMC*, p. 187 (ET, p. 175).
71. *LMC*, p. 321 (ET, p. 310).
72. *LMC*, p. 252 (ET, p. 239).
73. *LMC*, pp. 233–38 (ET, pp. 221–26).
74. *LMC*, p. 238 (ET, p. 225).
75. *LMC*, pp. 238–45 (ET, pp. 226–32).
76. *LMC*, pp. 245–49 (ET, pp. 232–36).
77. *LMC*, p. 250 (ET, p. 237).
78. *LMC*, p. 257 (ET, p. 244).
79. *LMC*, p. 315 (ET, p. 304).
80. *LMC*, pp. 355–78 (ET, pp. 344–67).
81. *LMC*, p. 366 (ET, p. 355).
82. *LMC*, pp. 362, 376 (ET, pp. 351, 364).
83. *LMC*, pp. 357–62 (ET, pp. 346–51).
84. See above, this chapter, "Man," in "The Birth of Man"; *LMC*, pp. 350–51, 323–46 (ET, pp. 339–40, 312–35).
85. *LMC*, p. 338 (ET, p. 327).
86. *LMC*, pp. 330–31 (ET, pp. 319–20); cf. Hayden White, "Foucault Decoded: Notes from the Underground," *History and Theory* 12, no. 1 (1973): 43.
87. *LMC*, pp. 364–65 (ET, p. 353).
88. *LMC*, p. 365 (ET, p. 354).
89. *LMC*, p. 368 (ET, pp. 356–57).
90. *LMC*, pp. 368–69 (ET, p. 357).
91. *LMC*, p. 370 (ET, p. 358).
92. *LMC*, pp. 371–72 (ET, pp. 359–61).
93. *LMC*, pp. 372–74 (ET, pp. 361–62).
94. *LMC*, p. 374 (ET, p. 362).
95. *LMC*, pp. 375–76 (ET, p. 364).
96. *LMC*, p. 376 (ET, p. 364).
97. *LMC*, pp. 385–98 (ET, pp. 373–86).

98. *LMC*, pp. 385–87 (ET, pp. 374–75).
99. *LMC*, pp. 389–90 (ET, pp. 377–78).
100. *LMC*, p. 391 (ET, p. 379). Since Foucault mentions Lévi-Strauss at this point, the reference is probably to *The Savage Mind* (Chicago: University of Chicago Press, 1966), p. 247: "So I accept the characterization of aesthete in so far as I believe the ultimate goal of the human sciences to be not to constitute, but to dissolve man."
101. *LMC*, pp. 392–93 (ET, p. 381).
102. *LMC*, pp. 307–11 (ET, pp. 294–98).
103. *LMC*, p. 398 (ET, p. 387).
104. *LMC*, pp. 224, 256, 396 (ET, pp. 211, 243, 384).
105. *LMC*, pp. 232–33, 262 (ET, pp. 221, 250).
106. *LMC*, p. 318 (ET, p. 307).
107. Bellour, "Entretien," p. 140.
108. Ibid., p. 140; *LMC*, p. 312 (ET, pp. 298–99).
109. *LMC*, p. 220 (ET, p. 207).
110. Cf. *LMC*, pp. 332, 336–37 (ET, pp. 321, 325–26).
111. As examples, see R. Bakker, *Het Anonieme Denken: Foucault en het structuralisme* (Baarn: Wereldvenster, 1973), esp. pp. 156–57; "Système et liberté," a discussion in *Structuralisme et marxisme* (Paris: Union Generale, 1970), pp. 267–316; Jean Langlois, "Michel Foucault et la mort de l'homme," *Science et Esprit* 21 (May–September 1969), pp. 209–30; Peter Sloterdijk, "Michel Foucaults strukturale Theorie der Geschichte," *Philosophisches Jahrbuch* 79 (1972), pp. 161–84; and Karl Baltheiser's dissertation, *Die Wegbereiter des linguistischen Strukturalismus und dessen sprachphilosophische Aspekte bei Michel Foucault* (University of Salzburg, 1971).
112. Chapsal, p. 14.
113. *LMC*, pp. 353, 221 (ET, pp. 342, 208). In this context, however, it should be pointed out that Foucault did not consider the diachronic-synchronic relationship the essential issue in the thinking of history; see his remarks to Caruso, p. 109.
114. See Bellour, "Entretien" (1966), pp. 139–40; Bellour, "Deuxième Entretien," pp. 196–97.
115. *LMC*, p. 221 (ET, p. 208).
116. "Réponse à une question," p. 860 (ET, p. 218); cf. Bellour, "Deuxième Entretien," p. 201: "A la différence de ceux qu'on appelle les structuralistes, je ne suis pas tellement intéressé par les possibilités formelles offertes par un système comme la langue."
117. *LMC*, p. 312 (ET, p. 299).
118. "Réponse à une question," p. 859 (ET, p. 217).
119. See *LMC*, pp. 351–53, 258, 331 (ET, pp. 340–42, 245, 320).
120. "Foucault répond à Sartre," an interview with Jean-Pierre El Kabbach, *La Quinzaine Littéraire* 46 (March 1–15, 1968): 21; cf. Caruso, p. 103.
121. Henri Lefebvre, *Au-delà du structuralisme* (Paris: Anthropos, 1971), p. 299; Olivier Revault D'Allonnes, "Michel Foucault: les mots contre les choses," *Structuralisme et marxisme* (Paris: Union Generale d'Editions, 1970), p. 34.
122. Jean-Paul Sartre, "Jean-Paul Sartre répond," an interview with B. Pingaud, *L'Arc* 30 (1966): 87–96; Revault D'Allonnes, pp. 14–15; Lefebvre, pp. 272–73. In addition, for related criticism or discussion of it, see Michel Amiot, "Le relativisme culturaliste de Michel Foucault," *Les Temps Modernes* 248 (January 1967): 1271–98, esp. p. 1296; "Système et liberté," *Structuralisme et marxisme,*

pp. 267–316; J. M. Domenach, "Le système et la personne," *Esprit* 360 (May 1967): 771–80.

123. Bellour, "Deuxième entretien," p. 189, and Caruso, p. 104. For an example of such a reaction, see "Entretiens sur Michel Foucault," *La Pensée* 137 (February 1968): 3–37.

124. Bellour, "Deuxième Entretien," pp. 190, 204–5; cf. *LMC*, p. 13 (ET, p. xxii).

125. Bellour, "Entretien," p. 138.

126. *LMC*, p. 139 (ET, p. 128).

127. *LMC*, p. 64 (ET, p. 50).

128. *LMC*, pp. 287–88, 272–74 (ET, pp. 274–75, 260–62). For a rich investigation of the fruitfulness of this approach, see W. R. Albury and D. R. Oldroyd, "From Renaissance Mineral Studies to Historical Geology in the Light of Michel Foucault's *The Order of Things*," *The British Journal for the History of Science*, 10, no. 36 (November 1977): 187–215.

129. Chapsal, p. 15.

130. "Réponse à une question," *Esprit*, p. 872 (ET, p. 230).

131. See above, chapter 2, Section 3 Aiii, "Thought and History."

132. *LMC*, p. 179 (ET, p. 168): "Dans une culture et à un moment donné, il n'y a jamais qu'une épistemè, qui définit les conditions de possibilité de tout savoir."

133. *LMC*, pp. 64–65 (ET, pp. 50–51); Bellour, "Deuxième Entretien," p. 193.

134. "La situation de Cuvier dans l'histoire de la biologie," p. 89; Bellour, "Deuxième Entretien," p. 195; Bellour, "Entretien," p. 138.

135. *LMC*, pp. 353–54 (ET, pp. 342–43).

136. For the attempted refutation, see G. S. Rousseau, "Whose Enlightenment? Not Man's: The Case of Michel Foucault," *Eighteenth Century Studies* 6 (1972–73): 255; as examples of the cautions expressed regarding such a misunderstanding, see Georges Canguilhem, "Mort de l'homme ou épuisement du cogito?" *Critique* 242 (July 1967): 599–618, and Michel de Certeau, "Les sciences humaines et la mort de l'homme," *Etudes* 326 (March 1967): 344–60.

137. Sartre, "Jean-Paul Sartre répond," 85; Levinas's remark, made in a letter, is reported by Bakker, 168.

138. "Réponse à une question," p. 850 (ET, p. 208).

139. Ibid.

140. Chapsal, p. 15.

141. See *LMC*, pp. 338–39 (ET, pp. 327–28).

142. "L'homme, est-il mort?" p. 9.

143. "Réponse à une question," pp. 860–66 (ET, pp. 218–24).

144. Ibid., p. 865 (ET, p. 223).

145. Ibid., pp. 866–72 (ET, pp. 224–30).

146. Ibid., p. 871 (ET, p. 229).

147. See "Entretien" with Claude Bonnefoy (October 5, 1966), p. 9, and Chapsal, p. 15; *LMC*, p. 16 (ET, p. xxiv). "C'était un nageur entre deux mots," an interview with Claude Bonnefoy, *Arts et Loisirs* 54.

148. "L'homme, est-il mort?" 9; *LMC*, pp. 353, 396–97 (ET, pp. 342, 385).

CHAPTER 4

1. This chapter is based on the writings from 1969 to 1971. The major items are: *L'archéologie du savoir* (Paris: Gallimard, 1969, hereafter *AS*) (ET: *The Archaeol-*

ogy of Knowledge, trans. A. M. Sheridan Smith [New York: Harper Colophon, 1971]); *L'ordre du discours* (Paris: Gallimard 1979, hereafter *OD*) (ET: "The Discourse on Language," trans. Robert Swyer and published as appendix to *The Archaeology of Knowledge*, pp. 215–37); "Qu'est-ce qu'un auteur?" *Bulletin de la Société française de Philosophie* 64 (1969): 73–104 (ET: "What is an Author?" in *Language, Counter-Memory, Practice*, pp. 113–38); "Jean Hyppolite (1907–1968)," *Revue de Metaphysique et de Morale* 74 (April–June, 1969): 131–36; "Michel Foucault explique son dernier livre," conducted by J. J. Brochier, *Magazine littéraire* 28 (April–May, 1969): 23–25; "La naissance du monde," a conversation with Jean-Michel Palmier, *Le Monde* 7558 (May 3, 1969): viii; "La situation de Cuvier dans l'histoire de la biologie 2," *Revue d'histoire des science et de leurs applications* 23 (January–March 1970): 63–92; "Theatrum Philosophicum," *Critique* 282 (November 1970): 885–908 (ET, with the same title, in *Language, Counter-Memory, Practice*, pp. 165–96); Foreword to the English edition of *LMC* in *The Order of Things*, pp. ix–xiv; "Sept propos sur le 7ᵉ ange," preface to Jean Pierre Brisset, *La grammaire logique* (Paris: Tchou, 1970), pp. vii–xix; "Mon corps, ce papier, ce feu," *Paideia* (September 1971), reissued as appendix to 1972 edition of *HF*, pp. 583–603; "Justice versus Power," a discussion between MF and Noam Chomsky in 1971, in *Reflexive Water: The Basic Concerns of Mankind*, ed. Fons Elder (London: Souvenir Press, 1974), pp. 134–97; "Par delà le bien et le mal," *C'est demain la veille* (Paris: Seuil, 1973), pp. 21–43, originally published in *Actuel* 14 (November 1971) (ET: "Revolutionary Action: 'Until Now'" in *Language, Counter-Memory, Practice*, pp. 218–33); "Monstrosities in Criticism," *Diacritics* 1, 1 (Fall 1971): 57–60; "Foucault Responds 2," *Diacritics 1*, 2 (Winter 1971): 60; "Nietzsche, la généalogie, l'histoire," in *Hommage à Jean Hyppolite* (Paris: Presses Universitaires de France, 1971), pp. 145–72 (ET: "Nietzsche, Genealogy, History" in Bouchard, *Language, Counter-Memory, Practice*, pp. 139–64); "A Conversation with Michel Foucault," conducted by John Simon, *Partisan Review* 38 (1971): 192–201. In addition, because of their greater relevance to this chapter, I have cited the second edition of *NC* (1972) and "Gaston Bachelard, le philosophe et son ombre: Piéger sa propre culture," *Le Figaro* (September 30, 1972): 16.

2. *LMC*, p. 13 (ET, p. xxii).
3. *AS*, p. 31 (ET, p. 21).
4. *AS*, pp. 26, 177 (ET, pp. 16, 135).
5. Caruso, p. 117; Boulez will later speak of a common commitment between serial music and the method of Foucault: a "renovation of thought by the renewal of the very foundations of language, whether that language is philosophical or musical." See "Quelques souvenirs de Pierre Boulez," *Critique* 471–72 (August–September 1986): 747. See also the discussion between MF and Boulez, "La musique contemporaine et le public," *FNAC Magazine* 15 (1983): 10–12, and MF's reflection on Boulez, "Pierre Boulez ou l'écran traversé," *Le Nouvel Observateur* 934 (October 2–8, 1982): 51–52. For a general consideration of MF and music, see Michel Fano, "Autour de la musique," *Le débat* 41 (September–November 1986): 137–39.
6. Arnold Schönberg, *Style and Idea* (London: Faber and Faber, 1975), pp. 216–17. On the meaning of the notion for Schönberg, see Charles Rosen, *Schönberg* (Glasgow: William Collins Sons, 1975), especially pp. 28–35.
7. *OD*, p. 60 (ET, p. 231).
8. *AS*, pp. 172–73 (ET, p. 131).

9. *AS*, p. 266 (ET, p. 204).
10. For just two examples of a manner that runs through his writings and interviews, see his remarks to Simon in "A Conversation with Michel Foucault," p. 192, and "Une mise au point de Michel Foucault," *La Quinzaine Littéraire* 47 (March 15–31, 1968): 21.
11. *OD*, p. 61 (ET, p. 231).
12. *AS*, p. 273 (ET, p. 209).
13. *OD*, pp. 38–47, (ET, pp. 224–27).
14. *OD*, pp. 23–28 (ET, pp. 220–24). For greater elaboration on the author-function in particular, see "Qu'est-ce qu'un auteur?"
15. *OD*, pp. 11–23 (ET, pp. 216–20).
16. *OD*, pp. 16–18 (ET, p. 218).
17. *OD*, pp. 47–51 (ET, pp. 227–28).
18. "Theatricum Philosophicum," p. 889 (ET, p. 171).
19. Ibid., p. 901 (ET, p. 187).
20. Ibid., pp. 892–93 (ET, pp. 175–76).
21. Ibid., p. 893 (ET, p. 176).
22. This part of this section is based upon Foucault's article "Nietzsche, la généalogie, l'histoire."
23. Ibid., p. 160 (ET, p. 154).
24. Ibid., p. 145 (ET, p. 140).
25. Ibid., p. 163 (ET, p. 156).
26. "Theatricum Philosophicum," p. 894 (ET, p. 178).
27. *AS*, p. 32 (ET, p. 21).
28. For an informed discussion of the various traditions to which MF was exposed as a student, see Pinguet, "Les années d'apprentissage."
29. Bellour, "Entretien," p. 139.
30. *LMC*, p. 233 (ET, p. 221).
31. Gerard Mendel, *La révolte contre le père* (Paris: Payot, 1974, 4th ed.), p. 320.
32. Caruso, p. 120.
33. "L'homme, est-il mort?" p. 9.
34. See "Foucault répond à Sartre," 22; Chapsal, p. 14; Bellour, "Entretien," p. 140; *LMC*, p. 312 (ET, p. 299).
35. *AS*, p. 149 (ET, p. 114).
36. *OD*, p. 73 (ET, p. 235). Dumézil, Canguilhem, Hyppolite, the three thinkers specifically mentioned in *OD*, are the same three (out of four) who were thanked by Foucault as far back as the 1961 Préface to *HF*, p. x.
37. In his 1961 *Le Monde* interview with Weber, "La folie n'existe que dans une société," Foucault had already named Dumézil as the source for his notion of structure. Dumézil was for many years a director of studies in the Section des Sciences Religieuses in the Ecole des Hautes Etudes of the Sorbonne, and was the retired professor of Indo-European civilization at the Collège de France until his death in 1987. Dumézil added to the traditional comparative study of the myths and epics of the Indo-European peoples a sociological and anthropological interest that was influenced by the work of Durkheim and Mauss. C. Scott Littleton has written an excellent study of Dumézil's extensive work, *The New Comparative Mythology: An Anthropological Assessment of the Theories of Georges Dumézil* (Berkeley: University of California, 1973). See pp. 202–3 and 215 for the contrast he draws between Dumézil's (inductive) and Lévi-Strauss's (deductive) concepts of structure.

38. *OD*, pp. 73–74 (ET, p. 235).
39. *AS*, p. 11 (ET, p. 4).
40. "Theatrum Philosophicum," p. 900 (ET, p. 186). In his later Introduction to the English translation of Canguilhem's *On the Normal and the Pathological* (Boston: Reidel, 1978), pp. ix–xx, Foucault will elaborate on Canguilhem's importance for current thought. His major works are *La formation du concept de réflexe aux XVIIIe et XVIIIe siècles* (Paris: Vrin, 1977); *Etudes d'histoire et de philosophie des sciences*, 2d ed. (Paris: Vrin, 1970). In this last volume there are three essays on Gaston Bachelard (1884–1962), who was of major importance in shaping Canguilhem's thought. While Bachelard was the first to make the notion of discontinuity significant for today's French philosophy (see his volume *Le rationalisme appliqué* [Paris: Presses Universitaires de France, 1949] for the terminology of "ruptures épistemélogiques"), there is no evidence to suggest that Bachelard was of major importance for Foucault himself. In Foucault's work, he is mentioned in a general context (see *AS*, p. 11 [ET, p. 4]), and his specific article on Bachelard is only a general statement of praise for his refusal to totalize (see "Gaston Bachelard, le philosophe et son ombre: Piéger sa propre culture").

In connection with this acknowledgement of Canguilhem, a word on the relationship between Foucault and his teacher at the Ecole Normale Supérieure, Louis Althusser, is warranted. Foucault acknowledges that he was marked by Althusser (see Bellour, "Deuxième entretien," pp. 191–92), and the specific point of praise for the Marxist thinker is his analysis of the notion of history contained in the first section of Althusser and Etienne Balibar's *Reading Capital* (London: NLB, 1977, 2d ed.). This study, first published in 1965, and with occasional references to Foucault's own work, systematizes, by the author's own admission, some of Canguilhem's concepts as a vehicle for understanding Marx. Other than transmitting the approaches of Bachelard (director of Althusser's thesis) and Canguilhem, there is not a close connection between Foucault and Althusser, as the latter himself recognizes (see his "A Letter to the Translator," in Balibar, pp. 323–24).

Perhaps the best study on Bachelard and Canguilhem, in terms of certain common interests with Foucault, is Dominique Lecourt's *Marxism and Epistemology: Bachelard, Canguilhem and Foucault* (Atlantic Highlands, N.J.: Humanities Press, 1975). On Althusser, see Alex Callinicos, *Althusser's Marxism* (London: Pluto Press, 1976).

41. *OD*, pp. 79–82 (ET, pp. 235–37). For the extraordinary influence exercised by Hyppolite in his teaching of Hegel, see Mark Poster, *Existential Marxism in Postwar France* (Princeton, N.J.: Princeton University Press, 1975), pp. 18–28. In addition to his translation of Hegel's *Phenomenology of Spirit* between 1939 and 1941, his major works are: *Genesis and Structure of Hegel's Phenomenology of Spirit* (Evanston: Northwestern, 1974, original French, 1946); *Introduction à la philosophie de l'histoire de Hegel* (Paris: Presses Universitaires de France, 1952); *Studies on Hegel and Marx* (New York: Harper and Row, 1973, original French, 1955); *Figures de la pensée philosophique*, in two volumes (Paris: Presses Universitaires de France, 1971).

42. See "Theatrum Philosophicum," p. 899 (ET, 184–85).

43. On Hyppolite's continuing discipleship, see, for example, his 1965 piece, "La situation de la philosophie dans le monde contemporain," *Figures de la pensée philosophique 2*, p. 1037.

44. *OD*, pp. 74–75 (ET, p. 235).
45. *OD*, p. 79 (ET, p. 236).
46. "Jean Hyppolite (1907–1968)," p. 131.
47. See Hyppolite's "Project d'enseignement d'histoire de la pensée philosophique" and his "Leçon inaugurale au Collège de France," *Figures de la pensée philosophique 2*, pp. 998, 1005, 1022.
48. Bellour, "Entretien," p. 144.
49. Bellour, "Deuxième entretien," p. 204.
50. See "Theatrum Philosophicum," p. 908 (ET, p. 196).
51. *OD*, p. 76 (ET, p. 236).
52. Bellour, "Deuxième entretien," p. 206. See Caruso, pp. 115–17, for a testimony of Nietzsche's unique status in an interview published three months after that of Bellour. In this regard it is interesting to note that the specific piece of music connected with Barraqué, whom Foucault identified as having been the occasion for his liberation from dialectical thinking, was a 1955 composition derived from a text of Nietzsche (see Caruso). Foucault is most likely making reference to Barraqué's "Séquence sur les poèmes de Nietzsche," 1950–55.
53. *LMC*, p. 316 (ET, p. 305).
54. *LMC*, p. 353 (ET, p. 342).
55. *LMC*, p. 275 (ET, p. 263).
56. *Thèse complémentaire 1*, p. 128.
57. *Logique et existence*, p. 243.
58. Caruso, pp. 116–17.
59. *Studies in Marx and Hegel*, pp. 154–55.
60. See the 1961 Préface to *HF*. For the change in *NC* to which I refer, see Appendix 2, Example 1.
61. Caruso, p. 117: "Le dirò solo che sono rimasto, ideologicamente, 'storicista' ed hegeliano, finché non ho letto Nietzsche."
62. See Foucault's later discussion with Gérard Raulet, "Structuralism and Post-Structuralism: An Interview with Michel Foucault," trans. Jeremy Harding, *Telos* 55 (Spring 1983); Préface (1961) to *HF*, p. v.
63. *AS*, p. 21 (ET, p. 11).
64. *AS*, pp. 22–23 (ET, pp. 12–13). The importance MF attributes to Marx here need not be interpreted as in contradiction to the position that *LMC* took in his regard, namely, that on the level of economic analysis, Marx introduced no epistemological break (see *LMC*, pp. 273–74 (ET, pp. 260–62)). As Foucault points out in his 1967 interview with Bellour, however, the level of historical analysis is a totally different matter ("Deuxième entretien," pp. 191–93).
65. "Nietzsche, le généalogie, l'histoire," pp. 148–50 (ET, pp. 142–44).
66. *AS*, pp. 22–23 (ET, pp. 12–13).
67. *AS*, pp. 10–13 (ET, pp. 4–6).
68. Ferdinand Braudel, *The Mediterranean and the Mediterranean World in the Age of Philip II* (New York: Harper Torchbooks, 2 vols., 1975), p. 16. First published in France in 1949, the translation is of the second revised edition of 1966. See also his "L'histoire des civilisations: le passé explique le present," *Ecrits sur histoire* (Paris: Flammarion, 1969), pp. 255–314, esp. pp. 301–5.
69. See Bellour, "Deuxième entretien," p. 190, and MF, "La naissance du monde," p. viii. In addition to Bloch and Febvre, MF singles out Braudel, François Furet, Denis Richet, and Le Roy Ladurie. See his later tribute to Philipe Ariès in "Le souci de la vérité," *Le Nouvel Observateur* 1006 (February 17–23, 1984), pp. 56–57.

70. See Jean Glénisson, "L'historiographie française contemporaine," in *La recherche historique en France de 1940 à 1965* (Paris: CNRS, 1965), pp. ix–lxiv, esp. pp. lxii–lxiii.
71. *AS*, pp. 13–14 (ET, pp. 6–7).
72. *AS*, pp. 13–14 (ET, pp. 6–7). In his "Réponse au Cercle d'épistémologie," p. 19 (ET, p. 127), MF had pointed out that he owed this formulation of documents as monuments to Canguilhem.
73. *AS*, pp. 14–20 (ET, pp. 7–11).
74. Braudel, p. 1243.
75. *OD*, pp. 56–57 (ET, p. 230).
76. On this theme, see Michel de Certeau, *L'écriture de l'histoire* (Paris: Gallimard, 1975), pp. 63–120.
77. See Bloch's manifesto, presented the year before the actual publication of *Annales*: "A Contribution Toward a Comparative History of European Societies," *Land and Work in Medieval Europe: Selected Papers by Marc Bloch* (Berkeley: University of California Press, 1967), pp. 47–81. Although it would be a large theme in itself to establish the impact of Foucault upon the work of historians writing in the *Annales* tradition, see, as an example, the reactions of Robert Mandrou, "Trois clefs pour comprendre la folie à l'époque classique," *Annales* 17 (1962), pp. 761–71, and the extraordinary praise that Braudel adds in a note to Mandrou's piece, pp. 771–72. See also Paul Veyne, "Foucault révolutionne l'histoire," an appendix to the second edition of his influential *Comment on écrit l'histoire* (Paris: Seuil, 1978), pp. 345–85.
78. *AS*, p. 24 (ET, p. 14).
79. *AS*, p. 26 (ET, p. 16).
80. *AS*, p. 26 (ET, p. 16).
81. *AS*, p. 25 (ET, p. 15).
82. For example, see *NC*, p. xii (xii) (ET, p. xvi); *LMC*, pp. 256, 262 (ET, pp. 243, 250); Bellour, "Deuxième entretien," pp. 196–97.
83. See *AS*, pp. 27, 74 (ET, pp. 16, 54). Foucault had been uncomfortable with the term "expérience" since at least 1963, but was stymied as to a replacement (see "Guetter le jour qui vient," *La Nouvelle Revue Française* 130 [October 1963], p. 710). As examples of his use of experience, see *HF*, p. 359: ". . . la réduction de l'expérience classique de la déraison à une perception strictement morale de la folie . . ." (ET, p. 161). In connection with perception, see *HF*, p. 548: ". . . perception médicale . . ." and *HF*, p. 411: ". . . perception asilaire . . ." and in *NC*, Appendix 2, Example 2, for the transformation of "codes perceptifs" into "codes de savoir." With respect to the gaze, see *RR*, p. 209 (ET, p. 166), and Appendix 2, Example 2, for an example that persists into the second edition.
84. *HF*, p. i (ET, p. ix); cf. *AS*, pp. 64, 26–27 (ET, pp. 47, 16–17).
85. See Appendix 2, Example 3 for a major example of this change, but also *NC*, pp. 18, 70, 199, 201 (and 18, 70, 201–3).
86. *AS*, p. 27 (ET, p. 16).
87. See "Réponse à une question," pp. 851–54 (ET, pp. 209–12).
88. *AS*, p. 41 (ET, p. 29).
89. *AS*, pp. 41–43 (ET, pp. 29–30).
90. *AS*, pp. 233–34 (ET, p. 179).
91. *AS*, pp. 44–47, 86 (ET, pp. 31–33, 65).
92. *AS*, pp. 47–48, 86 (ET, pp. 33–34, 65).
93. *AS*, pp. 48–53, 86 (ET, pp. 34–37, 65).
94. *AS*, p. 177 (ET, p. 135).

95. *AS*, p. 145 (ET, p. 111).
96. *AS*, p. 37 (ET, p. 25).
97. *AS*, p. 31–39 (ET, pp. 21–27).
98. *AS*, pp. 39–40, 105, 145–46 (ET, pp. 27–28, 79, 110–11).
99. *AS*, pp. 155–65 (ET, pp. 118–25).
100. *AS*, pp. 114–15, 138 (ET, pp. 86–87, 105).
101. *AS*, pp. 116–21 (ET, pp. 88–92).
102. *AS*, pp. 121–26 (ET, pp. 92–96).
103. *AS*, pp. 126–31 (ET, pp. 96–100).
104. *AS*, pp. 131–38 (ET, pp. 100–105).
105. Cf. *AS*, pp. 106–12 (ET, pp. 80–84).
106. *AS*, pp. 151, 141 (ET, pp. 115, 107).
107. *OD*, p. 55 (ET, p. 229).
108. *AS*, pp. 153–54 (ET, p. 117).
109. *AS*, pp. 44–47, 55–67 (ET, pp. 31–33, 40–49).
110. *AS*, p. 152 (ET, p. 116).
111. *AS*, pp. 47–48, 68–74 (ET, pp. 33–34, 50–55).
112. *AS*, pp. 48–49, 75–84 (ET, pp. 34–35, 56–63).
113. *AS*, pp. 49–52, 85–93 (ET, pp. 35–37, 64–70).
114. *AS*, p. 167 (ET, p. 127).
115. *AS*, pp. 167–69 (ET, pp. 127–28).
116. Préface to *HF* (1961), p. i (ET, p. ix); *NC*, pp. vii–viii (vii–viii) (ET, p. xi); *LMC*, p. 11–13 (ET, pp. xx–xxi).
117. *AS*, p. 81 (ET, p. 60); Foreword to ET of *LMC*, p. xi.
118. This particular formulation of *savoir* is to be found only in the English edition of *AS* (ET, p. 15) in a note in which the translator cites a specific definition of Foucault's for the distinction. For other formulations, see *AS*, pp. 236–40 (ET, pp. 181–84). Consult Appendix 2, Examples 4 and 5 for illustrations of how Foucault introduces this *savoir-connaissance* distinction into his revision of *NC*, and the greater precision that was permitted Foucault as a result of specifying the elements of a discursive formation. In translating *connaissance* as "cognition" and *savoir* as "knowledge," I have broken with the English translation of *AS* as well as with the common practice of most English language commentators who translate both as "knowledge." "Cognition" and "knowledge" seem to me superior in capturing Foucault's distinction, as well as having the advantage of allowing us two English terms for the two French words.
119. *AS*, pp. 62–63 (ET, pp. 45–46).
120. *AS*, p. 212 (ET, p. 162).
121. *AS*, p. 215 (ET, p. 164).
122. *AS*, pp. 95–96 (ET, p. 72).
123. *AS*, pp. 215 (ET, p. 165).
124. *AS* 173 (ET, p. 131); cf. "Michel Foucault explique son dernier livre," p. 23, and "La naissance du monde," p. viii.
125. *AS*, p. 171 (ET, p. 129).
126. *AS*, p. 171 (ET, p. 130).
127. *AS*, p. 173 (ET, p. 131).
128. For example, see his comments in *NC*, p. 197 (199) (ET, p. 195).
129. *AS*, p. 179 (ET, p. 136).
130. *AS*, p. 181 (ET, p. 138).
131. *AS*, p. 184–94 (ET, p. 141–48).

132. *AS*, p. 186 (ET, p. 142).
133. *AS*, p. 190 (ET, p. 145).
134. *AS*, pp. 195–204 (ET, pp. 149–56).
135. *AS*, p. 203 (ET, p. 155).
136. *AS*, pp. 205–15 (ET, pp. 157–65).
137. As an example of this general type of criticism, see de Certeau, p. 360.
138. *AS*, pp. 216–31 (ET, pp. 166–77).
139. See chapter 3, Section B, "The Task for Thought."
140. *AS*, p. 228 (ET, p. 175).
141. In his dispersal of discontinuities here, Foucault is attempting to make it impossible to interpret his view of break or rupture according to the model of a shift in *Weltanschauung*. In the light of certain of his formulations, such an interpretation would not have been without foundation, as I have already pointed out. For example, in *LMC*, he states: "Discontinuity—the fact that within the space of a few years a culture sometimes ceases to think as it has been thinking up till then and begins to think other things in a new way . . ." (*LMC*, p. 64 [ET, p. 50]).
142. *AS*, pp. 232–55 (ET, pp. 178–95).
143. *LMC*, pp. 262, 179 (ET, pp. 250, 168).
144. The notion of the archive is not new, and MF refers to it as early as 1964 ("La bibliothèque fantastique," p. 12 (ET, p. 92); its function as a general horizon for archaeology already appears in 1966 (see Bellour, "Entretien," p. 139, as well as his "Deuxième entretien," p. 201). Its value in the clarification of the episteme, however, does not appear until *AS*.
145. *AS*, pp. 243–47 (ET, pp. 186–89).
146. *AS*, pp. 240–41, 244–45 (ET, pp. 184, 187–88).
147. *AS*, pp. 247–49 (ET, pp. 189–91).
148. *AS*, pp. 250 (ET, p. 191).
149. *AS*, pp. 251–55 (ET, pp. 192–95).
150. For example, see Lecourt, pp. 187–90, and Jean-Paul Brodeur, "McDonnell on Foucault: Supplementary Remarks," *Canadian Journal of Philosophy* 7 (September 1977), pp. 558–59.
151. There is a tendency (Brodeur's article cited in n. 150 is a good example) to see Foucault's use of the term *episteme* as inextricably linked to a dalliance with structuralism. It might then be connected to the notion of "mytheme" in Lévi-Strauss's approach to myths (see Robert Scholes, *Structuralism in Literature* [New Haven: Yale University Press, 1974], pp. 69–70). My own speculation is that the term was employed in *LMC* originally because it permitted a sharp contrast between archaeology and the doxology of the history of ideas. See *LMC*, pp. 11–13 (ET, pp. xx–xxi).
152. "Nietzsche, la généalogie, l'histoire," p. 145 (ET, p. 139).
153. *OD*, pp. 55–56 (ET, p. 230). Since the English translation is inaccurate at this point, I cite the French: "Quatre notions doivent donc servir de principe régulateur à l'analyse: celle d'événement, celle de série, celle de régularité, celle de condition de possibilité. Elles s'opposent, on le voit, terme à terme: l'événement à la création, la série à l'unité, la régularité à l'originalité, et la condition de possibilité à la signification. Ces quatre dernières notions (signification, originalité, unité, création) ont, d'une manière assez générale, dominé l'histoire traditionelle des idées, où, d'un commun accord, on cherchait le point de la création, l'unité d'une oeuvre, d'une époque ou d'un thème, la marque de

l'originalité individuelle, et le trésor indéfini des significations enfouies."
154. See in chapter 3, "Archaeology and the Thinking of History."
155. See Colette Ysmal, "Histoire et archéologie: Note sur la recherche de Michel Foucault," *Revue Française de Science Politique* 22, no. 4 (August 1972): 796–97; Lecourt, pp. 208–9; Dreyfus and Rabinow, pp. 79–100.
156. "Par delà le bien et le mal," p. 25 (ET, p. 220).
157. Ibid., p. 26 (ET, p. 221).
158. "Human Nature: Justice Versus Power," p. 168.
159. *AS*, p. 138 (ET, p. 105). Cf. *OD*, p. 12 (ET, p. 216).
160. "Human Nature: Justice Versus Power," pp. 171, 184.

CHAPTER 5

1. The following are the most important texts from this period: *Moi, Pierre Rivière, ayant égorgé ma mère, ma soeur et mon frère*, ed. Michel Foucault (Paris: Gallimard, 1973) (ET: *I, Pierre Rivière, having slaughtered my mother, my sister and my brother*, trans. Frank Jellinek [New York: Pantheon, 1975], hereafter *MPR*); *Surveiller et punir: Naissance de la prison* (ET: *Discipline and Punish: The Birth of the Prison*, trans. Alan Sheridan [New York: Pantheon, 1977], hereafter *SP*); *Histoire de la sexualité 1: La volonté de savoir* (Paris: Gallimard, 1976) (ET: *The History of Sexuality 1: An Introduction*, trans. Robert Hurley [New York: Pantheon, 1978], hereafter *VS*); "Les intellectuels et le pouvoir: *L'Arc* 49 (1972): 3–10 (ET: "Intellectuals and Power," in *Language, Counter-Memory and Practice*, 205–17); "Sur la justice populaire," *Les Temps Modernes* 310 (1972): 335–66 (ET: "On Popular Justice: A Discussion with Maoists," in *Power/Knowledge*, ed. Colin Gordon [New York: Pantheon, 1980], pp. 1–36); "Michel Foucault on Attica," *Telos* 19 (1974): 154–61; "Médecine et lutte de classes," *La Nef* 49 (October–December 1972): 67–73; "Entretien avec Michel Foucault: à propos de l'enfermement pénitentiaire," *Pro Justicia: Revue politique de droit* 3–4 (October 1973): 5–14; "Pouvoir et corps," *Quel corps?* (Paris: François Maspéro, 1978), pp. 27–35 (ET: "Body/Power" in *Power/Knowledge*, pp. 55–62); "Entretien sur la prison," *Magazine littéraire* 101 (June 1975), pp. 27–33 (ET: "Prison Talk," in *Power/Knowledge*, pp. 37–54); "Questions à Michel Foucault sur la géographie," *Hérodote* 1 (January–March 1976): 71–85 (ET: "Questions on Geography," in *Power/Knowledge*, pp. 63–77); "Intervista a Michel Foucault, *Microfisica del Potere*, ed. Alessandro Fontana and Pasquale Pasquino (Torino: Einaudi, 1977), pp. 3–28 (ET: "Truth and Power," in *Power/Knowledge*, pp. 109–33); "L'extension sociale de la norme," *Politique hebdo* 212 (March 4, 1976): 14–16; "Pouvoirs et stratégies," *Les révoltes logiques* 4 (1977): 89–97 (ET: "Power and Strategies," *Power/Knowledge*, pp. 134–45); "L'oeil du pouvoir," introduction to Jeremy Bentham, *La panoptique* (Paris: Pierre Belfond, 1977), pp. 7–31 (ET: "The Eye of Power," in *Power/Knowledge*, pp. 146–65); "Les rapports de pouvoir passent à l'intérieur des corps," *La quinzaine littéraire* 247 (January 1–15, 1977), pp. 4–6 (ET: "The History of Sexuality," in *Power/Knowledge*, pp. 183–93); "Non au sexe roi," *Le Nouvel Observateur* 644 (March 12, 1977): 93–130 (ET: "Power and Sex: An Interview with Michel Foucault," trans. D. Parent, *Telos* 32 [Summer 1977]: 152–61); "La grande colère des faits," *Faut-il brûler les nouveaux philosophes?* ed. Sylvie Boucasse and Denis Bourgeois (Paris: Nouvelles Editions Oswald, 1978), pp. 63–70; "Le jeu de Michel Foucault," *Ornicar?* 10 (July 1977)

(ET: "The Confession of the Flesh," *Power/Knowledge*, pp. 194–228); "Enfermement, Psychiatrie, Prison," *Change: La folie encerclée* 32–33 (October 1977) : 76–110; Introduction to Canguilhem, *On the Normal and Pathological*, pp. ix–xx; "La poussière et le nuage" and "Table ronde du 20 mai 1978," both in *L'impossible prison: Recherches sur le système pénitentiare au XIXe siècle*, ed. Michelle Perot (Paris: Seuil, 1980), pp. 29–39, 40–56 (the table ronde was translated as "Questions of Method" in *Ideology and Consciousness* 8 (Spring 1981): 3–14; "Inutile de se soulever?" *Le Monde* 10, 661 (May 11, 1979): 1–2 (ET: "Is it useless to revolt?" *Philosophy and Social Criticism* 8, 1 [Spring 1981]: 1–19). In addition, see Foucault's course summaries in the *Annuaire du Collège de France* 1972–79. Several other works from this period will be taken up in the next chapter.

2. See in chapter 4, "The Fields of Application."
3. See in chapter 1 a consideration of his approach to the painting of Rebeyrolle as an example of the intimate association of thought and the political theme in Foucault.
4. *OD*, p. 10 (ET, p. 216). On the Collège itself and its history, see the volume that was published on the occasion of its 400th anniversary, *Le Collège de France* (1530–1930) (Paris: Les Presses universitaires de France, 1932).
5. "Enfermement, psychiatrie, prison," p. 91; cf. "Pouvoirs et strategies," p. 97 (ET, pp. 144–45).
6. See above, chapter 3, "Archaeology and Politics."
7. See above, chapter 4, "The Constraints on Thought," and *OD*, pp. 10–47 (ET, pp. 216–27).
8. See "Human Nature: Justice versus Power" (1971), pp. 168–87, and "Par delà le bien et le mal" (1971), pp. 38–39 (ET, pp. 230–31).
9. See *NC*, pp. 201–2 (199–200) (ET, pp. 197–98); "Nietzsche, Marx, Freud" (1964); "Pouvoirs et corps," p. 35 (ET, p. 62). The studies conducted under MF's direction in *Politiques de l'habitat 1800–1850* (Paris: Comité pour la Recherche et le Développement en Architecture [CORDA] 1977) are largely concerned with the relationships among political, health, and architectural discourses.
10. *VS*, p. 191 (ET, p. 145).
11. "Les intellectuels et le pouvoir," p. 6 (ET, p. 210).
12. "Michel Foucault on Attica," p. 156.
13. *SP*, p. 35 (ET, p. 30). For the impact of the prison revolts on Foucault, see Michelle Perrot, "La leçon des ténèbres. Michel Foucault et la prison," *Actes* 54 (Summer 1986): 74–79.
14. *SP*, pp. 234–35 (ET, pp. 232–33).
15. Beccaria, *Des délits et des peines* (1974, ed. 1856), cited in *SP*, p. 93 (ET, p. 90).
16. B. Rush in 1787, in an address to the Society for Promoting Political Inquiries, cited in *SP*, p. 16 (ET, p. 10).
17. Van Meenen, in an 1847 address to the Congrès pénitentiaire de Bruxelles, cited in *SP*, p. 234 (ET, p. 232).
18. *SP*, pp. 269–73 (ET, pp. 264–68).
19. *SP*, pp. 274–75 (ET, pp. 268–70).
20. *SP*, p. 274 (ET, p. 269).
21. See *SP*, pp. 122–31, 235–51 (ET, pp. 121–28, 233–48).
22. *SP*, p. 90 (ET, p. 87).
23. *SP*, p. 84 (ET, p. 82).
24. *SP*, pp. 77–80, 84–90 (ET, pp. 75–78, 84–87).

25. *SP*, p. 93 (ET, p. 90).
26. J. M. Servan, *Discours sur l'administration de la justice criminelle*, 1767, cited in *SP*, p. 105 (ET, p. 103).
27. *SP*, pp. 118–21 (ET, pp. 116–118).
28. *SP*, p. 132 (ET, pp. 128–29).
29. *SP*, pp. 201–3 (ET, pp. 200–201); "L'oeil du pouvoir," p. 10 (ET, p. 14). Bentham's *Panopticon; or the Inspection House* was written in 1787. Another version of the volume was published, by order of the National Assembly, in 1791 in Paris. English texts can be found in *The Works of Jeremy Bentham* 4, ed. John Bowring (1843, reprint ed., New York: Russel and Russel, 1971), pp. 37–172.
30. C. Lucas, *De la réforme des prisons*, 1, 1836, p. 69 and N. H. Julius, *Leçons sur les prisons*, 1, 1831, p. 384, cited in *SP*, pp. 252, 218 (ET, pp. 249, 216).
31. "L'oeil du pouvoir," p. 11 (ET, p. 147).
32. *SP*, pp. 143–70 (ET, pp. 141–68).
33. *SP*, pp. 172–96 (ET, pp. 170–94).
34. *SP*, p. 140 (ET, p. 138).
35. The full title of Bentham's *Panopticon* states that it is a study that contains the "idea of a new principle of construction applicable to any sort of establishment, in which persons of any description are to be kept under inspection; and, in particular to penitentiary-houses, prisons, houses of industry, work-houses, poor-houses, manufactories, mad-houses, lazarettos, hospitals and schools."
36. *SP*, pp. 197–229 (ET, pp. 195–228).
37. See *SP*, pp. 233–60 (ET, pp. 231–56).
38. *SP*, p. 229 (ET, p. 228).
39. Préface to Livrozet, *De la prison à la révolte*, (Paris: Mercure de France, 1973), 8; *SP*, pp. 292–93 (ET, pp. 286–87).
40. See *SP*, pp. 31–32, 189–91 (ET, pp. 26–27, 187–89).
41. *SP*, p. 196 (ET, p. 194).
42. *SP*, pp. 31–33 (ET, pp. 26–28).
43. *SP*, pp. 27–28 (ET, pp. 22–23).
44. *SP*, pp. 195–96, 185 (ET, pp. 194, 182–83).
45. *SP*, p. 143 (ET, p. 141).
46. *SP*, p. 312 (ET, p. 305).
47. *SP*, p. 311 (ET, p. 304).
48. *SP*, pp. 308–14, 186 (ET, pp. 301–7, 184).
49. See "Les rapports de pouvoir passent à l'intérieur des corps," p. 5 (ET, pp. 187–88).
50. The notion of the norm provides the major unifying concept of Ulrich Raulf's dissertation, *Das normale Leben: Michel Foucaults Theories der Normalisierungsmacht* (Marburg University, 1977, directed by Prof. Dr. Kamper). Its analyses are primarily directed to *SP*.
51. See "Vorwort zu deutschen Ausgabe," a presentation to the German edition of *VS: Sexualität und Wahrheit I: Die Wille zum Wissen* (Frankfurt: Suhrkamp, 1977), p. 7; "Non au sexe roi," p. 93 (ET, p. 152).
52. *VS*, pp. 16, 190 (ET, pp. 8, 144).
53. This common history of sexual repression is scattered through *VS*, but see especially pp. 9–12, 25–49, 152 (ET, pp. 3–5, 17–35, 115).
54. *VS*, p. 10 (ET, p. 4).
55. *VS*, pp. 25–49 (ET, pp. 17–35).

56. *VS*, p. 46 (ET, p. 33).
57. *VS*, pp. 50–67, 138–51 (ET, pp. 36–49, 103–14).
58. *VS*, p. 139 (ET, p. 105).
59. *VS*, pp. 71–98 (ET, pp. 53–73).
60. *VS*, p. 85 (ET, p. 63).
61. *VS*, p. 49 (ET, p. 35).
62. *VS*, p. 139 (ET, pp. 105–6).
63. *VS*, p. 207 (ET, p. 157); see also *VS*, pp. 198–207 (ET, pp. 150–56). The function it does in fact play is mentioned in our next section, on "Bio-politics."
64. See *VS*, pp. 30, 137–38, 150–51 (ET, pp. 21, 104–5, 113–14). The titles were those provided by Gallimard, the publisher of *VS*.
65. *VS*, pp. 152–61 (ET, pp. 115–22).
66. Cf. *VS*, pp. 57–65 (ET, pp. 41–47).
67. *VS*, pp. 119–27 (ET, pp. 90–96).
68. *VS*, p. 135 (ET, p. 102).
69. *VS*, pp. 177–82 (ET, pp. 135–39).
70. *VS*, p. 181 (ET, p. 138).
71. *VS*, p. 187 (ET, p. 142).
72. *VS*, p. 188 (ET, p. 143). Cf. "Histoire des systèmes de pensée." 1979, p. 367.
73. *VS*, p. 191 (ET, p. 145).
74. *VS*, p. 192 (ET, p. 146).
75. *VS*, p. 211 (ET, p. 159).
76. *VS*, p. 114 (ET, p. 86).
77. *VS*, p. 188 (ET, p. 143).
78. *VS*, p. 180 (ET, p. 137).
79. *VS*, p. 180 (ET, p. 137).
80. *SP*, p. 143 (ET, p. 141); see also *SP*, pp. 34, 312 (ET, pp. 29–30, 305), *VS*, pp. 93–94 (ET, p. 70).
81. See *VS*, p. 128 (ET, p. 97), and "Entretien sur la prison: le livre et sa méthode," p. 33 (ET, p. 52).
82. As examples of the former view, see Dominique Wolton, "Qui veut savoir?" *Esprit* 7–8 (July–August 1977): 36–47, and Donald J. McDonell, "On Foucault's Philosophical Method," *Canadian Journal of Philosophy* 7, no. 3 (September 1977): 537–53. For the latter view, see François Ewald, "Anatomie et corps politique," *Critique* 343 (December 1975): 1228–65, and Dreyfus and Rabinow.
83. See *AS*, pp. 251–55 (ET, pp. 192–95).
84. His study of the prison is portrayed at one point as a genealogy (*SP*, p. 27 [ET, p. 23]). A terminological function for genealogy was first indicated by Foucault in *OD*, where it designated the application of three principles of archaeological analysis: discontinuity, specificity, and exteriority (see *OD*, pp. 53–63 [ET, pp. 229–32]). Later Foucault suggested that genealogy might be best employed to mean the tactic of putting into play the fruit of archaeology's examination of specific discursive formations (see "Corso del 7 gennaio, 1976," p. 170 [ET, p. 85]).
85. Bellour, p. 138.
86. "Table ronde du mai 1978," p. 48 (ET, p. 9).
87. Ibid., p. 55 (ET, p. 14).
88. This formulation of the *dispositif* comes from the important 1977 conversation, "Le jeu de Michel Foucault," in *Ornicar?* pp. 63–66 (ET, pp. 194–98).
89. See "Intervista a Michel Foucault," pp. 8–9 (ET, pp. 114–15).

90. *VS*, pp. 19–29, 121–29 (ET, pp. 11–12, 92–97).
91. *VS*, pp. 129–35 (ET, pp. 98–102).
92. *VS*, p. 129 (ET, pp. 98).
93. See "L'oeil du pouvoir," p. 13 (ET, pp. 149–50).
94. For the beginnings of this reflection on the strategic model, see his summary of the 1976 course at the Collège, his "Corso del 7 gennaio, 1976," and "Des questions de Michel Foucault à *Hérodote*," *Hérodote* 3 (July–September 1976): 9–10.
95. "Inutile de se soulever?" p. 2 (ET, p. 9).
96. "Non au sexe roi," p. 113 (ET, p. 159).
97. See *AS*, p. 231 (ET, p. 177); "La grande colère des faits," pp. 67–68; "Histoire des systèmes de pensée," 1973, p. 217.
98. Jean-Pierre Peter and Jeanne Favret, "L'animal, le fou, le mort," *MPR*, p. 251 (ET, "The Animal, the Madman and Death," pp. 184–85).
99. "Non au sexe roi," pp. 113, 124 (ET, p. 160).
100. See chapter 3, "*Archaeology and Politics.*"
101. *SP*, p. 314 (ET, p. 305).
102. See *SP*, p. 32 (ET, p. 27); for transgression theme, see chapter 2, "Literature: A 'Within' and a 'Without'"; and "Pouvoirs et stratégies," p. 93 (ET, pp. 139–41).
103. *VS*, p. 126 (ET, pp. 95–96).
104. "L'oeil du pouvoir," p. 24 (ET, p. 159).
105. "Non au sexe roi," p. 124 (ET, p. 160).
106. *AS*, p. 272 (ET, p. 209). In his 1972 Préface to the new edition of *HF*, Foucault deprives himself of this sovereignty even over his own discourse. Asked to write a new introduction, he suppressed the 1961 preface as representative of that sovereignty over writing exercised in the author function.
107. Simon, p. 201.
108. "Pouvoirs et stratégies," pp. 94–95 (ET, pp. 141–42).
109. *VS*, p. 127 (ET, p. 96).
110. "Non au sexe roi," p. 124 (ET, p. 160).
111. "Pouvoirs et corps," p. 34 (ET, p. 62).
112. See "Questions à Michel Foucault sur la géographie," p. 72 (ET, pp. 64–65), "Non au sexe roi," p. 130 (ET, p. 161), and "Intervista a Foucault," pp. 22–23 (ET, pp. 127–29).
113. "Intervista a Michel Foucault," pp. 20–23 (ET, pp. 126–29). It goes without saying that Foucault's understanding of the intellectual is of a figure who could not be associated with any particular sociological group. He refers to Oppenheimer as an example of the transition from universal to specific intellectual: with him, "I think, the intellectual was hounded by political powers, no longer on account of a general discourse he conducted, but because of the knowledge at his disposal: it was at this level that he constituted a political threat." (Ibid., p. 22 [ET, p. 128]).
114. See "Corso del 14 gennaio, 1976," Pasquino, p. 180 (ET, pp. 93–94).
115. See *VS*, pp. 80–81, 98 (ET, pp. 60, 73), and "Non au sexe roi," pp. 93, 105 (ET, pp. 153, 157).
116. *OD*, p. 53 (ET, p. 229).
117. *OD*, pp. 15–23, 35–37 (ET, pp. 217–20, 223–4).
118. "Histoire des systèmes de pensée, 1971," p. 195 (ET, p. 199).
119. *VS*, p. 90 (ET, p. 67).

120. *SP*, pp. 186–96 (ET, pp. 184–94).
121. See "Histoire des systèmes de pensée, 1972," and *SP*, pp. 46, 99–100, 225–29 (ET, pp. 42, 96–98, 224–28).
122. See "Histoire des systèmes de pensée, 1972," pp. 204–5, and *MPR*.
123. On this point, see *MPR*, especially Foucault's "Les meurtres qu'on raconte," pp. 274–75 (ET, pp. 209–11), and Patricia Moulin, "Les circonstances atténuantes," pp. 277–83 (ET, pp. 212–18); Philippe Riot, "Les vies parallèles de P. Rivière," pp. 295–314 (ET, pp. 229–50); Robert Castel, "Les médecins et les juges," pp. 315–31 (ET, pp. 250–69).
124. *SP*, pp. 24–27 (ET, pp. 19–22).
125. *SP*, p. 100 (ET, p. 98). See also "About the Concept of the 'Dangerous Individual' in 19th-Century Legal Psychiatry," *International Journal of Law and Psychiatry* 1 (1978), pp. 1–18.
126. *VS*, p. 73 (ET, p. 54).
127. "Intervista a Michel Foucault," pp. 26–27 (ET, p. 132).
128. Ibid., p. 25 (ET, p. 131).
129. Ibid., pp. 27–28 (ET, pp. 131–33).
130. On the critique of education, see "Par delà le bien et le mal" (1971) and "Le piège de Vincennes" (1970); on the matter of secrecy, see his letter to the former prime minister of Iran, "Lettre ouverte à Mehdi Bazargan," *Le Nouvel Observateur* 753 (April 14, 1979): 46; on the matter of torture, see "Le supplice de la vérité," in the issue on torture of *Chemin de Ronde* 1 (1977): 162–63; on his advocacy, see "La stratégie du pourtour," *Le Nouvel Observateur* 759 (May 28, 1979): 57. His involvement with groups struggling against imperialism took the form of his sponsorship of a journal that attempted a radical critique of imperialistic policies. Its first issue was *Nouvel Africasia* 1 (January 1973), and was suppressed on the grounds that its title duplicated that of another journal. While Foucault saw this as a pretext, its following two issues bore the title *Zone des tempêtes* 2 (May–June 1973) and 3 (July–August 1973). For the general statement of the magazine's purpose, see the first issue, pp. 3–4. For Foucault's statement on the suppression, cf. no. 2, "Un nouveau journal," p. 3. While the suppressed *Nouvel Africasia* was not made available by the Bibliothèque Nationale, it may be consulted at the library of the Foundation Nationale des Sciences Politiques. The best account of Foucault's political activity is to be found in Claude Mauriac, *Le temps immobile* 3: *Et comme l'espérance est violente* (Paris: Grasset, 1976). Most of this volume's second part (pp. 261–592) is a diary account of political actions and debates in which Foucault played a prominent part. The major period covered runs from June 12, 1971 to September 29, 1975. Since I have not included in my list of MF's writings those letters regarding specific political issues to which he added his name, I wish to cite only three more recent statements as examples of this sort of intervention. See the letter on behalf of Doctor Martha Frayde, a prisoner in Cuba, and his leter in defense of a nonapproved "open" university in Poland, both of which appeared in the *New York Review of Books*, December 7, 1978, 2, and January 24, 1980, 49. See *Le Nouvel Observateur* 792 (January 14, 1980) for his letter of protest to a French television station against its choice of Georges Suffert to act as moderator of a series. Suffert was accused in the letter of having made grave accusations against a leftist who later came to be assassinated.
131. See "Une mort inacceptable," the preface to Bernard Cuau, *L'affaire Mirval ou*

comment le récit abolit le crime (Paris: Les Presses d'aujourd'hui, 1976), pp. vii–xi.

132. See "Intervista a Michel Foucault," pp. 20–23 (ET, pp. 126–29).
133. On specific abuses, see "Le discours de Toul," *Le Nouvel Observateur* 372 (December 27, 1971): 15; "Les deux morts de Pompidou," *Le Nouvel Observateur* 421 (December 4, 1972): 56–57; "Du bon usage du criminel," *Le Nouvel Observateur* 722 (September 11, 1978): 40–42. On *GIP*, see n. 138 below.
134. *SP*, pp. 61–68 (ET, pp. 57–65).
135. *SP*, pp. 261–99 (ET, pp. 257–92).
136. See "Sur la justice populaire"; "Michel Foucault on Attica"; "Gefängnisse und Gefängnisrevolten," an interview with MF conducted by Budo Morawe in *Dokumente: Zeitschrift für Zusammenarbeit* 29 (1973): 133–37; "Sur la sellete," an interview with Jean-Louis Ezine in *Les nouvelles littéraires* 2477 (March 17, 1975): 3; "Crimes et châtiments en U.R.S.S. et ailleurs," *Le Nouvel Observateur* 585 (January 26, 1976): 34–37 (ET: "The Politics of Crime," trans. M. Horwitz, *Partisan Review* 43 [1976]: 453–59); "Enfermement, psychiatrie, prison"; "Manières de justice," *Le Nouvel Observateur* 743 (February 5, 1979): 2–21; "Entretien avec MF: à propos de l'enfermement."
137. "Crimes et châtiments en U.R.S.S. et ailleurs," p. 35 (ET, pp. 455–56).
138. See "Michel Foucault on Attica" and "Gefängnisse und Gefängnisrevolten." The GIP was voluntarily dissolved in December 1972 as a result of the formation of other groups, particularly one formed by prisoners themselves, to continue the political struggle of the prison. The best statement of its purpose is contained in the introduction to its first study, *Enquête dans 20 prisons* (Paris: Editions Champ Libre, 1971), pp. 3–5. Its other studies under the general title of *Intolérable* were No. 2: *Le GIP enquête dans une prison-modèle: Fleury-Merogis* (Paris: Editions Champ Libre, 1971); No. 3: *L'assassinat de George Jackson*, with a preface by Jean Genet (Paris: Gallimard, 1971); No. 4: *Suicides de prison* (Paris: Gallimard, 1972). For a brief consideration of GIP, see Marc Kravetz, "Qu'est-ce que le gip?" *Magazine littéraire* 101 (June 1975): 13.
139. See "Enfermement, psychiatrie, prison," pp. 76–82.
140. "En guise de conclusion," *Le Nouvel Observateur* 435 (March 13, 1972): 92; "Convoqués à la P. J.," *Le Nouvel Observateur* 468 (October 29, 1973): 53.
141. See "L'asile illimité," *Le Nouvel Observateur* 646 (March 28, 1977): 66–67; "Sorcellerie et folie," *Le Monde* 9720 (April 23, 1976); "L'extension sociale de la norme." On Szasz's position, see his *The Myth of Mental Illness* (New York: Harper, 1971); *Schizophrenia: The Sacred Symbol of Psychiatry* (New York: Basic Books, 1976); *The Manufacture of Madness* (New York: Harper and Row, 1977).
142. See *Généalogie des équipements de normalisation: Les équipements sanitaires* (Fontenay-sous-Bois: Centre d'études, de recherches et de formation institutionelles [CERFI], 1976). The contents of this study conducted under Foucault's direction may be found in the bibliography.
143. See *Politiques de l'habitat 1800–1850* (Paris: Comité pour la Recherche et le Développement en Architecture [CORDA], 1977). The studies contained in this work are identified in the bibliography.
144. For information regarding the purposes of *GIS*, see the article by MF and others of the group, "Médecine et lutte de classes," and *GIS, La médecine désordonnée: d'une pratique de l'avortement à la lutte pour la santé* (Paris: Solon, 1974), pp. 7–10, 95–98. Other publications of the group have included:

Oui, nous avortons: Bulletin special du G.I.S. (Paris: Editions Gît-le-Coeur, 1973); *Le contrôle patronal sur les ouvriers malades* (Paris: Solin, 1974); *Travailler dans les égouts en 1976* (Paris: Les Imprimeurs libres, 1976).

145. "Intervista a Michel Foucault," pp. 23–25 (ET, pp. 130–32); "Gefängnisse und Gefängnisrevolten," p. 134.

146. See "Les rapports de pouvoir passent à l'intérieur des corps," p. 6 (ET, pp. 188–92) and "Gefängnisse und Gefängnisrevolten," p. 137. Foucault's course at the Collège in 1974 was largely taken up with an examination of the antipsychiatry movement that is contemporary with psychiatry's development, and that he felt did not want to annul the power of medicine itself. See "Histoire des systèmes de pensée," 1974. For a discussion on this topic, see A. F. Zoila, "Michel Foucault, Anti-Psychiatrie?" *Revue Internationale de Philosophie* 123 (1978), pp. 59–74.

147. For particular examples, see Foucault's conversation with José, a worker, "Pour une chronique de la mémoire ouvrière," *Libération* no. 00 (sic) (February 22, 1973), p. 6, and his Préface to *De la prison à la révolte*. On providing a voice for the worker, see especially the *GIS* publication *Travailler dans les égouts en 1976*.

148. See his discussion with MF, "Les intellectuels et le pouvoir," p. 5 (ET, p. 209).

149. "Non au sexe roi," p. 113 (ET, p. 159).

150. "La grande colère des faits," p. 66.

151. "Non au sexe roi," pp. 93, 105 (ET, pp. 153, 157) and Vorwort to the German edition of *VS*, 8.

152. The importance of three factors was stated in a personal communication to the editor of a Spanish language edition of some of MF's interviews. See Miguel Morey, *Sexo, Poder, Verdad: Conversaciones con Michel Foucault* (Barcelona: Editorial Materiales, 1978), pp. 48–49.

153. "Intervista a Michel Foucault," pp. 3–5, 9–10 (ET, pp. 115–16).

154. See "Non au sexe roi," pp. 113, 124 (ET, p. 160).

155. *VS*, pp. 126–27 (ET, p. 96).

156. See Foucault, "Pour une moral de l'inconfort," *Le Nouvel Observateur* 754 (April 23, 1979): 82–83, and "Vivre autrement le temps," *Le Nouvel Observateur* 755 (April 30, 1979): 88.

157. "Inutile de se soulever?" p. 2 (ET, p. 8).

CHAPTER 6

1. For examples of responses to his death, see *Le Monde* 12260 (June 27, 1984), with articles by Pierre Bourdieu, Philippe Boucher, Roger-Pol Droit, Bertrand Poirot-Delpech, and Paul Veyne; a special dossier of *Libération* (June 30–July 1, 1984) carried essays by François Ewald and Robert Maggiori, among others; *Le Nouvel Observateur* 1025 (June 29–July 5, 1984) contained responses of Jean Daniel, Georges Dumézil, Roger Chartier, and Pierre Nora; *University Publishing* 13 (Summer 1984) provided a forum for largely American and English responses by such writers as Michael Ignatieff, Thomas Laqueur, Ian Hacking, Allan Megill, and Paul Rabinow. In the years since his death, there has been a proliferation of texts with a large number of studies, many of which have been mentioned in the course of my study. Among these are *Michel Foucault: Une histoire de la vérité* (Paris: Syros, 1985); *Anschlüsse: Versuche nach Michel*

Foucault (Tübingen: Diskord, 1985); *Actes* 54 (Summer 1986); *Critique* 471–72
(August–September 1986); *Le débat* 41 (September–November 1986); *Foucault:
A Critical Reader*, ed. David Couzens Hoy (Oxford: Blackwell, 1986); *Philosophy and Social Criticism* 12 (1987).

2. *UP*, p. 11 (ET, p. 5).
3. *UP*, pp. 17–18 (ET, pp. 11–12).
4. *UP*, p. 12 (ET, p. 6).
5. *PSY*, p. 103 (ET, p. 87).
6. *RR*, p. 14 (ET, p. 7).
7. Daraki, "Michel Foucault's Journey to Greece," *Telos* 67 (Spring 1986): 105;
   Wolin, "Foucault's Aesthetic Decisionism," in the same issue of *Telos*, p. 78.
8. For my remarks on Foucault's 1975 course, I am indebted to a transcription of
   several of the lectures as well as the course description published in *Annuaire du
   Collège de France* 75 (1975), pp. 335–39; Foucault told me of Illich's suggestion
   in a March 1980 conversation I had with him; *OD*, p. 63 (ET, p. 232).
9. *VS*, p. 82 (ET, p. 61).
10. Course lecture of February 19, 1975.
11. For example, in his 1983 discussion, "On the Genealogy of Ethics: An Overview
    of Work in Progress" in Dreyfus and Paul Rabinow, pp. 229–64, and in his
    account of his project's modifications in the second volume of his history of
    sexuality, *UP*, pp. 9–19 (ET, pp. 3–13).
12. *VS*, p. 188 (ET, p. 143).
13. *VS*, p. 192 (ET, p. 146).
14. See in chapter 5, "The History of Sexuality: An Overview."
15. See his course descriptions of these years, which appeared in English as "War in
    the Filigree of Peace" (1976), trans. Ian Mcleod, *The Oxford Literary Review* 4,
    2 (1980): 15–19; "Foucault at the Collège de France I & II" (1978, 1979), trans.
    James Bernauer, *Philosophy and Social Criticism* 8, 2–3 (Summer and Fall 1981):
    235–42, 351–59.
16. Foucault, "La gouvernementalité," *Actes* 54 (Summer 1986): 7 (ET: "Governmentality," trans. Rosi Braidotti, *I & C* 6 [Autumn 1979]:6). This is a translation
    of an important lecture from Foucault's 1978 course.
17. Foucault's summary of the 1980 course may be found in the *Annuaire du
    Collège de France* 80 (1980): 449–52. The Stanford lectures were published as
    'Omnes et Singulatim: Towards a Criticism of 'Political Reason,'" in *The
    Tanner Lectures on Human Values* 2 (Salt Lake City: University of Utah Press,
    1981), pp. 225–54; this was later translated into French by P. E. Dauzat as
    "Omnes et Singulatim: Vers une critique de la raison politique," *Le débat* 41
    (September–November 1986): 5–35. The French will be cited first in these notes.
    Other publications are: "Sexuality and Solitude," *Humanities in Review* 1
    (1982), ed. David Rieff (New York: Cambridge University Press, 1982), pp.
    3–21; "La combat de la chasteté," *Communications* 35 (May 1982): 15–25 (ET:
    "The Battle for Chastity," trans. A. Foster in *Western Sexuality: Practice and
    Precept in Past and Present Times*, ed. Philippe Ariès and André Béjin (Oxford:
    Basil Blackwell, 1985), pp. 14–25; "L'écriture de soi," *Corps écrit* 5 (1983): 3–23.
    In addition, there are several discussions: "On the Genealogy of Ethics," in
    Dreyfus and Rabinow; "Le souci de la vérité," an interview conducted by
    François Ewald, *Magazine littéraire* 207 (May 1984): 18–23 (ET: "The Regard
    for Truth," trans. Paul Patton, *Art and Text* 16 [Summer 1984]: 20–31); and "Le
    retour de la morale," an interview conducted by Gilles Barbedette and André

Scala for *Les Nouvelles* 2937 (June 28–July 5, 1984): 36–41 (ET: "Final Interview," *Raritan* 5, 1 [Summer 1985]: 1–13). There are also several observations in *UP* as well as *SS*. A closely related summer course, "The Discourse of Self-Disclosure," was presented at the University of Toronto in 1982. In November 1980, Foucault presented two important lectures at Dartmouth College: "Subjectivity and Truth" and "Christianity and Confession." I was able to attend the 1980 and 1982 courses, and have transcripts of the Dartmouth lectures.

18. "Omnes et Singulatim," pp. 8–11, 16–19 (ET, pp. 228–31, 236–38).
19. Ibid., p. 18 (ET, p. 237). Lectures from the 1980 course on March 19 and 26.
20. "Sexuality and Solitude," p. 14.
21. Ibid., pp. 10–11.
22. 1980 course, lectures of March 5 and 12; "Christianity and Confession"; Toronto course, "The Discourse of Self-Disclosure," June 15, 1982.
23. "Le combat de la chasteté," p. 23 (ET, p. 20); 1980 course, lecture of March 26.
24. Ibid., p. 25. For a study of the important fifth-century leader of monasticism, Cassian, see Owen Chadwick, *John Cassian* (Cambridge: Cambridge University Press, 1968).
25. Ibid., p. 22 (ET, p. 23); "Christianity and Confession"; "Sexuality and Solitude," pp. 15–16; Toronto course, "The Discourse of Self-Disclosure," June 15, 1982.
26. "Christianity and Confession."
27. "Sexuality and Solitude," p. 10.
28. Foucault's summary of his 1982 course in *Annuaire du Collège de France* (82), p. 403.
29. "Le combat de la chasteté," p. 23 (ET, p. 25).
30. See "Omnes et Singulatim," pp. 19–20 (ET, p. 239); "Christianity and Confession"; Toronto course, "The Discourse of Self-Disclosure," June 15, 1982; "Sexuality and Solitude," pp. 10, 15; *UP*, pp. 74, 82 (ET, pp. 63, 70).
31. *Herculine Barbin dite Alexina B.* (Paris: Gallimard, 1978). Foucault's essay was published as the introduction to the English translation of the work, *Herculine Barbin, Being the Recently Discovered Memoirs of a Nineteenth Century Hermaphrodite*, trans. Richard McDougall (New York: Pantheon, 1980), pp. vii–xvii.
32. *Herculine Barbin*, p. 155 (ET, p. 144).
33. "Omnes et Singulatim," p. 20 (ET, p. 239).
34. Foucault, "The Subject and Power," in Dreyfus and Rabinow, p. 215.
35. "Sexuality and Solitude," pp. 11, 16.
36. "Christianity and Confession."
37. "The Subject and Power," pp. 212, 216.
38. *UP*, p. 275 (ET, p. 251).
39. "Politics and Ethics: An Interview" (1983) in *The Foucault Reader*, p. 375.
40. *UP*, p. 11 (ET, p. 5).
41. "What Is Enlightenment?" in *The Foucault Reader*, p. 46.
42. *VS*, p. 172 (ET, p. 130). I treat this archaeology within the perspective of psychosis in an essay, "Oedipus, Freud, Foucault: Fragments of an Archaeology of Psychoanalysis," published in the collection edited by David M. Levin, *Pathologies of the Modern Self: Challenges to the Orthodoxy* (New York: New York University Press, 1987), pp. 349–362.
43. *HF*, p. 360 (ET, p. 162); *LMC*, p. 372 (ET, p. 361); cf. Foucault's *PSY*, p. 103 (ET, p. 87).

44. *VS*, p. 158 (ET, p. 119).
45. Sigmund Freud, *The Interpretation of Dreams*, in *The Standard Edition* 4, ed. James Strachey (London: Hogarth, 1973), p. 262.
46. "Introduction to Pfister, *The Psycho-Analytic Method*" (1913), in *The Standard Edition* 12, ed. James Strachey (London: Hogarth, 1973), p. 329.
47. *NC*, pp. 154, 200 (156, 201) (ET, pp. 153, 198).
48. See *HF*, pp. 523–30 (ET, pp. 216–22), and *NC*, p. 207 (202–3) (ET, p. 199).
49. *LMC*, p. 372 (ET, p. 361).
50. Introduction to *Herculine Barbin*, p. xi. Cf. *VS*, pp. 137–39, 91, 94 (ET, pp. 104–5, 68, 70).
51. *VS*, pp. 108–9 (ET, pp. 82–83); cf. *VS*, pp. 136–51, 172–73 (ET, pp. 103–14, 130).
52. See *UP*, Parts 2, "Dietetics," and 3, "Economics," pp. 109–203 (ET, pp. 95–184).
53. *UP*, pp. 243–48 (ET, pp. 221–25).
54. *UP*, p. 243 (ET, p. 221).
55. *UP*, p. 243 (ET, pp. 220–21).
56. *UP*, p. 101 (ET, p. 88).
57. *UP*, pp. 263–64 (ET, p. 240).
58. See *SS*, Parts 4, "The Body," 5, "The Wife," and 6, "Boys," pp. 119–266 (ET, pp. 97–232).
59. See *SS*, Part 3, "Self and Others," pp. 87–117 (ET, pp. 69–95).
60. See *SS*, Part 2, "The Cultivation of the Self," pp. 51–85 (ET, pp. 37–68).
61. "On the Genealogy of Ethics," p. 246.
62. *SS*, p. 62 (ET, p. 47).
63. See Foucault's 1982 course description, "Histoire des systèmes de pensée," *Annuaire du Collège de France* (1982), pp. 395–406; "L'écriture de soi," pp. 3–23.
64. *IRE*, pp. 64–65 (ET, pp. 51–52).
65. *PER*, pp. 109–10; cf. *IRE*, pp. 127–28 (ET, pp. 74–75).
66. "La folie, l'absence d'oeuvre" (1964), published as appendix to the 1972 edition of *HF*, 578.
67. Foucault, "Inutile de se soulever?" *Le Monde* 10, 661 (May 11, 1979): 1 (ET: "Is it useless to revolt?" trans. James Bernauer, *Philosophy and Social Criticism* 8 [Spring 1981]: 5.)
68. "Politics and Ethics: An Interview," p. 377. For Foucault's viewpoint on Poland and the crisis generated by Solidarity, see "En abandonnant les Polonais, nous renonçons à une part de nous-mêmes," *Le Nouvel Observateur* 935 (October 9, 1982): 36; "L'expérience morale et sociale des Polonais ne peut plus être effacée," *Le nouvelles littéraires* 2857 (October 14–20, 1982): 8–9; "La Pologne, et après? Edmond Maire: Entretiens avec Michel Foucault," *Le débat* 25 (May 1983): 3–34. For a personal recollection of Foucault in Poland, see the essay by the former French Ambassador, Etienne Burin des Roziers, "Une rencontre à Varsovie," *Le débat* 41 (September–November 1986): 132–36.
69. *LMC*, p. 7 (ET, p. xv).
70. See "Omnes et Singulatim," 16–20 (ET, pp. 236–39).
71. *UP*, pp. 33–35 (ET, pp. 26–28).
72. See "On the Genealogy of Ethics," pp. 236, 251–52.
73. *UP*, p. 35 (ET, p. 28).
74. "Le retour de la morale," 41 (ET, p. 12).
75. See ibid., p. 38 (ET, p. 2); "What Is Enlightenment?" p. 39; and "Politics and Ethics: An Interview," p. 375.

76. For example, see the first preface he wrote for the second volume of the history of sexuality in *The Foucault Reader*, pp. 336–38; "Polemics, Politics and Problematizations," an interview conducted by Paul Rabinow, in *The Foucault Reader*, pp. 388–89.

77. Foucault, "Table ronde du 20 mai 1978," p. 51 (ET, p. 11); "Est-il donc important de penser?" an interview conducted by D. Eribon, *Libération* (May 30–31, 1982): 21 (ET: "Is it really important to think?" trans. T. Keenan, *Philosophy and Social Criticism* 9, 1 [Spring 1982]: 33).

78. "Est-il donc important de penser?" p. 21 (ET, p. 33); "Table ronde du mai 1978," pp. 51–52 (ET, p. 11).

79. "Est-il donc important de penser?" p. 21 (ET, p. 33).

80. "Polemics, Politics, and Problematizations," p. 388. As examples of his desire to claim coherence, see *UP*, pp. 17–18 (ET, pp. 11–12); "Le retour de la morale," and the opening pages of "L'éthique du souci de soi comme pratique de liberté," a conversation with Raul Fornet-Betancourt, Helmut Becker, and Alfredo Gomez-Müller in *Concordia* 6 (1984): 99–116 (ET: "The Ethics of Care of the Self as the Practice of Freedom," trans. Joseph Gauthier, *Philosophy and Social Criticism* 12 [1987]).

81. "La pensée du dehors," *Critique* 229 (June 1966): 526. I elaborate this theme of negative theology as the central experience of Foucault's thought in an article, "The Prisons of Man: An Introduction to Foucault's Negative Theology," published in the *International Philosophical Quarterly* (December 1987) 365–380.

82. "La pensée du dehors," pp. 526–27. The analogy was employed again in a lecture at the Collège de France on January 30, 1980.

83. In a 1967 interview with P. Caruso published in Caruso's *Conversazioni con Lévi-Strauss, Foucault, Lacan*, p. 120. In the context of this religious interest, it is interesting to note that in 1957, while he was in Sweden, Foucault offered a course devoted to "religious experience in French literature from Chateaubriand to Bernanos." (See Jean Piel, "Foucault à Uppsala," *Critique* 471–72 [August–September 1986]: 749.)

84. Bataille's dialogue with negative theology runs throughout his writings. See Roger Verneaux, "L'athéologie mystique de Georges Bataille," in *Recherches de philosophie* 3–4: *De la connaissance de Dieu* (1958), pp. 125–58.

85. Jean-Paul Sartre, *Being and Nothingness* (New York: Washington Square Press, 1966), p. 784.

86. See "Foucault répond à Sartre," pp. 20–22. However Foucault's faith or absence of it is described, it seems singularly inappropriate to claim, as Jean-Marie Auzias has in his recent book, that "radical atheism" is the point of convergence between Sartre and Foucault. On this topic too, the two thinkers would be quite far from one another. (See Auzias, *Michel Foucault* [Paris: La Manufacture, 1986], p. 240.)

87. See Eric Voegelin's collection of essays edited by John Hallowell, *From Enlightenment to Revolution* (Durham, N.C.: Duke University Press, 1975), especially "The Apocalypse of Man: Comte," pp. 136–59.

88. See "What is Enlightenment?" p. 34.

89. "Le souci de la vérité," p. 22 (ET, p. 29); *UP*, p. 14 (ET, p. 8).

90. Wolin, p. 83.

91. "Une esthétique de l'existence," a conversation between MF and Alessandro Fontana in *Le Monde* (July 15–16, 1984), p. xi. Cf. *UP*, p. 37 (ET, p. 30).

92. "The Power and Politics of Michel Foucault," an interview with MF in the *Daily Californian* (April 22, 1983): 20.
93. "Christianity and Confession."
94. *AS*, p. 28 (ET, p. 17).
95. Allan Stoekl, *Politics, Writing, Mutilation* (Minneapolis: University of Minnesota Press, 1985), p. 109.
96. Georges Bataille, *Death and Sensuality* (New York: Walker and Company, 1962), pp. 229–30.
97. "Inutile de se soulever?" p. 2 (ET, p. 8).
98. Wolin, pp. 84, 85.
99. "The Subject and Power," p. 222.
100. Reiner Schürmann, "What Can I Do? in an Archaeological-Genealogical History," *The Journal of Philosophy* 82, 10 (October 1985): 545.
101. For examples of this view, see Stephen White, "Foucault's Challenge to Critical Theory," *American Political Science Review* 80, 21 (June 1986): 428–30; Daraki, p. 108.
102. For accounts of Foucault's political work, see Claude Mauriac, *Le temps immobile* 3: *Et comme l'espérance est violente*, especially pp. 261–592; and Bernard Kouchmer, "Un vrai samourai," in *Michel Foucault: Une histoire de la vérité* (Paris: Syros, 1985), pp. 85–89.
103. "La vie des hommes infâmes," *Les Cahiers du Chemin* 29 (January 15, 1977): 13 (ET: "The Life of Infamous Men," trans. Paul Foss and Meaghan Morris, in Michel Foucault, *Power, Truth, Strategy*, ed. Meaghan Morris and Paul Patton [Sydney: Feral, 1979], p. 77).
104. I believe that Gilles Deleuze's sensitive study, *Foucault* (Paris: Editions de Minuit, 1986) errs in linking Foucault too closely with Nietzschean aspirations. Foucault has transcended even them.
105. Foucault, "La bibliothèque fantastique," p. 10 (ET, p. 90).
106. *UP*, p. 17 (ET, p. 11); cf. *VS*, p. 81 (ET, p. 60).
107. "Discourse and Truth," p. 113. For a presentation of Foucault's last course, see Thomas Flynn, "Foucault as Parrhesiast: His Last Course at the Collège de France," *Philosophy and Social Criticism* 12 (1987).
108. "La force de fuir," p. 63.
109. Daraki, p. 110.

The Works of Michel Foucault 1954–1984

INTRODUCTORY NOTE

This bibliography is divided into three sections. Section A lists all of Foucault's writings and interviews in their chronological order of composition when such exactness has been possible to establish. English translations are also noted. Section B identifies miscellaneous items that have been utilized in this text or are of some importance. Many other materials such as letters and unpublished notes may be consulted in the archive of Foucault at the Bibliothèque du Saulchoir in Paris. Section C takes note of the contents of studies which were conducted under his direction. The occasional symbols which are employed refer either to Foucault or to the principal words of his French titles. I wish to acknowledge a special debt to the Centre Michel Foucault for its assistance and especially to Thomas Keenan with whom I have worked for several years to establish this bibliography.

A) THE PUBLICATIONS

1) *Maladie mentale et personnalité*. Paris: Presses Universitaires de France, 1954. Cf. #10 below.

2) "Introduction." To Ludwig Binswanger, *Le rêve et l'existence* ("Traum und Existenz"). Translated from the German by Jacqueline Verdeaux. Paris: Desclée de Brouwer, 1954, 9–128.

> 2ET) "Dream, Imagination, and Existence." Translated by Forrest Williams. *Review of Existential Psychology and Psychiatry* XIX, 1 (1984–1985) 29–78.

3) "La recherche scientifique et la psychologie." In *Des chercheurs francais s'interrogent*. Edited by Jean-Edouard Morère. Paris: Presses Universitaires de France, 1957, 171–201.

4) "La psychologie de 1850 à 1950." In A. Weber and Denis Huisman, *Histoire de la philosophie européenne II: Tableau de la philosophie contemporaine*. Paris: Fischbacher, 1957, 591–606.

5) Translation into French with Daniel Rocher of Viktor von Weizsaecker, *Le cycle de la structure (Der Gestaltkreis)*. With a preface by Henry Ey. Paris: Desclée de Brouwer, 1958.

6) *Thèse complémentaire* for the doctorat ès lettres, University of Paris, Faculty of

Letters and the Human Sciences, 1961. The Director of Studies: Jean Hyppolite. A typescript in two volumes that is available at the Bibliothèque Sorbonne, Paris. This thesis is an introduction and translation, with notes, of
Immanuel Kant, *Anthropologie (Anthropologie in pragmatischer Hinsicht)*.
Vol. I: Introduction, 128 pp.; Vol II: Translation and Notes, 347 pp. The
second volume was published as *Anthropologie du point de vue pragmatique*.
Paris: Vrin, 1964.

7) *Folie et déraison. Histoire de la folie à l'âge classique*. Paris: Plon, 1961.
Published in an abridged form in 1964, Paris: Union Générale d'Editions.
Reissued in original complete form as *Histoire de la folie à l'âge classique*
(Paris: Gallimard, 1972) with different preface and two appendices: "La folie,
l'absence d'oeuvre" (*La Table Ronde*, May, 1964) and "Mon corps, ce papier,
ce feu" (*Paideia*, September, 1971). Reissued in the TEL collection without
the appendices, Paris: Gallimard, 1978.

    7ET) *Madness and Civilization*. Translated by Richard Howard. Intro-
duction by José Barchilon. New York: Pantheon, 1965. The English
version is a translation of the drastically abridged edition of 1964 with
some slight additions from the original edition.

8) "La folie n'existe que dans une société." *Le Monde* 5135 (July 22, 1961) 9. An
interview with Jean-Paul Weber.

9) Review of Alexander Koyre, *La révolution astronomique, Copernic, Kepler,
Borelli. La Nouvelle Revue Francaise* 108 (December, 1961) 1123–1124.

10) *Maladie mentale et psychologie*. Paris: Presses Universitaires de France, 1962,
1966. This is the revised edition of #1 above with a totally different second
part and conclusion.

    10ET) *Mental Illness and Psychology*. Translated by Alan Sheridan. New
York: Harper and Row, 1976.

11) "Introduction." To *Rousseau juge de Jean-Jaques: Dialogues*. Paris: Librarie
Armand Colin, 1962, vii–xxiv.

12) "Le 'non' du père." *Critique* 178 (March, 1962) 195–209. An essay on Jean
Laplanche's *Hölderlin et la question du père*.

    12ET) "The Father's 'No'." In *Language, Counter-Memory, Practice:
Selected Essays and Interviews*. Edited by Donald Bouchard. Translated by Donald Bouchard and Sherry Simon. Ithaca: Cornell University Press, 1977, 68–86.

13) Les déviations religieuses et le savoir médical." *Hérésies et sociétés dans l'Europe
pré-industrielle 11e–18e siècles*. Communications et débats du Colloque de
Royaumont présentés par Jacques LeGoff. Paris: Mouton, 1968, 19–29.
Foucault's presentation and the discussion which followed took place at a
conference held May 27–30, 1962.

14) "Le cycle des grenouilles." *La Nouvelle Revue Francaise* 114 (June, 1962)
1159–1160. Presentation of a text by Jean-Pierre Brisset.

15) "Un si cruel savoir." *Critique* 182 (July, 1962) 597–611. An essay on Claude
Crébillon's *Les égarements du coeur et de l'esprit* and J. A. Reveroni de
Saint-Cyr, *Pauliska ou la perversité moderne*.

16) "Dire et voir chez Raymond Roussel." *Lettre Ouverte* 4 (Summer, 1962) 38–51.
In a modified version much of this essay was published later as the first
chapter of his volume on Raymond Roussel. Cf. #19 below.

17) Translation into French of Leo Spitzer, "Art du langage et linguistique." *Etudes*

de style. Paris: Gallimard, 1962, 45–78. Original English: "Linguistics and Literary History," in Spitzer's *Linguistics and Literary History*. Princeton: Princeton University Press, 1948, 1–39.

18) *Naissance de la clinique. Une archéologie du regard médical*. Paris: Presses Universitaires de France, 1963. Revised edition published in 1972; cf. #99 below.

    18ET) *The Birth of the Clinic: An Archaelogy of Medical Perception*. Translated by Alan Sheridan Smith. New York: Pantheon, 1973. (A translation of revised edition with some exceptions.)

19) *Raymond Roussel*. Paris: Gallimard, 1963.

    19ET) *Death and the Labyrinth: The World of Raymond Roussel*. Translated by Charles Ruas, with an introduction by John Ashberry. New York: Doubleday and Company, 1986.

    19A) "Le métamorphose et le labyrinthe." *La Nouvelle Revue Francaise* 124 (April, 1963) 638–661. This is chapter 5 of *Raymond Roussel*.

20) "Wächter über die Nacht der Menschen." In Hans Ludwig Spegg, ed., *Unterwegs mit Rolf Italiaander: Begegnungen, Betrachtungen, Bibliographie*. Hamburg: Freie Akademie der Kunst, 1963, 46–49.

21) "Un grand roman de terreur." *France-Observateur* 1963. Reissued in Jean-Edern Hallier, *Chaque matin qui se leve est une lecon de courage*. Paris: Editions Libres, 1978, 40–42.

22) "Préface à la transgression." *Critique* 195–196 (August–September 1963) 751–769.

    22ET) "A Preface to Transgression." In *Language, Counter-Memory, Practice*, 29–52.

23) "L'eau et la folie." *Medecine et hygiène* 613 (October 23, 1963) 901–906.

24) "Un 'Fantastique de bibliothèque'." *Cahiers Renaud-Barrault* 59 (March, 1967) 7–30. Republished as the introduction to G. Flaubert, *La tentation de Saint Antoine* with the title "La bibliothèque fantastique." Paris: Le Livre de Poche, 1971, 7–33. This essay, written in 1964, was originally published in a German translation by Anneliese Botond and used as the afterword to Flaubert, *Die Versuchung des Heiligen Antonius*. Frankfurt: Insel, 1964, 217–251.

    24ET) "Fantasia of the Library." In *Language, Counter-Memory, Practice*, 87–109.

25) "Débat sur le roman." *Tel Quel* 17 (Spring, 1964) 12–54. A discussion held at Cérisy la Salle in September, 1963, directed by MF.

26) "Débat sur la poésie." *Tel Quel* 17 (Spring, 1964) 69–82. A discussion, held at Cérisy la Salle in September, 1963, in which MF participated.

27) "Le langage à l'infini." *Tel Quel* 15 (Autumn, 1963) 44–53.

    27ET) "Language to Infinity." In *Language, Counter-Memory, Practice*, 53–67.

28) "Guetter le jour qui vient." *La Nouvelle Revue Francaise* 130 (October, 1963) 709–716. On Roger Laporte, *La Vielle*.

29) "Distance, aspect, origine." *Critique* 198 (November, 1963) 931–945.

30) "La prose d'Actéon." *La Nouvelle Revue Francaise* 135 (March, 1964) 444–459. On Pierre Klossowski.

31) "Le langage de l'espace." *Critique* 203 (April, 1964) 378–382.

32) "La folie, l'absence d'oeuvre." *La Table Ronde* 196 (May, 1964) 11–21. Republished as appendix to 1972 edition of *Histoire de la folie*, 575–582.

33) "Nietzsche, Freud, Marx." *Cahiers de Royaumont 6: Nietzsche*. Paris: Éditions de Minuit, 1967, 183–200. Conference, at which this paper was first delivered, took place in July, 1964.

    33ET)"Nietzsche, Freud, Marx." Translated by Jon Anderson and Gary Hentzi. *Critical Texts* III, 2 (Winter, 1986) 1–5. This version does not include the discussion which followed Foucault's paper.

34) "Pourquoi réédite-t-on l'oeuvre de Raymond Roussel? un précurseur de notre littérature moderne." *Le Monde* 6097 (August 22, 1964) 9.

35) "Les mots qui saignent." *L'Express* 688 (Aug. 29, 1964) 21–22. Review of Pierre Klossowski's translation of Virgil's *Aeneid*.

36) "Le Mallarmé de J.-P. Richard." *Annales* 19, No. 5 (Sept.–Oct., 1964) 996–1004. A review of Richard's *L'univers imaginaire de Mallarmé*.

37) "L'obligation d'écrire." *Arts* 980 (Nov. 11–17, 1964) 7. On Gérard de Nerval.

38) "Philosophie et psychologie." *Dossiers pédagogiques de la radio télévision scolaire* 10 (February 15–27, 1965) 61–67. An interview conducted by A. Badiou.

39) "Philosophie et vérité." *Dossiers pédagogiques de la radio-télévision scolaire* (March 27, 1965) 1–11. A discussion among MF, Hyppolite, Canguilhem, Ricoeur, D. Dreyfus. and Badiou.

40) *Les mots et les choses: une archéologie des sciences humaines*. Paris: Gallimard, 1966.

    40ET) *The Order of Things: An Archaelogy of the Human Sciences*. Unidentified collective translation. New York: Pantheon, 1971.

    40A) "Les suivants." *Mercure de France* 1221–1222 (July–August 1965) 366–384. Identical to first chapter in *LMC*.

    40B) "La prose du monde." *Diogène* 53 (Jan.–March, 1966) 20–41. This is a shortened version of the second chapter of *LMC*, in which it bears the same title. This was also published as "The Prose of the World." Translated by Victor Velen. *Diogènes* 53 (Spring, 1966) 17–37.

41) "L'arrière-fable." *L'arc* 29 (1966) 5–12. On Jules Verne.

42) "Entretien: Michel Foucault, 'les mots et les choses.'" *Les Lettres Francaises* 1125 (March 31, 1966) 3–4. An interview with Raymond Bellour. Republished in Bellour's *Le livre des autres*. Paris: Éditions de l'Herne, 1971, 135–144.

43) "A la recherche du présent perdu." *L'Express* 775 (April 25–May 1, 1966) 114–115. Review of Jean Thibaudeau, *Ouverture*.

44) "Entretien." *La Quinzaine Littéraire* 5 (May 16, 1966) 14–15. An interview with Madeleine Chapsal.

45) "L'homme, est-il mort?: Un entretien avec Michel Foucault." *Arts et loisirs* 38 (June 15, 1966) 8–9. An interview with Claude Bonnefoy.

46) "La pensée du dehors." *Critique* 229 (June, 1966) 523–546. On Maurice Blanchot. Reprinted in book form: *La pensée du dehors*. Montpellier: Editions Fata Morgana, 1986.

    46ET) "Maurice Blanchot, The Thought from Outside." Translated by Brian Massumi. In *Foucault/Blanchot*. New York: Zone Books, 1987, 7–60. Published with Blanchot's "Michel Foucault, As I Imagine Him," translated by J. Mehlman, 61–109.

47) "Une histoire restée muette." *La Quinzaine Littéraire* 8 (July 1, 1966) 3–4. Review of Ernst Cassirer, *The Philosophy of the Enlightenment*.

48) "Qu'est-ce qu'un philosophe?" *Connaissance des Hommes* 22 (Autumn, 1966) 9. Interview with Marie-Geneviève Foy.

49) "Michel Foucault et Gilles Deleuze veulent rendre à Nietzsche son vrai visage." *Le Figaro littéraire* 1065 (September 15, 1966) 7. An interview with Claude Jannoud on Nietzsche.

50) "C'était un nageur entre deux mots." *Arts et loisirs* 54 (Oct. 5, 1966) 8–9. An interview with Claude Bonnefoy on André Breton.

51) "Message ou bruit?" *Le concours médical* 88, #43 (Oct. 22, 1966) 6285–6286.

52) "Un archéologue des idées: Michel Foucault." *Synthèses* 245 (October, 1966) 45–49. An article on *LMC* by Jean-Michel Minon, with extensive quotations from an interview with MF.

53) "Introduction générale." To Friedrich Nietzsche, *Oeuvres philosophiques* Vol. 5: *Le gai savoir*. Texts and variations established by G. Colli and M. Montinari. Translated from the German by Pierre Klossowski. Paris: Gallimard, 1967, i–iv.

54) "Des espaces autres." *Architecture-Mouvement-Continuité* 5 (October, 1984) 46–49.

    54ET) "Of Other Spaces." Translated by Jay Miskowiec. *Diacritics* 16, 1 (Spring, 1986) 22–27.

55) "Deuxième entretien: Sur les facons d'écrire l'histoire." *Les Lettres Francaises* 1187 (June 15, 1967) 6–9. Second interview with Raymond Bellour. Republished in R. Bellour, *Le livre des autres*. Paris: Éditions de l'Herne, 1971, 189–207.

56) "Conversazione con Michel Foucault." *La Fiera Letteraria* 39 (Sept. 28, 1967). An interview conducted by P. Caruso and published in Italian. Republished in Caruso's *Conversazione con Levi-Strauss, Foucault, Lacan*. Milano: U. Mursia and Co., 1969, 91–131. There is a German translation by Walter Seitter published as "Gespräch mit Michel Foucault" in the collection of MF's writings: *Von der Subversion des Wissens*. Frankfurt: Ullstein, 1978, 7–31.

57) "Préface." To Antoine Arnaud and Pierre Nicolle, *Grammaire générale et raisonée*. Paris: Paulet, 1969, iii–xxvii.

    57A) "La grammaire générale de Port Royal." *Langages* 7 (September, 1967) 7–15. An extract from #57.

58) "Les mots et les images." *Le Nouvel Observateur* 154 (Oct. 25, 1967) 49–50. A review of Irwin Panofsky's *Essais d'iconologie* and *Architecture Gothique et Pensée Scolastique*.

59) "Ceci n'est pas une pipe." *Les cahiers du chemin* 2 (Jan. 15, 1968) 79–105. This essay on the painter René Magritte was reissued in an enlarged version as *Ceci n'est pas une pipe*. Montpellier: Scholies, Fata Morgana, 1973.

    59ET) "Ceci n'est pas une pipe." Translated by Richard Howard. *October* 1 (Spring, 1976) 6–21. This translation was of the first edition but included some material from the enlarged version which was later translated and edited by James Harkness, *This Is Not a Pipe* (Berkeley: University of California Press, 1982).

60) "Linguistique et sciences sociales." *Revue tuniesienne de sciences sociales* 19 (December, 1969) 248–255. Presentation to a March, 1968 conference.

61) "En intervju med Michel Foucault." *B L M (Bonniers Litterara Magasin)* (Stockholm) 37, #3 (March, 1968) 203–211. Interview with Yngve Lindung. In Swedish.

62) "Foucault répond à Sartre." *La Quinzaine Littéraire* 46 (March 1–15, 1968) 20–22. A radio interview with Jean-Pierre El Kabbach. The publication of this unedited transcript provoked a sharp reply from MF in the journal's following issue (March 15–31) 21: "Une mise au point de Michel Foucault."

63) "Réponse à une question." *Esprit* 371 (May, 1968) 850–874.

  63ET) "History, Discourse, Discontinuity." Translated by Anthony Nazzaro. In *Salmagundi* 20 (Summer-Fall, 1972) 225–248, and reissued in *Psychological Man*, edited by Robert Boyers. Harper: Colophon, 1975, 208–231. A revised translation by Colin Gordon was published as "Politics and the Study of Discourse." *Ideology and Consciousness* 3 (Spring, 1978) 7–26.

64) "Lettre de Michel Foucault à Jacques Proust." *La Pensée* 139 (May–June, 1968) 114–117. This comments on the discussion which the same journal published as "Entretiens sur Michel Foucault." *La Pensée* 137 (Feb., 1968) 3–37.

65) "Réponse au Cercle d'épistémologie." *Cahiers pour l'analyse* 9: *Généalogie des sciences* (Summer, 1968) 9–40. Excerpted as "Réponse au Cercle d'épistémologie." *Les Lettres Francaises* 1240 (July 10, 1968) 3–6.

  65ET) "On the Archaeology of the Sciences." *Theoretical Practice* 3–4 (Autumn, 1971) 108–127. An abridged translation with no translator identified.

66) *L'archéologie du savoir*. Paris: Gallimard, 1969.

  66ET) *The Archeology of Knowledge*. Translated by A. M. Sheridan Smith. New York: Harper Colophon, 1976.

67) "Médecins, juges et sorciers au XVIIe siècle." *Médecine de France* 200 (1969) 121–28.

68) "Jean Hyppolite (1907–1968)." *Revue de Métaphysique et de Morale* 74, 2 (April–June, 1969) 131–136. This was originally presented at the memorial session for Hyppolite on Jan. 19, 1969, at the Ecole Normale Supérieure.

69) "Ariane s'est pendue." *Le Nouvel Observateur* 229 (March 31, 1969) 36–37. A review of G. Deleuze's *Différence et répétition*.

70) "En bref: Précision." *Le Nouvel Observateur* 229 (March 31, 1969) 39. Correction to "Une petite histoire," *Le Nouvel Observateur* 227 (March 17, 1969) 43. On MF's being prevented from speaking in London.

71) "La naissance du monde." *Le Monde des Livres* 7558 (May 3, 1969) viii. A conversation with Jean-Michel Palmier.

72) "Michel Foucault explique son dernier livre." *Magazine littéraire* 28 (April–May, 1969) 23–25. An interview on *AS* conducted by J. J. Brochier.

73) "Qu'est-ce qu'un auteur?" *Bulletin de la Société francaise de Philosophie* 63 (July–September, 1969) 73–104. First presented as a lecture on Feb. 22, 1969. Foucault's remarks are followed by a discussion in which the following participated: M. de Gandillac, L. Goldmann, J. Lacan, J. d'Ormesson, J. Ullmo, J. Wahl.

  73ET) "What Is An Author" In *Language, Counter-Memory, Practice*, 113–138. Translation is slightly abridged and the discussion is omitted.

74) "La situation de Cuvier dans l'histoire de la biologie II." *Revue d'histoire des sciences et de leurs applications* XXIII, 1 (Jan.–March, 1970) 63–92. The presentation was made at a conference held May 30–31, 1969, and was followed by a discussion. Foucault also made comments on another paper delivered at the conference, that of Francois Dagonet, "La situation de Cuvier dans l'histoire de la biologie I" (presentation is on pp. 49–60 in the same issue of the journal with Foucault's comments on pp. 61–62).

  74ET) "Cuvier's Position in the History of Biology." Translated by Felicity Edholm. *Critique of Anthropology IV*, 13–14 (Summer, 1979) 125–130.

75) Two letters from MF to Pierre Klossowski, dated July 3, 1969, and Winter 1970–71, reproduced in *Cahiers pour un temps: Pierre Klossowski*. Paris: Centre Georges Pompidou, 1985, 85–88 and 89–90.

76) *L'ordre du discours*. Paris: Gallimard, 1971. MF's inaugural lecture at the Collège de France, Dec. 2, 1970.

76ET) "Orders of Discourse." Translated by Rupert Swyer, *Social Science Information* (April, 1971). Republished as "The Discourse on Language," an Appendix to the ET of *AS* (cf. #66 above), 215–237.

77) "Présentation." To Georges Bataille, *Oeuvres Complètes I: Premiers Écrits 1922–1940*. Paris:: Gallimard, 1970, 5–6.

78) "Sept propos sur le 7e ange." A preface to Jean-Pierre Brisset, *La grammaire logique*. Paris: Tchou, 1970, vii–xix. Republished in book form as *Sept propos sur le septième ange*. Montpellier: Editions Fata Morgana, 1986.

79) "Le piège de Vincennes." *Le Nouvel Observateur* 274 (Feb. 9, 1970) 33–35. An interview with Patrick Loriot.

80) "Il y aura scandale, mais . . ." *Le Nouvel Observateur* 304 (Sept. 7, 1970) 40. A note on Pierre Guyotat's *Eden, Eden, Eden*.

80ET) "Open Letter to Pierre Guyotat." Translated by Edouard Roditi. *Paris Exiles* 2 (1985) 25.

81) "Croître et multipler." *Le Monde* 8037 (Nov. 15–16, 1970) 13. A review of Francois Jacob, *La logique du vivant*.

82) "Theatrum Philosophicum." *Critique* 282 (November, 1970) 885–908. This is a reflection on two books of Gilles Deleuze, *Différence et répétition* and *Logique du sens*.

82ET) "Theatrum Philosophicum." In *Language, Counter-Memory, Practice*, 165–196.

83) "Foreword." To the 1971 English edition of *LMC*. In *The Order of Things*, ix–xiv. Cf. #40 above.

84) "Entrevista com Michel Foucault." In *O homem e o discurso*. Rio de Janeiro: Tempo Brasileiro, 1971, 17–42. An interview conducted by Sergio P. Rouanet and J. G. Merquior. In Portuguese.

85) "Nietzsche, la généalogie, l'histoire." In *Hommage à Jean Hyppolite*. Paris: Presses Universitaires de France, 1971, 145–172.

85ET) "Nietzsche, Genealogy, History." In *Language, Counter-Memory, Practice*, 139–164.

86) "A Conversation with Michel Foucault." *Partisan Review* 38 (1971) 192–201. An interview by John Simon.

87) "Mon corps, ce papier, ce feu." *Paideia* (Sept., 1971). Reissued as Appendix to 1972 edition of *Histoire de la folie*, 583–603. Cf. #7 above.

87ET) "My Body, this Paper, this Fire." Translated, with an introduction, by Geoff Bennington. *Oxford Literary Review* IV, 1 (Autumn, 1979) 5–28.

88) "Enquête sur les prisons: Brisons les barreaux du silence." *Politique-Hebdo* 24 (March 18, 1971) 4–6. Interview with MF and P. Vidal-Naquet conducted by C. Angeli.

89) "La prison partout." *Combat* (May 5, 1971).

90) "L'Affaire Jaubert." *La Cause du Peuple* (June 3, 1971).

91) "Je percois l'intolérable." *Journale de Genève* (samedi littéraire, August, 1971). Interview with Geneviève Armleder.

92) "Lettre." In *La Pensée* 159 (Sept.–Oct., 1971) 141–144. Foucault wrote in

criticism of an article by Jean-Marc Pelorson, "Michel Foucault et l'Espagne." *La Pensée* 152 (August, 1970) 88–99.

93) "Human Nature: Justice versus Power." Published in *Reflexive Water: The Basic Concerns of Mankind*, edited by Fons Elders. London: Souvenir Press, 1974, 139–197. A discussion between MF and Noam Chomsky. Televised in November, 1971 by the Dutch Broadcasting Company and moderated by Fons Elders.

94) "Par delà le bien et le mal." *Actuel* 14 (Nov., 1971) 42–47. Interview with M. A. Burnier and P. Graine. Republished with slight modifications as "Entretien." *C'est demain la veille*. Paris: Seuil, 1973, 19–43.

    94ET) "Revolutionary Action: 'Until Now.'" In *Language, Counter-Memory, Practice*, 218–233.

95) "Monstrosities in Criticism." Translated by Robert J. Matthews. *Diacritics I*, 1 (Fall, 1971) 57–60. This was written in reply to a review of *The Order of Things* by George Steiner: "The mandarin of the hour—Michel Foucault." *The New York Times Book Review* (Feb. 28, 1971) 8, 23–31.

96) "Foucault responds 2." *Diacritics I*, 2 (Winter, 1971) 60. Foucault's response to Steiner's own reply to the preceding entry. Steiner's piece was published as "Steiner Responds to Foucault" *Diacritics I*, 2 (Winter, 1971) 59.

97) "Le discours de Toul." *Le Nouvel Observateur* 372 (December 27, 1971) 15.

98) "Histoire des systèmes de pensée." *Annuaire du Collège de France* 71 (1971). Summary of the course given at the Collège de France in 1971. Lecture: "La volonté de savoir." Seminar: "Le fonctionnement du système pénal en France à partir du XIXe siècle." Republished as Appendix in Angèle Kremer-Marietti, *Michel Foucault* (Paris: Seghers, 1974) 195–200. Foucault's courses have been published as a separate volume: *Résumé des cours 1970–1982*. Paris Julliard, 1989.

    98ET) "History of Systems of Thought." In *Language, Counter-Memory, Practice*, 199–204.

99) *Naissance de la clinique: Une archéologie du regard médical*. Revised, second edition. Paris: Presses Universitaires de France, 1972.

    99ET) Cf. # 18 above.

100) "Préface." To new edition of *Histoire de la folie à l'âge classique*. Paris: Gallimard, 1972, 7–9.

101) "Sur la justice populaire: Débat avec les maos." *Les Temps Modernes* 310 (1972) 335–366. A discussion with Philippe Gavi and Pierre Victor.

    101ET) "On Popular Justice: A discussion with Maoists." Translated by John Mepham. In *Power/Knowledge: Selected Interviews and Other Writings, 1972–1977*, edited by Colin Gordon. New York: Pantheon, 1980, 1–36.

102) "Les intellectuels et le pouvoir." *L'arc* 49 (1972) 3–10. A conversation between MF and Gilles Deleuze which took place on March 4, 1972.

    102ET) "Intellectuals and Power." In *Language, Counter-Memory, Practice*, 205–217.

103) "Michel Foucault on Attica." *Telos* 19 (1974) 154–161. An interview with John Simon in 1972.

104) "Table ronde." *Esprit* 413 (April–May, 1972) 678–703. A discussion, in which MF participated, on questions relating to social work and its clients.

105) "Les grands fonctions de la médecine." *Psychiatrie Aujourd'hui* 10 (September, 1972) 15–16.

106) "Gaston Bachelard, le philosophe et son ombre: Piéger sa propre culture." *Le Figaro* 1376 (Sept. 30, 1972) Litt. 16.

107) "Un dibattito Foucault-Preti." *Bimestre* 22–23 (Sept.–Dec., 1972) 1–4. A debate in Italian conducted by Michele Dzieduszycki.

108) "Médecine et lutte de classes." *La Nef* 49 (Oct.–Dec., 1972) 67–73. An edited round-table discussion between MF and members of the Health Information Group (Groupe Information Santé).

109) "Les deux morts de Pompidou." *Le Nouvel Observateur* 421 (Dec. 4, 1972) 56–57. Excerpts reprinted as "Deux calculs." *Le Monde* 8676 (Dec. 6, 1972) 20.

    109ET) "The Guillotine Lives." Translated in abridged form by Paul Auster. *The New York Times* (April 8, 1973) section 4, p. 15.

110) "Histoire des systèmes de pensée." *Annuaire du Collège de France* 72 (1972) 283–286. A summary of the course given at the Collège de France in 1972. Lecture: "Théories et institutions pénales." Seminar: "Psychiatrie et pénalité au XIXe siècle."

111) "Préface." To Serge Livrozet, *De la prison à la révolte*. Paris: Mercure de France, 1973, 7–14.

112) "Présentation." To *Moi, Pierre Rivière, ayant égorgé ma mère, ma soeur et mon frère*. Edited by Michel Foucault. Paris: Gallimard, Julliard, 1973, 9–15.

    112ET) "Foreword." To *I, Pierre Rivière, having slaughtered my mother , my sister and my brother*. Edited by Michel Foucault. Translated by Frank Jellinek. New York: Pantheon, 1975, vii–xiv.

    112A) "Une crime fait pour être raconté." *Le Nouvel Observateur* 464 (October 1, 1973) 80–112. This article is an abbreviated version of his "Présentation" to *MPR* with excerpts from the memoir itself.

113) "Les meutres qu'on raconte." *MPR*, 265–275.

    113ET) "Tales of Murder." In *I, Pierre Rivière . . .*, 199–212.

114) "Pour une chronique de la mémoire ouvrière." *Libération* (Feb. 22, 1973) 6. A brief conversation with MF, a journalist and a worker named José.

115) "En guise de conclusion." *Le Nouvel Observateur* 435 (March 13, 1973) 92. A commentary on David Rosenhan, "Je me suis fait passer pour fou," 72–93.

116) "La force de fuir." *Derrière le Miroir* 202 (March, 1973) 1–8. On the artist Rebeyrolle.

117) "L'intellectuel sert à rassembler les idées, mais . . . 'son savoir est partiel par rapport au savoir ouvrier.'" *Libération* 16 (May 26, 1973) 2–3. A conversation between MF and a worker named José.

118) "Un nouveau journal?" *Zone des tempêtes* 2 (May–June, 1973) 3.

119) "A verdade e as formas juridicas." Translated into Portuguese by R. Machado. *Cadernos do P.U.C.*, 1974, 5–102. Translated into Spanish by Enrique Lynch as *La verdad y las formas juridicas*. Barcelona: Gedisa, 1980. Five conferences by Foucault at the Catholic University of Rio de Janeiro on May 21–25, 1973. A discussion with MF is on 103–133 in *Cadernos*.

120) "Entretien avec Michel Foucault: à propos de l'enfermement pénitentiaire." *Pro Justicia: Revue politique du droit* 3–4 (October, 1973) 5–14. An interview conducted by A. Krywin and F. Ringelheim.

121) "Gefängnisse und Gefängnisrevolten." *Dokumente: Zeitschrift für übernationale Zusammenarbeit* 29 (June 1973) 133–137. An interview conducted by Bodo Morawe.

122) "Convoqués à la P. J." *Le Nouvel Observateur* 468 (Oct. 29, 1973) 53. Written in collaboration with Alain Landau and Jean-Yves Petit.

123) "Entretien avec Gilles Deleuze, Felix Guattari." *Recherches* 13 (December, 1973) 27–31, 183–186.
124) "Histoire des systèmes de pensée." *Annuaire du Collège de France* 73 (1973) 255–267. A summary of the course given at the Collège de France in 1973. Lecture: "La société punitive." Seminar: "Pierre Rivière et ses oeuvres." Reprinted as appendix in Kremer-Marietti, *Michel Foucault*, 206–221.
125) "Les rayons noirs de Byzantios." *Le Nouvel Observateur* 483 (Feb. 11, 1974) 56–57. A review of *Trente dessins de Byzantios*.
126) "Carceri e manicomi nel congegno del potere." *Avanti!* 78, #53 (March 3, 1974) 6. Interview with Marco D'Eramo.
127) "Sexualité et politique." *Combat* 9274 (April 27–28, 1974) 16.
128) "Entretien." *Cahiers du Cinéma* 251–252 (July–August, 1974) 5–15. An interview with Pascal Bonitzer and Serge Toubiana.
    128ET) "Film and Popular Memory." Translated with some omissions by Martin Jordin. *Radical Philosophy* 11 (Summer, 1975) 24–29.
129) Three lectures on the history of medicine delivered at the Instituto de Medicina Social. Centro Biomédico, Universidad Estatal de Rio de Janeiro, Brazil, in October, 1974. "Crisis de un Modelo en la medicina?" *Revista Centroamericana de Ciencias de la Salud* 3 (Jan.–April, 1976) 197–210; "El nacimiento de la mediciana social." *Ibid.* 6 (Jan.–April, 1977) 89–108; "Incorporacion del hospital en la tecnologia moderna." *Ibid.* 10 (May–August, 1978) 93–104.
130) "Table ronde sur l'expertise psychiatrique." *Actes: Cahiers d'action juridique* 5–6 (Dec. 1974–Jan. 1975). Reprinted in *Actes: Délinquances et ordre* (Paris: Maspero, 1978) 213–228. Other participants were Y. Bastie, A. Bompart, Diederichs, F. Domenach, P. Gay, J. Hassoun, J. Lafon, C. Marechal, P. Sphyras, F. Tirlocq. MF's interventions collected and republished as "L'expertise psychiatrique." *Actes* 54: La gouvernementalité (Summer, 1986) 68.
131) "Histoire des systèmes de pensée." *Annuaire du Collège de France* 74 (1974) 293–300. A summary of the course given at the Collège de France in 1974. Lecture: "Le pouvoir psychiatrique." Seminar: "Explication des textes médicaux et juridiques du XIX siècle."
    131A) A longer version of this text was later published as "La casa della follia." Translated by C. Tarroni. In Franco Basaglia and Franca Basaglia-Ongaro, ed., *Crimini di Pace*. Torino: Einaudi, 1975, 151–169. The original complete French text was then published in Basaglia and Basaglia-Ongaro, ed., *Les Criminels de paix: Recherches sur les intellectuels et leurs techniques comme préposés à l'oppression.* Translated by Bernard Fréminville. Paris: Presses Universitaires de France, 1980, 145–160.
132) *Surveiller et punir: Naissance de la prison.* Paris: Gallimard, 1975.
    132ET) *Discipline and Punish: The Birth of the Prison.* Translated by Alan Sheridan. New York: Pantheon, 1977.
    132A "La naissance des prisons." *Le Nouvel Observateur* 536 (Feb. 17, 1975) 69–86. This article is made up of excerpts from *SP*.
133) "La peinture photogénique." An introduction to an exhibition of paintings by Fromanger: *Fromanger: Le désir est partout.* Paris: Galérie Jeanne Bucher, 1975. (10 pages, no pagination).
134) "Préface." To Bruce Jackson, *Leurs Prisons.* Paris: Plon, 1975, i–vi.
135) "Un pompier vend la mèche." *Le Nouvel Observateur* 531 (Jan. 13, 1975) 56–57. A review of Jean-Jacques Lubrina, *Enfer des Pompiers*.

136) "Des supplices aux cellules." *Le Monde* 9363 (Feb. 21, 1975) 16. An interview with MF conducted by Roger Pol Droit.

136ET) "Michel Foucault on the Role of Prisons." *The New York Times* (Aug. 5, 1975) 31. Excerpts translated by Leonard Mayhew.

137) "Sur la sellette." *Les nouvelles littéraires* 2477 (March 17, 1975) 3. An interview conducted by Jean-Louis Ezine.

137ET) "An Interview with Michel Foucault." Translated by Renée Morel. *History of the Present 1* (Feb., 1985) 2–3, 14.

138) "Il carcere visto da un filsofo francese." *L'Europeo* 1515 (April 3, 1975) 63–65. Interview on *SP* with Ferdinando Scianna.

139) "La Fête de l'Écriture." *Le Quotodien de Paris* 328 (April 25, 1975) 13. MF and J. Almira interviewed by Jean Le Marchand on Almira's *Voyage à Naucratis*.

140) "La Mort du Père." *Libération* 421 (April 30, 1975) 10–11. Discussion on Marx and communism with P. Daix, P. Gavi, J. Rancière and Yannakakis.

141) "Entretien sur la prison." *Magazine littéraire* 101 (June, 1975) 27–33. An interview conducted by J. J. Brochier.

141ET) "Prison Talk: an interview with Michel Foucault." Translated by Colin Gordon. *Radical Philosophy* 16 (Spring, 1977) 10–15. Republished in *Power/Knowledge*, 37–54.

142) "Pouvoir et corps." A June interview with MF in *Quel corps?* 2 (1975). Reissued in a collection of texts from the review and published as *Quel corps?* Paris: Francois Maspero, 1978, 27–35.

142ET) "Body/Power." In *Power/Knowledge*, 55–62. Translated by Colin Gordon.

143) "Foucault, passe-frontières de la philosophie." *Le Monde* (Sept. 6, 1986). An interview conducted by Roger-Pol Droit on June 20, 1975.

144) "La machine à penser s'est-elle detraquée?" *Le Monde Diplomatique* 256 (July, 1975) 18–21. Quotes MF, among others in an inquiry into "crisis of thought?," conducted by Maurice Maschino.

145) "Aller à Madrid." *Libération* 538 (Sept. 24, 1975) 1, 7. An interview conducted by Pierre Benoit concerning a delegation of seven French intellectuals, including MF, expelled from Madrid while denouncing death sentences imposed on anti-Franco militants.

146) "Faire les fous: Réflexions sur *Histoire de Paul*." *Le Monde* 9559 (Oct. 16, 1975) 17. On the film by René Feret.

147) "À propos de Marguerite Duras." *Cahiers Renaud Barrault* 89 (October, 1975) 8–22. A conversation between MF and Hélène Cixous.

148) "Sade, sergent du sexe." *Cinématographe* 16 (Dec., 1975–Jan., 1976) 3–5. Interview conducted by Gérard Dupont.

149) "Histoire des systèmes de pensée." *Annuaire du Collège de France* 75 (1975) 335–339. A summary of the course given at the Collège de France in 1975. Lecture: "Les anormaux." Seminar: "L'expertise médico-légale en matiere psychiatrique."

150) *Histoire de la sexualité I: La volonté de savoir*. Paris: Gallimard, 1976.

150ET) *The History of Sexuality I: An Introduction*. Translated by Robert Hurley. New York: Pantheon Books, 1978.

151) "Les têtes de la politique." A preface to *En attendant le grand soir*, a book of sketches by Wiaz. Paris: Denoël, 1976, 7–12.

152) "Un mort inacceptable." A preface to Bernard Cuau, *L'affaire Mirval ou Comment le récit abolit le crime*. Paris: Les presses d'aujourd'hui, 1976, vii–xi.

153) "La politique de la santé au XVIIIe siècle." The introduction to Part I, "L'Institution hospitaliere au XVIIIe siècle," of a three part study done under the direction of MF and published as *Généalogie des équipements de normalisation: Les équipements sanitaires*. Fontenay-sur-Bois: Centre d'Études, de Recherches et de Formation Institutionelles (CERFI), 1976, 1–11.

    153ET) "The Politics of Health in the Eighteenth Century." Translated by Colin Gordon. In *Power/Knowledge*, 166–182.

154) "La crisis de la medicina o la crisis de la antimedicina." *Education medica y salud* 10, 2 (1976) 152–170.

155) "Sur *Histoire de Paul*." *Cahiers du Cinéma* 262–263 (January, 1976) 63–65. A conversation between MF and René Féret.

156) "Questions à Michel Foucault sur la géographie." *Hérodote* 1 (Jan.–March, 1976) 71–85.

    156ET) "Questions on Geography." Translated by Colin Gordon. In *Power/Knowledge*, 63–77.

157) "Crimes et châtiments en U. R. S. S. et ailleurs." *Le Nouvel Observateur* 585 (Jan. 26, 1976) 34–37. An interview with K. S. Karol.

    157ET) "The Politics of Crime." A translation of large excerpts by Mollie Horwitz. *Partisan Review* 43 (1976) 453–459.

158) "Corso del 7 gennaio 1976," and "Corso del 14 gennaio 1976." In *Microfisica del Potere*. Edited by Alessandro Fontana and Pasquale Pasquino. Torino: Einaudi, 1977, 163–177, 179–194. Italian translation of two lectures, unpublished in France, which were delivered in January, 1976 at the Collège de France.

    158ET) "Two Lectures." Translated by Kate Soper. In *Power/Knowledge*, 78–108.

159) "L'extension sociale de la norme." *Politique hebdo* 212 (March, 1976) 14–16. An interview, with P. Werner, on Szasz's *Fabriquer la folie*.

160) "Sorcellerie et folie." *Le Monde* 9720 (April 23, 1976) 18. A conversation with MF conducted by Roland Jaccard on Thomas Szasz's *Fabriquer la folie*.

161) "Intervista a Michel Foucault." An interview in June, 1976, conducted by Alessandro Fontana and Pasquale Pasquino. It serves as an introduction to their *Microfisica del Potere*, 3–28. Cf. #158 above for full entry.

    161ET) "Truth and Power." Translated by Colin Gordon. In *Power/Knowledge*, 109–133.

    161A) This interview was released in French as "Vérité et pouvoir." *L'Arc* 70 (1977) 16–26. Excerpts had appeared earlier as "La fonction politique de l'intellectuel." *Politique hebdo* 247 (Nov. 29, 1976) 31–33. An English translation of the latter was made by Colin Gordon and published as "The Political Function of the Intellectual." *Radical Philosophy* 17 (Summer, 1977) 12–14.

162) "Des question de Michel Foucault à *Hérodote*." *Hérodote* 3 (July–Sept., 1976) 9–10. Foucault's questions were replied to in the same journal, issue #6 (April–June, 1977) 7–30.

163) "Bio-histoire et bio-politique." *Le Monde* 9869 (Oct. 17–18, 1976) 5. Remarks on J. Ruffie's *De la biologie à la culture*.

164) "L'Occident et la vérité du sexe." *Le Monde* 9885 (Nov. 5, 1976) 24.

    164ET) "The West and the Truth of Sex." Translated by Lawrence Winters. *Sub-Stance* 20 (1978) 5–8.

165) "Entretien avec Michel Foucault." *Cahiers du Cinéma* 271 (Nov. 1976) 52–53. An interview conducted by Pascal Kane on the Réné Allio film of *Moi, Pierre Rivière*.

166) "Pourquoi le crime de Pierre Rivière?" *Pariscope* (November 10–16, 1976) 5–7. Conversation with Francois Chatelet on the Rivière case.

167) "Malraux." *Le Nouvel Observateur* 629 (Nov. 29, 1976) 83.

168) "Histoire des systèmes de pensée." *Annuaire du Collège de France* 76 (1976) 361–366. A summary of the course given at the Collège de France in 1976. Lecture: "'Il faut défendre la societé.'" Seminar: "L'utilisation des techniques psychiatriques en matière pénale."

      168ET) "War in the Filigree of Peace. Course Summary." Translated by Ian McLeod. *Oxford Literary Review* IV, 2 (1980) 15–19.

      168A) *Vom Licht des Krieges zur Geburt der Geschichte*. Edited by Walter Seitter. Berlin: Merve Verlag, 1986. This volume is made up of German translations of two of the lectures from this course (Jan. 21 and Jan. 28).

169) "Preface." To the English translation of Gilles Deleuze and Felix Guattari, *Anti-Oedipus: Capitalism and Schizophrenia*. Translated by Robert Hurley, Mark Seem, and Helen Lane. New York: Viking, 1977, xi–xiv.

170) "Vorwort zu deutschen Ausgabe." An introduction to the German edition of *VS: Sexualität und Wahrheit: I: Die Wille zum Wissen*. Translated by Ulrich Raulf. Frankfurt: Suhrkamp, 1977, 7–8.

171) "Avant-propos." Foreword to *Politiques de l'habitat 1800–1850*, a study done under the direction of MF. Paris: CORDA, 1977, 3–4.

172) "L'oeil du pouvoir." Introduction to Jeremy Bentham's *Le panoptique*. Paris: Pierre Belfond, 1977, 7–31. A conversation with Jean-Pierre Barou and Michelle Perrot.

      172ET) "The Eye of Power." Translated by Colin Gordon. In *Power/Knowledge*, 146–165.

173) "Le supplice de la vérité." *Chemin de Ronde* 1 (1977) 162–163.

174) "Die Folter, das ist die Vernunft." *Literaturmagazin* 8 (1977) 60–68. A conversation with Kurt Boesers.

175) "Préface." To Mireille Debard and Jean-Luc Hennig, *Les juges kaki*. Paris: Editions Alain Moreau, 1977, 7–10. Also published as "Les juges kaki." *Le Monde* 10214 (Dec. 1–2, 1977) 15.

176) "Historia de la medicalizacion." *Education medica y salud* 11, 1 (1977) 3–25.

177) "La sécurité et l'Etat." *Tribune socialiste* (1977).

178) "Les rapports de pouvoir passent à l'intérieur des corps." An interview conducted by Lucette Finas. *La quinzaine littéraire* 247 (Jan. 1–15, 1977) 4–6.

      178ET) "The History of Sexuality." Translated by Leo Marshall. In *Power/Knowledge*, 183–193.

179) "La vie des hommes infâmes." *Les Cahiers du Chemin* 29 (Jan. 15, 1977) 12–29. This piece was to serve as the introduction to a volume to be edited by Foucault and published under the same title by Gallimard.

      179ET) "The Life of Infamous Men." Translated by Paul Foss and Meaghan Morris. In the collection of essays they edited, *Power, Truth, Strategy* (Sydney, Australia: Feral, 1979) 76–91.

180) "Michel Foucault: à bas la dictature du sexe!" *L'Express* 1333 (Jan. 24, 1977) 56–57. A review of *VS* by Madeleine Chapsal, with extensive quotations from an interview with MF.

181) "Pouvoirs et stratégies." *Les révoltes logiques* 4 (Winter, 1977) 89–97.
    181ET) "Powers and Strategies." Translated by Colin Gordon. In *Power/Knowledge*, 134–145.

182) "Le poster de l'ennemi public no. 1." *Le Matin* 6 (March 7, 1977) 11. On Jacques Mesrine's *L'Instinct de mort*.

183) "Non au sexe roi." *Le Nouvel Observateur* 644 (March 12, 1977) 92–130. An interview conducted by Bernard-Henri Levy.
    183ET) "Power and Sex: An Interview with Michel Foucault." Translated by David Parent. *Telos* 32 (Summer, 1977) 152–161.

184) "Les matins gris de la tolérance." *Le Monde* 9998 (March 23, 1977) 24. A review of a film by P. Pasolini, *Enquête sur la sexualité (Comizi d'Amore)*.

185) "L'asile illimité." *Le Nouvel Observateur* 646 (March 28, 1977) 66–67. A review of Robert Castel's *L'ordre psychiatrique*.

186) "La géométrie fantastique de Maxime Defert." *Les Nouvelles Littéraires* 2582 (April 28, 1977) 13. On an exhibit of paintings by Defert.

187) "La grande colère des faits." *Le Nouvel Observateur* 652 (May 9, 1977) 84–86. Reissued in *Faut-it brûler les nouveaux philosophes?*, edited by Sylvie Bouscasse and Denis Bourgeois. Paris: Nouvelles Editions Oswald, 1978, 63–70. A reflection on André Glucksmann's *Les maîtres penseurs*.

188) "L'angoisse de juger." *Le Nouvel Observateur* 655 (May 30, 1977) 92–126. A debate on capital punishment with Robert Badinter and Jean Laplanche, edited by Catherine David.

189) "Michel Foucault à Goutelas: La redéfinition du 'Justiciable.'" *Justice: Syndicat de la Magistrature* 11'5 (June, 1987) 36–39.

190) "Le jeu de Michel Foucault." *Ornicar?* 10 (July, 1977) 62–93. A discussion with MF. Participants were: Alain Grosrichard, Gérard Wajeman, Jacques-Alain Miller, Guy Le Gaufey, Catherine Millot, Dominique Colas, Jocelyne Livi, Judith Miller.
    190ET) "The Confession of the Flesh." Translated by Colin Gordon. In *Power/Knowledge*, 194–228.

191) "Une mobilisation culturelle." *Le Nouvel Observateur* 670 (Sept. 12, 1977) 49.

192) "Enfermement, Psychiatrie, Prison." *Change: La folie encerclée* 32–33 (Oct., 1977) 76–110. A dialogue between MF, David Cooper, Victor Fainberg, and Jean-Pierre Faye.

193) "About the Concept of the 'Dangerous Individual' in 19th-Century Legal Psychiatry." Translated by Alain Baudot and Jane Couchman. *International Journal of Law and Psychiatry I* (1978) 1–18. Originally delivered in English at a symposium in Toronto, October 24–26, 1977.
    193A) This was later issued in French as "L'évolution de la notion d'"individu dangereux' dans la psychiatrie légale." *Revue déviance et société V* (1981) 403–422.

194) "Va-t-on extrader Klaus Croissant?" *Le Nouvel Observateur* 679 (Nov. 14, 1977) 62–63.

195) "'Désormais, la sécurité est au-dessus des lois.'" *Le Matin* 225 (Nov. 18, 1977) 15. An interview conducted by Jean-Paul Kauffman.

196) "Lettre à quelques leaders de la gauche." *Le Nouvel Observateur* 681 (Nov. 28, 1977) 59.

197) "'Wir fühlten uns als schmutzige Spezies.'" *Der Spiegel* 31 (Dec. 19, 1977) 77–78.

198) "Préface." To *My Secret Life*. Translated from the English by Christiné

Charnaux et al. Paris: Editions les Formes du Secret, 1978, 5–7.

199) "Introduction." To Georges Canguilhem's *On the Normal and the Pathological*. This is the English translation of *Le normal et le pathologique*. Translated by Carolyn Fawcett. Boston: D. Reidel, 1978. ix–xx.

    199A) This was later issued in French as "La vie: l'expérience et la science" in *Revue de métaphysique et de morale* 90 (January–March, 1985) 3–14.

200) "Note." *To Herculine Barbin dite Alexina B.* Presented by MF. Paris: Gallimard, 1978, 131–132.

    200A) "Introduction." To the English translation: *Herculine Barbin, Being the Recently Discovered Memoirs of a Nineteenth Century French Hermaphrodite*. Translated by Richard McDougall. New York: Pantheon Books, 1980, vii–xvii. This introduction is a totally new work dated January, 1980. The original brief note to the French edition is on pages 119–120 of the translation.

    200B) "Le vrai sexe." *Arcadie* 323 (November, 1980) 617–625. A slightly modified version of the "Introduction" to the English translation.

201) "La grille politique traditionelle." *Politique-Hebdo* 303 (1978) 20.

202) "M. Foucault. Conversazione senza complessi con il filosofo che analizza le 'strutture del potere.'" A discussion with J. Bauer. *Playmen* 12, 10 (1978) 21–30.

203) "Incorporacion del hospital en la tecnologia moderna." *Educacion medica y salud* 12, 1 (1978) 20–35.

204) "Un jour dans une classe s'est fait une film." *L'Educateur* 51, 12 (1978) 21–25.

205) "Eugène Sue que j'aime." *Les nouvelle littéraires* 2618 (Jan. 12–19, 1978) 3. A reflection on the reissued *Les mystères du peuple* by Sue.

206) "Une érudition étourdissante." *Le Matin* 278 (January 20, 1978) 25. A review of Philippe Ariès' *L'Homme devant la mort*.

207) "Alan Peyrefitte s'explique . . . et Michel Foucault lui répond." *Le Nouvel Observateur* 689 (Jan. 23, 1978) 25.

208) "Precisazioni sul potere. Riposta ad alcuni critici." *Aut Aut* 167–168 (Sept.–Dec., 1978) 3–11. Response to written questions from Pasquale Pasquino in February, 1978.

209) "La gouvernamentalità." *Aut Aut* 167–168 (Sept.–Dec., 1978) 12–29. The Italian transcript, translated by Pasquale Pasquino, of a lecture given at the Collège de France in February, 1978.

    209ET) "Governmentality." Translated by Rosi Braidotti. *Ideology and Consciousness* 6 (Autumn, 1979) 5–12.

    209A) This lecture was released in a French translation by Jean-Claude Oswald as "La gouvernementalité," *Actes* 54 (Summer, 1986) 7–15.

210) "Attention: danger." *Libération* 1286 (March 22, 1978) 9.

211) "Sekai-ninshiki no Hoho: Marukusushugi o do shimatsusuruka [The strategy of world-understanding: How to get rid of Marxism]." *UMI* (Tokyo) 53, #7 (July, 1978) 302–328. Dialogue with Ryumei Yoshimoto on April 25, 1978.

212) "Sei to Seiji Wo Kataru (On Sex and Politics)." *Asahi janaru* 20, #19 (May 12, 1978) 15–20. An interview with Moriaki Watanabe and Chobei Nemoto.

213) Le poussière et le nuage." *L'impossible prison: Recherches sur le système pénitentiaire au XIXe siècle*. Edited by Michelle Perrot. Paris: Seuil, 1980,

29–39. Although not published until May, 1980, this was written in 1978 as a reply to a text by Jacques Léonard which appears in the same volume: "L'historien et le philosophe: A propos de: *Surveiller et punir; naissance de la prison.*" Both papers served as the basis for a discussion with MF which was published as the following entry.

214) "Table ronde du 20 mai 1978." In *L'impossible prison*, 40–56 (cf. #213 for full details). While specific interventions were not cited by name with the exception of those from MF, participants in this discussion were: Maurice Agulhon, Nicole Caston, Catherine Duprat, François Ewald, Arlette Farge, Alexandre Fontana, Carlo Ginzburg, Remi Gossez, Jacques Léonard, Pascal Pasquino, Michelle Perrot, Jacques Revel.

   214ET) "Questions of Method." Translated by Colin Gordon. *Ideology and Consciousness* 8 (Spring, 1981) 3–14.

215) "Postface." To *L'impossible prison* (cf. #213), 316–318.

216) "Vijftien vragen van homosexuele zijde san Michel Foucault." *Interviews met Michel Foucault*, ed. by M. Duyves and T. Maasen. Utrecht: De Woelrat, 1982, 13–23.

217) "Du pouvoir." *L'Express* 1722 (July 13, 1984) 56–62. An interview with MF, conducted by Pierre Boncenne in July, 1978 but not published until after Foucault's death.

218) "Il misterioso ermafrodito." *La Stampa Supp. Litt.* 4, #30 (August 5, 1978) 5. Interview with Elena Guicciardi on *Herculine Barbin*.

219) "Du bon usage du criminel." *Le Nouvel Observateur* 722 (Sept. 11, 1978) 40–42.

220) "Taccuino Persiano: L'esercito, quando la terra trema." *Corriere della Sera* 103, No. 228 (Sept. 28, 1978) 1–2. The first of a series of articles in Italian on the revolution in Iran.

221) "Teheran: la fede contro lo Scia." *Corriere della Sera* 103, No. 237 (Oct. 8, 1978) 11.

222) "A quoi rêvent les Iraniens?" *Le Nouvel Observateur* 726 (Oct. 9–16, 1978) 48–49.

223) "Le citron et le lait." *Le Monde* 10, 490 (Oct. 21, 1978) 14. A review of Philippe Boucher's *Le ghetto judiciaire*.

224) "Ein gewaltiges Erstaunen." An interview on the exposition "Paris-Berlin" which took place in Paris in 1978. *Der Spiegel* 32 (Oct. 30, 1978) 264.

   224ET) "Interview with Michel Foucault." Translated by J. D. Steakley. *New German Critique* 16 (Winter, 1979) 155–156.

225) "Une rivolta con le mani nude." *Corriere della Sera*, 103, No. 261 (Nov. 5, 1978) 1–2.

226) "Sfida all'opposizione." *Corriere della Sera*, 103, No. 262 (Nov. 7, 1978) 1–2.

227) "I 'reportages di idee.'" *Corriere della Sera*, 103, No. 267 (Nov. 12, 1978) 1.

228) "Réponse de Michel Foucault à une lectrice iranienne." *Le Nouvel Observateur* 731 (Nov. 13, 1978) 26.

229) "La rivolta dell'Iran corre sui nastri delli minicasette." *Corriere della Sera*, 103 No. 273 (Nov. 19, 1978) 1–2.

230) "Il mitico capo della rivolta nell'Iran." *Corriere della Sera*, 103, No. 279 (Nov. 26, 1978) 1–2.

231) *Colloqui con Foucault.* Salerno: 10/17 Cooperative editrice, 1981. A series of 1978 interviews between MF and Duccio Trombadori.

232) "Lettera di Foucault all'Unita." *L'Unita* 55, no. 285 (December 1, 1978) 1.

233) "Histoire des systèmes de pensée." *Annuaire du Collège de France* 78 (1978) 445–449. A summary of the course given at the Collège de France in 1978. Lecture: "Securité, territoire, et population." Seminar: "La Médicalisation en France depuis le XIXe siècle."

    233ET) "Foucault at the Collège de France I: A Course Summary." Translated, with an introduction, by James Bernauer. *Philosophy and Social Criticism VIII*, 2 (Summer, 1981) 235–242.

    233A) An edited version of the course's lectures has been translated into German by Andreas Pribersky and published as "Vorlesungen zur Analyse der Macht-Mechanismen 1978: Das Denken des Staates." In MF, *Der Staub und die Wolke* (Bremen: Verlag Impuls, 1982) 1–44.

234) "L'espirit d'un monde sans esprit." A conversation with MF conducted by Claire Brière and Pierre Blanchet. Published as an appendix to their *Iran: la révolution au nom de Dieu*. Paris: Seuil, 1979, 225–241.

235) "Préface." To Peter Brückner and Alfred Krovoza, *Ennemi de l'Etat*. Calix: La pensée sauvage, 1979, 4–5.

236) "La phobie d'etat." *Libération* 967 (June 30–July 1, 1984) 21. An excerpt from a lecture by Foucault on Jan. 31, 1979 at the Collège.

237) "Manières de justice." *Le Nouvel Observateur* 743 (Feb. 5, 1979) 20–21.

238) "Une polveriera chiamata Islam." *Corriere della Sera* 104, no. 36 (Feb. 13, 1979) 1.

239) "Michel Foucault et l'Iran." *Le Matin* 647 (March 26, 1979) 15. A short reply to an article which had attacked his position on Iran's revolution. Cf. Claudie and Jacques Broyelle. "A quoi rêvent les philosophes?" *Le Matin* 646 (March 24, 1979) 13.

240) "La loi de la pudeur." *Recherches* 37 (April, 1979) 69–82. A transcript of a radio discussion on April 4, 1978 with Guy Hocquenghem and Jean Danet.

    240ET) Excerpts from Foucault's remarks were translated by Daniel Moshenberg and published in *Semiotext(e)* (Summer, 1980) 44, 40–42.

241) "Une plaisir si simple." *Le Gai Pied* 1 (April, 1979) 1, 10.

    241ET) "The Simplest of Pleasures." Translated by Mike Riegle and Gilles Barbedette. *Fag Rag* 29, p. 3.

242) "Lettre ouverte à Mehdi Bazargan." *Le Nouvel Observateur* 753 (April 14, 1979) 46.

243) "Pour une morale de l'inconfort." *Le Nouvel Observateur* 754 (April 23, 1979) 82–83. A review of Jean Daniel's *L'ère des ruptures*.

244) "Le moment de vérité." *Le Matin* 673 (April 25, 1979) 20. On the death of Maurice Clavel.

245) "Vivre autrement le temps." *Le Nouvel Observateur* 755 (April 30, 1979) 88. A testimony to Maurice Clavel.

246) "Inutile de se soulever?" *Le Monde* 10,661 (May 11, 1979) 1–2.

    246ET) "Is it useless to revolt?" Translated, with an introduction, by James Bernauer. *Philosophy and Social Criticism VIII*, 1 (Spring, 1981) 1–9.

247) "La stratégie du pourtour." *Le Nouvel Observateur* 759 (May 28, 1979) 57.

248) "Omnes et Singulatim: Towards a Criticism of 'Political Reason.'" Lectures delivered at Stanford University on Oct. 10 and 16, 1979. In Sterling McMurrin, ed., *The Tanner Lectures on Human Values II* (1981). Salt Lake City: University of Utah Press, 1981, 225–254.

248A) "Omnes et Singulatim: Vers une critique de la raison politique."
Translated by P. E. Dauzat. *Le débat* 41 (Sept.–Nov., 1986) 5–35.

249) "Luttes autour des prisons." *Esprit* 35 (Nov., 1979) 102–111. A discussion
between MF (under the pseudonym of "Louis Appert"), Antoine Lazarus,
and François Colcombet, on the prison movements of the 1970s.

250) "Histoire des systèmes de pensée." *Annuaire du Collège de France* 79 (1979)
367–372. A summary of the course given at the Collège de France, in 1979.
Lecture: "Naissance de la biopolitique." Seminar: "Problèmes de méthode
en histoire des idées."

　250ET) "Foucault at the Collège de France II: A Course Summary."
Translated, with an introduction, by James Bernauer. *Philosophy and
Social Criticism* VIII, 3 (Fall, 1981) 349–359.

251) "Les quatre chevaliers de l'Apocalypse et les vermisseaux quotidiens." *Cahiers
du Cinéma* hors série 6: Syberberg (February, 1980) 95–96. Interview with
Bernard Sobel on Syberberg's *Hitler, a film from Germany*.

252) "'Le Nouvel Observateur' e l'unione della sinistre." *Spirali* 15 (Jan., 1980)
53–55. Excerpts from a conversation between MF and Jean Daniel, first
broadcast on a France-Culture radio program conducted by Denis Richet.

253) "Lettre." *Le Nouvel Observateur* (Jan. 14, 1980).

254) "Préface." To Roger Knobelspiess, *Q. H. S.: Quartier de haute sécurité*. Paris:
Stock, 1980, 11–16 (March 31, 1980).

255) "Le philosophe masqué." *Le Monde Dimanche* 10, 945 (April 6, 1980) I and
XVII. An interview conducted by Christian Delacampagne and originally
published without identifying Foucault.

256) "Conversation with Michel Foucault." *The Threepenny Review* I, 1 (Winter-
Spring, 1980) 4–5. An interview conducted by Millicent Dillon.

257) "Sexuality and Solitude." *London Review of Books* (May 21–June 3, 1981) 3,
5–6. The text of Foucault's James Lecture, delivered Nov. 20, 1980 at the
New York Institute for the Humanities. This was later published in *Humanities in Review* I (1982), edited by David Rieff. New York: Cambridge
University Press, 1982, 3–21.

258) "Roland Barthes." *Annuaire du Collège de France* 80 (1980) 61–62.

259) "Histoire des systèmes de pensée." *Annuaire du Collège de France* 80 (1980)
449–452. A summary of the course given at the Collège de France in 1980.
Lecture: "Du gouvernement des vivants." Seminar: "Liberalisme et Etatisme
à la fin du XIXe siècle."

260) "De l'amitié comme mode de vie." *Le Gai Pied* 25 (April, 1981) 38–39.

　260ET) "Friendship as a Lifestyle: An Interview with Michel Foucault." *Gay Information* 7 (Spring, 1981) 4–6. No translator identified.

261) "L'intellectuel et les pouvoirs." *La Revue Nouvelle* 80 (1984) 338–345. Interview conducted on May 14, 1981 by Christian Panier and Pierre Watté.

262) "Est-il donc important de penser?" *Libération* (May 30–31, 1981) 21. An
interview with MF conducted by Didier Eribon.

　262ET) "Is it really important to think?" Translated, with an afterword,
by Thomas Keenan. *Philosophy and Social Criticism* 9, 1 (Spring,
1982) 29–40.

263) "Face aux gouvernements, les droits de l'Homme." *Libération* 967 (June
30–July 1, 1984) 22. A statement by Foucault in June, 1981, but published
only after his death. It concerned Southeast Asian "boat people."

264) "Il faut tout repenser la loi et la prison." *Libération* 45 (July 6, 1981) 2. On hunger strikes by prison inmates.

265) "Lacan, il 'liberatore' della psicanalisi." *Corriere della Sera* 106, no. 212 (Sept. 11, 1981) 1. An interview with MF conducted by Jacques Nobécourt after the death of Jacques Lacan.

266) "De la nécessité de mettre un terme à toute peine." *Libération* 108 (Sept. 18, 1981) 5.

267) "Les réponses de Pierre Vidal-Naquet et de Michel Foucault." *Libération* 185 (Dec. 18, 1981) 12. Concerns the French government's reaction to the imposition of martial law in Poland.

268) "Conversation." In Gérard Courant (ed.). *Werner Schroeter.* Paris: Cinématheque Francaise et Goethe Institute, 1982, 38–47. A discussion between MF and Werner Schroeter as recorded by Courant on Dec. 3, 1981.

269) "Notes sur ce qu'on lit et entend." *Le Nouvel Observateur* 893 (Dec. 19, 1981) 21. On the imposition of martial law in Poland.

270) "Histoire des systèmes de pensée." *Annuaire du Collège de France* 81 (1981) 385–389. A summary of the course given at the Collège de France in 1981. Lecture: "Subjectivité et vérité." Seminar: "Problèmes du liberalisme au XIXe siècle."

271) *Le désordre des familles: Lettres de cachet des Archives de la Bastille.* A collection of police documents, edited with introductions by MF and Arlette Farge. Paris: Gallimard/Julliard, 1982.

272) "Nineteenth Century Imaginations." Translated by Alex Susteric. *Semiotext(e) IV*, 2 (1982) 182–190.

273) "The Subject and Power." An afterword to Hubert Dreyfus and Paul Rabinow. *Michel Foucault: Beyond Structuralism and Hermeneutics.* Chicago: University of Chicago Press, 1982, 214–232. Part I was written in English. Part II was translated by Leslie Sawyer. Republished in *Critical Inquiry* 8 (Summer, 1982).

274) "Non aux compromis." *Gai Pied* 43 (1982) 9. A conversation with R. Surzur.

275) Response to speech by Susan Sontag. *The Soho News* (March 2, 1982) 13.

276) "Space, Knowledge and Power." *Skyline* (March, 1982) 16–20. An interview with Paul Rabinow, translated by Christian Hubert.

277) "Histoire et Homosexualité: Entretien avec M. Foucault." *Masques* 13 (Spring, 1982) 14–24. An interview conducted by J. P. Joecker, M. Ouerd and A. Sanzio.

278) "Sexual Choice, Sexual Act: An Interview with Michel Foucault." *Salmagundi* 58–59 (Fall, 1982–Winter, 1983) 10–24. Conducted by James O'Higgins in March, 1982.

    287A) This appeared in French as "Lorsque l'amant part en taxi." *Gai Pied Hebdo* 151 (Jan. 5, 1985) 22–24, 54–57.

279) "La combat de la chasteté." *Communications* 35 (May 1982) 15–25.

    279ET) "The Battle for Chastity." In *Western Sexuality: Practice and Precept in Past and Present Times*, edited by Philippe Ariès and André Béjin and translated by Anthony Foster. Oxford: Basil Blackwell, 1985, 14–25.

280) "The Social Triumph of the Sexual Will." *Christopher Street* 64 (May, 1982) 36–41. A conversation with MF, conducted by Gilles Barbedette and translated by Brendan Lemon.

281) "Des caresses d'homme considérées comme un art." *Libération* (June 1, 1982)

27. A review of K. J. Dover's *Homosexualité grecque*.

282) "An Interview." *Ethos I*, 2 (Autumn, 1983) 4–9. Conducted by Stephen Riggins on June 22, 1982.

283) "Michel Foucault, An Interview: Sex, Power and the Politics of Identity." *The Advocate* 400 (Aug. 7, 1984) 26–30, 58. Conducted by Bob Gallagher and Alexander Wilson in June, 1982.

> 283A) This later appeared in a French translation by Jacques Hess as "Que fabriquent donc les hommes ensemble?" *Le Nouvel Observateur* 1098 (Nov. 22–28, 1985) 54–55.

284) "Le terrorisme ici et la." *Libération* (Sept. 3, 1982) 12. A discussion with D. Eribon.

285) "Pierre Boulez ou l'écran traversé." *Le Nouvel Observateur* 934 (Oct. 2, 1982) 51–52.

286) "En abandonnant les Polonais, nous renonçons à une part de nous-mêmes." *Le Nouvel Observateur* 935 (Oct. 9, 1982) 36. A conversation with Bernard Kouchner and Simone Signoret, conducted by Pierre Blanchet.

287) "L'expérience morale et sociale des Polonais ne peut plus être effacée." *Les nouvelles littéraires* 2857 (Oct. 14–20, 1982) 8–9. An interview with MF conducted by Gilles Anquetil.

288) "Truth, Power, Self: An Interview with Michel Foucault." An interview with Rex Martin on Oct. 25, 1982. In *Technologies of the Self: A Seminar with Michel Foucault*. Edited by Luther H. Martin, Huck Gutman, and Patrick H. Hutton. Amherst: University of Massachusetts Press, 1988, 9–15.

289) "Technologies of the Self." In *Technologies of the Self: A Seminar with Michel Foucault*, 16–49.

290) "The Political Technology of Individuals." In *Technologies of the Self: A Seminar with Michel Foucault*, 145–162.

291) "La Pensée, L'Emotion." In *Duane Michals: Photographies de 1958 à 1982*. Paris: Paris Audiovisual, Musée d'Art Moderne de la Ville de Paris, 1982, iii–vii. An exposition at the Musée d'Art Moderne in Paris, Nov. 9, 1982–Jan. 9, 1983.

292) "L'âge d'or de la lettre de cachet." *L'Express* 1638 (Dec. 3, 1982) 35–36. An interview with MF and Arlette Farge, conducted by Yves Hersant, on *Le Désordre des familles* (# 271 above).

293) "Histoire des systèmes de pensée." *Annuaire du Collège de France* 82 (1982) 395–406. A summary of the course given at the Collège de France in 1982. Lecture: "L'hermeneutique du sujet." An abridged presentation of Foucault's lectures was edited and published by Helmut Becker and Lothar Wolfstetter as "Michel Foucaults Hermeneutik des Subjekts" in their collection *Freiheit und Selbstsorge* (Frankfurt: Materialis Verlag, 1985) 32–60.

294) "L'écriture de soi." *Corps écrit* 5 (1983): *L'autoportrait*, 3–23.

295) "Rêver de ses plaisirs: sur l'onirocritique d'Artémidore." *Recherches sur la philosophie et le langage* 3 (1983) 53–78. A slightly altered version of this material became chapter 1 of *Le souci de soi*. Cf. # 312 below.

296) "Un système fini face à une demande infinie." In *Sécurité sociale: l'enjeu*. Paris: Editions Syros, 1983, 39–63. An interview with R. Bono.

> 296ET) "The Risks of Security." *History of the Present* 2 (Spring, 1986) 4–5, 11–14.

297) "Un cours inédit." *Magazine littéraire* 207 (May, 1984) 35–39. A lecture at the

Collège de France, January 5, 1983, on the question of enlightenment in Kant.

297ET) "Kant on Enlightenment and Revolution." Translated by Colin Gordon. *Economy and Society* 15 (February, 1986) 88–96.

298) "A propos des faiseurs d'histoire." *Libération* (Jan. 21, 1983) 22. An interview with Didier Eribon.

299) "An Exchange with Michel Foucault." An exchange of letters between MF and Lawrence Stone. *The New York Review of Books* (March 31, 1983) 42–44. Foucault's letter was written in criticism of Stone's earlier essay, "Madness," in *The New York Review of Books* (Dec. 16, 1982) 28–36.

300) "Structuralism and Post-Structuralism: An Interview with Michel Foucault." *Telos* 55 (Spring, 1983) 195–211. An interview conducted by Gérard Raulet and translated by Jeremy Harding. First published in German as "Um welchen Preis sagt die Vernunft die Wahrheit?" *Spuren* 1–2 (1983).

301) "The Power and Politics of Michel Foucault." *Inside* (April 22, 1983) 7, 20–22. An interview in the weekly magazine of the *Daily Californian* (University of California at Berkeley) conducted by Peter Maas and David Brock.

302) "Politics and Ethics: An Interview." Translated by Catherine Porter. In *The Foucault Reader*, edited by Paul Rabinow (New York: Pantheon Books, 1984) 373–380. Edited interviews conducted in April, 1983, by Paul Rabinow, Charles Taylor, Martin Jay, Richard Rorty and Leo Lowenthal.

303) "On the Genealogy of Ethics: An Overview of Work in Progress." In the 2nd edition of *Michel Foucault: Beyond Structuralism and Hermeneutics*. Chicago: University of Chicago Press, 1983, 229–252. An interview conducted by Hubert Dreyfus and Paul Rabinow. An abridged French translation by Jacques B. Hess appeared as "Le sexe comme une morale." *Le Nouvel Observateur* (June 1, 1984) 62–66.

304) "La Pologne, et après? Edmond Maire: Entretien avec Michel Foucault." *Le débat* 25 (May, 1983) 3–34.

305) "La Musique contemporaine et le publique." *CNAC Magazine* 15 (May–June, 1983) 10–12. A discussion between MF and Pierre Boulez, in the magazine of the Pompidou Center.

306) "Vous êtes dangereux." *Libération* 639 (June 10, 1983) 20.

307) "Archéologie d'une passion." *Magazine littéraire* 221 (July–August, 1985) 100–105. An edited interview conducted by Charles Ruas on Sept. 15, 1983.

307ET) "An Interview with Michel Foucault." Postscript to Ruas's translation of *Raymond Roussel* (cf. #19 above) 169–186.

308) "Usage des plaisirs et techniques de soi." *Le débat* 27 (November, 1983) 46–72. This is a very slightly modified version of the introductory chapter to *L'usage des plaisirs*. Cf. #311 below.

309) "Qu-appelle-t-on punir?" *Revue de l'université de Bruxelles* (1984): *Punir mon bon souci, Pour une raison penale*, 35–46. An interview with Foulek Ringelheim, conducted in December, 1983.

310) "Histoire des systèmes de pensée." *Annuaire du Collège de France* 83 (1983) 441. Foucault's last submitted course description reads simply: "Le cours a porté sur: 'Le gouvernement de soi et des autres.'"

311) *Histoire de la sexualité 2: L'usage des plaisirs*. Paris: Gallimard, 1984.

311ET) *The Use of Pleasure*. Translated by Robert Hurley. New York: Pantheon, 1985.

311A) Earlier version of "Preface." Translated by William Smock. In *The Foucault Reader*, 333–339.

312) *Histoire de la sexualité 3: Le souci de soi*. Paris: Gallimard, 1984.

312ET) *The Care of the Self*. Translated by Robert Hurley. New York: Pantheon, 1986.

313) "Interview met Michel Foucault." *Krisis: Tijdschrift voor filosofie* 14 (1984) 47–58. A discussion with J. Francois and J. de Wit.

314) "Foucault, Michel, 1926–   ." Entry, under the pseudonym Maurice Florence, in Jean Huisman, ed., *Dictionnaire des Philosophes*. Paris: Presses Universitaires de France, 1984, I, 941–944.

315) "L'éthique du souci de soi comme pratique de liberté." *Concordia* 6 (1984) 99–116. An interview with Raul Fornet-Betancourt, Helmut Becker and Alfredo Gomez-Müller, conducted on Jan. 20, 1984.

315ET) "The Ethics of Care of the Self as a Practice of Freedom." Translated by Joseph Gauthier. *Philosophy and Social Criticism* XII, 2–3, 112–131.

316) "Philippe Ariès: Le souci de la vérité." *Le Nouvel Observateur* 1006 (Feb. 17–23, 1984) 56–57.

317) "Le style de l'histoire." *Le Matin* 2168 (Feb. 21, 1984) 20–21. Interview conducted by Francois Dumont and Jean-Paul Iommi-Amunstegui, with Arlette Farge, on Philippe Ariès.

318) "A Last Interview with French Philosopher Michel Foucault." *City Paper* 8, 30 (July 27–Aug. 2, 1984) 18. Conducted by Jamin Raskin in March, 1984.

319) "Interview de Michel Foucault." *Actes* 45–46 (1984): *La prison autrement?*, 3–6. An interview conducted by Catherine Baker in April, 1984.

320) "Le souci de la vérité." *Magazine littéraire* 207 (May, 1984) 18–23. An interview conducted by François Ewald.

320ET) "The Regard for Truth." An abridged translation, with an introduction, by Paul Patton. *Art and Text* 16 (Summer, 1984) 20–31.

321) "What is Enlightenment?" A translation by Catherine Porter of an unpublished French text. In *The Foucault Reader*, 31–50.

322) "Parla Michel Foucault: Alle fonti del piacere." *Panorama* 945 (May 28, 1984) 186–193. Radically different version published in French as "Une esthétique de l'existence." *Le Monde Aujourd'hui* (July 15–16, 1984) xi. Interview with Alessandro Fontana on April 25, 1984.

323) "Polemics, Politics and Problematizations." Translated by Lydia Davis. In *The Foucault Reader*, 381–389. Foucault's written responses to questions from Paul Rabinow and Tom Zummer in May, 1984, based on the transcript of an interview conducted earlier.

324) "Pour en finir avec les mensonges." *Le Nouvel Observateur* 1076 (June 21–27, 1985) 76–77. An interview conducted by Didier Eribon.

325) "Le retour de la morale." *Les Nouvelles* 2937 (June 28–July 5, 1984) 36–41. An interview conducted by Gilles Barbedette and André Scala. Conducted on May 29, 1984, this is probably the last interview which Foucault gave.

325ET) "Final Interview." Translated by Thomas Levin and Isabelle Lorenz. *Raritan* V,1 (Summer, 1985) 1–13.

B) MISCELLANEOUS MATERIALS

1) Letter to Roger Caillois on May 25, 1966. In *Cahiers pour un temps: Roger Caillois*. Paris: Centre Georges Pompidou/Pandora Editions, 1981, 228.

2) Letter to René Magritte on June 4, 1966. In René Magritte, *Ecrits complets.* André Blavier, ed. Paris: Flammarion, 1972, 521. Responds to letter from Magritte of May 23, 1966 in *Ceci n'est pas une pipe* (cf. #59 above).

3) Excerpt from an April, 1968 letter from MF to Maurice Clavel. Published in Clavel's *Ce que je crois* (Paris: Grasset, 1975) 138–139.

4) "Création d'un 'Groupe d'Information sur les prisons.'" *Esprit* 401 (March, 1971) 531–532. Co-signed by MF, Jean-Marie Domenach, and Pierre Vidal-Naquet.

5) "Ceremonie, Théatre, et Politique au XVIIe Siècle." *Acta 1. Proceedings of the Fourth Annual Conference of XVIIth Century French Literature.* Minneapolis: University of Minnesota Graduate School, 1972, 22–23. A summary in English by Stephan Davidson of a lecture given at the University on April 7, 1972.

6) "Power and Norm: Notes." Notes from a lecture at the Collège de France on March 28, 1973. Translated by W. Suchting, in *Power, Truth, Strategy*, 59–66.

7) A radio interview of an hour between MF and Jacques Chancel, "Radioscopie," on March 10, 1975. A tape of this interview is available at the library of the Georges Pompidou Center in Paris.

8) "Punir ou guérir." Dialogues, Radio-France (Oct. 8, 1976).

9) "Toujours les prisons." An exchange of letter with Paul Thibaud and Jean-Marie Domenach in *Esprit* 37 (January, 1980) 184–186.

10) Otto Friedrich. "France's Philosopher of Power." *Time* 118, No. 20 (Nov. 6, 1981) 147–148. A news article with extensive quotations from an interview with MF.

11) *Discourse and Truth: The Problematization of Parrhesia.* Notes to the Fall, 1983 seminar given by MF at the University of California, Berkeley. A privately printed transcription of Foucault's presentations by Joseph Pearson.

12) A July, 1983 letter to Hervé Guibert. In "L'autre journal d'Hervé Guibert." *L'Autre Journal* 10 (December, 1985) 5.

13) Letters of and conversations with MF quoted extensively in Claude Mauriac's series "Les Temps immobile," published by Grasset in Paris: vol. 2, *Les Espaces imaginaires* (1975); vol. 3, *Et comme l'espérance est violente* (1976); vol. 7, *Signes, rencontres, et rendez-vous* (1983); vol. 9, *Mauriac et fils* (1986); and in *Une Certain rage*. Paris: Laffont, 1977.

C) STUDIES CONDUCTED UNDER THE DIRECTION OF MF

1) *Moi, Pierre Rivière, ayant égorgé ma mère, ma soeur et mon frère.* Paris: Gallimard, 1973. A study done under Foucault's direction at the Collège de France. For his own contributions to this volume, cf. the preceding section of the bibliography, #112 and 113. The other contents of the study are listed here. The English translations were done by Frank Jellinek and published as: *I, Pierre Riviere, having slaughtered my mother, my sister and my brother* (New York: Pantheon, 1975).

I: "Le dossier" of the parricide, Pierre Rivière.
    ET) "The Dossier." This translation omits several passages from the Dossier as well as several documents included in the original.
    A) Rivière's memoir was made into a movie by René Allio and released under the same title in 1976 (Paris: Planfilm). Its screenplay is available in *Cinéma* 183 (1977).

II: Notes
    1) "L'animal, le fou, le mort," by J. P. Peter and Jeanne Favret.

ET) "The Animal, the Madman and Death."
2) "Les circonstances atténuantes," by Patricia Moulin.
ET) "Extenuating Circumstances."
3) "Regicide-parricide," by Blandine Barret-Kriegel.
ET) "Regicide and Parricide."
4) "Les vies parallèles de P. Rivière," by Ph. Riot.
ET) "The Parallel Lives of Pierre Rivière."
5) "Les médecins et les juges," by Robert Castel.
ET) "The Doctors and the Judges."
6) "Les intermittences de la raison," by Alexandre Fontana.
ET) "The Intermittences of Rationality."
2) *Généalogie des équipements de normalisation: les équipements sanitaires.* Fontenay-sous-Bois: Centre d'études, de recherches et de formation institutionnelles (CERFI), 1976. Although the entire volume was identified as under Foucault's direction, it seems that he was actually involved only with Part I. "L'institution hospitalière au XVIIIe siècle." The members of the group he directed are unidentified. For Foucault's introduction to the study, cf. the preceding section of the bibliography, #153.
3) *Politiques de l'habitat 1800–1850.* Paris: Comité pour la Recherche et le Développement en Architecture (CORDA), 1977. For Foucault's brief introduction, cf. the first section of the bibliography, #171. The following studies make up the volume.
1) "Reflexions sur la notion d'habitat aux XVIIIe et XIXe siècles," by Ann Thalamy.
2) "Les demeures de la misère. Le choléra-morbus et l'émergence de l'‘Habitat,'" by Blandine Barret-Kriegel.
3) "Anatomie des discours de réforme." by Jean-Marie Alliaume.
4) "‘La loi du 13 juillet 1850 sur le logements insalubres.' Les philanthropes et le problème insoluble de l'Habitat du pauvre." by Danielle Rancière.
5) "Savoirs de la ville et de la maison au début du XIXe siècle," by Francois Béguin.

Index

———◆———